The Word in the World

The WORD in the WORLD

Evangelical Writing, Publishing, and Reading in America, 1789~1880

CANDY GUNTHER BROWN

THE WORD IN THE WORLD

EVANGELICAL WRITING,

PUBLISHING, AND READING

IN AMERICA, 1789–1880

Candy Gunther Brown

The University of North Carolina Press
Chapel Hill and London

The paper in this book meets the guidelines for permanence and
durability of the Committee on Production Guidelines for Book
Longevity of the Council on Library Resources.

The publication of this book was supported by a subvention from
the Department of American Studies and the College of Arts and
Sciences of Saint Louis University.

Portions of this book are reprinted with permission in revised form
from "Domestic Nurture versus Clerical Crisis: The Gender Dimension in Horace Bushnell's and Elizabeth Prentiss's Critiques of
Revivalism," in *Embodying the Spirit: New Perspectives on North American Revivalism*, edited by Michael J. McClymond (Baltimore: Johns
Hopkins University Press, 2004).

Frontispiece: "Christian Union," by Thomas S. Sinclair (1845).
(Courtesy of The Library of Congress)

Library of Congress Cataloging-in-Publication Data
Brown, Candy Gunther.
The Word in the world : evangelical writing, publishing, and reading
in America, 1789–1880 / Candy Gunther Brown.
p. cm.
Includes bibliographical references and index.
ISBN 0-8078-2838-6 (cloth: alk. paper)
ISBN 0-8078-5511-1 (pbk.: alk. paper)
1. Christian literature — Publishing — United States — History —
18th century. 2. Christian literature — Publishing — United States —
History — 19th century. 3. Evangelicalism — United States —
History — 18th century. 4. Evangelicalism — United States —
History — 19th century. 5. Christians — Books and reading — United
States — History. 6. Religious newspapers and periodicals — United
States — History. 7. Music — Religious aspects — Christianity.
8. Christianity and culture — United States — History. I. Title.
Z480.R4 B76 2004
070.5'0973'09034 — dc22
2003016297

cloth   08 07 06 05 04   5 4 3 2 1
paper   08 07 06 05 04   5 4 3 2 1

To my husband Josh

and my daughter Katrina,

with love

This book it chalketh out before thine eyes
The man that seeks the everlasting prize;
It shows you whence he comes, whither he goes;
What he leaves undone, also what he does;
It also shows you how he runs and runs,
Till he unto the gate of glory comes.

—John Bunyan, *The Pilgrim's Progress*

This is the testimony of all the good books, sermons, hymns, and memoirs I read . . . that this life is but a scene of probation through which we pass to the real life above.

—Elizabeth Prentiss, *Stepping Heavenward*

CONTENTS

ILLUSTRATIONS

ACKNOWLEDGMENTS

It is a pleasant duty to recognize the many debts that I have accumulated in the process of writing this book. Several generous financial grants facilitated the completion of the first stage of this project, a dissertation in the History of American Civilization program at Harvard University. I benefited from a Louisville Institute Dissertation Completion Fellowship; Packard Fellowship; Institute for the Study of American Evangelicals Hymnody Project Grant; Harvard Graduate Student Council Travel Grant; American Antiquarian Society Kate B. and Hall J. Peterson Research Fellowship; Harvard Graduate Society Research Fellowship and Travel Grant; Sarah Bradley Gamble Fellowship; Mazur Fellowship; and Lilly Endowment Fellowship. Mellon Faculty Development Grants and a subvention from Saint Louis University have aided manuscript revisions and illustration procurement and production.

The thoughtful assistance of library staff at a number of institutions has proven invaluable. I warmly thank the librarians at the American Antiquarian Society, Worcester, Massachusetts; American Baptist Historical Society, Rochester, New York; Library Company of Philadelphia, Pennsylvania; Presbyterian Historical Society, Philadelphia, Pennsylvania; Gebbie Archives and Special Collections, Wheaton College, Wheaton, Illinois; Oral Roberts University Library, Tulsa, Oklahoma; Rauner Special Collections Library, Dartmouth College, Hanover, New Hampshire; Library of Congress, Washington, D.C.; Vanderbilt University Library, Nashville, Tennessee; Saint Louis University Library, St. Louis, Missouri; Washington University Library, St. Louis, Missouri; Kenneth J. LaBudde Department of Special Collections, University of Missouri–Kansas City; Andover Newton Theological Library, Newton, Massachusetts; Boston University Library, Boston, Massachusetts; Boston Public Library, Boston, Massachusetts; and Harvard University libraries in Cambridge, Massachusetts: Andover-Harvard Theological, Houghton, Schlesinger, Widener, Lamont, and Hilles.

Several individuals graciously commented on a version of the entire manuscript: Lawrence Buell, Ann Braude, Paul Gutjahr, Matthew Mancini, Doug Kasischke, and Ronald Norricks. As readers for the University of

North Carolina Press, Philip Gura and Mark Noll provided a wealth of useful advice. I am also very thankful for suggestions and encouragement offered by William Hutchison, Alan Heimert, David Nord, Alexis Mc-Crossen, David Morgan, Grant Wacker, Scott Casper, Donald Mathews, Stephen Marini, and colleagues in the Harvard Divinity School Colloquium on American Religious History, especially Heather Curtis, David Bains, John O'Keefe, Timothy Milford, Virginia Brereton, Christopher White, Mark Sherrod, Scott Erikson, Emma Anderson, Stephen Shoemaker, Kirsten Sword, and Dean Grodzins. I thank my research assistants, Nancy Thompson, Renée Davidson, Jody Sowell, and Rob Wilson, for their immense aid. Editors at the University of North Carolina Press have been fabulous, particularly Elaine Maisner, Paula Wald, and Julie Bush. I owe a great deal to my undergraduate advisers, Bernard Bailyn and Louis Masur, for setting my feet on the path toward this project.

I leave my greatest obligations for last. I am indebted beyond measure to my graduate school adviser and friend, David Hall, for his piercing insights and steady words of wisdom and counsel over the course of a decade. Finally, I am grateful to my husband, Josh, for his constant support, feedback, and love, and to my parents and siblings, Raymond, Cecilia, Brian, Carlton, Sherry, and Lindy, for a lifetime of love and encouragement.

The Word in the World

The Struggle for
Purity and Presence

"In nothing is this age more distinguished from the past," mused John Waller, editor of Kentucky's *Western Baptist Review*, in the summer of 1850, "than in the increased facilities for multiplying books and publications of every description — of sending on the wings of the press the opinions of men to all parts of the earth." Waller's tone of cautious optimism captured the mood of many of his contemporaries; "for good or for evil" the printed word had become the "lever which moves the moral world."[1]

This book explains how evangelical Protestants like John Waller used the Word of the Bible and printed words of their own to transform the world of mid-nineteenth-century America. By 1850, the year of Waller's reflections, self-identified evangelicals had forged a burgeoning print culture with a dual mission: *purity* and *presence* in the world. Amid the contentious milieu of American culture, evangelical writers, publishers, and readers self-consciously strove to sanctify their own pilgrim community and redeem American society without allowing themselves to become worldly.

This study conceptualizes "evangelical print culture," as it developed between 1789 and 1880, as a distinctive set of writing, publishing, and reading practices centered on the power of the Word to transform the world. I argue, first, that evangelicals shared a set of assumptions about how the Holy Spirit used the Word to convey sanctifying influences across time, space, and language to permeate the world. Second, I demonstrate that evangelicals viewed participation in a textual community defined by an informal canon of texts as aiding one another's pilgrimage through the world. Third, I reveal that using the Word and their own words to influence the world's redemption, evangelicals dialogically enacted a set of core narrative structures to contend for the faith, set themselves apart as the priest-hood of all believers, sanctify the surrounding world, and unite as the church universal. Evangelical print culture diversified over time as clerical arbiters and a lay priesthood decided that more and more profane words functioned to convey sacred meanings.

Evangelicals and the Word

Christianity, like Judaism, has always been a text-centered religion that envisions God as the living and creative "Word." The Hebrew Bible opens by declaring that God created the world by speaking: "In the beginning God created the heaven and the earth. . . . God said, Let there be light: and there was light." The New Testament book of John starts with an allusion to the Genesis account: "In the beginning was the Word, and the Word was with God, and the Word was God. . . . All things were made by him. . . . And the Word was made flesh, and dwelt among us." The Word existed before the world's creation and spoke the world into being. In the incarnation, the Word became flesh, Jesus Christ, in order to redeem creation from its fall to sin. Shortly before Jesus' crucifixion, he promised to send his disciples the Holy Spirit—from the same root as "inspired" or "God-breathed" word—to guide Christians into all truth.[2]

The term "evangelical," translated from the Greek *euaggellion* and the Anglo-Saxon *godspel*, originates in the New Testament. Mark commences: "The beginning of the gospel of Jesus Christ, the Son of God," and reaches its climax in reporting Jesus' postresurrection instructions to his disciples: "Go ye into all the world, and preach the gospel to every creature." This so-called Great Commission has for 2,000 years motivated Christians to preach the gospel, or good news of salvation from sin through faith in Jesus Christ, around the world. Early church leaders dispatched evangelists, cir-culated books, and formed libraries since they interpreted the Great Com-mission as authorizing them to proclaim the gospel both by quoting Scrip-ture and through their own creative use of spoken and written language.[3]

Protestants first called themselves evangelicals during the Reformation of the sixteenth century, when Martin Luther's (1483–1546) followers in Germany adopted the name Evangelische Kirche, or Evangelical Church. In identifying themselves as evangelicals, Protestants defined their break from the Roman Catholic Church as centrally concerned with the doc-trines of *sola gratia, sola fides, solus Christus,* or salvation by grace through faith in the gospel of Jesus Christ, revealed in the Bible alone, *sola scriptura,* independent of good works, the sacraments, or ecclesiastical tradition. Repudiating the church hierarchy's claim to mediate between the Word and lay Christians, Protestants affirmed that they belonged to a priesthood that included all Christian believers.[4]

Arguing that Roman Catholic clergy had used their control of the Word to tyrannize over the people, Protestant ministers nevertheless worried that because sin had corrupted every human faculty, full lay autonomy would atomize the church universal. This tension between a lay priesthood and clerical regulation has constituted an enduring theme in the history of evangelicalism. Protestants have resolved the dilemma, in part, by using preached and printed words to serve the priestly function of applying the Word to the world of lived experience. Nearly thirty European towns laid claim to the invention of printing as early as the 1420s, and a German edition of the Bible circulated by 1466. Many of the early Reformers welcomed the "divine and miraculous inventing of printing" as a providential gift from God designed to promote true religion. From 1517 to 1520, Martin Luther oversaw the printing of an estimated 300,000 copies of thirty sermons, tracts, and broadsides. The Geneva Bible (1560), one of six major English translations produced in the sixteenth century, included commentaries, verse separations, and interpretive woodcuts, all of which interposed between the Word and the reader.[5]

Both the Geneva Bible and the King James Version (1611) that superseded it reflect the Protestants' privileging of plain-style, vernacular language in contrast to the ornate Latin rhetoric that they believed the Catholic clergy had used to conceal truth from the masses. Early Protestants understood "sacred" language to consist of human words (*verba*) that communicated the substance (*res*) of God's word in a manner easily grasped by the ordinary reader. The nonconformist minister Richard Baxter, a leading advocate of the plain style in seventeenth-century England, considered it the responsibility of clergy to preach and write so as to make the Word accessible to the laity and thus "give the children their meat in due season." At the same time, Baxter recognized the ease with which textual corruption could enter Bibles and other publications, whether by careless printing or intentional scheming. Indeed, printings of the King James Bible included an estimated 24,000 textual variations by the 1830s. In order to counteract erroneous texts produced by others, Baxter wrote prolifically, even as he wrote plainly, producing 130 books, the most influential of which was *The Saints' Everlasting Rest* (1650), a bulky volume of more than 800 quarto pages. Criticized for writing too much, Baxter responded, "And as to the *number* and length of my Writings, . . . the World cannot be sufficiently instructed and edified by fewer words." Baxter saw his multiplication of words as communicating the pure Word to a corrupt world.[6]

By the mid-nineteenth century, evangelicals who continued to read Baxter's writings, the King James Version of the Bible, and, after 1881, a new Revised Version of Scripture had developed what I term a "functionalist" view of sacred language. Evangelicals became increasingly optimistic that the Holy Spirit could reveal the pure Word through a wide range of linguistic styles, genres, and forms. The distinction between sacred and profane language came to rest less on the kinds of words adopted than on their usefulness in interfacing the Word with human experience. Extending the logic of Baxter and others like him, nineteenth-century evangelicals reasoned that the world could be sufficiently instructed and edified only if their words, activated by the indwelling Holy Spirit, permeated every arena of a shifting cultural landscape. Divergent refined and vernacular, or folk, aesthetics of the sacred employed everyday language (whether poetic or uncultivated but heartfelt) to incarnate an ineffable sacred story into the world of lived experience. As high and low literary cultures differentiated, new "middling styles," to adopt a phrase from Kenneth Cmiel, intermingled the refined and the vulgar. The language of refinement appealed particularly to the sensibilities of the well-heeled urban middle classes, while vernacular discourse better met the needs of rural folk communities. At the same time, as widespread literacy and democratic values created what Richard Bushman terms "vernacular gentility," more and more people mixed the formal and the folksy in both urbane and rustic settings. Evangelicals endeavored to go into all the world to preach the gospel, entering the railway car, Victorian parlor, and sharecropper farmhouse with words adapted to the needs and preferences of varied audiences and contexts.[7]

Evangelicals articulated this more inclusive, functionalist understanding of sacred language at the same time that they expressed a more restrictive, or what I will call an "ontological," view of the Bible's special status as actually being the inspired Word of God. The freedom that evangelicals felt to enlarge the meanings of sacred language alleviated mounting cultural pressures to tamper with the biblical text itself. The Bible, uniquely, remained the same, even as other sacred and profane texts readily bent to connect with changing cultural needs. The evangelical doctrine of biblical inspiration evolved substantially from the sixteenth through the nineteenth centuries. All the early Reformers distinguished between the words of the Bible and the living Word, affirming that the Holy Spirit spoke through the biblical authors and convinced readers of the Word's truth by illuminating the Bible's meaning, usually in its simplest grammatical reading. During the seventeenth century, Lutherans and Calvinists who continued to differentiate the Spirit from the letter of the Bible developed a doctrine of inspiration that emphasized the Holy Spirit's role in guarding the Bible's authors from error in content or in words.[8]

The doctrine of verbal, plenary inspiration and its corollary, biblical inerrancy, solidified in the nineteenth century in response to the challenges of European biblical-historical criticism and American romanticism. Practitioners of biblical criticism, such as F. C. Baur and D. F. Strauss in Germany and J. E. Renan in France, assumed that the Bible was a text like any other, subject to historical and scientific analysis of its human composition and transmission. American romantics like Ralph Waldo Emerson (1803–82) and Henry David Thoreau (1817–62) focused on the Bible's symbolic rather than literal meaning. By the 1850s, Charles Hodge (1797–1878), at the helm of the Old School Presbyterian Princeton Seminary, took the lead in formulating an evangelical response through the columns of the *Princeton Review*. Hodge insisted that the Holy Spirit guaranteed the accuracy of the Bible by inspiring its human authors to select not only correct ideas but also correct words. Drawing on the philosophical school of Scottish common sense realism, forged in the mid-eighteenth century, Hodge minimized the gap between the Spirit and the letter of the Bible by asserting that even uninspired readers could understand the Bible's meaning by employing common sense. Hodge's successors elaborated the doctrine in an 1881 *Presbyterian Review* article, which proclaimed that "the Scriptures not only contain, but ARE THE WORD OF GOD, and hence that all their elements and all their affirmations are absolutely errorless, and binding the faith and obedience of men." Equating the Bible with the Word of God marked a significant theological development. My narrative treats nineteenth-century evangelical efforts to conceptualize the Word but stops short of the regimentation of such an exalted view of the Bible by the Fundamentalist movement at the end of the century.[9]

Although mid-nineteenth-century evangelicals resisted altering the Bible's words, they did not hesitate to experiment with physical presentation. The doctrine of the incarnation, the Word made flesh, encouraged interest in the Bible's material form. Evangelicals understood physical Bibles, and by extension other sacred texts, as demonstrating the Word's relevance to human experience. Beginning in the fifteenth century, printed Bibles sold throughout Europe as ordinary market wares, advertised by handbills, circulars, and catalogs; transported by waterways; and marketed at annual book fairs. Nineteenth-century evangelicals fashioned the production, distribution, sales, and consumption of Bibles and other printed artifacts as means to permeate European and American cultures with sacred influences. This idea of sacred texts as words, artifacts, and commodities had theological significance. By entering the print market with physically attractive, commercially competitive, and distinctively evangelical products, authors and publishers hoped to transform the purchasing and reading habits of the general market. That the Bible could be formatted in more ways than any other text seemingly provided evidence of its unique adaptability to every cultural need.[10]

The Word became incarnate in American culture by the 1850s as publishers demonstrated its relevance to diverse cultural settings, ranging from the refined Victorian parlor to the rough-hewn frontier farm. The mammoth family Bible as well as the cheap tract society edition accumulated layers of religious meanings that went much deeper than Thorstein Veblen's well-worn interpretation of commodities as status symbols. A long lineage of more recent commentary has similarly overlooked the theology of commercialization by too readily assuming that nineteenth-century evangelicals grew more interested in packaging than contents and confused religious values with the ideals of middle-class consumer culture. In the give and take of human experience, the sacred and profane cannot be so easily disentangled or collapsed.[11]

Evangelicals living in mid-nineteenth-century America nevertheless struggled with an inherent tension between their goal of purity, or keeping that which they defined as sacred uncontaminated by the profane world, and their goal of presence, or infusing the world with sanctifying influences. Always their own harshest critics, evangelicals feared attaining either goal apart from the other: purity without presence undermined transformative influence, while presence without purity eliminated the sense of being set apart upon which sacred status depends. As evangelicals intensified their participation in the American print market, they worked through the relationship between the secular and the sacred, or between the things of this world and the things of the world to come.[12]

Nineteenth-century evangelicals worried not about the mingling of the sacred and the secular in American culture but about their confusion. Christians have more or less always set apart particular texts, spaces, and times, such as the Word and the Sabbath, as sacred while presuming that Providence dispensed profane, or ordinary, resources for use in achieving transcendent purposes. The commission to go into all the world presupposed the permeability of boundaries between the sacred and the secular and the possibility of exerting an influence that sanctified the profane for holy uses. In connecting the worlds of religion and the book trades, evangelicals hoped to infuse the secular with the sacred without allowing the Holy Word and profane words to become indistinguishable.

Creating an Evangelical Canon

In their efforts to transform the world of print, nineteenth-century evangelicals forged an informal, open-ended "canon" of texts that embedded core values and assumptions about the relationships connecting writers, publishers, texts, and readers. I do not mean to suggest that all evangelicals read exactly the same body of publications at any point in time or that they always agreed upon which texts belonged in the canon. Indeed, favored texts and genres shifted over time, even as certain "steady sellers," to borrow David Hall's term, never went out of print. The terms "old" and "new," applied to canonical texts, coded the goals of adhering to the Word while maintaining relevance to a changing world. The canon embraced older texts, like Baxter's *Saints' Everlasting Rest*, as well as the newest press releases, written in genres as diverse as poems, histories, memoirs, hymns, sermons, and novels.[13]

Frequently reprinted texts, or those recognized by most evangelicals as belonging to the canon, included a variety of contributions. Nineteenth-century evangelicals often expressed an affinity for doctrinal volumes such as the English nonconformist Joseph Alleine's *Alarm to Unconverted Sinners: In a Serious Treatise on Conversion* (1672) and the Presbyterian Charles Hodge's *Way of Life* (1841); memoirs of the Congregationalist David Brainerd (1749), the British Methodist Hester Ann Rogers (1804), and the Baptist Adoniram Judson (1853); and certain novels like *Uncle Tom's Cabin* (1852), written by the Congregationalist Harriet Beecher Stowe. Texts that expressed controversial doctrines, adopted suspect fictional devices, or otherwise dissatisfied portions of the reading community usually occupied a more tenuous place in the canon. The same readers chose from among market options written in multiple genres and forms, interpreting each in the context of the wider canon and assuming that one kind of text could not replace another.

Rules for evaluating evangelical texts differed from the standards of secular literature. New publications gained entrance to the canon if they shared certain marks of membership, in other words, if they reinforced the same values as texts previously recognized as canonical. Usefulness, rather than genre or form, was the primary characteristic that marked texts as evangelical. At the same time, narrative qualities, physical packaging, and commercial value all presumably contributed to each text's usefulness or functionally sacred status. Evangelicals assumed that texts did not belong to their authors but to the Christian community, and members of this community could appropriate any printed matter for particular purposes. This understanding of texts contributed to the fluidity of the canon and the disregard of copyrights. Editors and publishers readily modified texts and crossed the boundaries between evangelical and nonevangelical or sacred and secular whenever useful.

The Bible, not surprisingly, occupied a privileged position in the evangelical canon. Nineteenth-century evangelicals, unmindful of the struggles of sixteenth- and seventeenth-century Reformers to define a Protestant biblical canon, considered the biblical canon closed, unalterable, self-authenticating, and ontologically sacred since it was inspired by the Holy Spirit. By contrast, the evangelical canon was open, fluid, conditionally authoritative, and functionally sacred. Texts could be added, subtracted, abridged, or altered, and they gained or retained their status as evangelical on the condition that they were useful in reinforcing the Word of the Bible. Although evangelicals did not usually claim that the Holy Spirit inspired extrabiblical words, they did assert that certain texts functioned to convey sacred influences. Evangelicals revered the Bible as articulating a divinely authored, comprehensive structure of universal meaning and saw their own narratives as partial, imperfect reflections of this God-given plot. The texts that comprised the evangelical canon, when taken together, elaborated the complex, meaningful patterns of significance that God presumably first revealed through the Bible.[14]

This study sets aside the question of whether evangelicals were correct in asserting that God authored all meaning or whether modern scholars are right in assuming that all cultures write their own meaningful stories and weave their own webs of significance. Sharing Clifford Geertz's goal of accessing the "conceptual world in which our subjects live so that we can . . . converse with them," this book focuses on how evangelical textual practices functioned in the lives of nineteenth-century participants.[15]

Widely shared story structures both enabled evangelicals to view their lives in specific ways and limited their interpretive options. Texts played a central role in sustaining certain great narratives, for example of evangelicals as members of a pilgrim community traveling through this world toward the holiness of heaven. The Bible introduced the pilgrimage concept, and Christian writers took up the theme repeatedly, most influentially John Bunyan in *The Pilgrim's Progress from This World to That Which is to Come* (1678). The pilgrimage metaphor, among numerous tropes for the Christian life, captured the imagination of the mobile society of colonial and nineteenth-century America.[16]

As American evangelical publishers reprinted Bunyan's text, the book exerted a tremendous cultural influence by providing a framework within which readers saw secular, or worldly, experience in terms of a sacred, or otherworldly, journey. Bunyan's subtitle offered readers a map of the pilgrim's journey, outlining the *Manner of His Setting out, His Dangerous Journey, and Safe Arrival at the Desired Countrey*. At the moment of conversion, or justification, the pilgrim received forgiveness from the guilt of sin through the imputation of Christ's righteousness. The pilgrim then commenced a dangerous journey toward heaven, assisting and assisted by other pilgrims whom he met along the way. A lifelong process of growth in holiness, or sanctification, progressively purified the pilgrim community from the pollution and power of sin. Arrival at the desired country, or glorification, abolished sin completely, thereby reinstating the long-severed relationship between Christ and the church in heaven. Bunyan's work, and many comparable texts, portrayed the visible church's progress as aided by the interactions of readers and writers in an invisible, textually defined pilgrim community.[17]

Such universalizing frameworks exalted individual experience, in an age of emergent self-identity, as significant within the scheme of God's redemptive purposes for the world. Narrative conventions allowed readers to envision their lives as typical, conforming to the same patterns that had guided generations of Christians. Deeply embedded atemporal structures provided a model for interpreting linear series of events as they occurred in one person's life. The world of meanings unfolded and elaborated by the evangelical canon oriented readers to their everyday lives as evangelicals used texts to translate the world of lived experience into transcendent biblical categories of meaning.[18]

Participating in an Evangelical Textual Community

Nineteenth-century evangelical writers, publishers, and readers used the evangelical canon to participate in a textually defined community that constituted a distinctive culture. Joan Jacobs Brumberg's pioneering study, *Mission for Life*, conceptualized evangelicalism as a culture in which texts functioned as converting instruments. I consider the role of texts in sustaining and transmitting evangelical culture among the already converted. In speaking of participation in a "textual community," I refer to a set of practices and to the assumptions that informed and made them meaningful, connecting authors, publishers, texts, and readers in an interlocking "web of relationships," to use Hannah Arendt's phrase. The practices of an evangelical textual community linked individual experiences with social processes. Thus, I use the term "evangelical" in its most generous, inclusive sense as a style that structured personal and social experience. Similarly, Glenn Hendler, building on the work of Jürgen Habermas and Raymond Williams, has described "public sentiment" as just such a "structure of feeling" that articulated meanings and values as people lived and felt them in nineteenth-century America. I contend that, in an analogous manner, identification with an evangelical textual community mediated and structured seemingly private experiences to connect with a larger social experience in the process of forming. Individuals felt their textual practices to be spiritually transformative since the Holy Spirit presumably worked through evangelical relationships to influence each individual's and the entire community's sanctification.[19]

Skillful interaction with any textual community requires literacy. Historians continue to debate early American literacy levels and the best indices for measurement, nevertheless agreeing for the most part that white men enjoyed higher attainments than blacks or white women and that oral and written cultures overlapped even in highly literate communities. In part because of evangelical efforts to establish Sunday and common schools and to make cheap, printed texts more readily available in rural areas, American literacy increased rapidly in the nineteenth century. An ability to decipher texts, however, did not always translate into an ability to apply knowledge gained from reading. By 1850, the U.S. Census reported a literacy rate of 90 percent among white women and men, compared with an adult literacy rate of 60 percent in Britain. Rising literacy encouraged a shift in American evangelical culture from oral to print-based practices, especially as growing lay sophistication made it possible for texts other than the Bible and a few steady sellers to shape cultural identities.[20]

A crucial caveat is that a majority of black evangelicals participated in print-centered communities on a more limited basis and in different ways than did white evangelicals. Literate white and black evangelicals shared textual practices and narratives of the Christian life, and oral and print cultures overlapped considerably, even among the illiterate. Yet literacy rates for African Americans, particularly slaves, remained much lower in America throughout the nineteenth century. Free black, like white, evangelicals debated among themselves the relative merits of refined and vernacular aesthetics of the sacred, with the lines of division falling according to class and region as well as education. Nevertheless, black and white evangelicals lived in distinct cultural worlds. For both free and enslaved African Americans, oral cultural modes predominated, and textual practices shared with whites gained variant meanings. Black evangelicals were more likely to apprehend the living Word as intervening in the world directly without mediation by the written word. Great narratives, such as the pilgrimage trope, focused in antebellum African American communities less on Bunyan's model than on an all-encompassing vision of deliverance that blended Moses with Jesus in leading God's chosen people from bondage to freedom both in this world and in the world to come. After emancipation, black and white evangelicals interacted increasingly in print and local communities with the result that each group influenced the cultural development of the other, even when such exchanges remained unacknowledged.[21]

The meanings of evangelical print culture emerged at the moving intersection of what Paul Ricoeur terms the "world of the text" and the "world of the reader." Conventions embedded in the evangelical canon partially determined the choices available to nineteenth-century writers, publishers, and readers, while interactions among print market participants contributed to the development of larger patterns of meaning. A dialectical process of textual "sedimentation" and "innovation," to again quote Ricoeur, alternately stabilized narrative structures and provided the rules that guided legitimate experimentation. Familiarity with previous texts affected authors' and publishers' organization of experiences and oriented readers to receive new texts in partially prescribed ways. Socialization into evangelical print culture involved learning conventionalized ways of writing, publishing, and reading, the practices of which continually re-created the evangelical canon as members chose from among interpretive options.[22]

Evangelicals used conventional textual practices to perform, or ritually enact, the frameworks inscribed in the evangelical canon, thereby appropriating these frameworks to make their own lives meaningful. In breaking with the Roman Catholic Church, sixteenth-century evangelicals to varying degrees deemphasized ritual and liturgy to privilege the Word. Yet evangelicals continued to use words to serve liturgical functions and, indeed, often envisioned Word and sacrament as conjoined. John Calvin viewed celebration of the Lord's Supper as verbally embodying the spiritual reality it represents. Nineteenth-century evangelicals extended Calvin's analysis to identify the use of any evangelical text as verbally embodying membership in the church universal. Readers and writers made progress in a spiritual journey through textual practices, giving and receiving encouragement from other readers and writers, by placing themselves within the story of the church's communal pilgrimage. In performing shared narrative frameworks, such as Christian pilgrimage, participants reenacted a story of redemption history and intensified that story's authority to structure their lives. Texts acquired ritual significance as evangelicals used words, in the context of relationships with other members of their textual community, to order experiences and formulate connections between embedded patterns and the details of everyday life.[23]

Through their participation in a textually defined community, evangelicals repositioned the boundaries between the authority of a lay priesthood and clerical regulation. Informally designated cultural arbiters, notably publishers and editors, increasingly shared authority with clergy to referee involvement in the textual community. Regulation took various forms: granting or withholding permission to publish, altering printed versions of texts, advising readers what and how to read, and inscribing implicit or explicit rules within texts that partially governed writing and reading practices. Expansion of the print market stimulated lay initiative by diminishing the expense of introducing new publications and by augmenting readers' choices. Consumer purchasing decisions influenced which texts publishers and booksellers could market profitably. Rules governing interaction in the textual community to some degree mirrored prevailing social and political assumptions about the proper spheres of groups such as women and African Americans. At the same time, evangelical assumptions about the priesthood of all believers opened up rhetorical spaces for politically disempowered individuals.[24]

The idea of a textual community provided an alternative to viewing the Christian church as centered in the local congregation. As the market revolution, westward migration, denominational rivalries, immigration, and political divisions fragmented local communities across the United States, shared textual practices alleviated anxieties caused by physical and social dislocations. By 1860, more than a third of free Americans lived outside the state of their birth, and population persistence rates for any given town often sank below 50 percent in a single decade. From the 1850s to the 1880s, Americans were twice as likely as the British to move across counties, and Americans, on average, traveled greater distances. Disoriented by ceaseless mobility, frustrated by religious controversies, and weary of the intermittent nature of revivals, scattered individuals and congregations longed for a sense of connection with a timeless, placeless, unified church. Evangelicals used texts to envision themselves as belonging to the church universal, which included Christians from all time periods, countries, and denominations. Relationships with other members of a textual community often proved more harmonious and intimate than everyday religious and social exchanges. In such instances, writing and reading potentially heightened individuals' dissatisfaction with the messiness of day-to-day interactions, thereby intensifying the contentiousness of local communities.[25]

Even as an expanding print market depersonalized communication among authors and readers, ritualized textual practices sustained evangelicals' sense of personal connection with one another. Separated friends and family members continued to share experiences by reading the same books or books that transmitted similar narratives. Writers and readers who had never met saw themselves as closely related and sometimes formed deep emotional attachments. Even when an author had been dead for centuries, readers, intermingling oral and print cultural practices, used texts to engage in intimate conversations in which the author spoke almost audibly. Evangelicals likewise attributed personal qualities to favorite texts, which they viewed as repositories of the Holy Spirit's living presence and as faithful companions throughout the pilgrimage of life.[26]

Printed texts extended the reach of evangelical community to encompass every life event, from early childhood to the deathbed, in all moments and places of experience. The relative stability of printed texts added continuity to devotional practices that supplemented the sporadic bursts of piety fostered by revivals. By the 1820s, revivals themselves were becoming routinized, though never entirely predictable, and maturing churches began the long-term work of institution-building. As first-generation revival converts pursued ongoing growth as Christians and socialized their children into the life of the church, congregations and denominations built more elaborate structures and auxiliary agencies, many of which employed new printing technologies. Scholars have expressed skepticism about this pattern of institutional thickening, characterizing the process, in the words of Roger Finke and Rodney Stark, as shifting attention "toward this world and away from the next." This book instead emphasizes the ways in which evangelicals used printed texts to address difficult new questions as they progressed through physical and spiritual life cycles, coped with generational transitions, and adjusted to their changing social and economic status.[27]

Religious publications, presented by clergy and editors as operating within and strengthening the family unit, coupled a narrowing inward of communal identity toward a domestic center with a broadening outward to intensify individuals' sense of membership in the church universal. As evangelical communities emerged in the eighteenth century, the need for fellowship encouraged church members to see one another as spiritual kin. By the mid-nineteenth century, both northern and southern churches increasingly relied upon the nuclear family, centered in the sacred space of the domestic hearth, rather than the local congregation to stimulate weekday religious devotion. At the same time, as evangelical publishing expanded, any time or space in which people sold, bought, wrote, or read religious texts could potentially be viewed as sacred. Market participants gained flexibility to configure religious meanings separate from church institutions or specifically religious rituals. As publishing accentuated extrainstitutional, and especially domestic, religious practices, evangelical culture spilled outside the confines of the church service or Sabbath to the everyday places and times in which American culture took shape.[28]

As evangelicalism and American culture intermingled, cultural identities blurred at the edges. The textual community imagined by evangelicals had permeable boundaries that allowed for and even invited exchange with European and especially English evangelicalism and with what evangelicals termed unevangelical alternatives, including Catholicism, Unitarianism, and secular literature. Evangelical print culture embraced both texts written by nonevangelicals and texts that contended for the faith by bitterly attacking cultural outsiders. As Tessa Watt has elegantly said of an earlier period, "The profane and the pious, the verbal and the visual: all were accommodated within the same room, the same mind, the same experience. . . . [C]ulture could absorb new belief while retaining old ones, could modify doctrines, could accommodate words and icons, ambiguities and contradictions." The print culture that evangelicals formed and maintained in nineteenth-century America was meaningful because of, rather than despite, its most contradictory elements. This cultural universe contained and reconciled a multiplicity of strains in dialectical tension: individual and community, local and universal, temporal and timeless, presence and purity, Word and world.[29]

The evangelical mandate to influence the world did not presuppose that evangelical culture already contained every element worth possessing or that evangelicals had nothing to gain from the world. Although twenty-first-century terminology often confuses the terms "evangelical" and "fundamentalist," nineteenth-century evangelicals were not fundamentalists in the sense of being culturally defensive, frozen in a world withdrawn from the broader milieu. To the contrary, evangelicals critiqued the deficiencies of their own cultural universe and incorporated useful resources from wherever they found them. Participation in the world of print did not represent an inevitable compromise as much as a proactive choice: to make the gospel more accessible by appealing to popular tastes while appropriating means of grace from extra-Christian sources. Likewise, nonevangelical communities sometimes accepted religious contributions and at other times vehemently opposed evangelical ideals — as did members of the anti-Sabbatarian and antitemperance movements. To be sure, strident conflicts surfaced repeatedly over religious, ethnic, racial, regional, gender, class, and political differences, and those with the most power tended to enforce their agendas on others. But a more fluid relationship existed between evangelical and nonevangelical cultures than we might expect. Such complex interactions among evangelicals and other groups suggest the need to reenvision American evangelicalism as a densely layered cultural system.[30]

Context and Scope

Although the history of Christian textual practices dates back to the first century, my narrative begins in 1789, with the formation of the Methodist Book Concern, and ends in 1880, with Harper & Brothers' publication of the best-seller *Ben-Hur*. Over the course of a century, evangelical culture embraced diverse writing, publishing, and reading practices while defining these practices as functioning to preserve core beliefs and values. Starting in the mid-eighteenth century and picking up speed in the nineteenth, evangelicalism and the book trades grew explosively, and the histories of these developments intersect. I focus especially on the middle decades of the nineteenth century, when possibilities for participating in the world of print multiplied.

The Methodist Episcopal Church made some of the earliest coordinated efforts to use the press to disseminate evangelical values throughout the new United States. From the outset, Methodists, as well as other evangelicals, expressed readiness to experiment with different genres, material packaging, and marketing strategies. By the 1840s, early experiments had blossomed into the beginnings of an integrated publishing industry that crossed regional and racial boundaries to create a national print culture. The costs of production and distribution decreased while the quality of paper, bindings, illustrations, and type improved dramatically. Meanwhile, contents and narrative styles diversified, so much so that by the 1860s, evangelical histories, biographies, essays, hymnals, and novels easily outran sermons in number and size of print runs. By the time the Methodist-influenced trade press of Harper & Brothers published *Ben-Hur*, which would eventually sell 2.5 million copies, evangelicals had been long accustomed to reading and writing best-sellers.[31]

By 1880, the contours of evangelicalism had become increasingly difficult to delineate. Confronting challenges posed by higher biblical criticism, evolution, scientific naturalism, urbanization, immigration, and Reconstruction, Protestants reconfigured their religious landscape. As some clergy, such as Henry Ward Beecher (1813–87), leaned toward a new religious liberalism, and as others, including Dwight L. Moody (1837–99), worked to revive conservative evangelicalism through nondenominational channels, denominational labels lost much of their usefulness in discriminating between evangelical and liberal theologies. Liberal Protestants, some of them joining the Social Gospel movement, trained their attention more on this world than on the world to come; they privileged morality as the essence of religion and deemphasized the supernaturalism of the gospel. Another subgroup of Protestants, who became known as Fundamentalists during the early twentieth century, invoked commitment to the fundamentals of the Word as an antidote to perceived modernist heresies while expressing increasingly pessimistic ideas regarding the possibility of transforming the world. Reversing the previous half century's emphasis on gaining a hearing in the world, Moody urged every Christian to draw a line "between the church and the world, and . . . get both feet out of the world." As racial and social tensions mounted, more and more evangelicals withdrew from mainstream churches to form new African American, Holiness, and Pentecostal denominations that accentuated the Word's purifying power.[32]

Most lay evangelicals did not experience these large-scale cultural shifts as intensely as did theologians and seminary professors but instead continued to choose from among options articulated by leaders who were much like their predecessors. I do not, in this book, intend primarily to trace the attenuation of evangelical cultural dominance. Indeed, evangelicals continued to exert a tremendous cultural influence throughout the nineteenth century and beyond. Other scholarship has admirably described late-nineteenth- and early-twentieth-century religious and cultural adaptation. Rather, I tease out some of the ways that evangelicals used the printed word to work through alternatives and tensions during an equally rich but less examined earlier phase in American cultural history.[33]

Popular and academic writings alike have favored evangelicals as a subject of inquiry in recent decades. Authors interested in topics such as America's "Christian origins" and the presidency of George W. Bush agree that evangelicals have continued to play a significant, though shifting, role in shaping American culture. Much of this literature uses the term "evangelical" without a great deal of historical precision. The tendency toward vagueness is problematic since the term has accreted conflicting connotations over the years; the mere mention of evangelicals evokes strongly favorable or unfavorable ideas and emotive responses depending upon personal assumptions and experiences.[34]

My use of the term "evangelical" instead of "conservative Protestant" — which, though not unproblematic, stirs fewer immediate responses — requires explanation. I write about evangelicals because the people whose story I tell used that label to describe themselves and because the term accentuates what I consider one of the central themes in American religious history: the goal of using the Word to transform the world. To paint the aims of this project in its broadest strokes, this book strives to rehabilitate the analytical usefulness of the term "evangelical," much as the scholarship of Perry Miller resuscitated the label "puritan." As a corollary, this book seeks to illuminate how print cultures work, using the evangelical case to deepen our understanding of problems in the interpretation of cultures.[35]

This interdisciplinary study approaches evangelical print culture from the perspectives of the histories of religion, the book trades, writing, and reading, employing literary and cultural analysis to consider textual transmission, authorship, genre, and language in relation to identity formation. I am indebted to the theoretical work of cultural anthropologists and literary critics as well as to practitioners of the interdisciplinary history of the book. Looking beyond the uses of texts as converting instruments, this study asks how writing, publishing, and reading practices reflected, sustained, and transmitted evangelical culture while influencing the broader processes of American cultural formation.

This project grows out of my dissatisfaction with the assumptions and methods that have governed two streams of academic discourse, one in religious history and the other in cultural studies. First, I rethink approaches taken by American religious historians. Analysts have generally understood evangelicalism in terms of emotional revivalism, affirmation of core doctrines, or membership in certain denominations. Such accounts privilege crisislike, individual conversion as the apex of evangelical experience. Studies typically classify groups according to doctrinal standards such as original sin and justification by faith or offer denominational roll calls that include, for instance, Methodists, Baptists, Presbyterians, and Congregationalists. Scholars have at times deployed the term "evangelical" with tremendous interpretive power, yet traditional definitions have also reified dynamic experiences and silenced fresh historical insight.[36]

By shifting the terrain for discussions of evangelicalism, I invite frustration. Conventional classifications provide convenient checklists for determining which individuals and groups should count as evangelicals. My goal, however, is to problematize and work through the variable meanings of

American evangelical print culture. One way of framing evangelical diversity would be to say that several evangelical cultures competed for dominance. This statement, however, implies a higher level of stability within cultural communities than I believe existed. In their attempts to harmonize purity and presence, self-identified evangelicals simultaneously inhabited overlapping cultural worlds and felt substantial freedom to move across communities and to employ a range of resources and strategies in their interactions with the world. To cite a few prominent examples, Henry Ward Beecher, Harriet Beecher Stowe (1811–96), and Horace Bushnell (1802–76), in certain phases of their lives, identified themselves and were identified by others as evangelicals, although each stretched the meaning of this classification. Many other individuals and groups espoused values that may seem to us contradictory, in some instances finding ways to reconcile perceived tensions and in other cases experiencing no tension at all. In part, this study aims to discover what people meant when they called themselves evangelical and to determine how it was possible for so much variety and even antagonism to exist among those who shared this self-understanding.[37]

This project expands our picture of evangelicalism by bringing into fuller view some of the day-to-day relationships, concerns, and practices of lay and clerical individuals who identified themselves as evangelical. The story of evangelical culture-building is much thicker than a focus on institutional development, conversion experiences, or doctrinal controversies might suggest. Evangelicals understood everyday activities, such as writing, publishing, and reading, within the same framework as revival meetings or specifically religious rituals, interfacing doctrine and emotion, denominational and evangelical identity, social and religious experience.

I argue that individual conversion marked the beginning rather than the culmination of evangelicals' day-to-day, communal pursuit of holiness, or sanctification. Printed texts played a prominent role in sustaining and transmitting cultural values among communities of the already converted. The categories of conversion, democratization, denominationalism, and evangelicalism, as people generally define them, inadequately describe the dynamic processes of cultural transmission, exchange, and negotiation that together molded beliefs and experiences throughout individual and communal life cycles. In reorienting the thrust of evangelical studies, I probe the manifold intersections of lived religion and American cultural formation, linking religious and social practices and loyalties based on doctrine, denomination, region, gender, class, and race.[38]

In addition to revising interpretations of American religious history, my second concern is to qualify certain claims made by American cultural historians and literary critics. Scholars have generally contended that commercialization of the print market implicated Protestantism in secularization and cultural decline. Beginning with the present and working backward in search of the origins of contemporary "problems," these cultural analysts trace declension from an earlier golden age free of the taint of capitalism, advertising, and sentimentalism. Grouping evangelicals with other religious Americans and emphasizing elite New Englanders, interpreters argue that religious leaders, in their bid to win and keep an audience, reduced religion to a commodity. Anxious about declining social authority, clergy and women in particular disingenuously used the popular press to influence American culture. Would-be religious, but market-conscious, writers and publishers made a series of cultural concessions, replacing doctrine with narrative, intellect with emotion, and self-scrutiny with narcissism. These shifts putatively reflected and produced a secularized, feminized, and commodified religious landscape and confirm the primacy of economic and social forces in shaping even religious cultures[39]

I question the premise that commercialized religious publishing inevitably led to secularization or cultural declension. This book differentiates evangelical uses of print from other political, social, and religious uses and takes into account evangelicals from multiple regional, denominational, racial, and class backgrounds. Unlike theologically liberal, elite New Englanders whose social authority diminished in the nineteenth century, evangelical clergy and churches enjoyed consistent growth in every region of the expanding nation. I find little evidence that evangelicals used influence manipulatively to regain lost attention.[40]

The mere presence of secular elements in religious texts or marketing strategies does not constitute secularization. The question, as I would pose it, is whether nineteenth-century evangelicalism refocused its core concerns from a heavenward to an earthbound orientation. My basic answer to this question is negative, qualified by recognition of evangelicals' ongoing struggle to perform a difficult balancing act. What some scholars have interpreted as cultural compromise meant something different to the historical actors. Rather than accommodating religion to advancing capitalism, evangelicals configured commerce as a religious instrument. Writers, publishers, and readers self-consciously and strategically developed marketing strategies and narrative styles to bring orthodox doctrine to bear on everyday experience. Innovative packaging and advertising, instead of subverting textual authority, enhanced the power of the printed word to direct the currents of American culture.

The partnership between religion and the press created tensions for evangelicals who identified themselves both as Christians and as book trades participants. It does not follow, however, that commerce inexorably overshadowed religion. Evangelicals anxiously acknowledged that their project of going into the world to preach the gospel could be derailed in either of two directions: if they withdrew from the world to maintain purity or if, in their zeal to transform the world, they diluted their distinctive message. Nineteenth-century evangelicals constantly and, for the most part, successfully steered between these extremes. As twenty-first-century Americans strive to interpret the evolving relationship between religion and commercialized media, the nineteenth-century encounters offer instructive parallels.

Although I do not find secularization narratives persuasive, I avoid an opposite, triumphal account. I have tried to enter into, or at least draw closer to, the ambiguous, conflicted world conceptualized by nineteenth-century evangelicals. I ask how these people understood and represented what they were doing. With the goal of learning about the hopes, struggles, nonnegotiables, and compromises that together constituted evangelical print culture, I work through alternatives expressed by its participants and assess the choices they made and the implications of these choices for the development of evangelicalism and the book trades. As evangelicals interacted with the world of print, tensions surfaced repeatedly as individuals and communities sought to navigate the tempestuous milieu of American culture. Several overlapping dialectics played themselves out: evangelical and denominational identities, clerical and lay authority, local and textual communities, domestic and institutional sites of religious growth, conservative and radical views of race and gender, print and oral modes of expression, and refined and vernacular aesthetics of the sacred.[41]

In focusing on evangelical print culture, this book necessarily omits much. My approach is thematic rather than encyclopedic or chronological. I do not enter into a full history of evangelicalism or the book trades, nor do I emphasize questions of change over time. An examination of writing, publishing, and reading practices provides an illuminating vista onto evangelical culture, but it represents only one of several possible approaches. Evangelical identity developed partially through the use of printed texts but also through other religious rituals and church-building strategies. My account must be viewed alongside studies that emphasize the preached word, activities of churches and voluntary societies, oral rituals such as prayer and worship, revivals, camp meetings, and Sunday school attendance, to name but a few of the cultural practices that reflected and formed evangelical identities. The evangelical press supplemented other vehicles used to build and sustain churches and denominations and, in some instances, provided an alternative to those other strategies.

Religious commitments, moreover, intersected with social and political concerns. Indeed, Mark Noll has persuasively argued that American evangelicals transferred "religious commitment from the church to the nation." This book says little about politics, although religious and political ideologies and affiliations often informed one another. I also resist using the political term "democratization" to describe lay religious participation; regulation always accompanied lay empowerment, and the exercise of influence to mediate between Word and world differed in significant respects from political power. Another important omission is the cultural experience of non-English-speaking evangelicals. This decision flows from my concern with the formation and sustenance of a textual community that depended on the use of a shared language.[42]

The first half of this book depicts the cultural universe of evangelical writing, publishing, and reading practices. Chapter 1 distinguishes evangelical print culture from other political, social, and religious uses of the press. The discussion explores how evangelicals balanced purity and presence by interweaving the religious and commercial meanings of print artifacts as words, objects, and commodities. Evangelicals used words incarnated in the print market to transform the world by performing core narrative structures: contending for the faith, exemplifying the priesthood of all believers, infusing the world with sanctifying influences, and uniting as the church universal. The interplay of these story frameworks contributed to the simultaneous maturation of evangelical and denominational identities and to the differentiation of evangelical from nonevangelical cultural strands. A distinctive linguistic style of relating to the Word and the world set evangelical print culture apart from the textual practices of other religious or morally oriented groups, such as Catholics, Mormons, and romantics.

The next three chapters view evangelical print culture from the vantage of publishers, texts, and readers and writers. Chapter 2 asks how denominational, nondenominational, and evangelical trade publishers located themselves relative to the structures of the book trades and how they reconciled their identities as evangelicals and as book trades participants. Denominational publishers, out of concern for correct doctrine and practice, published controversial texts that fueled religious rivalries. Nondenominational houses, aiming to make the Word accessible to all, promoted evangelical unity by disseminating inexpensive publications nationally. Evangelical trade publishers, envisioning themselves as members of a priesthood of all believers, sanctified the general print market. Despite tensions between religious and trade goals and anxieties about the dangers of conforming to the world, evangelicals retained their drive for distinctiveness while influencing an American print market.

The discussion turns from publishers to texts in chapter 3, identifying a fluid canon that shared certain marks of membership. Informally designated cultural arbiters altered, abridged, and refashioned canonical texts whenever useful and appropriated texts and genres originating outside evangelicalism. Works of doctrine, history, and devotion portrayed everyday experiences as contributing to spiritual progress. Memoirs used Christian examples to provoke emulation. Fiction was more controversial; evangelicals debated among themselves whether imaginative writing merely excited the passions or employed the sentiments to stimulate sympathetic action on behalf of others. Sunday school libraries, by gradually forming readers' character, promoted ongoing sanctification.

Chapter 4 examines how idealized and actual readers and writers interacted with the evangelical canon to forge a sense of membership in a textual community that transcended space and time. Authors, editors, and publishers inscribed in evangelical texts informal rules that oriented readers to texts and partially shaped reading practices. Advice literature outlined reading programs and urged strategies such as prayer, memorization, and meditation. Actual readers and writers who reflected on their experiences often used the strategies prescribed in advice manuals. Individuals also had expectations and agendas of their own that reconfigured the boundaries between author, text, and reader. Evangelicals pursued reading and writing as sacred disciplines, recording meditations through marginalia, inscriptions, albums, diaries, and memoirs. Participants moved with ease among old and new genres, steady sellers and recently popular titles, and intensive and extensive reading styles, confidently crossing back and forth from evangelical to nonevangelical print communities.

The second half of the book explores the uses of evangelical print culture by focusing more narrowly on one form and one genre, the periodical and the hymnal. Chapters 5 and 6 assess how periodicals empowered a priesthood of all believers to contend for the Word in the world. Chapter 5 asks how writers and readers used periodicals to defend pure gospel truth by refuting religious errors and adapting market strategies to religious purposes. Evangelical efforts to control the forces impacting American culture fueled denominational controversies and facilitated dialogue among religious and secular reading communities. The relatively low price, speed of production, and geographic range of distribution of periodicals made them effective in transmitting versions of evangelical culture across space to shape the American landscape.

The communication networks established by periodicals, as chapter 6 argues, functioned ritually to sustain evangelical identity over time as members of the priesthood of all believers. Predictably frequent communication among evangelicals enforced shared narratives that explained how things are in the world. Periodicals connected textual and domestic models of community to supplement or even replace local community relationships. The periodical form encouraged regular communication among geographically scattered individuals and invited widespread participation that involved clergy, laity, women, and African Americans in the ongoing process of reinventing the evangelical canon.

In contrast to the cultural work done by the periodical form, chapters 7 and 8 explain, the hymnal genre silenced disagreements to exert a sanctifying and unifying influence on a pilgrim community traveling through this world toward that which is to come. As chapter 7 illustrates, by repeatedly performing hymns in settings as diverse as Sunday worship, midweek gatherings, private devotions, camp meetings, and gospel-song services, evangelicals sanctified the world around them by positioning daily life experiences within a universalizing narrative framework. In seeking to sing with the spirit and with the understanding, evangelicals balanced competing aesthetics of sacred language: ontologically and functionally sacred words, oral and literate expression, African and European traditions, and vernacular and refined styles.

Chapter 8 demonstrates that hymnals functioned in evangelical culture to elide denominational differences in order to unify the pilgrim community. Editors, compilers, and translators actively molded an informal canon of hymns by framing, selecting, and altering the texts included in published collections. These cultural mediators promoted a textual model of community imagined as transcending temporal, geographic, and denominational barriers to collective identity.

Evangelicals have long used the Word and printed words to sustain a communal pilgrimage and to transform the world. As the epilogue suggests, twenty-first-century alliances between religion and the media bear the imprint of earlier cultural negotiations. This book tells the story of how nineteenth-century evangelicals balanced purity and presence in the world and how, along the way, their struggles to navigate among linguistic alternatives reshaped the worlds of evangelicalism and American culture.

Part One

The Cultural Universe of Evangelical
Writing, Publishing, and Reading

1

What Is Evangelical
Print Culture?

The opening passage of Kate M'Clellan's children's book *Two Christmas Gifts* (1866), published by the Protestant Episcopal Society for the Promotion of Evangelical Knowledge, provides a window onto the tension-ridden world of evangelical print culture:

> The man with the huge basket moved away at last, and Johnny Lee slipped into his place before the bright store-window, which was unlike any other in the long street; for it contained only Bibles, Prayer-Books, and markers; but never before had Johnny seen such elegant book-marks nor such handsomely-bound books. The one that pleased him most was a monstrous Bible in rich morocco binding, with very large, clear type. If he only were rich enough to buy that, what a beautiful present it would be for him to give to his lame brother Willy, and surely no person's eyes ever could ache while looking at such large letters, even if the lamp-light were very dim. And the Bible was opened at one of Willy's favorite chapters: "The Lord is my shepherd." If he only were rich! Then the poor boy drew the thin scarf over his red ears, rubbed his cold hands, and looked far into the store. How full it seemed, and no wonder; for wasn't it Christmas Eve? and was not the book that contained the tidings of great joy brought to earth on the first Christmas night, the best possible present to make whenever that time came round?

The passage captures a number of the hopes and contradictions that characterized the entrance of evangelical writers, publishers, and readers into the print marketplace of nineteenth-century America. The elegance of the

Bible-store window attracts Johnny's attention; he eyes the brightness and fullness of all the shops lining the long street on Christmas Eve and the unique products in this particular shop. What first catches his attention is not the content of the Bibles and prayer books; he doubtless would have seen these kinds of books before. He notes the books' handsome bindings and quality type and fantasizes about being rich.[1]

Johnny's interactions with the open Bible suggest the close connection between religious and commercial meanings. Johnny at first perceives worldly riches as requisite to the possession of the otherworldly wealth contained within the Bible's pages. Johnny does not neglect to notice that the Bible is opened to a favorite chapter, but the passage is ironic in this context. "The Lord is my shepherd," begins the Twenty-third Psalm, the next line of which reads "I shall not want," implying that the Lord provides for every need. Reading this passage does not lead Johnny to rest content but causes him to long for riches. Yet Johnny does not simply equate worldly and otherworldly wealth. After adjusting his thin scarf and rubbing his cold hands, he refocuses his attention on the power of the Word itself, incarnated by a full range of more and less expensive packaging into the world of human relationships.

Johnny's longing to give his brother a Bible, even if not a fancy one, on Christmas Eve reflects the campaign of Victorian evangelicals to Christianize Christmas, formerly celebrated as a secular holiday, and to reshape popular literary markets, like that for giftbooks. Evangelical giftbooks not only sentimentalized relationships between givers and recipients and expressed middle-class standards of taste and status, as did secular giftbooks, but also invoked participation in a textual community inhabited by all Christians (figure 1.1). The Bible occupied a privileged position among a dense constellation of evangelical texts, such as *Two Christmas Gifts*, that writers, publishers, buyers, recipients, and readers used to influence one another's spiritual progress from this world to the next. M'Clellan purportedly aims not to replace Bible sales or reading but to promote Bible study. Even as the text explicitly encourages the buying and giving of Bibles and advertises its own suitability as a Christmas gift, it concludes by urging its "dear reader" to receive "that most precious of all Christmas gifts," Jesus Christ. The language of the text simultaneously embraces its own market participation and claims to transcend mere consumerism by offering its readers the most precious gift of all, Jesus Christ, the incarnate Word.[2]

Two Christmas Gifts exemplifies the struggle of nineteenth-century evangelicals to balance purity with presence as they used the Word and words to transform their world. The book represents one of the largest branches of

Figure 1.1. "Christmas Day," *The Christian Year* (1864). This illustration depicts one child giving a book to another to celebrate Christmas Day and defines the holiday exchange as Christian by quoting Luke 2:14: "Glory to God on high, on Earth be peace." (Courtesy of the American Antiquarian Society)

evangelical publishing, Sunday school literature, and is typical in themes and style of texts produced by several expanding denominational publishing boards. Like many evangelical publications, this one was manufactured and sold in New York, the center of the book trades by midcentury. The book's author, Kate M'Clellan, belonged to an expanding class of prolific women authors who sacralized home and family by portraying pious mothers presiding over fireside religion. In alternating between third-person narrative and direct address to the reader, the text characteristically blends imaginative and didactic styles and blurs the genres of fiction and lay sermon. The book points to the commercialization not only of Bibles but also of a wide range of evangelical literary productions — such as *Two Christmas Gifts* itself — marketed as Christmas gifts and sold in bright-windowed stores (figure 1.2). In the world of evangelical publishing, print artifacts functioned simultaneously as words, objects, and commodities. Evangelical texts possessed cultural value both because of the purity of their message and because they exhibited qualities such as fine craftsmanship esteemed by those within and without evangelicalism. The two Christmas gifts of M'Clellan's story suggest that the cultural practices of bookmaking, selling, buying, giving, and reading have overlapping commercial and religious significance.[3]

As the story line of *Two Christmas Gifts* develops, the dialectic of Bibles as sacred texts and as material artifacts plays itself out. Johnny's mother, Mrs. Lee, shares his desire to buy for Willy (her son and Johnny's brother) not just any Bible, but a "nice" one. Indeed, the story makes clear that the lame boy, Willy, already owns a personal copy of the Bible, although the print is "too fine" for him to read it easily. The high quality of the large Bible adds not only to its material value but also to its religious meaning. Mrs. Lee, with a hint of disappointment, selects a smaller Bible with large type and "bound in red," which costs all her remaining money. Every time the author mentions this Bible throughout the rest of the story, she calls attention to its red binding. As the family later gathers to admire the gift, all pronounce the red Bible "the most precious book in the house," even though there is at least one other Bible in the house, and likely more than one, since the Bible with the fine print is described as Willy's. When Mrs. Lee visits the Bible store, she secures not only the red volume for Willy but also a job for Johnny working as a shop assistant; the whole family benefits economically because Mrs. Lee buys and gives a sacred gift to her son.[4]

This first Christmas gift of the story empowers an evangelical priesthood of all believers to contend for the Word in the world. Every night Willy selects a passage in his red Bible, and every morning Johnny turns the leaves of the "great," "beautiful" Bible in the store to that same page. By catching the attention of passersby, first through its beauty and then through its contents, the open Bible does "good" to many. Willy rejoices that he with his cheap red Bible can indirectly exert a moral influence through the great, beautiful Bible: "It was such a comfort to be doing something daily for Jesus, and to feel that, though only a poor lame boy, he might still be the means, under God, of doing much good." M'Clellan depicts the respective values of the red and morocco Bibles as, in one sense, equivalent: both possess the "words of life." The display Bible is positioned to do more good than the red privately owned Bible possibly could, yet the

Figure 1.2. G. G. Evans Gift Book Store, established in Philadelphia in 1854, was one of many large urban stores that sold books like *Two Christmas Gifts* to middle-class consumers. (Courtesy of The Library Company of Philadelphia)

careful selection of passages from the smaller Bible enhances the larger Bible's influence. Paradoxically, the larger Bible is both more and less valuable than the smaller, from which it partially derives its efficacy. The red Bible is more valuable to Willy since it is just cheap enough that his mother can afford it; the morocco Bible's high commercial value makes it useless to him, because it is unattainable.[5]

The second Christmas gift presented in the story is the great Bible itself, which extends poor Willy's influence into the home of his wealthy cousin, Little Marian, the recipient of the Bible. This second Bible, through its fine packaging, sanctifies the worldly domain of high fashion and, by the influence it exerts, unifies diverse members of the church universal. Marian, the child of nominally Christian parents, has previously demonstrated little interest in religion; she rarely opened her own "handsome," "tiny" "blue-velvet" Bible. The morocco Bible begins a spiritual transformation in Marian's life. The great Bible first draws Marian when displayed in the bookshop window; every day she stops to read the passage to which the Bible has been opened. The morocco Bible is "not at all like" any other Bible she has tried to read; its value as a material artifact attracts Marian, inducing her to read it, submit to its authority, and apply its teachings. Although other expensive textual embodiments of the Bible have failed to win Marian or her family to Christian faith, this large, superbly crafted Bible opens "a new home . . . to Jesus." The episode portrays the Bible's material value as augmenting, even as essential to achieving, its spiritual value; the red Bible could not have produced the same effect. The reader knows, however, what Marian does not: that the great Bible would not have attracted her notice had it not been for the passages selected by Willy from the cheap red Bible. This scene reveals the instability of hierarchies between material and religious wealth exemplified by the contrasts of fine and cheap Bibles and by the distant worlds of the well-stocked shop and the poor lame boy's family. Marian's conversion shows that every Christian, even Willy who seemingly has no power, can influence others to join and grow as members of the church universal.[6]

The twin centers of religious activity, for poor Johnny and Willy's family and for wealthy Marian's, are the bookstore and domestic fireside, the scenes where all the text's actions take place. The shop window is sanctified as a meeting ground for poor and rich Christians, both of whom can at least afford to look at fine commercial and religious artifacts. The worlds of print and commerce mediate between Christians otherwise separated by social difference, allowing the poorer family to influence the richer one for good. Nineteenth-century evangelicals simultaneously narrowed the focus of Christian fellowship from church to home and expanded it out again to encompass all participants in a textually defined community. The textual community invoked by *Two Christmas Gifts* represents an alternative to the contentiousness of socially and religiously fragmented local communities. Throughout the narrative, no character attends a single church service or meeting or mentions the name of a specific church or denomination, even though a denominational publishing society printed the book. This pattern, too, suggests several key tensions in evangelical print culture at midcentury: between domestic and institutional religion, clerical and lay religious discourse, and evangelical and denominational identity.

Evangelical Uses of the Printed Word

Evangelicals used printed texts, like M'Clellan's *Two Christmas Gifts*, to enact a set of sometimes competing core narrative structures that envisioned the Christian life as contending for the faith, exemplifying the priesthood of all believers, sanctifying the world, and uniting as the church universal. Each of these story frameworks, discussed at length in later chapters, balanced the goals of maintaining the Word's purity and creating a transformative presence in the world. Evangelicals, though often themselves divided along denominational lines, participated in a loosely organized print culture that constituted an alternative to "unevangelical" uses of the press — those founded upon divergent assumptions about the Word or the world.

As evangelicals used the press, alongside other means, to achieve both purity and presence, evangelical and denominational identities blossomed simultaneously and in tension. Protestants, like Catholics, affirmed that all Christians belonged to one church universal, united under Christ. Yet much as zeal for purity led the early Reformers to break from the Roman Catholic Church, subsequent generations who read the Bible for themselves often felt the need for deeper reformation. Henry VIII's notorious withdrawal of England's church from Roman leadership in 1534, for the purpose of gaining a divorce, left Calvinists dissatisfied with the vestiges of Catholicism they perceived in the reorganized Church of England. These so-called Puritans, named by their opponents for thinking themselves purer than anyone else, used both the pulpit and the press to carry on the work of reformation.[7]

Dissenters from the Church of England developed an ecclesiology, or view of the church, as a single, universal body manifested plurally and locally. Puritan publications crystallized disagreements between the church and dissenters, which erupted in the English Civil War of the 1640s. Puritans such as John Bunyan, deprived of his pulpit and imprisoned in 1660, employed the printed word to articulate grievances against the established church. The resilience of dissent led ultimately to the Glorious Revolution and Toleration Act of 1689, which legally recognized loyal but nonconformist religious groups, namely Presbyterians, Congregationalists, Baptists, and subsequently Quakers. Print was one factor among many that encouraged such a balance between a lay priesthood's yearning for purity and the needs of political and ecclesiastical leaders to maintain national and religious unity.[8]

By the mid-nineteenth century, purity-minded Christians often thought of themselves as evangelicals, but no less often they described themselves as members of a "denomination." Denominational rivalries cut across the shared fabric of evangelicalism, generating fierce polemics around issues such as baptism and free will. Denominations worked hard to create and sustain a sense of difference, using their own publishing boards or agencies to this end. Although the historian of religious publishing must respect the denominational dimensions of this enterprise, many evangelicals rejected the very idea of difference, insisting, as Methodist founder John Wesley (1703–91) did, on "fellowship" among all Christians, even as he gathered around himself those who shared his religious views: "But from real Christians, of whatsoever denomination they be, we earnestly desire not to be distinguished at all. . . . Dost thou love and serve God? It is enough. I give thee the right hand of fellowship." George Whitefield (1714–70), the Great Awakening's most influential evangelist, similarly envisioned himself as a spokesman for a broadly evangelical movement rather than seeking to found a single religious society. Denominational theory, as it developed during the next half century, recognized the existence of one Christian church divided into multiple branches, each legitimate and vital to the growth of the whole.[9]

Revivalists such as Wesley and Whitefield managed simultaneously to evade and reinforce divisions within Protestantism by classifying some, but not all, Protestants as "evangelical." Self-proclaimed evangelicals reserved the label, which had up until the mid-eighteenth century referred to all Protestants, for a subset of church leaders and members whom they approved. Evangelicals distinguished themselves from sacramentalist High Churchmen, whom they accused of relying on the sacraments instead of the gospel, and from rationalist liberals, whom they accused of denying the gospel's power. Evangelical leaders used the printed and the preached word to set themselves apart from other Protestants and to cultivate in their followers a sense of membership in a transatlantic evangelical community. Whitefield kept a journal of his local activities and reception, which he published in periodicals that circulated internationally. Wesley wrote or republished hundreds of evangelical tracts and books, beginning with Thomas à Kempis's *Imitation of Christ* (1471–72) and including Charles Wesley's (1707–88) numerous hymns. John Wesley stimulated the rapid growth of Methodist societies by deploying circuit riders in Britain and America with a joint theological and commercial charge, commissioning them as preachers and booksellers. The establishment of the Methodist Book Concern in America in 1789 formalized ministers' dual responsibilities, creating means for the production of a centrally sanctioned literature and for its distribution through a corps of itinerant preachers.[10]

Opponents of the revivals, who similarly turned to the press to gather a following, used the term "evangelical" as a label of reproach to denote presumed fanaticism. Self-titled liberals claimed to be more rational than evangelicals in their reading of the Word and more charitable in accommodating diverse viewpoints. In America, Charles Chauncy (1705–87) led the antievangelical party, pronouncing the classic expression of liberal ideals in *Seasonable Thoughts* (1743). William Ellery Channing's (1780–1842) sermon "Unitarian Christianity" (1819) further developed the liberal position. Liberals, who formed Unitarian and Universalist churches, emphasized the importance of human reason in interpreting the Bible, consequently denying the rationality of such doctrines as human depravity and Jesus' divinity. Although liberalism swept across New England's upper classes and sacramentalists retained control of branches of the Episcopal and Lutheran churches, evangelicals dominated the American religious landscape.[11]

Cross-fertilization between European and American evangelicalism persisted throughout the nineteenth century as revivalists and publications traversed the Atlantic, but American expressions developed in a distinctive political and social context. Throughout most of Europe, as in England, the state established the church, mandating tax support and religious tests for public office and imposing financial and civil penalties on dissenters. In America, the religious diversity of immigrants, some of them fleeing persecution, destabilized religious establishments. Not only evangelical, sacramentalist, and liberal Protestants but also Catholics, Jews, Muslims, and other sects contributed to the American religious milieu beginning in the colonial period. Undergirded by republican ideology, the Establishment Clause of the First Amendment to the United States Constitution, ratified in 1791, separated church and state at the federal level. Although not required to do so by the constitutional provision, every state in the union had formally disestablished religion by 1833. With the collapse of established churches, denominational competition seemingly gained the upper hand relative to evangelical fellowship. Here too the story is more complex because denominational and evangelical allegiances continued to overlap throughout the nineteenth century.[12]

Under a new voluntary principle, denominations developed into a fuller institutional dimension, not as dissenting parties but as the predominant form of church organization in America. Lyman Beecher (1775–1863), the foremost Congregationalist spokesperson of his day and longtime opponent of disestablishment, voiced the best-known articulation of the new voluntary ethic. In his autobiography, Beecher reflected that losing the battle to keep Congregationalism established in Connecticut, in 1818, was the "best thing that ever happened" in the state. Thrown on "their own resources and on God," Congregationalist churches gained influence "by voluntary efforts, societies, missions, and revivals." Even denominations that had never enjoyed state support grew by participating in the institutional thickening that Beecher described.[13]

To gain and keep a following in the entrepreneurial milieu of antebellum America, every denomination relied upon both the pulpit and the press. Revivals ignited in many backwoods areas and African American communities from the 1780s forward, gaining particular notice from the press at Cane Ridge, Kentucky, in 1801, as the Great Revival birthed new churches throughout the South and West. The so-called Second Great Awakening reached its peak in the 1830s, most famously in the "burned-over" district of upstate New York. The revivals stimulated the formation of voluntary moral reform societies, many of which employed the press. The American Temperance Society, founded in 1826, supplemented its pledge campaigns and local mobilization efforts with the publication of hymns, tracts, and books, such as *Ten Nights in a Bar Room*, published in 1853. The American Sunday School Union, established in 1824 to encourage literacy as well as piety, paired Sabbath religious instruction with the dissemination of libraries of inexpensive publications. By 1837, an estimated 1 million children attended 16,000 Sunday schools in America. These children and their families borrowed Sunday school library books for Sabbath and midweek religious reading that socialized them into the evangelical cultural system. Churches grew and sustained themselves through the activities of Sunday school teachers and ministers who preached in churches and visited families in their homes; the laity's participation in midweek prayer, class, and praise meetings; the establishment of schools and colleges; and the publication of books, tracts, and periodicals. It is virtually impossible to disentangle the relative effectiveness of each of these measures, which evangelicals at the time perceived as complementary and mutually reinforcing.[14]

Through the combined influence of various church-building strategies, religious institutions in every region grew tremendously during the first half of the nineteenth century. In 1791 the United States population totaled 4 million, 5–10 percent of whom, or less than 400,000, belonged to any church. By 1870, 40 million people inhabited the United States, roughly 30 percent of whom, or 12 million Americans, affiliated with a Christian church. Catholics and Methodists each claimed memberships of 3.5 million, Baptists and Disciples together counted 2 million, Presbyterians 1,150,000, Congregationalists 480,000, Episcopalians and Lutherans 440,000 each, Universalists 140,000, German Reformed and Quakers 90–100,000 each, Dutch Reformed 55,000, and Unitarians 30,000. During the antebellum period, Methodists and Baptists significantly outran every other denomination, together accounting for two-thirds of Protestant church adherents. Denominational identity took deep root as church leaders and members used the pulpit and the press to articulate points of difference between denominations. Debates over doctrine, polity, and practice, which peaked from the 1840s to the 1860s, produced bitter divisions, even among denominations that affirmed their identity as evangelicals.[15]

Disagreements subdivided each of the major denominational families. The Methodists, first organized with an independent ecclesiastical structure in 1784, branched into the Methodist Episcopal Church, North, Methodist Episcopal Church, South, and African Methodist Episcopal (AME), African Methodist Episcopal Zion (AMEZ), Colored Methodist Episcopal, Methodist Protestant, Reformed, Wesleyan, Primitive, and Calvinistic Methodist churches. By 1815, 40,000 or nearly one-third of all Methodists were African American. Expanding tremendously during the early years of Reconstruction, the AME Church, founded in 1787, grew to 70,000 members by 1866 and 390,000 members by 1876. The AMEZ Church, formed in 1796, claimed 42,000 members in 1866 and 164,000 members in 1868. Baptists, never as centrally coordinated (or as adept at keeping membership statistics) as the Methodists, included congregations who classed themselves as Regular, Freewill, Free Communion, Old School, Six-Principle, Old Two-Seed-in-the-Spirit Predestinarian, German, English Seventh-Day, and German Seventh-Day churches and the black National Baptist Convention. Baptists attracted a similar number of blacks as did Methodists in the antebellum period. In the second half of the nineteenth century, African Americans more often joined Baptist churches than those of any other denomination.[16]

The press, employed by churches of every affiliation, contributed to denominational growth in part by fanning the flames of religious controversy. In one of the best-known instances of controversial religious publishing, the Landmark disputes exploded in the decades between 1850 and 1880. James Robinson Graves (1820–93), a Vermont Yankee transplanted to rural Tennessee, initiated the "Landmarkism" movement by arguing that certain landmarks, particularly congregational governance and adult baptism by immersion, distinguished local Baptist congregations as the only true Christian churches. Graves used periodicals, pamphlets, and books to discourage Baptists from cooperating with members of hierarchically organized "Pedobaptist" (child-baptizing) churches, such as Methodists, Presbyterians, and Episcopalians. Graves also attacked "Campbellites," or Disciples of Christ, who did organize congregationally and immerse adults, but for the wrong purpose of achieving regeneration. In 1860, Graves's heyday, his periodical, the *Tennessee Baptist and Reflector*, had the largest subscription list, 13,000, of any paper in Tennessee, Texas, Arkansas, and Missouri. As the Baptist *Religious Herald* of Richmond, Virginia, countered Graves's claims, the conflict reflected not only doctrinal concerns but also competing temperaments among Baptists that roughly split along urban-rural, southeastern-southwestern, and settled-frontier lines of social and religious identity. Eventually, in 1905, the Landmark controversies led to the formation of a separate denomination, the Landmark Baptists.[17]

In the Landmark disputes, publications hardened denominational divisions by accentuating disagreements among groups. In contrast, denominational leaders sometimes used the press to make a hegemonic bid for support by purposefully disregarding denominational rivalries. The journal for the avowedly nondenominational American Home Missionary Society published an article in 1827 appealing for funds to support a church in Niagara County of western New York. The article urged evangelicals of all denominations to support the proposed mission because the area was "destitute of the stated ministry of the gospel of every denomination." The article's author almost certainly knew that Baptist and Methodist churches had already been organized in Niagara County but omitted this information in an attempt to increase Congregational and Presbyterian influence.[18]

Yet this kind of cooperation among evangelicals did not erase differences in denominational, regional, ethnic, racial, class, gender, or political orientations. Even when not deployed to controversial ends, evangelical print culture revealed the diversity of its participants. Jarena Lee's 1836 autobiography demonstrates its author's sense of identification as a member of the AME Church, a preacher of the gospel, a servant maid, a resident of New Jersey and Pennsylvania, and a wife and mother. By comparison, Peter Cartwright's *Autobiography* (1856) illuminates his identity as a Methodist, an itinerant preacher west of the Appalachians, a husband, a father, a grandfather, a great-grandfather, and a political officeholder intensely loyal to the Democratic party. The 1863 memoir of William Simonds of Massachusetts includes no reference to his Congregational affiliation, since the volume targeted an interdenominational audience; the account describes Simonds as a Christian, an apprentice printer, a newspaper editor, and a published author of fiction. Lee, Cartwright, and Simonds shared many ideals, yet their published records of their experiences diverged significantly. Evangelical print culture is irreducibly complex in part because it embraced participants who struggled to balance competing affiliations, circumstances, values, and practices.[19]

Even as denominational identities solidified during the antebellum period, evangelicals continued to envision themselves as members of the church universal. Nineteenth-century denominational leaders worried about the atomistic tendencies of the priesthood of all believers and, much like Wesley and Whitefield, aggressively sought common ground with other denominations. Evangelical partnerships that crossed denominational lines complicated the balance between denominational and evangelical identities. The American Bible Society (ABS) (1816), American Sunday School Union (ASSU) (1824), and American Tract Society (ATS) (1825), all children of the London Religious Tract Society (1799), brought together members of several denominations. The ASSU board, for example, as of 1844 incorporated representatives of Episcopal, Congregationalist, Baptist, Presbyterian, Lutheran, Dutch and German Reformed, Methodist, Quaker, and Moravian denominations in united action.[20]

Joint ventures like those of the ASSU, ATS, and ABS at no point supplanted denominational identity. The Methodist Episcopal Church, which committed board members and resources to all three nondenominational publishing societies, resented Calvinist dominance of these organizations. Rather than withdraw completely from a cooperative stance, Methodists continued to support these nondenominational partnerships while accelerating denominational publishing initiatives, forming their own Tract Society (1817), Sunday-School Union (1827), and Bible Society (1828). The Baptists, often more controversy-minded than the Methodists, withdrew entirely from the ABS over a translation dispute. Adoniram Judson, renowned missionary to Burma, submitted his Burmese edition to the ABS for publication in 1834, translating the Greek word *baptizo* as "immerse" instead of "baptize." When the ABS refused to publish a "sectarian" translation, the Baptists exited the ABS to form a rival society. An unsuccessful attempt at interdenominational cooperation in this instance solidified denominational dividing lines.[21]

Despite frequent strains like those reflected by the Methodist and Baptist publishing experiences, calls for interdenominational cooperation proliferated. Alongside the publishing boards, nondenominational voluntary societies promoted such causes as missions, temperance, antislavery, educa-

tion, and ministerial training. Evangelicals felt optimistic about the potential for benevolent action to produce wide-reaching societal change. Many
nineteenth-century evangelicals held a postmillennial understanding of
world history and hoped to hasten the thousand-year period prefatory to
Christ's second coming to redeem the world. More than fifty American and
European denominations sent representatives to the first meeting of the
international Evangelical Alliance, held in London in 1846; an American
branch formed in 1867. The alliance aimed to promote fellowship, cooperation, and prayer for united action against the forces opposing evangelical
religion, enumerated by the convention as Roman Catholicism, ignorance,
strong drink, and an irreligious press. Delegates to the 1873 meeting of
the international alliance expressed confidence that, despite continual onslaughts by the "hosts of unbelief," the forces of "evangelical truth" were
progressively reshaping both Europe and America.[22]

Ultimately, the unifying tendencies of evangelical print culture outran
the most divisive intentions. Self-identified evangelical denominations, despite biting antagonisms with one another, strove to form a united front
against common opponents, including Roman Catholics, liberal Protestants, and other sects perceived as unevangelical. In rallying support for the
cause of evangelical religion and reform, nineteenth-century evangelicals,
like earlier generations, turned to the pulpit and the press. Robert Baird
(1798–1863), a leading spokesman for Presbyterianism and for the nondenominational ABS, ASSU, and Evangelical Alliance, used his influential
history, *Religion in America* (1844), to solidify popular perceptions of difference between what he termed evangelical and unevangelical denominations. Since, as Stanley Fish notes, the only proof of membership in an
interpretive community is a "nod of recognition" from other community
members, classifications such as Baird's are extraordinarily helpful in defining the contours of evangelical print culture. According to Baird, evangelicals, those who recognized "Christ as common head," included Protestant
Episcopal, Congregational, Baptist, Presbyterian, German and Dutch Reformed, Methodist, Moravian, Lutheran, United Brethren, Winebren-
narian, Mennonist, and Quaker denominational families. Baird classed the
Disciples of Christ as evangelical only "with much hesitation," since they,
in Baird's view, lacked "repentance toward God and faith in Jesus." Baird
felt particularly troubled that several vocal Disciples rejected the doctrines
of human depravity, eternal damnation, the Trinity, and substitutionary
atonement. The fifth largest denomination in America by 1860, partly
because of their relentless deployment of the press in verbal battles with

other denominations, Disciples — in the evaluation of Baird and many, though certainly not all, other evangelicals — occupied a precarious position on the fringes of evangelical print culture.[23]

Baird similarly compiled a list of unevangelical denominations, which he defined as those "not ranked with those for whom the whole Bible and only the Bible is a foundation." For Baird, as for other self-proclaimed evangelicals, attitudes toward the Word, as revealed in the Bible, constituted the principle criterion for membership in the evangelical family. Although recognizing that not all unevangelical churches shared the "same footing," Baird nonetheless listed together Roman Catholics, Unitarians, the Christian Connection, Universalists, Swedenborgians, Dunkers, Jews, Rappists, Shakers, Mormons, Atheists, Deists, Socialists, and Fourrierists. Not everyone would have compiled precisely the same lists, but Baird's division of the religious world into evangelical and unevangelical segments reflected and perpetuated a perception widely held by self-identified evangelicals.[24]

Unevangelical Uses of the Printed Word

Nineteenth-century evangelical print culture shared characteristics with other religious, social, and political uses of the press termed by Baird and others like him "unevangelical." In America, the rapid, uneven movement of peoples across a vast continent created novel needs for national communication networks. By the mid-nineteenth century, a broad spectrum of groups shared new confidence in the power of the printed word, if not the Word, to influence American culture. Commentators of every persuasion observed that movements that failed to employ the press seldom flourished. New religious groups, such as the Seventh-Day Adventists, Jehovah's Witnesses, and Christian Scientists, signaled their entrance into the nineteenth-century cultural milieu by issuing distinctive publications. Spiritualists, who did not establish churches or denominational structures, published prolifically since they depended on the press for communication and group identity to a greater degree than did more structured religious or social bodies. Older religious and ethnic groups, such as Jews, used the printed word to sustain their unique claims as minorities in the American cultural landscape. The press served a common set of purposes for these and other groups, including evangelicals: facilitating rapid exchange of information, forming and preserving collective identity, educating adherents about core values and beliefs, responding to criticism by outsiders, and contending for controversial viewpoints. Evangelical print culture can be differentiated from other religious or moral uses of the press, despite such common uses, as a distinctive linguistic style of relating to the Word and the world.[25]

Certain religious groups agreed with evangelicals that the world was corrupt and in need of transformation yet disagreed about the nature of the Word and words as agents of redemption. The evangelical doctrine of *sola scriptura*, that the Bible reveals all matters of faith and practice necessary for salvation, privileged the written Word. By contrast, the Catholic Church, having affirmed at the Council of Trent (1545–63) that God revealed the Word through the Bible and unwritten church traditions, encouraged a religious culture in which the Word was experienced orally and visually. Nineteenth-century lay Catholics, as the religious historian Colleen McDannell has observed, attended mass, partook of the sacraments, repeated the rosary and catechism, and performed private devotions before sacred heart pictures, candles, crucifixes, and holy water fonts. Catholics nevertheless developed a richly textured print culture. At least sixty Catholic publishers had entered business by 1850, most notably Mathew Carey, one of the pioneers in the wider American print market and a premier publisher of Catholic and Protestant Bibles. Catholic steady sellers included liturgical guides, hymnals, biographies, histories, children's literature, periodicals, and sentimental novels. Yet, given Catholic understandings of the Word and words, textual practices could never substitute for local church communities.[26]

Catholics envisioned Christian community as centered squarely in the church, superintended by a priest who set apart particular spaces, times, and practices as sacred. Catholics and Protestants shared certain great narratives of Christian experience, such as pilgrimage, but with key differences. Evangelicals conceived of themselves as lay priests, encouraging one another along a corporate pilgrimage through the world toward heaven. Catholics saw pilgrimage as individual withdrawal from the world, assisted by canonized saints and priests. Unlike internally divided evangelicals, Catholic authors and publishers limited contending for the faith to debating non-Catholic opponents. Higher views of ecclesiastical authority, awareness of Catholics' minority status in America, and sensitivity to Protestant criticisms sharply curtailed Catholic use of the press to voice internal controversies. To ensure public uniformity, the church hierarchy firmly regulated Catholic publishing, impressing its marks of approval on acceptable texts with the Latin phrases *Imprimatur, Nihil Obstat,* or *Permissu Superiorum,* meaning "Let it be printed," "Nothing hinders," or "By permission of superiors." Despite deep affinities between evangelical and Catholic assumptions about the world, differing understandings of the Word and words kept Catholic and evangelical print cultures distinct in content and function.[27]

Some religious groups placed less emphasis on ecclesiastical tradition than did Catholics yet, to a greater degree than most evangelicals, considered ongoing revelation a vital supplement to the written Word of the Bible. Shakers and many Quakers expected God to continue revealing the living Word orally. Mormons privileged oral, "latter-day" revelation and also insisted on the divine inspiration of extrabiblical written texts. From its inception, Mormonism stood outside the evangelical camp by choice as well as rejection of kinship by self-identified evangelicals. Mormons vigorously debated evangelicals in the press and produced a voluminous outpouring of diaries, journals, and letters asserting the group's distinctive identity. Joseph Smith, the movement's founder, claimed that God spoke to him in a vision, warning him not to join any existing religious denomination since they all were wrong and none belonged within the church universal. Denying the sufficiency of the Bible to reveal the living Word, Smith attested that God had appointed him to use special stones, Urim and Thummin, to translate the Book of Mormon, which proclaimed the "fullness of the everlasting Gospel." Smith procured a local publisher for his book in 1830, after a follower mortgaged his farm to pay the printing costs. The book was a market flop but stirred newspaper controversy that afforded Smith national notoriety. On the heels of the Book of Mormon's publication, Smith organized the one true "Church of Christ," which attracted 200,000 members by 1890.[28]

The Mormon canon, constructed as an alternative to the evangelical canon, encompassed the Bible, the Book of Mormon, and the Pearl of Great Price. The latter texts presumably had more authority than those in the evangelical canon — including the Bible — because they were inspired and translated by the power of God rather than man and were therefore free from the corruption of human language. The Mormon canon remained open, in a restricted sense, in that the prophet (Smith and his successors), but no one else, could add to the canon as he received new revelations from God to help the church adapt to a changing world. As a corollary to Smith's enlarged doctrine of the Word, he restricted the evangelical idea of the priesthood of all believers. All white Mormon men — but not women or blacks (until 1978) — could serve as priests, and some achieved higher priestly status than others did. Although anyone could receive individual revelations, priests conveyed revelations to others in their spheres of influence. Most men progressed from the Aaronic to the

Melchizedek priesthood, but few advanced to the rank of high priest or apostle. Although they agreed with evangelicals about the corruption of the world, Mormon interpretations of the Word set the group apart.[29]

Certain other religious groups shared evangelical assumptions about an inspired written Word and a corrupt world. Yet instead of seeking a transformative presence in the American cultural milieu, such groups withdrew from the world to avoid its corrupting influences. Ethnic and linguistic differences encouraged the cultural insulation of some Lutheran, German Reformed, Moravian, Quaker, and Amish communities. Feelings of alienation caused by low social status increased the importance for other groups, such as Disciples, Millerites, Mormons, and Holiness churches, of maintaining a sense of identity as separate from the world. Some of these groups could be classed with evangelicals, as they were by Robert Baird, on many doctrinal grounds, but their assumptions about the world created an important point of distinction.[30]

Still other religious or morally oriented groups did not perceive a need for the Word to transform the world since they saw neither words nor the world as fundamentally corrupted by sin. American romantics, for example, played a leading role in the emergence of a national literary culture that articulated a model for the moral life that diverged from evangelical print culture. During the second quarter of the nineteenth century, New England literary leaders such as Ralph Waldo Emerson and Henry David Thoreau espoused an American version of romanticism that opposed evangelicalism and domesticated the radical ideology of European romantics, such as Samuel Taylor Coleridge, Thomas Carlyle, and Johann Wolfgang von Goethe. American romantics aimed at moral improvement, cast primarily in terms of character formation, and felt hopeful that words could reform society. Interpreting language symbolically, romantics viewed the poetic expression of ideas as more significant than literal meaning. Romantics perceived imaginative language as spiritually powerful because it evoked the same states of feeling in the reader as the writer. For romantics, the distinction between Word and words, sacred and secular, worldly and otherworldly, Holy Spirit and human spirit, broke down. Rather than understanding the Bible as self-authenticating Word inspired by the Holy Spirit, romantics averred that the Bible and other texts were similarly authoritative to the extent that they expressed an inspired poetic vision. As the literary historian Lawrence Buell concludes, for romantics "piety merges with aestheticism." Romantics believed linguistic reform was superior to wholesale transformation of words or the world.[31]

Despite significant differences in foundational assumptions, romantic ideals shaped cultural dialogues in which evangelicals actively participated. Both romantics and evangelicals felt deeply interested in language and optimistic about the creative power of words, but for very different reasons. A majority of evangelicals, through at the least the 1870s, self-consciously differentiated their view of language from the romantic position. Evangelicals expressed a deeper commitment to both the literal and spiritual meanings of the Word and words. For evangelicals, the Word *was* God, and the Holy Spirit really, not symbolically, operated through divine and human words in radically transformative ways. Words so inhabited by the Holy Spirit did more than evoke common feelings in writers and readers; the words became vehicles by which God progressively purified human nature from sin, a process begun in this world but only completed in the world to come.[32]

Yet the boundaries between romantic and evangelical cultures cannot be rigidly drawn. Certain individuals, such as Horace Bushnell and Henry Ward Beecher, to some degree inhabited both romantic and evangelical cultural worlds and attempted to bridge the gap between them. Bushnell questioned traditional doctrines of the Trinity and atonement and interpreted the Bible more as poetry than literal truth. Beecher similarly rejected the orthodox doctrines of hell and plenary inspiration of the Bible, eventually leading his church out of the Congregational Association in 1882 to evade a heresy trial. Yet for decades, both Bushnell and Beecher, as their doctrinal positions developed, profoundly influenced evangelical ideas of sacred language. Other more orthodox evangelical proponents of a refined aesthetic began through their conversations with romantics to question the capacity of words to contain rather than merely approach spiritual truth. Such discussions encouraged the proliferation of genres and forms as evangelicals attempted to approximate successively the truth that the living Word expressed perfectly. The openness of the American print market facilitated dialogue among groups that could never in America constitute isolated cultural universes.[33]

Evangelical print culture, though internally divided along denominational lines and sharing characteristics with unevangelical uses of the press, reflected distinctive assumptions about the Word and the world. As the example of *Two Christmas Gifts* suggests, evangelicals struggled to maintain the Word's purity while using their own words, embodied in densely textured material and commercial forms, to enact a transforming presence in the world. Evangelical publishers made some of the crucial decisions about how to accomplish this balancing act, and it is to their practices that we now turn our attention.

2

The World of
Evangelical Publishing

As he opened the first office of the Methodist Book Concern in 1789, Thomas Coke reflected in his journal: "We have now settled our Printing business. . . . The people will thereby be amply supplied with Books of pure divinity for their reading, which is of the next importance to preaching." Others before Coke had endeavored to supply Americans with books of pure divinity, but the Methodist Book Concern was the first publishing house in America to initiate the systematic printing and distribution of evangelical books, ranging from Bibles and hymnals to medical advice, across the nation. Methodist successes inspired other denominational, non-denominational, and evangelical trade publishers to establish such an extensive network of publishing operations that it took half a century for secular publishers to catch up with religious innovations.[1]

Publishers like Thomas Coke played a crucial role in shaping evangelical print culture. They shared authority with clergy to mediate ongoing processes of textual sedimentation and innovation by deciding which steady sellers and new titles merited publication and how best to promote texts to win a readership. As they aggressively interacted with an expansive American print market, evangelical publishers negotiated between their identities as Christians and as book trades participants. They envisioned their secular work as functionally sacred because it was useful in communicating the gospel. Through their book trades activities, publishers ritually enacted core narratives that structured involvement in an evangelical textual community: contending for the faith, promoting Christian unity, and, as the priesthood of all believers, sanctifying the world of print. In seeking to advance religious truth, evangelical publishers engaged in some — but not all — practices of the trades; they often worked in partnership with each other, at other points in competition; sometimes they heeded the wisdom of the market, at other times they worked against it. By midcentury, some evangelical publishers occupied an uneasy position on the margins of the book trades even as others attained the highest levels of market influence. As their strategies diversified over time, publishers attempted to avoid corruption while maintaining an influential presence in a constantly evolving cultural milieu.[2]

Evangelicals in the Marketplace of Culture

Evangelical publishers stood at the vanguard as the American print market blossomed during the nineteenth century. When the Methodist Book Concern opened shop, American publishing was still in its infancy. Booksellers circulated a relatively small supply of mostly imported or pirated books, many of which the average consumer found unaffordable. By the 1850s, an American publishing industry had begun to shed its long-held disrepute as younger sibling to the British book trades, where vibrant retail and wholesale markets for new and used books had functioned since the 1660s. Technological advances that originated in Europe, including stereotyping (1812), steam-power printing (1823), machine papermaking (1820s), and cloth bindings (1830s), combined with improvements in railway transportation (1830s–50s) and more favorable postal fee schedules (1851) to encourage the establishment of printing presses throughout the United States and the expansion of subscription lists and cheap editions that reached national and international reading audiences. By midcentury, 400 publishing firms, 3,000 booksellers, and over 4,000 printing offices made texts available across America. During the second quarter of the nineteenth century, book and periodical production in the United States increased 500 percent, and the overall value of books sold grew from $2.5 million to $12.5 million annually. The per unit cost of a book ranged from a few cents for a cheap edition up to a dollar or more for a standard octavo volume. One source estimated in 1842 that there were 12 million books, 3 million periodicals, and 300 million newspaper sheets in annual circulation. In part because of evangelical publishing initiatives, in mid-nineteenth-century America every cause needed an effective publishing arm to survive as a cultural player.[3]

The American print market reached maturity as overall output grew. In 1804, American publishers offered approximately 1,300 titles for sale. From 1820 to 1850, at least 25,000 titles circulated, approximately the same number of works as the total published during the entire 1639–1791 time period. Reprints of British editions, generally reproduced without payment of copyright, accounted for many of these titles; over time, however, the market shifted toward original American productions. In 1820, publishers introduced seventy British texts for every thirty American; by 1856, the ratio had reversed: eighty American books appeared for every twenty British. Simultaneously, American newspaper and periodical production grew at a staggering pace. In the process, a distinctively American literary culture formed.[4]

Print shaped American cultural emergence as thickening publishing networks crisscrossed the nation. Publishing decentralized during the early stages of the transportation revolution, but by midcentury northeastern cultural hubs had regained dominance. In 1830, publishers operated out of 199 cities and towns in every state but Mississippi. Cincinnati, leading the western section of the country, had by 1850 advanced to fourth place among national publishing cities. By 1860, Nashville had developed into a major southern publishing center; although it ranked tenth in U.S. population, it came in eighth for religious periodicals and sixth in total monthly publications. Yet northeasterners consistently produced and consumed more texts overall than did westerners or southerners. In 1850, the total per capita circulation of periodicals among southern whites remained only a third of the level in the North, and southern book production accounted for less than 5 percent of the national market. The maturation of national communication networks pushed publishing dominance back toward East Coast centers. New York, Philadelphia, and Boston publishers controlled three-quarters of the market at midcentury. Texts produced in one region, most often the Atlantic seaboard, circulated among readers in every section of the country and overseas. Local, national, and international markets overlapped as readers simultaneously demonstrated provincial loyalty and cosmopolitan interest.[5]

Keenly aware of the increasing power of the press to shape American culture, evangelicals determined to sanctify the world of print. The *Methodist Quarterly Review* observed in 1846 that the "world is in motion" and "we must study the tactics of the opposing hosts, and throw up an impenetrable shield against all their fiery darts." Such analyses of rapid cultural change were scarcely new at midcentury; evangelicals had voiced similar concerns about the world's motion since the Reformation of the sixteenth century. Yet nineteenth-century evangelicals perceived their world as having reached a crucial historical juncture. Indeed, in America as in Britain the proliferation of cheap new editions of certain types of science, history, biography, and

fiction created market competition for religious titles. An anonymous "physician" warned in 1855 that the "popular literature" of the day had opened a
"floodgate" of "public poison . . . from beneath whose slimy jaws runs a
stream of pollution, sending forth its pestilential branches to one great
ocean of immorality." Such vivid diction did not represent fringe sen-
sationalism but conventional discourse among evangelicals of every denomination, including elite cultural guardians. Noah Porter, the Congregationalist president of Yale University, cautioned in 1870 that printed texts
could either "leave behind the most powerful impress for good, or . . . reduce
the soul to utter barrenness and waste, and even scathe it as with devouring
fire." The Baptist *Michigan Christian Herald* (1880) likewise depicted a po-
larity between pure and polluted uses of the press: "A stream of pure water
must rush forth on its cleansing way, resistless in its God-given strength; else
we and our children shall be swept away beneath the dark waves of pollution." Evangelicals employed elaborate imagery to express their sense of
urgency about the need to sanctify the American print market.[6]

The tone of evangelical commentary denoted optimism that publishers
could effectively deploy printed texts to contend for religious truth. Rather
than withdraw from market participation, evangelicals concluded almost
unanimously that to "counteract the influence of vile or worthless books,
something better must be offered." The *Christian Herald* (1823) proclaimed
boldly that "the PULPIT AND THE PRESS are inseparably connected. . . . The
Press, then, is to be regarded with a sacred veneration and supported with
religious care." The ATS, reflecting on the "Wants and Prospects of Our
Country" in 1866, perceived "almost no other recourse but to the vigorous
employment, and the universal diffusion of the moral and religious press."
Similarly, an anonymous writer for the nondenominational annual the
Christian Diadem of 1852 expressed confidence that when "corrupting"
error appeared in the press, "the friends of the Redeemer have only to
double their diligence, and oppose such error, wherever it appears, by gospel truth." Evangelicals strove to keep pace with secular publishers in an era
of increasing literary abundance.[7]

But did evangelicals succeed in their bid to shape the nineteenth-century
print market? Quantifying an evangelical market share is problematic both
because of the absence of comprehensive bibliographical data and because
of the difficulty of assessing which texts served evangelical purposes by
enhancing the gospel's influence in the world. The patchwork of figures
that does exist, particularly those numbers based on self-reported data,
should not be relied upon for precision. From 1640 to 1790, newspaper
issues accounted for nearly 80 percent of all texts published. Government

printing contributed another 5.8 percent, and sermons ranked third, at 2.6 percent of all publications. Texts that I classify as religious, including sermons, prayer books, psalmbooks, and hymnals, constituted approximately 4,000 out of 25,400 titles published, or around 16 percent of total production. By the mid-nineteenth century, the percentage of individually published sermons had declined. In my analysis of a sample of books published from 1852 to 1855, sermons accounted for only 8 percent of religious publications and less than 2 percent of the overall market. Yet these calculations veil the countless sermons printed in the columns of periodicals and literary annuals. For example, the ATS's *American Messenger*, which claimed to present in each issue "columns of searching spiritual truth adapted to the salvation of men," was one of the most widely circulated periodicals at midcentury; it grew steadily from its establishment in 1825, peaking at 200,000 subscribers in 1865. Like many similar publishing ventures, the *Messenger* incarnated sermonic contents in new market forms.[8]

Envisioning themselves as a lay priesthood responsible for shaping American textual practices, evangelical publishers actively promoted the diversification of the print market. The relative abundance of history, biography, travel, and science increased noticeably, together accounting for a third of all books published at midcentury. From one point of view, this shift reflected secularizing literary interests, but evangelicals saw many such texts as functioning in traditionally religious ways. Histories narrated the progress of God's redemption of the world; biographies offered models for Christian character formation; travel narratives encouraged interest in missions; and science explained God's providence. Textbooks, by 1860, accounted for 30 to 40 percent of total book production. Here, too, difference from an earlier era is less apparent than continuity, for nineteenth-century evangelicals viewed education and religion as deeply connected. *McGuffey's Readers*, adopted by schools across the nation, taught morality and religion in every lesson. Seven million copies of the *Readers* circulated from 1836 to 1850, and total sales approached 40 million by 1870. The less explicitly doctrinal tenor of later editions of the *Readers* can be interpreted as evidence of secularization or as indicating evangelical aptitude at presenting the gospel in ways that accorded with changing cultural tastes.[9]

Evangelicals conceived of themselves, as priests, to be standing in the gap between the sacred and the profane, appropriating secular resources for holy uses. Yet many evangelicals who welcomed the proliferation of textual forms expressed anxiety about the growing prominence of one particular genre, the novel. American publishers introduced just 90 fiction titles from 1774 to 1820. Between 1840 and 1850, 800 fiction titles appeared; in 1855, novels accounted for over half the books published. Here, too, the story of mounting secular influences is complicated because many evangelicals self-consciously wrote and read fiction, often explicitly arguing that fiction could be made to serve religious purposes. Some best-sellers were religious in theme and tone, such as Harriet Beecher Stowe's *Uncle Tom's Cabin*, Susan Warner's *Wide, Wide World*, and General Lew Wallace's *Ben-Hur*. Such texts might be seen as more concerned with entertainment and life in this world than with heavenly pilgrimage, yet this interpretation discounts the claims of evangelicals that such texts functioned to communicate sacred meanings.[10]

Publishers motivated by evangelical values in large measure succeeded in disseminating religious publications in every sector of the American print market. Of indisputably religious publications, Bibles not surprisingly surpassed every other class of text for extent of circulation. In just the year 1829–30, the ABS distributed over 1 million copies of the Bible, or one for every thirteen people. By 1852, American evangelical publishing societies had reputedly dispensed 40 million Bibles and hundreds of millions of pages of tracts. For the year 1855, estimating overall book production at 15.4 million copies, selling on average for one dollar apiece, the three largest nondenominational publishing societies, the ATS, ABS, and ASSU, by themselves sold 2.4 million volumes for just $1 million, or about forty cents each. Because the evangelical societies sold many titles for a third to half the price charged by trade publishers, the three houses accounted by themselves for approximately 7 percent of book revenue for 1855 while publishing close to 16 percent of all books produced. Viewing this number alongside the 16 percent that total religious publications claimed from 1640 to 1790 provides striking evidence that religion had gained ground in the print market, not lost it. This comparison, moreover, does not account for the rich variety of denominational and evangelical trade publications that abounded at midcentury, which in one sample sold for an average of sixty-six cents each compared with eighty-one cents for what scholars class as secular belles lettres. Although an absolute quantification of the ratio between evangelical and nonevangelical publications is elusive, the data point to a substantial, even an increasing, evangelical presence in the American print market at midcentury.[11]

Denominational Publishing Houses: Contending for the Faith

Every major religious denomination in America established its own publishing arm in the antebellum period. In entering the national print market, publishers tried to balance denominational mission and participation in a nondenominationally centered book trade, evangelical unity and denominational identity, an ever-widening geographic expansion and cultural coherence. Denominational publishers saw themselves as countering the errors of the secular press and rival religious denominations by proclaiming pure gospel truth. Because of the premium they placed on purity, denominational publishing houses occupied a peculiar position relative to the structures of the book trades. They competed in an open market against trade publishers but refused to engage in certain distribution practices for fear of corruption. Ironically, efforts to contend for an uncorrupted faith both inhibited denominational influence in the general market and compromised the goal of Christian unity by intensifying rivalries among evangelicals.

Distribution constituted the most pressing challenge that every secular and religious press faced. Since we lack a close, detailed history of any one denominational publisher's distribution practices, we must, for the purposes of the present study, paint denominational involvement in the book trades with a rather broad brush. We do know from comparisons with the secular and nondenominational religious press that publishers incurred their greatest expenses during the initial stages of book production; after paying fixed costs, additional copies required relatively little outlay. Because more sales resulted in greater profits, trade publishers sought to reach the largest markets possible, employing strategies such as wholesale vending to retail bookstores, subscription canvassing, and direct sales through the mail. Trade publishers exchanged book lists and took part in semi-annual trade auctions, through which they dispensed with excess stock and gained fresh supplies of new publications. Although trade publishers sold some books directly to consumers or bookstores, they also transacted business with wholesale middlemen jobbers, who resold their lots to booksellers in remote locations nationally or internationally. The wholesale business required a substantial capital base, augmented through exchanges and auctions, which made available sufficient resources to offer generous discounts to wholesalers and to keep an adequate stock on hand. Denominational publishers did not fully participate in any of these trade practices, thereby imposing an element of restriction on themselves that aggravated tensions between evangelical and market identities.[12]

Every denominational publisher grappled with the question of how to balance purity and presence in the world of print. The unique publishing record of the Methodist Book Concern made the problem all the more vexing. Although other denominations could not compete successfully in the general book trades, by the 1840s the Book Concern flourished by supplying a rapidly growing Methodist population with the "best possible" literature and by underselling the market. The Book Concern centrally sanctioned every Methodist publication, and only Methodist ministers served as authorized sales agents. Ironically, the very success of the Book Concern fueled unprecedented controversy when Southern Methodists withdrew to form the Methodist Episcopal Church, South, after the General Conference of 1844 deadlocked over the slavery issue. For the next decade, northern and southern Methodists bitterly disputed the allocation of denominational assets, especially those connected with Book Concern properties in New York and Cincinnati, until the courts forced the northern church to apportion funds and book stock to the southern seceders. The conflict contributed to sectional alienation that prepared the way for the Civil War and convinced many observers that greed had clouded the quest for purity. Nevertheless, Methodists, North and South, recovered sufficiently from the strain to enjoy continued success in the difficult task of book distribution. They accomplished this feat through itinerant ministers who doubled as traveling booksellers and by establishing an efficient system of denominational book depositories, which functioned as an alternative to trade distribution networks. The Western Book Concern, which opened as a book room in 1820, operated independently in Cincinnati by 1839, and the Southern Methodist Publishing House, founded in 1854, worked out of Nashville, Richmond, and Charleston. By 1872, the Book Concern, headquartered in New York, had established depositories in Boston, Pittsburgh, Auburn, Buffalo, Chicago, St. Louis, and San Francisco. Despite their embroilment in religious and sectional controversies, Methodists made denominational publications available in every region for the lowest prices offered.[13]

Judged by financial criteria, the New York Book Concern, by far the largest Methodist publishing house, succeeded well beyond any other denominational publisher. According to Book Concern statistics, in the forty years before 1848, 650,000 Methodists purchased $600,000 in books; in the next forty years, 2 million Methodists purchased nearly $7 million in books. The weekly circulation of Methodist newspapers grew from 80,000 in 1850 to 3 million by 1889. By 1875, Methodist publications accounted for over one-third the total value of all religious texts sold, or around $48 million. It is difficult to plot the exact connection between the Book Concern's publishing success and denominational growth, but nineteenth-century Methodists perceived a correlation. Although northern and southern Methodists would remain divided until 1939, one celebrant of the Book Concern's 1889 centennial thought the outcome of denominational publishing achievements abundantly clear: "The largest Protestant Church in the United States consolidated into unity!" Operating alongside other church-building strategies, publishing provided a sense of cultural cohesion for scattered individuals and churches who yet shared a common literature. The Book Concern expanded with the Methodist Episcopal Church and, conversely, publishing aided denominational growth.[14]

As the Book Concern enlarged operations, its leaders experimented with new packaging styles and marketing strategies calculated to enhance Methodist influence. In so doing, Methodists saw themselves as incarnating the gospel in functionally sacred cultural forms. As the *Christian Advocate and Journal* (1848) phrased the issue: "People will have the gilding and tinsel; and if we intend to supply them, we must give them what they want." Methodist books published in the 1850s commonly displayed muslin or morocco bindings with elaborate scrollwork and gilding on the front and spine, marbled edges, and an "elegant" style. In 1860, the Book Concern adopted what was for it a new strategy, although the practice had long been common in the general book trades: supplying publishing partners with editions of Sunday school and certain other cheap books, allowing purchasers to place their own imprints in the volumes retailed. This tactic alone expanded Book Concern sales by tens of thousands of volumes. Employing many of the same production and distribution tactics as did trade publishers, Methodists used profane resources to broadcast sacred influences.[15]

Methodist innovations extended beyond packaging and dispersal to selection of genres considered worthy of the Methodist imprint. Publication decisions shaped the processes of textual sedimentation and innovation that continually reconfigured the evangelical canon. As early as 1843, Methodists debated the strategic value of entering the general book trades rather than focusing exclusively on religious literature. Proponents of expanding the book lists hoped to educate Methodist readers more thoroughly and to attract more non-Methodist readers. The argument for expansion appealed to the Book Concern's goal as an evangelical publisher: to "prevent evil, promote good," by whatever lawful means possible. A more general publication list could enhance the Book Concern's ability to transform general market tastes. The opposing argument was less philosophical than economic: as long as the Methodist house limited itself to certain classes of religious publications, trade publishers would respect its "peculiar property" in this corner of the market. Once the Book Concern entered into open competition with trade publishers in other areas, it must expect "interference" even in those areas where its interests had been respected previously. By the late 1840s, the argument for open competition had prevailed, albeit to a limited degree, without producing the consequences that some leaders had feared. As the Methodist canon evolved to include more varied contents, the Book Concern still dominated the market for denominational teachings.[16]

On the eve of the Book Concern's centennial, in 1889, the range of "Methodist" texts had broadened considerably from a century before. Always "ready to adapt itself to modern methods," by the 1880s the Book Concern issued Methodist doctrine, commentaries, biographies, Sunday school books, periodicals, and general literature, including travel, "harmless" fiction, general biography, history, science, and "entertaining and elevating romances." Much had clearly changed as Methodists worked to keep a foothold in a shifting print market, but much had also stayed the same. John Wesley himself wrote texts that were not strictly religious, such as a *Complete English Dictionary: Explaining Most of the Hard Words Which are Found in the Best English Writers* (1753) and a medical textbook, *Primitive Physic* (1789), and edited nonreligious poetry in his *Arminian Magazine* (1788–91). Wesley encouraged participation in literary culture since Christians could grow in grace through the attainment of knowledge, even that derived from secular sources. The Book Concern's attempts to adapt to modern methods while struggling to maintain a distinctive Methodist identity accorded well with Wesleyan philosophy and practice.[17]

Throughout the nineteenth century, Methodist leaders worked to balance purity and presence, expressing anxiety about the difficulty of achieving both goals simultaneously. One Methodist observer worried in 1889 that the Book Concern had not exerted enough of a presence in the general market. The "*limitations* of a denominational literature are that the general public will invariably consider the institution a part of Methodist machinery, and infer, therefore, that what it publishes is primarily for the use of Methodists, and its imprint will constantly confirm that impression. So that, from a commercial point of view, what is its chief strength is of necessity an element of restriction." This particular spokesperson seemed almost to regret that the demand for purity prevented entrance into the most profitable branches of the book trades. The Book Concern could not of course sell the "sentimental" and "sensational" works of fiction "whose sales run up into the hundreds of thousands," nor could it obtain the "notoriety" that is "of immense business value to many other houses" by associating its name with such popular branches of literature. Rather than ruing the limitation of Methodist market competitiveness, other Methodists critiqued innovation as a dangerous compromise with the world. Despite such self-questioning, the Book Concern, to a greater extent than any other denominational publisher, maintained a distinctive, widely recognized identity yet remained competitive in the print market.[18]

Few denominations regulated book production or sales as rigidly as did the Methodist Episcopal Church, but all publishers had to address the problem of distribution in some manner. In fact, most denominational houses failed to establish adequate distribution networks, to appeal to sufficiently sizable markets, or to reap substantial enough profits to ensure viability as independent business enterprises. The Congregational Board of Publication, founded in 1829 and housed in Boston at the Massachusetts Sabbath-School Society headquarters, aspired to be more than a "mere business concern." Congregationalist supporters, rejecting financial success as a legitimate goal for a denominational publisher, viewed the board as a "channel of benevolence for the supply of a sound theology to the churches." Focusing on purity, the board reprinted "valuable" and "standard" works written by the "Fathers of New England" and by seventeenth-century English nonconformists. The works sponsored by the board could not be obtained from other publishers because there was insufficient demand to make their production profitable.[19]

From the perspective of business strategy, the Congregational Board faced a difficult task in endeavoring to specialize in unprofitable titles. Other publishers with more extensive catalogs could compensate for losses experienced with one title through profits gained from works that succeeded in winning a wide readership. The Congregational Board's evangelical mandate to make pure words affordable by all potential readers compounded its fiscal problems. The board undersold the market, pricing many of its titles at twenty to thirty cents per copy. The board also sent texts without charge to "needy churches, ministers, and theological students, particularly in the West." The Congregational Board not only refused to participate in trade distribution networks that could have increased sales but also rejected outright a basic rule of the market, namely that publishers should strategize to reap monetary returns on their investments.[20]

Not surprisingly, then, the Congregational Board experienced financial trouble from the start. In the 1849–50 fiscal year, sales totaled $15, compared with a startling $985 in expenses. "Surely, as a mere business operation, this looks badly," the board admitted. The board's financial record improved somewhat once it had produced a stock of stereotype plates from which to print subsequent editions of standard volumes. The stereotyping process, a usual trade practice by midcentury, involved the creation of papier-mâché molds that eliminated the need to keep standing type or to reset the type for each new edition. Prior to the widespread use of stereotyping, printed texts were highly unstable. Individual copies within a single edition contained textual variations as compositors corrected errors midway through a print run. Although stereotyping required a larger initial investment, the method proved extremely cost-effective in the long-term. Yet even by 1859, board sales of $2,760 could not cover $8,900 in expenses. Consistently operating at a loss, the Congregational Board depended upon donations to sustain its business operations. Ironically, disavowing "mere" market considerations impeded the achievement of denominational goals. Viewing "profit on sales" as antithetical to "spreading light and truth," the board restricted its appeal to a narrow market, centered in New England among Congregationalist church members. The board made little effort to sponsor publications that could compete in the open market or to sell its texts outside New England. Consequently, Congregationalists experienced limited success either in publishing or in denominational growth.[21]

Even denominational publishers that accepted the legitimacy of monetary profits strained to compete against nondenominational and trade publishers with better established distribution systems. The AME Church first organized a distinct publication arm in 1818, formally chartering the AME Publication Department in 1855. This department "struggled, with but little progress, for many years." Unwilling to participate in trade distribution practices, the AME publisher lacked the capital necessary to build alternate networks. The department could not afford to accumulate stock at such reduced prices as to compete with "large and influential firms" for prices charged consumers or for discounts and credits offered wholesalers. The AME Philadelphia depository kept a "fine assortment of Church books on hand," including a variety of hymnbooks, church disciplines, histories, and general reading. But the denomination failed to develop a depository system in the South or West, where nondenominational and general book dealers could, ironically, sell AME publications for lower prices than could AME agents. The publication department barely maintained financial stability through the 1880s, consistently appealing to members and outsiders for donations and running a deficit most years. Lacking adequate monetary reserves, the AME denomination had to rely on church-building strategies other than publishing to connect scattered individuals and congregations.[22]

Other denominational houses approached the problem of distribution by forming partnerships with select evangelical trade publishers, thus placing one foot in the general market. The multiple-imprint system, a strategy that regular trade houses also employed, allowed the New School Presbyterian Publication Committee to copublish works, thereby splitting financial risks and gaining assistance in retailing publications. The committee found two of its strongest allies in Robert Carter & Brothers and A. D. F. Randolph, both of New York. Carter and Randolph, two lay Presbyterians, were sympathetic to their denomination's publishing goals. Although the publication committee's partnerships aided its marketing success, Presbyterian sponsors felt uncomfortable with the arrangement, worrying about the loss of control over books bearing the Presbyterian imprint. Insecure about their need to rely on trade partnerships at all, Presbyterian leaders failed to grasp the significance of trade practices from which they remained partially aloof. Carter and Randolph consistently sold evangelical books at a profit, but the committee experienced monetary losses in publishing the same or similar titles on its own. Spokespersons for the committee explained this' seemingly anomalous pattern by complaining that they lacked the "influence and power" of large trade houses whose works won an audience simply because of the name of the publisher. The inconsistency of lay purchasing decisions suggests that few, if any, publishing houses had the kind of cultural valence that the Presbyterian lament attributed to Carter and Randolph. The Presbyterian imprint did limit the size of potential audiences, since some consumers dismissed books published by a denomination to which they did not belong. But Carter and Randolph had another, more significant advantage. Although both houses specialized in religious works, they also participated in trade distribution networks that allowed them to sell more copies and garner greater profits than could the isolated publication committee. Unfamiliar with the workings of trade practices yet dependent on trade partnerships, Presbyterian leaders were baffled by their inability to achieve a wider presence in the market on their own terms.[23]

The religious dimension of such commercial frustrations can scarcely be overstated. In the competitive milieu of the nineteenth-century religious landscape, denominational leaders perceived publishing success as essential to survival in the contest among denominations. The *Methodist Quarterly Review* noted anxiously in 1846 that "our sister denominations" had recently increased their use of the press. The *Review* urged renewed support of the Book Concern; otherwise, "if our books are not procured and read by our people, others will be." Lay evangelicals of every denomination possessed relative autonomy to choose among market alternatives and often demonstrated looser denominational loyalties in purchasing texts than publishers would have liked. The Presbyterian Publication Committee worried that denominational presses "out of sympathy" with New School Presbyterianism exerted more of an influence on Presbyterian readers than did the organs of their own denomination. The publication committee cautioned in 1863 that "with every other religious body in the land publishing its books and tracts, and sending them all over the West, in order to influence and control the minds of the people, it becomes a question of life or death with us, whether we, as a denomination, sustain this cause and publish our history, our polity, our doctrine." The Methodist and Presbyterian warnings, though calculated to motivate support of their respective publishing houses, reveal a perception widespread at midcentury: that competitive failure in the print market spelled disaster in the religious marketplace as well.[24]

The high esteem with which nineteenth-century evangelicals regarded publishing as a church-building strategy accelerated the development of rival publication societies. The Protestant Episcopal Society for the Promotion of Evangelical Knowledge formed in 1847 to counter the less evangelical tendencies of the Protestant Episcopal Sunday-School Union, founded in 1826. Operated as a voluntary society rather than as an official denominational organ, the Protestant Episcopal Society gained support from a majority of bishops, clergy, and laity. The oppositional activities of the two publishing boards clarified and intensified disagreements among Episcopalians. More starkly, Presbyterian intradenominational disputes culminated in formal separation into Old and New School branches in 1837. The Old School General Assembly established the Presbyterian Board of Publication in 1838, and the New School General Assembly commissioned the Presbyterian Publication Committee in 1852. The New and Old School assemblies both split along sectional lines, in 1857 and 1861; Old and New School southerners reunited in 1864, northerners in 1870. The larger northern bodies combined their publication societies in 1887, merging book lists and organizational structures to form a new Presbyterian Board of Publication and Sabbath-School Work. As disagreements arose within other denominational families, one party or another typically opened a new publishing house to promote its particular interests.[25]

Competition among denominational publishers intensified intergroup enmity. Whenever denominations attempted to sponsor a "catholic and national" evangelical literature, they confronted challenges specific to their position in the book trades. Most denominational publishers had significantly smaller market bases and economies of scale than did nondenominational and trade publishers who participated in extensive national distribution networks. Consequently, for a majority of genres, including broadly evangelical and miscellaneous texts, denominational editions could rarely compete for pricing with nondenominational and trade editions of the same or similar titles. For certain other genres, such as hymnals and Sunday school texts, denominational publications presented a sufficiently unique appeal to members of the sponsoring denomination that these texts could claim a significant segment of the market in spite of competition. Denominational publishers dominated, however, when it came to a third class of texts: denominational doctrine, history, and controversy with other denominations.[26]

The unparalleled financial success of denominational volumes led their promoters to focus on this class of texts with the effect that religious rivalries mounted. The Presbyterian Publication Committee succeeded as a business enterprise largely because it specialized in texts that differentiated New School Presbyterians from other denominations. By 1867, the committee had secured a working capital of $50,000 and sold over $45,000 in books for the year. The 1867 Presbyterian catalog listed 365 publications, including 1 periodical, 127 leaflets, 71 tracts, and 166 books, most of which could be classed as Calvinist doctrine, Sunday school literature, hymnals, history, and polemics against other religious groups. Paradoxically, efforts by denominational publishers to remain pure from market corruption hampered their ability to compete with trade publishers and disrupted already contentious relationships with other evangelical denominations.[27]

Nondenominational Publishing Societies: Promoting Christian Unity

Contention among evangelical denominations, as chapter 1 argues, developed in parallel with cooperative ventures by denominations committed to similar religious goals. Since evangelicals recognized the growing influence of the press and the limited effectiveness of denominational publishing alone, some church leaders and members minimized disagreements among themselves for the sake of combating mutual enemies. In London, the Religious Tract Society (1799) and the British and Foreign Bible Society (1804) joined Anglicans, Methodists, Baptists, and Congregationalists in an effective coalition that pioneered in using new technologies to shape the print market. By midcentury, the Religious Tract Society, acting in its self-assigned role as cultural arbiter, had adjusted to a changing market by introducing narratives set in urban, industrial landscapes and by adopting "secular subjects, treated in an evangelical manner." In the United States, the ABS, ASSU, and ATS, following the British examples, united members of the major evangelical denominations in using the press to incarnate the gospel in popular cultural forms. Nondenominational publishing societies developed into national institutions that consolidated resources for production and distribution in order to make evangelical publications available to all, regardless of ability to pay. By their nature, nondenominational publishers excluded the specifically denominational and controversial publications that constituted the bread and butter of denominational publishing. Cooperation among members of different denominations did not eliminate disagreements, which often remained acute, but it did foster participants' sense of unity as evangelical Christians.[28]

The ASSU contributed to evangelicals' sense of membership in a nationwide community by networking authors, booksellers, and readers across denominations and regions and by disseminating a common body of cheap printed texts. In so doing, the publishing society accelerated a larger process in which evangelical ideas of Christian fellowship shifted from membership in a local congregation to a more diffuse sense of belonging within a textually defined community. The ASSU self-consciously affiliated Protestants of diverse denominations in a partnership to reach all areas of the country. The governing board for 1844 consisted of members from ten denominations and published only those texts approved by all members. The ASSU confronted a problem common to all publishers ambitious for a market beyond their immediate regions: how to get books to a geographically dispersed readership. In response to this challenge, the ASSU developed a system of book depositories operated by evangelical booksellers of various denominational affiliations in New York, Philadelphia, Boston, Rochester, Louisville, St. Louis, and Charleston. The ASSU, from its New York headquarters, shipped books at wholesale prices to depositories in each city, where retailers took responsibility for selling cheap books to local reading audiences. In this manner, the ASSU connected major urban centers in the North, South, and West through relational ties with booksellers and the diffusion of a common literature. ASSU publications flowed primarily from northeastern self-identified cultural centers to outlying peripheries where communities were reputedly "destitute" of books, money, and religion.[29]

The ASSU specialized in providing cheap literature for Sunday school libraries, families, and communities, since children were presumably more susceptible to influence than adults, and children could reach their parents with the gospel. One Sunday school library contained one hundred volumes and sold for ten dollars; a similar library with seventy-five volumes sold for just five dollars (figure 2.1). The ASSU sold some books directly while urging wealthy northeastern Sunday schools to donate libraries to poorer communities, especially in the South and West. ASSU promoters appealed to donors' sense of responsibility to help their less privileged, distant neighbors by claiming that ASSU libraries might be the only books available in some regions. The New-York Sunday School Union estimated in 1831 that the city's fifty-three libraries housed over 15,000 volumes while frontier communities were lucky to possess a Bible and a hymnal. Such statements conveyed some degree of accuracy; books were indeed much more abundant in the Northeast than in other regions. But pleas for aid also reflected an element of rhetorical excess calculated to intensify evangelicals' sense of urgency to proclaim the gospel. Requests for northeastern support fostered evangelical identity in two ways: by disseminating a common literature nationally and by increasing northeasterners' sense of membership in a nationwide evangelical community.[30]

In point of fact, the South and West were not wholly destitute of print. Numerous readers had access to cheap newspaper sheets, fiction, almanacs, broadsides, and pamphlets, some of them considered "godly" by their writers and readers. The ASSU worried not only about the quantity of texts available but also about how to regulate the quality of texts read around the country. The story of Jonathan Cross, native of western Pennsylvania and Virginia, offers a picture of ASSU success in propagating evangelical culture. Sometime before 1858, Cross converted to Christianity by reading "old standard works" printed by northeastern evangelicals. Thereafter, Cross desired to "do something for others" by raising money to order an ASSU library and open a Sunday school in his home. Commissioned as a colporteur by the ATS, Cross claimed in his autobiography that many of his neighbors did not own Bibles and that most of the books people did have were published by one of the charitable societies. Converted not only to Christianity but also to a specific evangelical mandate, Cross expressed views similar to those of his sponsors. He appealed to northeastern generosity by emphasizing the duty of wealthy Christians to help their poorer neighbors: "It is well for those reared in the midst of church privileges and good libraries to consider how different the influence of a good book may be on such as have few books, or none at all." In the South or West, Cross argued, donated books were "devoured with greediness — not by a gospel-hardened sinner — but by one who has few or no gospel privileges. Is it strange that such a one, on reading the *Pilgrim's Progress*, the *Anxious Inquirer*, or *Come to Jesus*, is immediately awakened to seek for pardon and salvation?" Ironically, in urging the diffusion of evangelical texts, Cross suggested that overabundance might produce results as negative as scarcity could, "hardening" sinners to reception of the gospel.[31]

Reports from ASSU and ATS agents such as Jonathan Cross represent only one side of the story; it is more difficult to know how those targeted by publishing society beneficence viewed reading or their own supposed destitu-

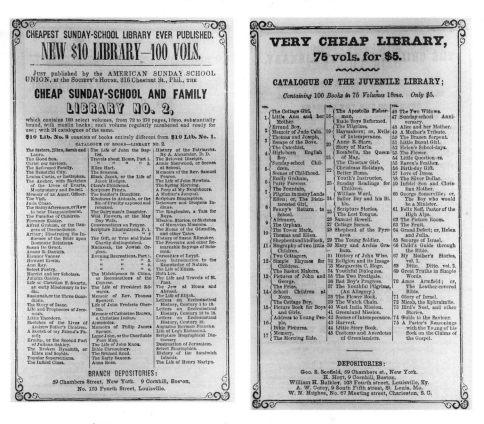

Figure 2.1. The ASSU *Catalogue* of 1856 advertised "cheap" and "very cheap" libraries for Sunday school children and their families. (Courtesy of the American Antiquarian Society)

tion. Some inhabitants of the South and West resented northeastern influence and clamored for distinctive regional literatures. Field reports undeniably reveal that not every house visited by colporteurs like Cross welcomed the proffered texts. Meanwhile, the number of periodicals and books produced outside the eastern seaboard grew steadily, presenting inland readers with new alternatives. Bridge figures like Jonathan Cross, himself a southwesterner converted by northeastern publications, nevertheless indicate the existence of at least some appreciative beneficiaries of evangelical cultural transmission. There were enough "Jonathan Crosses" to enable nondenominational publishers to find willing recipients of their wares throughout the nineteenth century, and even to find some paying customers.[32]

Jonathan Cross's connections with the ASSU and the ATS suggest the similarities among nondenominational publishing societies in sources of support and methods used to forge evangelical alliances across denominations and regions. ATS production and distribution practices illuminate a related way in which publishing societies promoted evangelical unity: by developing innovative tactics to produce and disperse the largest number of texts for the lowest possible cost. The ATS saw such strategies as functionally sacred because they were useful in proclaiming the gospel. As the historian David Nord has demonstrated, the ATS pioneered the modern business techniques of centralized national production and administration, localized distribution, systematic management, division of labor, economies of scale, differential pricing, capitalization, and mechanization that trade publishers later emulated. The ATS, unlike most denominational publishers, competed effectively against trade houses by cheaply and efficiently producing and distributing evangelical texts around the country and even internationally. At the same time, ATS goals differed fundamentally from the objectives of trade publishers: the society valued maximum readership over maximum profit. The ATS undersold trade publishers, gave many of its books away, and redirected the flow of publications away from the Northeast, where demand was high but "need" was low, toward the West and South, where there was less money, less demand, and, from the vantage of the ATS, greater need. The extensive diffusion of society publications expanded demand for still more ATS texts by encouraging a taste for religious reading.[33]

The style and packaging of ATS publications reflected evangelical zeal to incarnate the Word in attractive yet inexpensive cultural forms, thereby removing unnecessary barriers to acceptance of the gospel. The ATS, like the Methodist Book Concern, perceived that the desirability of publications to potential readers depended at least as much on presentation as on content. In order to reach the widest possible readership, the ATS offered high quality texts for low prices. ATS advertisements voiced the intention "to issue all its publications in good type, for the poor as well as the rich; and to sell them, as nearly as may be, at cost, that the Society may neither sustain loss nor make a profit by all its sales." Recognizing the appeal of middling rhetoric to diverse social classes, the ATS advertised even its cheapest texts as "elegant" and "beautifully illustrated" as well as "practical" in content. Rather than rejecting fine craftsmanship as worldly, the ATS considered packaging a religious instrument and endeavored to produce the most inviting volumes that it could.[34]

ATS marketing practices, nevertheless, reveal the difficulty of interacting with an American publishing industry yet retaining evangelical distinctiveness. In order to allocate texts efficiently, the ATS worked through local auxiliary societies with independent budgets. Auxiliaries in wealthier regions had ample funds to give books away, but those in economically depressed areas tended to sell books at higher prices, regardless of readers' inability to pay. Countering this inequity, the ATS adapted longstanding European bookselling strategies to pioneer a system of colportage in 1841, by which salaried agents sold or donated books and tracts throughout the South and West; the ATS employed an average of 400 agents annually in the antebellum period. Colporteurs reported starting Sunday schools where there were no day schools, supplying books that led to conversions where there had been no religious reading, and helping "Christians of different orders" to begin "living & laboring together." ATS promoters, like the sponsors of other nondenominational publishing initiatives, developed a complex relationship with the market, embracing some trade strategies, countering others, and unintentionally conforming to others still, as they negotiated among evangelical and publishing priorities. Despite inevitable strains, nondenominational publishers succeeded in deepening evangelicals' sense of membership in a relatively unified, textually defined Christian community.[35]

Evangelical Trade Publishers: Priesthood of All Believers Sanctifying the Print Market

A third kind of publishing house, the evangelical trade publisher, shared the market for religious texts with denominational and nondenominational societies. Unlike these publishing societies, which remained aloof from standard practices of the book trades, evangelical trade publishers strove to maintain their religious identities while engaging fully in trade practices. From a twenty-first-century perspective, the activities pursued and even the titles of books selected by nineteenth-century evangelical and general trade publishers appear quite similar. But evangelical publishers, understanding themselves to be members of the priesthood of all believers, interpreted their everyday business as a holy calling useful in refereeing participation in a community of print. Evangelicals viewed bookmaking and commerce as neutral tools rather than as independent agents with a compelling logic of their own. Publishers accordingly felt free to use market methods for what they considered functionally sacred purposes. Because nineteenth-century evangelicals placed a premium on the power of the printed word to shape American culture, publishers viewed their activities as effective means to sanctify the world of print. In interacting with the general market more closely than did the religious societies, trade publishers encountered more opportunities to influence the market and greater tensions between their evangelical and trade agendas.[36]

At midcentury, almost every major trade publisher affirmed a denominational affiliation while participating, to greater or lesser degree, in the regular book trades. Given their full access to national distribution networks, trade publishers cooperated with denominational and nondenominational representatives to make religious titles available in the general market. In so doing, trade publishers envisioned themselves as relationally connected to one another, to authors, and to potential readers as priests and fellow members of a pilgrim community. Gould & Lincoln of Boston worked with the Baptists; Crocker & Brewster of Boston the Congregationalists; Robert Carter & Brothers and A. D. F. Randolph, both of New York, the Presbyterians; J. B. Lippincott & Company of Philadelphia and E. P. Dutton & Company of Boston the Episcopalians; and most influential of all, Harper & Brothers of New York supported the Methodists (figure 2.2). Some publishers specialized in particular genres, forging partnerships with multiple denominations. A. S. Barnes & Company of New York produced hymnals for the Congregationalists, Presbyterians, Baptists, and Episcopalians. John E. Potter & Company of Philadelphia manufactured Bibles and prayer books for use by any denomination. In addition to working closely with denominational publishers, trade houses formed partnerships with nondenominational societies. Both the Riverside Press of Hurd & Houghton of New York and Lockwood & Brooks of Boston published works for the ATS. Henry Hoyt of Boston cooperated with the ASSU, the Massachusetts Sabbath-School Society, and the London Religious Tract Society. With one foot in denominational and nondenominational publishing networks, the other in business partnerships, trade houses diminished the distance between evangelical publishing practices and a wider American print market.[37]

Trade partnerships that crossed denominational and regional lines contributed to the formation of a geographically expansive evangelical textual community, even in years when sectional tensions were mounting, by making denominational and nondenominational texts available in every region of the country. The Presbyterian Robert Carter of New York regularly retailed books through the Baptist Gould & Lincoln of Boston. An independent Baptist bookseller in Louisville, Kentucky, claimed in 1845 to have made arrangements with other publishers that allowed him to "sell works as cheap" as could any other office, sending them anywhere in the United States, especially to purchasers living in "the country." By 1851, the American Baptist Publication Society (ABPS), headquartered in Philadelphia,

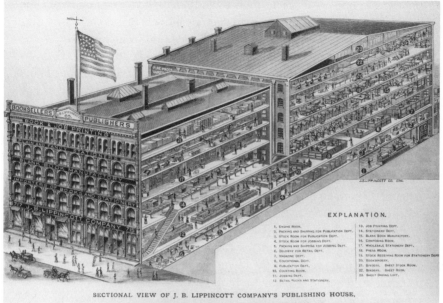

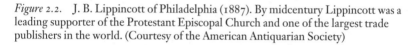

SECTIONAL VIEW OF J. B. LIPPINCOTT COMPANY'S PUBLISHING HOUSE,
715 and 717 Market St., and 714, 716, 718, and 720 Filbert St., Philadelphia.

Figure 2.2. J. B. Lippincott of Philadelphia (1887). By midcentury Lippincott was a leading supporter of the Protestant Episcopal Church and one of the largest trade publishers in the world. (Courtesy of the American Antiquarian Society)

wholesaled books through depositories run by booksellers in sixty-seven locations, North, South, and West, and promised every publisher's best productions for sale. The Southern Baptist Publication Society of Charleston likewise advertised in 1857 that its depositories sold approved texts published by the ATS and ASSU and by other denominational and private vendors from every region. The Presbyterian W. H. Bulkley of Louisville advertised in 1864 a "full assortment" of books from the ASSU, ABS, ATS, and other religious publishing houses, all suitable for Sunday school, family, and other libraries. Through broad-based trade partnerships, evangelical publishers and booksellers established distribution networks that increased the evangelical share of the American print market.[38]

Some individuals who bridged the worlds of evangelical and trade publishing balanced their dual identities with relative ease. New School Presbyterian Anson Davies Fitz Randolph began his publishing career in 1830 at the age of ten when he walked into a New York bookstore that housed business offices for the ASSU, the ATS, and the trade house of John P. Haven. Inspired to apprentice as a book publisher and retailer, Randolph pursued these trades until near his death in 1896. Randolph viewed publishing and bookselling as "more than the manufacture and sale of merchandise." The Christian bookmaker did a "beneficent" work: rather than making "men worse," he could "make them better." Not restricting himself to Presbyterian publications, Randolph sold religious titles and miscellaneous books on topics as diverse as flower arranging and support of the Union during the Civil War. Randolph's catalogs included a large proportion of hymnals and works of religious fiction, some of which were very profitable, selling hundreds of thousands of copies. Randolph participated fully in the book trades, even serving as president of the American Book-Trade Union, founded in 1874; this association organized publishers and booksellers, helping them to exchange their goods more efficiently. Randolph perceived his two callings, as a Christian and as a publisher, to be complementary.[39]

Publishers who, like Randolph, sought to maintain purity and presence in the world of print found themselves engaged in a difficult balancing act. The Boston Congregationalist Henry Hoyt adopted typically evangelical language in describing his publishing business as a means to "do good." Hoyt specialized in publishing children's books written by evangelicals; some of these texts fell into the genre of Sunday school literature, but others Hoyt marketed as holding more general interest. Among the "New Issues" for 1870, Hoyt urged that *Moth and Rust* "should be in every family and Sunday school in the land"; of *The Orient Boys*, he instead touted: "Every page full of interest and instruction. The most capital boy-book of the season." Such a text, in Hoyt's view, was functionally sacred because it instructed boys in moral values that encouraged receptivity to the gospel. A notice for *Both Sides of the Street* claimed to fulfill children's and parents' objectives simultaneously: the work was "full of originality, interest, and power; yet pervaded by a deep religious sentiment" (figure 2.3). The advertisement implied that a book could be both interesting and deeply religious; the conjunction "yet" suggests tension between the goals. Hoyt navigated through the potentially competing demands of supporting the Sunday school cause and influencing a more general audience.[40]

Hoyt balanced a second set of sometimes competing goals: making evangelical texts accessible to all, whether rich or poor, while maintaining a profitable business operation. Hoyt advertised a small number of inexpensive books designed to be affordable by anyone. The "Paper Series" sold for between two cents and eight cents. Yet the majority of Hoyt's publications sold for much higher prices, averaging about $1.50 each. Indeed, Hoyt participated in the lucrative holiday giftbook business. Advertisements for one giftbook, *The Cross of Our Lord Jesus Christ*, focused on the book's

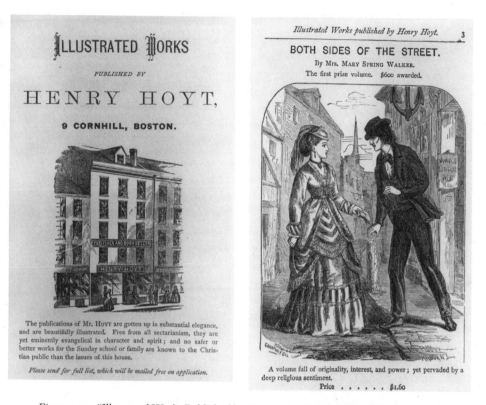

Figure 2.3. "Illustrated Works Published by Henry Hoyt" (1870). Henry Hoyt advertisements used illustrations to vaunt the intrinsic interest as well as the religious value of publications offered for sale. (Courtesy of the American Antiquarian Society)

packaging rather than on its specifically religious qualities. Five editions of this "beautiful," "tasteful," and "elegant" book sold for $1.50 up to $9, depending on the binding. Hoyt advertised another volume, *Under the Cross*, as one of the "beautiful books of the season, every way tasteful and elegant." Hoyt printed the Holiday Edition on heavy toned paper and used English cloth, full gilt, with nineteen illustrations, selling the volume for $4.25. This book was "valuable" both for its physical beauty and because its contents dwelt on the "sublimest theme, THE CROSS OF OUR LORD JESUS CHRIST." The book served both as a fitting "aid to private devotion" and as a suitable "presentation volume" that reflected sanctified relationships between givers and recipients. For readers who embraced middling cultural styles, finely crafted artifacts conveyed religious meanings by interpreting an event as humble as the crucifixion to be sublime by means of refined language and material packaging. Although the ATS sought to produce books that were both attractive and easily affordable, Hoyt weighted his publishing program toward wealthier audiences. Publishers like the ATS and Henry Hoyt reached different segments of the print market with comparable texts, packaged to meet divergent tastes and financial abilities. Hoyt's decision to emphasize refinement illustrates the complex relationship between perceptions of material and religious value and the pull of fiscal priorities for even evangelical publishers.[41]

As Hoyt's entrance into the holiday giftbook business indicates, evangelical and commercial markets overlapped at midcentury. Whatever the motives of publishers and booksellers, certain classes of religious texts were big business. A spectrum of consumers had a taste for religious reading but relatively weak loyalties to particular publishers. Trade publishers generally began their careers by printing an evangelical title, expecting, and usually finding, a ready market. Daniel Appleton, founder of D. Appleton & Company of New York and Philadelphia, was in the evaluation of his biographer a "highly religious" Protestant who opened business in 1831 by publishing three works of nondenominational religious devotion. Soon, the firm extended its operations to encompass the "whole range of literature" (figure 2.4). Even after entering the general book trades, Appleton's 1847 catalog allotted a full eight of thirty-three pages to books in the religious "department" of literature, making religion the most extensive section in the publisher's catalog and salesroom. Yet Appleton also published texts calculated to reap a monetary profit that, in the evaluation of the firm's critics, corresponded less well with evangelical purposes. Such titles included the "Catholicizing" *Tracts for the Times* produced by the Church of England's antievangelical Tractarian movement from 1833 to 1845 and books promoting scientific naturalism, for instance an 1860 edition of Darwin's *Origin of Species*. When denounced by the evangelical press for such publishing decisions, Appleton's sons took the decisively unevangelical position of denying that publishers should be concerned with the influence exerted by texts that bore their imprint.[42]

The unapologetic mingling of religion and commerce exhibited by Appleton's trade practices held the potential to reduce religious texts to commodities. The 1875 *Christmas Catalogue* of Lockwood & Brooks of Boston suggests one aspect of the dilemma faced by publishers who wanted to bridge the gap between religion and business. In a lighthearted tone, the *Catalogue*'s "Christmas Greetings" employed religious language as a marketing device. The book-loving Santa Claus is a "good saint," the "publishers are his prime ministers, the book-sellers his purveyors, and their shops his shrines." Lockwood's *Catalogue* "invites all the worshippers of the saint

Figure 2.4.   D. Appleton & Company of New York City was by 1875 a full participant in the general book trades. (Courtesy of the American Antiquarian Society)

to seek his shrine and pay happy tribute to the deity of the day." The article's diction hints at a fundamental cultural ambiguity surrounding the meaning of religious publishing. On the one hand, Christmas giftbooks sacralized what was for a majority of nineteenth-century Americans a secular holiday. Christmas provided an opportunity to market Christian titles to a large audience, thereby fulfilling a central evangelical mandate. On the other hand, the secular counterpart to Saint Nicholas had, for Lockwood's audience, apparently replaced Christ as the center of Christmas worship. Likewise, the bookstore and its attendants supplanted the church and its ministers as sites of religious pilgrimage. The catalog's ambiguous meaning reflects the difficulty of appropriating market strategies for evangelical uses.[43]

Some book trades participants apparently confused evangelical and commercial value. The marketing strategies of Cassell, Petter & Galpin of New York, London, and Paris offer a striking example of the conflation of material and religious attributes. Cassell's *Illustrated Catalogue* for 1874 devoted one-third of its pages to Bibles and "standard" religious texts. The remaining books included history, science, travel, fairy tales, and fiction.

Figure 2.5.   "Cassell's Illustrated Bunyan," in Cassell, Petter & Galpin's *Illustrated Catalogue* of 1874, appealed to refined audiences with a new edition of Bunyan's classic, *The Pilgrim's Progress*. (Courtesy of the American Antiquarian Society)

The catalog implicitly argued that beautiful presentation and quality materials were more important than content in determining a text's value. Cassell advertised each volume with an 8″ × 10″ illustration (figure 2.5). A new edition of Bunyan's *Pilgrim's Progress* sold for $3.50 in plain cloth and $5 in full gilt cloth with gilt edges, the same prices listed for general interest texts such as *Robinson Crusoe* (1719) and *Swiss Family Robinson* (1813).[44]

In marketing standard evangelical texts, material characteristics distinguished particular editions from numerous other renditions of the same titles. John Foxe's *Book of Martyrs*, first published in Latin in 1554, then in English in 1563, was like *Pilgrim's Progress* a steady seller printed by numerous houses, regardless of denominational affiliation. Cassell offered an edition for $5 in plain cloth and $6 in full gilt cloth with gilt edges. The advertisement for Foxe quoted English Baptist minister Charles Spurgeon as saying that this particular edition "should be *the* Christmas present to his children of every father who can afford it" since "it is profusely illustrated, beautifully printed, elegantly bound, and exceedingly cheap." This edition would uniquely serve the cause of "Protestant truth" because such a "handsome volume" would be "read and re-read by all young people into whose hands it may come." The advertisement said nothing about the book's content, since this would have been thoroughly familiar to potential purchasers. Instead, it dwelt exclusively on the book's material attributes, arguing that fine illustrations, print, and binding made the work religiously significant. Voicing middling cultural rhetoric, the advertisement correlated the beauty and quality of a volume with its religious utility. Vaunting the book's exceeding cheapness (relative to other Cassell products), the advertisement remained silent about those fathers who would *not* be able to afford this fine commodity and whether their children must remain bereft of religious truth.[45]

The most remarkable advertisement in Cassell's *Catalogue* is that for a Bible featured on the front cover, spectacularly illustrated by the renowned French artist Gustave Doré (1832–83). The two-volume Bible boasted 238 full-page engravings and four options for quality binding, ranging from cloth gilt at $64 to morocco antique with gilt edges for $100 to morocco antique extra at $125 up to rich morocco, paneled, extra gilt, with silk ends for $150 (figure 2.6). The Bible—quite like that displayed in Kate M'Clellan's shop window and bestowed on Little Marian in *Two Christmas Gifts*—was the showpiece for the entire catalog, the most beautiful and most expensive volume offered for sale. The least expensive books in the catalog—children's volumes in the *Half-Crown Library*—each sold for $1.25, or less than one one-hundredth the cost of the finest quality Bible. The Cassell catalog apparently transformed the most purely evangelical text into an extreme example of commodification. The publisher chose the Bible as its premier display because this particular book possessed the highest intrinsic value and the clearest appeal to potential purchasers. Adorning this most esteemed religious text with the finest publishing and print technologies available presumably increased its evangelical and commercial value. Yet texts such as this one occupied an ambiguous position in evangelical print culture. Cassell's Bible must be viewed alongside Bibles produced by publishers like the ABS, sold for around one one-thousandth the price of Cassell's. ABS Bibles resembled the cheap red Bibles of M'Clellan's *Two*

Figure 2.6. "Abraham and the Three Angels," by Gustave Doré, from the Doré Bible, served as the frontispiece of Cassell, Petter & Galpin's *Illustrated Catalogue* of 1874. (Courtesy of the American Antiquarian Society)

Christmas Gifts much more closely than Cassell's morocco Bibles and were vastly more influential, if judged by the standard of total distribution.[46]

Success in the commercial book trades did not lead to an inevitable sacrifice of evangelical to market values. No nineteenth-century trade publisher achieved a higher level of business success than did Harper & Brothers, established in 1818. All four Harper brothers were devoted members of the Methodist Episcopal Church and conceived of their publishing business as a priestly calling to sanctify the world of print. Harper opened shop by printing two evangelical publications: Thayer's *Religion Recommended to Youth* and the *Prayer Book of the Protestant Episcopal Church*. As its operations expanded, the house continued to print some evangelical works while participating extensively in the regular book trades. Harper's catalogs included a "Biblical and Theological" department, positioned alphabetically between Agriculture and Biography. According to James Harper, the firm conducted its business on the basis of "*character*, and not *capital*." Although not restricting themselves to religious titles, the brothers resolved to print only such books as were "interesting, instructive, and moral." As evangelicals, the Harpers saw themselves as sanctifying the print market by publishing religious texts and by using their influence to reinforce religious and moral standards. During all their years in business, the Harpers competed aggressively in the print market six days a week but never allowed themselves or any of their employees to work on a Sunday.[47]

As a full participant in the regular book trades, Harper & Brothers experienced few of the limitations that hindered the efforts of denominational and nondenominational publishing societies. Indeed, Harper gained a reputation as an innovator and leader in the trades. Even as the evangelical societies refrained from exchanging books with secular publishers, Harper strenuously promoted publishers' auctions. During these events of the trade, publishers sold their books in lots to the highest bidder; the bidding set a wholesale price that regulated sales to other booksellers and facilitated national distribution. Harper was also the first American trade house (preceded by British publishers and American religious societies) to adopt the strategies of stereotyping and of publishing series of books as libraries. Stereotyping, by minimizing per-unit production costs, made it easier to print as many copies of a volume as could be used. The idea behind the book series was that purchasers would buy a larger number of volumes, including lesser known titles, if they perceived the books as belonging together. Of all its series, *Harper's Family Library* attained the most extensive reputation. The series consisted primarily of biography, travel, and history, mostly reprinted from British editions. In 1840, 105 volumes sold for $46.40, in a case with lock and key for $47.50, or in half-morocco binding and marbled edges for $52.50. When Harper completed the series in 1845, 187 volumes sold for $80, representing a slight discount compared with the per volume price of forty-five cents. Books in the *Family Library* appealed to evangelical readers who viewed efforts to strengthen the family as tending to advance religion; the books also won a more general audience who appreciated access to quality literature for a relatively inexpensive price.[48]

Harper's most successful publications attracted evangelical and non-evangelical audiences alike. *Harper's New Monthly Magazine*, published from 1850 through 1900, was not a religious publication per se, yet evan-

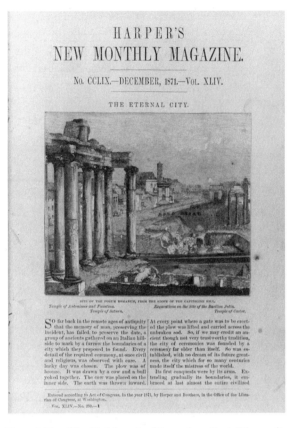

Figure 2.7.   Harper's New Monthly Magazine (December 1871). The quality articles and attractive format of *Harper's New Monthly Magazine* won an audience among both evangelical and nonevangelical readers. (Courtesy of the University of Missouri–Kansas City)

gelicals subscribed to the paper, considering its articles reliably moral (figure 2.7). In 1853, the paper had a distribution list of 130,000; by 1885, 200,000 copies circulated monthly in the United States and 35,000 copies in Britain. The periodical achieved one of the largest subscription lists in the world by offering its readers more quality material (144 two-column pages) for a lower per-column price ($3 per year for the magazine) than did any other monthly. *Harper's Illuminated and New Pictorial Bible*, though relatively modest when compared with Cassell's later, Doré Bible, was the most costly and elaborate illustrated volume published in the antebellum period. Printed in fifty-four parts between 1843 and 1846 at twenty-five cents per installment, the Bible included 1,600 engravings, produced through a new

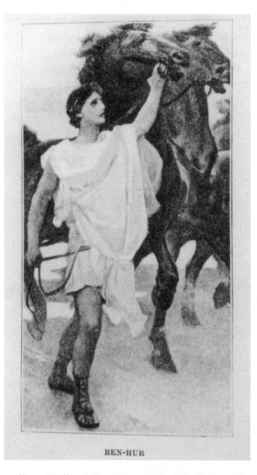

BEN-HUR

Figure 2.8. General Lew Wallace's *Ben-Hur: A Tale of the Christ* (1880) achieved best-seller status through its realistic historical details and captivating narrative. (Courtesy of the Saint Louis County Library)

electrotyping technique known as facsimile line work. The completed volume appeared in 1846, morocco-bound, hand-tooled, gold-embossed, and gilt-edged, and sold for $22.50. The Bible found an audience among those who appreciated its fine craftsmanship, whether or not they valued its message. Perhaps, like Little Marian of M'Clellan's *Two Christmas Gifts*, some of the Bible's readers learned to love the volume's contents after having been attracted by its appearance.[49]

Harper discovered its greatest publishing success of the century with a work that bridged the categories of religious and secular literature. General Lew Wallace's *Ben-Hur* first appeared in 1880 (figure 2.8). Within seven years, the book sold 230,000 copies. By 1913, sales had skyrocketed to 2.5 million. *Ben-Hur*, like the Harper publishing house, triumphed in the gap between evangelicalism and commerce. The book, more than any other *Tale of the Christ*, as its subtitle proclaimed, appealed to readers interested in its detailed historical narrative and emotionally charged plot as well as its doctrinal content. For many evangelical readers, the book's historical accuracy and realistic story line reinforced the authenticity of biblical claims to truth; for such readers, elements of the text that may appear purely secular to scholars conveyed religious meanings. Because publishers such as Harper acted simultaneously as evangelicals and as members of the book trades, boundaries separating their religious and commercial agendas frequently blurred.[50]

The financial success of Harper's publications provoked criticism by evangelicals at the time as well as more recently by cultural observers skeptical of commodification. By the 1870s, Charles Finney worried about a tendency that *Ben-Hur* would seemingly epitomize: "Now we are really too popular. The world does not hate us any more." Paradoxically, the evangelical commission to go into the world to win an audience for the gospel had succeeded, yet an element of failure was built into this success. Evangelicals feared the consequences of worldly entanglements even as they longed to sanctify the world. Denominational, nondenominational, and evangelical trade publishers all entered the world of print in order to transform it. In the process, they experienced tensions inherent to their mixed identities as evangelicals and as book trades participants.[51]

Yet the long-standing evangelical penchant for declension narratives cautions against an overly literal acceptance of Finney's critique. Throughout the nineteenth century, evangelical publishers struggled to balance purity and presence in the world as they embraced functionally sacred texts and marketing strategies. Denominational publishing tended especially to aid evangelical efforts to contend for the truth, while nondenominational activities unified evangelicals across denominational and regional lines. Trade publishers extended the reach of print artifacts — understood as religiously and commercially valuable — to expansive audiences. Evangelical publishing diversified between the Methodist Book Concern's 1789 printing of "pure divinity" and the more loosely Methodist-inspired trade house Harper & Brothers' publication of *Ben-Hur* in 1880. Yet the canon of evangelical texts circulating in 1880 bore many of the same marks of evangelical identity that characterized the previous century's steady sellers. The following pages examine the texts that populated this constantly evolving evangelical print universe.

3

Marks of Membership
in an Evangelical Canon

In 1585, an "obscure" English nonconformist minister named Edmund Bunny discovered a text written by a Jesuit, Robert Parsons, which had in it some things "too good to be lost." Bunny "cut the popery out" and published his own edition of *A Booke of Christian Exercise Appertaining to Resolution*. Forty-five years later, a poor, unnamed nonconformist cottager lent the volume to Richard Baxter's father when Richard was fifteen years old; this book provided the "means of awakening his soul." When Baxter matured, he wrote *A Call to the Unconverted* (1657), which led to Philip Doddridge's conversion. Doddridge's *Rise and Progress of Religion in the Soul* (1745) in turn resulted in the "conversions of hundreds and of thousands" and the lifelong religious growth of countless Christian pilgrims. The book stimulated one convert, British Parliamentarian William Wilberforce, to spend the rest of his political career pursuing moral reform causes— fighting for the abolition of the British slave trade and for the introduction of Christianity into India — and writing his own book, *A Practical View of the Prevailing Religious System of Professed Christians* (1797). This book convinced Scottish Presbyterian minister Thomas Chalmers in the nineteenth century to consecrate his "princely intellect to the cause of evangelical truth." Wilberforce's book, as read by Legh Richmond, produced a "first sacred impression" that prompted him to write the influential *Dairyman's Daughter* in 1813. This successive legacy, in the evaluation of a nineteenth-century Presbyterian interpreter, "all started" with Edmund Bunny's discovery of the Jesuit text 250 years earlier. A "single book" appropriated from outside evangelicalism aided the justification and sanctification of a pilgrim community envisioned as transcending time and place. The text linked "different generations together" in a common narrative universe of Christian theology and experience.[1]

Edmund Bunny's book opens a road inward to the universe of print artifacts written, published, purchased, and read by evangelicals in mid-nineteenth-century America. In chapter 1, I differentiated evangelical from nonevangelical print cultures, and in chapter 2, I traced the diversification of evangelical publishing by the mid-nineteenth century. This chapter classifies texts marked as evangelical by "genre." The literary historian Lawrence Buell offers a helpful definition of genres as "clusters of stylistic and thematic traits" loosely shared by a number of individual texts. Care must be taken in applying a term from literary studies to evangelical print culture since evangelicals distinguished sacred words from profane literature. Evangelicals viewed language not as an end in itself but as functioning to influence a scripted action pattern: texts moved their readers forward along a pilgrimage from the present world toward that which is to come. Usefulness in this pursuit, rather than formal qualities, constituted the essential mark of membership in the evangelical canon. Nineteenth-century evangelicals classed as sacred all those texts that functioned to promote Christian pilgrimage but considered some texts better suited than others to particular uses by the pilgrim community. The concept of genre is helpful in differentiating among the uses of certain classes of evangelical texts. Doctrine reinforced religious truth; memoirs gave examples worthy of emulation; fiction employed imagination to motivate action; and Sunday school texts socialized the rising generations into evangelical culture.[2]

Evangelical genres, because they were use-oriented, were inherently unstable. Texts presumably belonged to the entire pilgrim community rather than to authors, publishers, or readers in their roles as book trades participants. A lay priesthood and clerical arbiters negotiated uses of particular texts and regulated textual transmission to assist one another's pilgrimage. The lines differentiating evangelical genres and separating evangelical from nonevangelical words frequently blurred. Evangelicals even appropriated texts written by authors who clearly stood outside the confines of evangelicalism, such as the sixteenth-century Jesuit Robert Parsons. Evangelical genres must be discussed with a certain looseness of classification that extends to the term "evangelical" itself.[3]

The proliferation of genres populating the evangelical canon reflected the goal of balancing purity and presence in an expanding world of print. The Methodist *Christian Advocate* (1860) framed this dual agenda as an effort to maintain a "conservative-progressive spirit." With such a spirit, a "sanctified public temper" preserved "our blessed Theology unmarred," even as strategic adaptation to "changing circumstances" heightened evangelicals' influence on a wider cultural milieu. The terms "old" and "new," or "standard" and "modern," coded the project of incarnating the Word into nineteenth-century American society. The evangelical canon accordingly juxtaposed old and new titles and editions. Lockwood & Brooks of Boston advertised a "fine new edition" of Bunyan's *Pilgrim's Progress* as well as several other "old favorites in new styles and bindings." Side-by-side with new editions of old texts, Lockwood's 1875 *Catalogue* displayed more recent genres that had almost instantly accrued "standard and lasting value," such as Jacob Abbott's Rollo Series of children's fiction, first published in the 1830s. Evangelicals considered modern texts useful supplements to steady sellers. The ATS advertised Sarah E. Chester's *Proud Little Dody* (1875) as a new narrative that taught old Christian lessons in a pleasing style, in this case recounting a story that illustrates pride as a "besetting sin." Decades after their first publication, new editions of hymns written by the Unitarian Sarah Adams (1805–48) and the British Roman Catholic Frederick William Faber (1814–63) found their way into evangelical trade catalogs as suitable presents for "lovers of sweet religious poetry." Adopting the "latest," "best" styles of the market, new additions to the evangelical canon reinforced the work formerly accomplished by a much smaller, more uniform body of texts.[4]

Doctrine: The Usefulness of Truth

Doctrinal genres have occupied a privileged position in the evangelical canon since the formation of the early church. Evangelicals in the nineteenth as well as the first century took seriously Jude's command to "earnestly contend for the faith which was once delivered unto the saints," an objective further explored in chapter 5. The form taken by doctrinal exposition nevertheless shifted over time to correspond with changing reader tastes. Stand-alone sermons — as detailed by chapter 2 — accounted for a decreasing share of the nineteenth-century print market, while theological treatises, histories, devotional guides, and doctrinal libraries continued to find a ready audience. Many of those nineteenth-century readers who did relish sermons applauded preachers who shied away from analytical complexity and instead adopted a middling cultural style that blended tasteful elegance with emotionally persuasive personal anecdotes. Booksellers' catalogs prominently displayed the sermons of men who achieved fame on international preaching circuits, appealing to diverse audiences by interspersing refined and folksy speech: English Baptist Charles Spurgeon

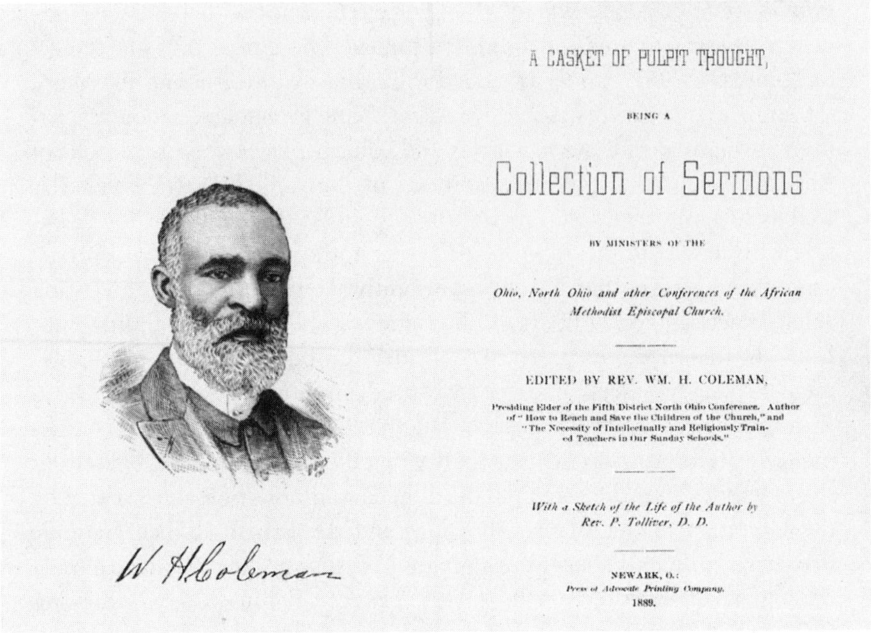

A CASKET OF PULPIT THOUGHT,

BEING A

Collection of Sermons

BY MINISTERS OF THE

Ohio, North Ohio and other Conferences of the African Methodist Episcopal Church.

EDITED BY REV. WM. H. COLEMAN,

Presiding Elder of the Fifth District North Ohio Conference. Author of " How to Reach and Save the Children of the Church," and " The Necessity of Intellectually and Religiously Trained Teachers in Our Sunday Schools."

With a Sketch of the Life of the Author by Rev. P. Tolliver, D. D.

NEWARK, O.:
Press of Advocate Printing Company.
1889.

Figure 3.1.   A Casket of Pulpit Thought (1889) demonstrated the literary refinement of AME ministers while disseminating evangelical doctrine. (Courtesy of The Library Company of Philadelphia)

(1834–92), Scottish Presbyterian Thomas Chalmers (1780–1847), and American Congregationalist Henry Ward Beecher. For urbane African American clergy, publication of volumes such as *A Casket of Pulpit Thought* (1889) functioned both to transmit doctrine and to demonstrate literary achievement (figure 3.1). Evangelical concern for doctrine did not so much diminish as did the forms for communicating doctrine change to reflect evolving literary sensibilities.[5]

Theological texts filled a market demand for instruction in evangelical and denominational teachings. Robert Carter & Brothers opened business in 1836 by reprinting a Scottish Presbyterian doctrinal treatise, William Symington's *On the Atonement and Intercession of Jesus Christ* (1834). Although other publishers had feared that the text's "strong doctrine" would limit its market appeal, Carter quickly sold more than 6,000 copies. Other strongly doctrinal, denomination-specific volumes appeared regularly in the lists of trade publishers, for instance, Episcopal bishop Charles McIlvaine's 500-page *Evidences of Christianity* (1832) and Presbyterian Charles Hodge's 2,000-page *Systematic Theology* (1871–72). Less denominationally oriented religious reference texts also found a steady place in salesrooms and catalogs, for example, Alexander Cruden's *Concordance* (1738), Howard Malcolm's *Bible Dictionary* (1830), Lyman Abbott and Thomas Conant's eclectic *Dictionary of Religious Knowledge* (1875), and Thomas Scott's *Comprehensive Commentary on the Holy Bible* (1834–38) (figure 3.2). Reader reports discussed in chapter 4 suggest that laity as well as clergy found such books indispensable aids to Bible study.[6]

Alongside more extensive treatises, denominational and nondenominational catechisms and tracts taught doctrine to lay Christians and non-Christians alike, using question-and-answer and narrative formats. By 1858, the Presbyterian Board had distributed over 1 million copies combined of its *Confession of Faith*, *Shorter Catechism*, and *Catechism for Young Children*. Even briefer and considerably more abundant than catechisms, tracts addressing particular doctrines reached audiences that included and extended beyond evangelical church members. The ATS scattered evangelical tracts printed in ten different languages across the nation. Denominational societies each disseminated tracts that taught more controversial doctrines; the Baptists used tracts to teach "Facts on Baptism," "Facts on Communion," and "Facts Concerning the Church." Theological texts ranging from comprehensive treatises to single-issue tracts instilled doctrine in readers with all levels of interest and expertise.[7]

Historical volumes, long established in the canon as reinforcing doctrine by demonstrating God's providential works, gained new prominence in the nineteenth century. Histories defended the Word's authority against the challenges of biblical-historical criticism and romanticism by documenting the circumstances surrounding characters and events in the Bible and throughout the stream of church history (figure 3.3). In applying the Word to the experiences of people living in diverse times and places, histories reaffirmed evangelicals' identity as participants in an enduring narrative of Christian and denominational experience. Thus, *From Exile to Overthrow: A History of the Jews from the Babylonian Captivity to the Destruction of the Second Temple* (1881), written by the Presbyterian minister John Mears, urged readers to consider themselves heirs to the exiled Jews. Mears aided readers in placing themselves in the narrative by connecting historical details with features of the American environment: the streets of Babylon were "straight and intersected each other at right angles," like those William Penn designed in Philadelphia.[8]

Histories not only depicted ancient times but also traced the church's development. Some books invoked a sense of transgenerational, transatlantic evangelical identity by recounting the story of the Reformation, focus-

The Great Theological Work of the Age.

DR. HODGE'S THEOLOGY.

Systematic Theology.

BY CHARLES HODGE, D.D., LL.D.,

of Princeton Theological Seminary.

To be completed in three volumes 8vo.   Tinted paper.   Price per vol., in cloth, $4.50.

IN these volumes are comprised the results of the life-long labors and investigations of one of the most eminent theologians of the age. The work covers the ground usually occupied by treatises on Systematic Theology, and adopts the commonly received divisions of the subject,—THEOLOGY, Vol. I.; ANTHROPOLOGY, Vol. II.; SOTERIOLOGY AND ESCHATOLOGY, Vol. III.

The plan of the author is to state and vindicate the teachings of the Bible on these various subjects, and to examine the antagonistic doctrines of different classes of Theologians. His book, therefore, is intended to be both didactic and elenchtic.

The various topics are discussed with that close and keen analytical and logical power, combined with that simplicity, lucidity, and strength of style which have already given Dr. HODGE a world-wide reputation as a controversialist and writer, and as an investigator of the great theological problems of the day.

CONTENTS OF VOLUME I.

INTRODUCTION.

Chapter I. On Method.
"   II. Theology.
"   III. Rationalism.
"   IV. Mysticism.
"   V. Roman Catholic Doctrine concerning the Rule of Faith.
"   VI. The Protestant Rule of Faith.

PART I.

Chapter I. Theology Proper.
"   II. Theism.

Chapter III. Anti-Theistic Theories.
"   IV. Knowledge of God.
"   V. The Nature and Attributes of God.
"   VI. The Trinity.
"   VII. The Divinity of Christ.
"   VIII. The Holy Spirit.
"   IX. The Decrees of God.
"   X. Creation.
"   XI. Providence.
"   XII. Miracles.
"   XIII. Angels.

SPECIAL NOTICE.   Volumes I. and II. of Dr. Hodge's SYSTEMATIC THE-OLOGY are now published; and Vol. III. is in preparation, and may be expected in September, 1872.

Figure 3.2.   Advertisements by Scribner, Armstrong for Charles Hodge's *Systematic Theology* (1872) and by J. B. Lippincott for Thomas Scott's *Comprehensive Commentary* (1860). Trade publishers included theological reference volumes in their general catalogs. (Courtesy of the American Antiquarian Society)

ing alternately on the movement's heroes and its enemies. Such works included a translation of the French writer Jean Henri Merle d'Aubigne's five-volume *History of the Reformation of the Sixteenth Century* (1847–53) and the German author Frederic Shoberl's *Persecutions of Popery: Historical Narratives of the Most Remarkable Persecutions Occasioned by the Intolerance of the Church of Rome* (1844). Most denominations supplemented general histories with accounts of their own history, doctrine, and polity, for example, E. H. Gillett's *History of the Presbyterian Church in the United States of America* (1864) and Augustus Green's *Treatise on the Episcopacy of the African Methodist Episcopal Church* (1845). By linking the Word with previous generations' experiences, historical texts reinforced evangelicals' sense of participation in a grand narrative of the progress of the church.

While histories emphasized past experience, devotional volumes applied

Comprehensive Commentary.

The Comprehensive Commentary on the Holy Bible, containing the text according to the authorized version; with marginal references; Matthew Henry's Commentary, condensed, but retaining the most useful thoughts; the practical observations of Rev. Thomas Scott, D.D., with extensive explanatory, critical, and philological notes, selected from Scott, Doddridge, Gill, Adam Clarke, Patrick, Poole, Lowth, Burder, Harmer, Calmet, Stuart Robinson, Bush, Rosenmueller, Bloomfield, and many other writers on the Scriptures. The whole designed to be a digest and combination of the advantages of the best Bible commentaries, and embracing nearly all that is valuable in Henry, Scott, and Doddridge. Conveniently arranged for family and private reading, and at the same time particularly adapted to the wants of Sabbath-school teachers and Bible classes; with numerous useful tables, and a neatly-engraved family record. Embellished with Engravings on wood and steel, of Scripture scenes, and illustrative of Scripture manners, customs, antiquities, etc. Including

A Supplement, containing a new concordance to the Holy Scriptures, with authentic illustrations on wood; a guide to the study of the Bible, embracing evidences of Christianity,

34

the Word to the experiences of the present generation. Devotional guides aided meditation on biblical truth by selecting and explicating short passages, often accompanied by hymns, a genre discussed at length in chapters 7 and 8. *Daily Steps Towards Heaven* (1869) presented readers with a verse or two of the Bible and a hymn or "pious reflection" for every day in the year. Many such guides were "pocket-sized" for easy carrying to individual or family worship or for travel away from home. Some devotional texts addressed the special needs of particular groups, for instance, sailors or sufferers. *An Epitome of the Art of Spiritual Navigation; Or, A Voyage to Heaven Recommended, by a Christian Mariner* (1845) developed concrete metaphors comparing sea travel and Christian pilgrimage. *The Christian Comforter: A Gift for the Afflicted and Bereaved* (1846) collected hymns and Bible verses suited to seasons of suffering. Still other volumes connected doctrine with social issues, such as *The Temperance Lyre: A Collection of Temperance Songs Adapted to Popular Melodies* (c. 1852). Indeed, the ATS

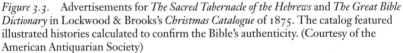

Figure 3.3. Advertisements for *The Sacred Tabernacle of the Hebrews* and *The Great Bible Dictionary* in Lockwood & Brooks's *Christmas Catalogue* of 1875. The catalog featured illustrated histories calculated to confirm the Bible's authenticity. (Courtesy of the American Antiquarian Society)

circulated 5 million copies of similar temperance publications by midcentury. In contrast to other doctrinal genres, relatively few devotional guides emphasized doctrines peculiar to particular denominations.[9]

Library series balanced evangelical and denominational priorities in making cheap editions of older doctrinal texts accessible to nineteenth-century readers. The ATS commenced one of the first and most influential libraries of "standard works in religious literature" in 1833, *The Evangelical Family Library.* The first fifteen volumes of what would grow to a forty-five volume series could be purchased as a set for $5.50; within a decade of the library's introduction, more than 2 million copies of books in the series had sold. An anonymous beneficiary of the library made it a "rule to read one volume every week"; the man's minister claimed that the "effect on his mind was visible to all around him." Because the books were so "cheap," the man had been able to purchase the entire set.[10]

The Evangelical Family Library elided doctrinal differences among denominations by embracing and modifying texts written by British and American evangelicals between the seventeenth and nineteenth centuries. The ATS excluded what its board evaluated as "controversial" or "sectarian" views and omitted references to denominational affiliation, although many of the authors were English nonconformists. The ATS altered most of the texts reprinted, abridging their contents to fit into uniformly sized and bound volumes and supplying new "pre-texts" (to borrow a term from Larzer Ziff), or supplementary information previous to the main text, that shaped readers' expectations about the books. The title page to the Congregationalist Jonathan Edwards's *Treatise on Religious Affections* (1746) announced that the text had been "rewritten and abridged." A prefatory note explained the nature of the textual changes: "The precise thoughts of Edwards" had been preserved "as far as practicable in his own language, but in a more modern and perspicuous style; with no addition, and the omission only of his tautologies, redundancies, repetitions, and more extended illustrations." English nonconformist Joseph Alleine's *Alarm to Unconverted Sinners: In a Serious Treatise on Conversion* (1672) similarly fell under the knife of ATS editors. A prefatory note acknowledged that "numerous obsolete or defective words or phrases have been altered, and some passages, including a few referring to denominational peculiarities, have been omitted." The ATS editorial committee felt no hesitancy in modifying texts written by authors whom it considered worthy of inclusion in the series. This editorial freedom reflects an understanding of doctrinal texts as the common property of all Christians. When editing made denominational texts more useful for evangelical purposes, publishers saw no reason to transmit texts in their original form.[11]

In response to ATS success with *The Evangelical Family Library*, denominational publishers commenced series of their own to instruct readers in controversial doctrines. *The Baptist Library* (1843) presented thirty-three "rare and costly" "Standard Baptist Works" to readers for a mere "trifle." Although the ATS rigidly excluded sectarian publications, the Baptists printed both evangelical and denominational volumes. John Bunyan's nonsectarian *Holy War* (1682) functioned in the "promotion of piety," as did "works of controversy" such as Abraham Booth's *Vindication of the Baptists from the Charge of Bigotry in Refusing Communion at the Lord's Table to Paedobaptists* (1778). *The Baptist Library*, and other similar denominational

series, used older works of doctrine to remember and reinforce denominational identity. Old and new doctrinal texts and genres served evangelical
and denominational purposes in contending for the faith by informing and
reminding readers of the truth of the Word in all times and places of human
experience.[12]

Memoirs: The Usefulness of Example

Like doctrinal volumes, memoirs, one of the most abundant genres in the
nineteenth century, grew out of a long-standing tradition in Christian writing. Hagiographies, stories of the lives of the saints, had for centuries described how noteworthy Christians modeled their lives on the life of Christ
as an invitation for others to follow their examples. Nineteenth-century
hagiographical texts included third-person authored biographies of Christians as well as non-Christians who exhibited exceptional moral qualities
and third-person edited memoirs of a subject's own diaries and letters.
Since biographies and memoirs functioned similarly in evangelical culture,
and since the boundaries dividing the genres readily collapsed, the terms
can for our purposes be used interchangeably. Biographical volumes occupied a prominent position in the catalogs of religious and trade publishers alike. As one index to their popularity, out of a cross section of trade
books published from 1852 to 1855, nearly 10 percent were biographical.
In contrast to doctrinal texts that contended for the faith by explicating
biblical truth, evangelical memoirs used example to strengthen the priesthood of all believers and to deepen Christian unity. Unlike Catholic hagiographies of canonized saints, evangelical memoirs took as their models
ordinary "saints" whose everyday experiences qualified them to influence
other Christian pilgrims. At the same time, memoir editors and biographers acted as cultural arbiters who reshaped the experiences of their subjects in order to provide useful models that any Christian could and should
emulate.[13]

Evangelicals privileged memoirs because they considered example a
powerful tool to mold Christian "character." Nineteenth-century Americans were obsessed with character formation, even as various groups con-
tested the definition of the term. Evangelicals associated character with
habits of the mind and heart that led to habitual actions calculated to
promote growth in holiness. Memoirs prepared readers for action by encouraging them to identify sympathetically with eminent models of Christian experience while engaging readers' interest in the scenes and events
described. Studying the "written lives of those who have gone to their rest,"

asserted the nondenominational *Mothers' Magazine* (1849), "exerts a heavenly influence upon the mind and heart" readily translatable into sanctified action. The nondenominational *Beauty of Holiness* (1855) similarly evaluated biographies as the "cream of literature in every age, and generally the only portion which leaves any permanent impress on the morals of a people." By illustrating how memoir subjects applied the Word to life experiences, biographical texts stimulated readers to pursue a similarly holy character.[14]

The memoirs that populated the evangelical canon evoked a pilgrim community that transcended time, place, or denomination. In catalogs and on bookshelves, steady sellers appeared side-by-side with a continual stream of more recent publications. Thanks to such books, the names of Congregationalist David Brainerd (1718–47), Scottish Presbyterian (later Episcopal archbishop) Robert Leighton (1611–84), Congregationalist Edward Payson (1783–1827), Anglican Henry Martyn (1781–1812), Methodist Hester Ann Rogers (1756–94), and Baptist Adoniram Judson (1788–1850), among others, were household words among nineteenth-century evangelicals. In emphasizing experiences shared by all Christians, editors glossed over denominational differences to reinforce evangelical unity. A review in *Mothers' Magazine* (1849) approved a new edition of Payson's *Life and Works* (1829) for the reason that contemplating the life of "such a devoted servant of Christ in his journey heavenward" is both "profitable and pleasant" for the "warm-hearted Christian" of any denomination. One biographical compendium, *Heroes and Martyrs of the Modern Missionary Enterprise* (1852), condensed the "lives" of twenty-nine missionaries from different denominations. All of the volume's subjects, regardless of when or where they lived, purportedly demonstrated a common Christian character that made doctrinal differences irrelevant.[15]

Indicative of evangelicals' emphasis on a priesthood of all believers, the presumptive usefulness of a memoir depended less on the theological training or social status of its subject than on the exemplar's experiences struggling to live as a Christian in the world. Although numerous memoirs recorded the lives of religious and social elites, others told the stories of less prominent Christians, including African Americans, women, and children. Many evangelicals classed the latter groups as especially near to Christ on account of what Harriet Beecher Stowe termed their "lowly" status in *Uncle Tom's Cabin; Or, Life Among the Lowly*. One such volume described *The Life of the Rev. Dandridge F. Davis* (1850), missionary of the AME Church (figure 3.4). As an itinerant minister, Davis traveled throughout Kentucky, Virginia, North and South Carolina, Georgia, and Indiana, preaching wher-

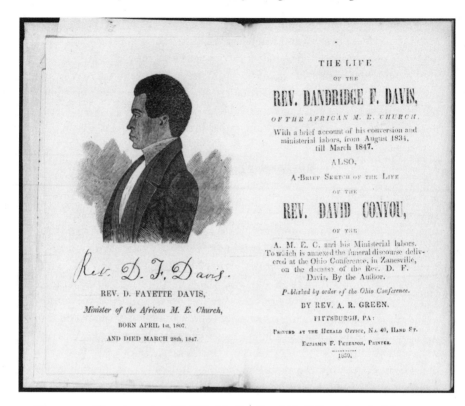

THE LIFE

OF THE

REV. DANDRIDGE F. DAVIS,

OF THE AFRICAN M. E. CHURCH.

With a brief account of his conversion and
ministerial labors, from August 1834,
till March 1847.

ALSO,

A BRIEF SKETCH OF THE LIFE

OF THE

REV. DAVID CONYOU,

OF THE

A. M. E. C. and his Ministerial labors.
To which is annexed the funeral discourse delivered at the Ohio Conference, in Zanesville,
on the decease of the Rev. D. F.
Davis, By the Author.

Published by order of the Ohio Conference.

BY REV. A. R. GREEN.

PITTSBURGH, PA:

PRINTED AT THE HERALD OFFICE, No. 40, HAND ST.

Benjamin F. Peterson, Printer.

1850.

Rev. D. F. Davis.

REV. D. FAYETTE DAVIS,

Minister of the African M. E. Church,

BORN APRIL 1st, 1807.

AND DIED MARCH 28th, 1847.

Figure 3.4.   Memoirs such as *The Life of the Rev. Dandridge F. Davis* (1850) of the AME Church presented evangelical readers with models for how to live as Christians in the world. (Courtesy of The Library Company of Philadelphia)

ever he went to "white and colored, and even to the red man of the forest." Davis's life merited remembrance because of the influence he had exerted and which he could continue to exert as readers emulated his example. Truman Pratt (1776–1876), centenarian and Colored Methodist Episcopal minister of Baltimore, deserved a biography that conveyed the "storehouse of experience" he had gathered during his long life. Pratt's story aided other Christian pilgrims as they heard his "sweet recollections of his journey past." Baptist Charity Richards (1845) gained her experience through "complicated and protracted sufferings." Her biography depicted a Christian's attainment of a "good degree of eminence in piety, together with the process" through which she had grown in holiness. The "pious reader breathing out his soul after God and holiness" would be encouraged through reading the narrative to "press forward with a holy zeal through the crowd of obstacles which oppose his onward progress." The depth of

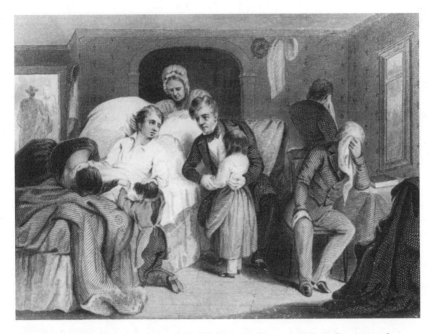

Figure 3.5. "The Christian's Death Bed," *Christian Souvenir* (1851). Sentimental portrayals of scenes of sanctified suffering invited readers' sympathetic participation. (Courtesy of the American Antiquarian Society)

Christian experience that exemplars gained by overcoming obstacles to pursue purity made these individuals useful models for readers.[16]

To heighten the influence of noteworthy examples, biographers and editors advised readers to identify sympathetically with memoir subjects. Editorial interventions reminded readers that each shared the subject's mortality: "It is but a little while, my dear reader, at longest, that you will tarry in this world." Deathbed narratives invited the reader's emotional participation by detailing the last few days or hours of an eminent Christian's life, including hymns and Scriptures read and requested, last words, extent and duration of suffering, and hopes of happiness and heaven (figure 3.5). One such account, *Saved by Grace; Or, The Last Week in the Life of Davis Johnson, Jr.* (1860), traced the final days of a nineteen-year-old who suffered a "mortal wound bathing." The biographer asked the reader to reflect that he or she could as easily succumb to an untimely accident; would the reader as patiently and cheerfully walk with Jesus through the "fire kindled to refine him"? Another volume compared the *Death Bed Triumphs of Eminent Christians* (1842) in a variety of circumstances to demonstrate that true religion not only blesses life but also "sanctifies affliction" and makes death "triumphant and happy." The author avowedly designed the book to "encourage those who are traveling to Zion, and to allure others to ask for this good path and walk therein." Readers who identified sympathetically with the characters described would hopefully be moved to pursue the path toward heaven.[17]

Deathbed accounts of children provided models with which child readers could specifically identify. As narrated in *Lizzie Ferguson; Or, the Sabbath-School Scholar* (1856), a young girl approached her death repeating a hymn she had "known and loved" long: "I want to be an angel . . . I'll join the heavenly music, / And praise him day and night." The text asked its reader, "Does your heart feel sober as you look at her? Do you wish that your own dying-bed may be as peaceful a place as hers?" If so, the reader must follow Lizzie's example while still healthy. Similarly, an advertisement for children's memoirs in the AME *Christian Recorder* (1862) prompted: "You know, children, that the good example of a good child like yourselves is a great help to you in trying to be good." Memoirs of pious children aimed to be useful to child readers who could identify with other children's experiences and through this identification process emulate worthy examples.[18]

Missionary memoirs, another prominent biographical form, inspired imitation by combining "interesting" records of foreign or domestic travel and customs with models of exemplary piety (figure 3.6). The term "interest" functioned as a code word for evangelicals' goal of motivating holy action. *Spicy Breezes from Minnesota Prairies* (1886) offered "racy and interesting sketches of missionary life and work in that new and growing State," including its "hardships, its discouragements, and its happy results." Thomas Upham endorsed the memoir of George Thompson (1857), missionary to western Africa, by affirming that the work would "increase the interest and efforts of Christians for the good of their fellow-men." The memoirs of women and children missionaries appealed in a special way to evangelical readers. Beginning with the life of Congregationalist Harriet Newell, missionary to India (1813), a stream of memoirs recorded the experiences and sufferings of women who left the comforts of the domestic fireside to die overseas. Several texts narrated the experiences of the three successive Mrs. Judsons, wives of the pioneer Baptist missionary Adoniram Judson of Burma. Other missionary memoirs combined the interest of foreign scenes with the pathos of a child's early death. *Myra* (1876), daughter of Congregationalist missionaries to Turkey, would be "useful to parents and children" because of the "interest attaching to the account of her life in Asia and her journey home" to heaven. Whether or not readers followed the particular example of missionary service, their interest in the

CARTERS' PUBLICATIONS.

FOX—Memoir of the Rev. H. W. Fox, Missionary to the Teloogoo people. With an Introductory Essay by Bishop McIlvaine. Illustrated with a fine portrait, and seven highly finished wood engravings by Howland. 12mo. $1 00.

"No appeal that I know of—not even the Memoir of Henry Martyn—has blown the trumpet in our Zion with so loud and so stirring a note, as that which sounds forth in this volume. It speaks to the Church of Christ; it speaks to

16

Figure 3.6. Missionary memoirs such as the *Memoir of the Rev. H. W. Fox, Missionary to the Teloogoo People*, in Robert Carter's 1851 *Catalogue*, stimulated readers' interest in foreign scenes and exemplary piety. (Courtesy of the American Antiquarian Society)

scenes and events described prepared them to imitate a model of sacrificial Christian action.[19]

Since evangelicals viewed memoir subjects as models for emulation, editors felt justified in modifying narratives in order to present more worthy models to the public gaze. Despite evangelical assumptions about the priesthood of all believers, some Christians, particularly white clerical editors, assumed that they had the authority to regulate the influences that memoirs exerted. Editors concerned themselves first of all with selecting appropriate subjects. Because biographies conveyed a permanent impress on Christian character, the entire Christian community suffered a "real misfortune when misdirected genius sets the seal of indestructibleness upon inferior objects." Even the holiest lives included "many blots" and "many blanks in the most important passages" of the Christian story; editors sought to minimize the negative effects of these imperfections.[20]

The memoir of David Brainerd illustrates this process of textual transmission. Jonathan Edwards published *An Account of the Life of the Late Reverend Mr. David Brainerd* in 1749. In selecting passages from Brainerd's diary for inclusion in his *Life*, Edwards elided words and entire paragraphs that suggested religious enthusiasm, despair, unorthodox sentiments, or confidence in human ability to prepare for the reception of divine grace. Subsequent editors representing multiple denominations likewise appropriated Brainerd for their own theological uses, generally deemphasizing what these editors considered excesses of Edwardsean Calvinism and revival-oriented religion. Methodist John Wesley published a condensed version of the *Life* in 1768 in which he excised passages that were strongly predestinarian or committed to an extreme view of human depravity. Methodist, Anglican, and Baptist missionaries all claimed to find inspiration in the Congregationalist Brainerd's religious experiences. Over thirty editions of Brainerd's *Life* appeared in the nineteenth century, making it the most frequently reprinted, and most often altered, of all Edwards's works.[21]

Clerical editors felt even greater freedom in appropriating the experiences of pious women, children, and African Americans as pedagogical aids. White clergy, as the historian Christine Heyrman has argued, frequently promoted the memoirs of such subjects precisely because their "natural capacities" seemed to the arbiters "so limited that supernatural intervention alone could account for such piety and eloquence." ATS secretary Rev. Israel P. Warren wrote a biography of *The Sisters: A Memoir of Elizabeth H., Abbie A., and Sarah F. Dickerman* in 1859. An advertisement for the book adopted conventional language from Hebrews 11:4 to boast of the women: "Though dead, they yet speak." In point of fact, the women only speak through the mediating voice of their "pious and learned pastor," who used the text to admonish other young women toward advances in "personal piety." The memoir of the English Methodist Mary Fletcher (1739–1815) clarifies the process by which editors intervened to reshape women's experiences, choosing what to retain and omit as well as reconfiguring texts through organizational strategies, prefaces, and footnotes. In editing Fletcher's diaries, Rev. Henry Moore intruded at several points to explain and qualify Fletcher's assertions, assuring readers that her emphasis on good works bore no resemblance to Roman Catholic monasticism and that her claims to hear from God in dreams did not make her an enthusiast. Moore's voice, rather than Fletcher's, interprets the significance of Fletcher's experiences for those who would follow her example.[22]

The biographers of African Americans commonly rewrote the meanings of subjects' lives to accord with white editorial standards of religious and social character. The eighteenth-century free black Methodist shoemaker Henry Evans attracted large audiences of blacks and whites when he preached in Fayetteville, North Carolina. Evans's bold addresses to racially mixed audiences so alarmed the town council that they forced him to limit his preaching to venues in the surrounding countryside. Evans's nineteenth-century biographer represented him as far more deferential in death than he ever appeared to observers in life: "never speaking to a white man but with his hat under his arm; never allowing himself to be seated in their houses; and even confining himself to the kind and manner of dress proper for negroes in general, except his plain black coat in the pulpit." Mediated by his editor, Evans's life reinforced white ideals of Christian character and racially prescribed patterns of social deference. Such examples point to a tense balancing act within evangelical culture between the religiously and socially radical notion of a priesthood of all believers and the conservative efforts of white male clergy to regulate a unified community of print.[23]

Fiction: The Usefulness of Imagination

Although doctrine and biography both emphasized direct connections between religious truth and human experience, fiction gave freer play to the imagination as an influence on character. Fiction opened new possibilities for evangelicals to sanctify the popular print market and raised new questions about the possibility of balancing purity and presence in the world. In responding to the rise of the novel in the secular print market, evangelicals asked whether all literary forms could be bent to religious purposes or whether some genres were inherently corrupt and corrupting. Nineteenth-century evangelicals objected to secular novels more vehemently than to any other genre. At the same time, an increasing number of evangelicals, confident of the usefulness of imagination as a religious instrument, employed fictional devices and even wrote novels. Debates over the meanings of fiction illuminate evangelical understandings of the ideal relationship—one characterized by usefulness—linking writers, publishers, texts, and readers in a textually defined pilgrim community. As means to an end and as the property of the Christian community, texts should induce readers to promote their own and others' progress in holiness.[24]

Evangelicals agreed about the immorality of many popular novels, but they differed as to whether Christian authors could safely appropriate fiction for religious uses. Charles Wesley Andrews, in *Religious Novels: An Argument Against Their Use* (1856), argued that the gradual appearance of fiction between the eighteenth and nineteenth centuries had caught unsuspecting Christians off guard. Andrews blamed not the bad novelists but the good ones for opening the floodgates of immoral fiction. By the early nineteenth century, Sir Walter Scott, the best of the novelists in Andrews's evaluation, broke "down the walls of the Church, and brought in the wooden horse. He was read and praised by bishops, priests, and people. To object to *his* novels was a scouted mark of spiritual prudishness. . . . But the breach was left open. . . . Our stores, railroad cars, offices, shops, counting-rooms, parlors, nurseries, nay, our very bedchambers, were infested with books, magazines, and papers of every form filled with tales, tales, interminable tales." For Andrews, fiction was so corrupt that it stood beyond the pale of acceptable genres. Attempts to preach "truth through fiction" could be no more effective than trying to produce "temperance through rum." Fiction appeared to Andrews not as a neutral tool but as an agent with evil power of its own.[25]

Evangelical critiques of fiction, and especially novels, stemmed from the assumption that writers should use texts to provoke moral action. *Confessions and Experience of a Novel Reader*, written by "a physician" in 1855, articulated some of the arguments typically raised against novels. High market demand for fiction encouraged authors to write for the wrong reasons: to secure "*merely* ambitious notoriety" and "*purely* pecuniary" gain. In the evangelical framework, authors should use the medium of print, like every other resource, to influence others for good. Evangelicals assumed that Christians were responsible not only for their own spiritual growth but also for the growth of others in their physical and textual communities. Novelists with no intention in writing but to profit personally were the "moral pests of community." Instead of seeking to be useful, such novelists were "devoid of any definite aims, and dead to any practical efforts for the amelioration of society, or the good of mankind." Wrong motives in the composition process presumably corrupted the texts produced and compromised their usefulness to readers.[26]

Many evangelicals saw fiction as inherently worse than useless. They distinguished between inciting interest in true characters and events, the province of memoirs, and merely "exciting" the passions through fictional devices. Although interest engaged the reader's intellectual faculties, excitement drew out the reader's feelings, which many evangelicals viewed as an inferior mode of constructing religious knowledge. Interest led to knowledge that induced action, but excitement consumed energy in a fire of passion that resulted in idleness of mind and body. As one critic argued, "There is no need of fiction to interest the young. There are *incidents* enough, without a particle of fiction about them, which will secure the attention of the young or old better, we believe, than romance." Once a text had secured its readers' mental attention, it could influence them to act in a particular way. Novels, by contrast, were "not only useless, but positively injurious" because they tended "wrongly to excite the imagination." The "inflammation" of the passions, rather than inducing readers to fulfill their Christian duties, gave readers a "disrelish for the most ordinary duties of life." Instead of increasing readers' usefulness to others, novels encouraged the indulgent to "shrink away up in a corner of the room," away from other people, where they could do no one any good. Isolated readers shed "rivers of sentimental tears, and caverns full of agonizing sighs." Sentimentalism purportedly replaced meaningful knowledge and consequent action on behalf of others by stirring up and then releasing emotions in self-absorbed excess.[27]

In the narrative framework of evangelicalism, every life activity potentially had eternal significance; every action properly conceived constituted a step along a heaven-bound pilgrimage and a way to help others in their journeys toward salvation. By contrast, novels — even those not on the surface immoral — consumed time, money, and energy that should have been invested in an urgent struggle against the forces of evil. Evangelicals believed that the world was filled with deceptions that could derail growth in holiness. Novels threatened to deceive the unwary: "The poison is the more dangerous, because served up in styles so relishful to the youthful fancy." Instead of leading heavenward, novels "hurled" readers into the "fire of consuming passion, and then, at last, into the fire which is unquenchable." In short, novels represented the inverse of the proper relationship among members of a textually defined pilgrim community.[28]

Although some evangelicals voiced sharp criticisms of novels throughout the nineteenth century, by the 1850s many evangelicals evaluated the potential of religious fiction more positively as a powerful means to sanctify the world of print. Yale's president Noah Porter led educated evangelicals in a move to oppose the "New Infidelity" in scholarship, exposing the atheistical assumptions that hid in apparently harmless secular guises. As a part of this reforming agenda, Porter approved the use of novels that offered a "healthful" combination of "instruction" and "amusement." Other evangelicals themselves wrote fiction. Intensely concerned with distancing themselves from the authors of immoral novels, some evangelical authors used novelistic literary conventions while denying that they were writing novels. A number of the women authors who achieved literary notice in the nineteenth century, such as Susan Warner, author of the best-selling *Wide, Wide World* (1850), interpreted their books as means to evangelical ends. As literary historian Jane Tompkins has described the agenda of such authors, they had "designs upon their audiences," desiring to lead readers to think and act by the rules of a domestic model of piety.[29]

Religious fiction, because it influenced audiences wider than church members, seemed to many evangelicals useful in sanctifying American culture. Harriet Beecher Stowe's *Uncle Tom's Cabin*, which sold more than 3 million copies in the nineteenth century and awoke the nation's conscience, achieved popularity by employing a sentimental style deplored by fiction's opponents. Yet Stowe shared evangelical assumptions about the correct relationship among writers, publishers, texts, and readers, namely, that reading should induce moral action on behalf of others and that writers and publishers should influence readers through their texts. In using sentimentalism to achieve these goals, Stowe's work reflected certain evangelicals' growing appreciation of feeling, as opposed to intellect, as a legitimate, even superior, faculty of religious knowledge that promoted useful action rather than idleness. Her novel stirred religious feelings in order to move readers to fight slavery and oppression; engrossed audiences identified with her fictionalized characters and sympathized with their dilemmas. Stowe prefaced the novel by articulating her theory of evangelical fiction: "Every influence of literature, of poetry and of art, . . . under the allurements of fiction, breathe a humanizing and subduing influence, favorable to the development of the great principles of Christian brotherhood. The hand of benevolence is everywhere stretched out, searching into abuses, righting wrongs, alleviating distresses, and bringing to the knowledge and sympathies of the world the lowly, the oppressed, and the forgotten." Stowe had not written a merely literary text with self-referential value; *Uncle Tom's Cabin* served a definite function. Readers motivated to "feel right" necessarily acted to resist the inherent wrong of slavery. Even as Stowe claimed a transformative power for fiction, she adopted the third person to deny her own agency in writing: "The story can less be said to have been composed by her than imposed upon her. . . . The book insisted upon getting itself into being, and would take no denial." By disavowing authorship, Stowe marked her novel as a religious work, in a sense inspired by the Holy Spirit; the text did not belong to her, as an author or as a woman, but to the Christian community.[30]

Stowe was but one member of that "damned mob of scribbling women" that Nathaniel Hawthorne jealously condemned, largely because their market successes exceeded his own. Many such women wrote fiction since it provided one of the only venues through which they could not only earn money but also preach evangelical doctrine without violating religious and social strictures against women's public speech. As the literary historian David Reynolds has argued in *Faith in Fiction*, works of fiction could serve as potent vehicles for religious discussion, enabling women to participate in theological discourses otherwise dominated by men. Unfortunately, in recovering women's religious fiction, it is all too easy to confuse the adoption of imaginative styles for doctrinal liberalization, the narration of secular experience for secularization, and the voicing of women's concerns for the replacement of male intellectual rigor with weakly feminine emotion. Such a perspective suggests that nineteenth-century evangelical publishing underwent an inexorable progression from orthodox doctrinal treatises to subversively heterodox, commodified sentimental fiction. The problem with this line of reasoning is that it obscures the extent to which theology mattered to nineteenth-century women and to the imaginative texts they produced and consumed.[31]

Elizabeth Prentiss (1818–78), born in Portland, Maine, to Ann Shipman and Congregationalist revival preacher Edward Payson, was one of many nineteenth-century evangelical women who used fiction to sanctify the print market by translating doctrinal preaching into a popular cultural medium. As Prentiss described her agenda, she "preached the Bible doctrine of an indwelling Christ, with the conviction that just in proportion to this indwelling will be the holiness of the soul." From 1834 to 1878, Prentiss wrote thirty-one book-length volumes, including novels, poems, hymns, plays, and children's stories, and contributed regularly to religious periodicals, such as the ATS *Sabbath at Home*, and two denominational papers, the *New York Observer* and the *Advance*. During Prentiss's lifetime, publishers sold over 200,000 copies of her works in the United States, not counting British editions and multiple translations into French and German. Prentiss's *Stepping Heavenward* (1869), which by itself accounts for over 100,000 nineteenth-century sales, is doctrinally rigorous, privileges intellectual principle over fluctuating feelings, calls its readers to higher levels of piety, and legitimates women's experiences — not by undercutting theology but by imbuing domestic life with theological significance (figure 3.7). In the evaluation of her 1884 biographer, Prentiss won an audience, not because she wrote anything extraordinary or subversive, but because her writings flowed "squarely in the center of a stream of evan-

Figure 3.7.   Elizabeth Prentiss's *Stepping Heavenward* (1869) exemplified evangelical print culture's concern with sanctification. (Courtesy of Jeremy Huggins Collection and the University of Missouri–Columbia)

gelical preaching which made her interpretation of the daily Christian life utterly familiar to a large section of churchgoing America." Prentiss's readers bought her books since they wanted to hear confirmed through fiction a view of the world that they already knew well from reading many comparable texts in the evangelical canon.[32]

As the daughter of three generations of Calvinist ministers and the wife of yet another, George L. Prentiss, Elizabeth Prentiss's "preaching" illuminates some of the ways nineteenth-century evangelicals in the Calvinist doctrinal tradition used fiction to adapt theology to changing cultural needs. When asked whether she had taken her doctrine from her father, Edward Payson, Prentiss claimed to be old enough to have the right to a theology of her own. *Stepping Heavenward* stakes out a position distinct from Payson's Calvinism, yet it shares the same consciousness of original sin and passion for renewed relationship with God through faith in Jesus Christ. Prentiss reserved her sharpest censure not for her father but for contemporary novelists whom she understood to have lost sight of Christ in their fictionalization of doctrine, including Harriet Beecher Stowe in her later works such as *The Minister's Wooing* (1859) and Elizabeth Stuart Phelps Ward in *The Gates Ajar* (1868). After reading one of the many offshoot novels inspired by Phelps, *Gates Off the Hinges*, Prentiss quipped that the next volume ought to be titled "There Aint no Gates." Payson and Prentiss did not disagree about human or divine nature — doctrines that authors such as Stowe and Phelps revised — but about the salvation process. Payson's generation of Calvinists had emphasized the doctrine of justification, exemplified by a momentous one-time conversion experience under the influence of a minister's revival preaching. Prentiss and her peers renewed seventeenth-century Calvinism's priority on the lifelong, gradual sanctification process; the nineteenth-century version of this doctrine heightened the role that women played in guiding spiritual as well as physical growth in the domestic circle.[33]

Formally, *Stepping Heavenward* is an imaginative rendering of a young woman's diary kept from adolescence through marriage and motherhood. In the unfolding narrative of everyday experiences, the reader witnesses the process by which the protagonist, Katy, takes daily steps heavenward. Through dialogue, correspondence, and private journal entries, Katy and other women, lay men, and clerical characters each offer explicitly theological interpretations of their ordinary daily activities as helping them to grow in holiness. The text follows in the Calvinist literary tradition of the *exemplum fidei* and is a fictionalization of the Calvinist self-examination journal; in imaginatively rendering a step-by-step progression from sin to sanctification, it has no less a model than Bunyan's *Pilgrim's Progress*. Prentiss used the clerical figure, Dr. Cabot, as a mouthpiece to authorize theological opinions, but simultaneously she challenged clerical/lay and male/female hierarchies by placing doctrinal instruction into the mouths of Mrs. Cabot, Katy, her mother, and her lay husband, Ernest.[34]

Stepping Heavenward self-consciously preaches Prentiss's interpretation of holiness. Prentiss warns — through the character of Dr. Cabot — against falling into errors "only too common," for example, believing that after conversion "the great work of life is done" or spending the rest of life asking "whether you are really in a state of grace." Dr. Cabot gives practical counsel to help Christians grow subsequent to justification. He teaches that sanctification, like redemption, is God's work, but "at the same time," one must not "sit with folded hands." Instead, growing Christians must use "every means of grace appointed by God," such as listening to sermons, studying the Bible and devotional books, choosing godly associates, praying, caring for the poor and sick, and even consenting to suffer when ordained by God.[35]

Prentiss used fiction to argue that all theology should be useful. Developing a relationship with Christ through daily experience was better than "all the theological discussions in the world." It was by "doing and suffering" God's will that "we shall learn the doctrine." Since dwelling on one's own suffering produces "great weariness and heaviness of soul," Katy's mother encourages her to try sympathizing with others. As Katy, like Prentiss herself, visits the poor, nurses the sick, and gives her time and money to the needy, she discovers "how much suffering and sickness there is in this world, and how delightful it is to sympathize with and try to relieve it." The redemptive power of sympathy consists in the fact that no one need suffer alone. Sympathy transforms the isolating experiences of sickness and grief into the relational bonds of community. Prentiss envisioned a kind of community in which the hierarchies between men and women, rich and poor, and privileged and suffering have been undermined by the power of sympathetic identification with others.[36]

Fiction afforded Prentiss a vehicle to critique indirectly her father's austere Calvinism through the character of Katy's father-in-law. Father, as Katy calls him, can only see "a great and good and terrible God who cannot look upon iniquity, and does not see His risen Son who has paid the debt we owe." Father urges Katy that being faithful to her four-year-old son means telling him he is a sinner and "in a state of condemnation." Katy has as deep a sense of human sin and divine holiness as does Father but an even deeper sense of Christ's redeeming love. She responds to Father that her son "will learn that he is a sinner only too soon; and before that dreadful day arrives, I want to fortify his soul with the only antidote against the misery that knowledge will give him. I want him to see his Redeemer in all His love and all His beauty." Katy neither romanticizes her children's nature as innocent nor waits for a clerically led revival to convert them. Much as the theologian Horace Bushnell argues in *Christian Nurture* (1847), Katy and Dr. Cabot teach through informal conversation that "the influence of Christian parents might work so gradually" that their children "rarely can point to any day or hour when they began to live this new life." Even as Father objects to Dr. Cabot's preaching as "not doctrinal enough," Cabot leads Father to "think of God, as manifested in Christ, far more than he used to do." Rather than weakening religious devotion, Dr. Cabot's and Katy's Bushnellian theology and conversational style help not only Katy and her children but even Father to take steps heavenward.[37]

Prentiss sought to demonstrate the usefulness of her generation's modifications of Calvinist doctrine in elevating piety and infusing new life into stale doctrine. Father "seems to abhor anything like a merry-making" and sits "in his corner so penetrated with gloom." Katy encourages Father that "if you would indulge yourself in a little harmless mirth now and then, your mind would get rested, and you would return to Divine things with fresh zeal." Instead of demonstrating a weakened religious commitment or an emasculated view of God, Katy reveals her desire to pursue divine things more zealously. Father admits to feeling distant from God, but Katy lives "very near" to God every day.[38]

Prentiss's — and other nineteenth-century evangelicals' — theological and stylistic adaptations represented attempts to bring Christian doctrine into closer connection with daily life. The growing presence of secular settings in mid-nineteenth-century fiction need not indicate a trend toward secularization. As Prentiss herself put it, "It is *because* I believe — fully believe that I shall be saved through Christ — that I want to be like Him here upon earth." Mirroring language from the Westminster Shorter Catechism, Mother shows Katy that the way to grow in holiness "is to make all our employments subserve the one great end and aim of existence, namely, to glorify God and to enjoy Him for ever." How can one help "carrying religion into everything" if it is "a vital part of one's self, not a cloak put on to go to church in, and hang up out of the way against next Sunday?" As Katy learns to practice daily religion, she in turn teaches her husband, Ernest, to cease viewing ordinary daily work as one thing and religion as quite another.[39]

Katy's domestic example has transformative power not only within her home but also beyond it through the influence she exerts on her husband and his business practices. Ernest exclaims that applying Katy's principles will "transmute our drudgery into acts of worship. Instead of going to prayer-meetings to get into a 'good frame,' we should live in a good frame from morning till night, . . . and prayer and praise would be only another form for expressing . . . love and faith and obedience." *Stepping Heavenward* is not a feminist text in the sense of advising women to step outside the domestic sphere, yet the book has radical implications, suggesting that women, by their private, domestic practice of Christianity, have a kind of political power to transform the masculine sphere of business. This is not to say that Prentiss equated the Christian life with domesticity or that she portrayed women's religious experience as qualitatively different or better than men's. Katy, Ernest, and Father all exhibit their sinful natures and their potential to take steps heavenward, indicating that for Prentiss, theology was a more compelling category than gender in explaining human nature and development.[40]

Although concerned with speaking to experiences shared by all Christians, Prentiss particularly addressed women readers whose influence was similarly contained within their families. Mrs. Cabot assures Katy that God intended, "in making us wives and mothers, to put us into the very conditions of holy living." Prentiss offered women a theological lens that defined "all the little homely tasks that return with each returning day" as eternally significant. Every "tiresome visitor" and unwelcome interruption, "every negligence on the part of the servants," and every inattention by her overworked husband help Katy to grow toward sanctification and pave the way for her ultimate joy and fulfillment. As an imaginative work replete with autobiographical parallels, *Stepping Heavenward* gave theological meaning to Prentiss's own suffering. Both Prentiss and Katy suffered the loss of a father at an early age and endured the burdens of debt, chronic illness, the deaths of young children, and the neglect of busy husbands. Katy declares that she has "learned Christ" in the school of suffering. Counterintuitively, suffering not only prepares the Christian for eternal joy but also makes possible the "sweetest enjoyment of earthly good." One "young wife and mother" who read *Stepping Heavenward* claimed that the book had "formed an era in her religious life"; she had read it fifty or sixty times and kept it by the side of her Bible. This reader seized upon the empowerment that Prentiss offered her female readers: by choosing self-denial and sacrifice, and by voluntarily consenting to suffer God's discipline, women could obtain the very agency, self-fulfillment, and joy that they desired. By portraying women as the greater sufferers, Prentiss indirectly argues that they, rather than men, are better positioned for growth in sanctification. She thus legitimates and infuses hope into women's experiences and challenges hierarchies that had privileged men's religious identity and authority to preach. Women, the text suggests—and reinforces by the very fact of its publication—may actually be better prepared to preach to both women and men.[41]

Stepping Heavenward, and countless other fictional texts similar in both doctrine and imaginative style, formed an era in many women's and men's religious lives. A reviewer for the nondenominational *Sunday School Times* praised the book as "full of gospel teachings, and free from the conventional forms of such teachings." The *New York Clergyman* similarly accounted for the book's popularity: *Stepping Heavenward* "gives in popular form, depths and lights of religious experience to which those who read will aspire, and which are found elsewhere only in treatises too learned, or too mystical for the popular mind." Rather than representing an inevitable progression from doctrine to imagination, from theology to secular experience, or from masculine reason to feminine sentimentalism, the text exemplifies an evangelical hermeneutics of daily experience as intrinsically sacred in meaning. Prentiss used imagination in the service of doctrine. As a Christian woman author, she found in fiction a unique medium through which she could legitimately preach her own modified Calvinist theology; her teaching on sanctification indirectly empowered other women to understand their lives as theologically and socially significant. Even so, evangelicals who used fiction and those who opposed the genre as inherently corrupting shared a common set of beliefs about the purposes of writing and reading and about the relationships among writers, publishers, texts, and readers. As with their many other struggles between purity and presence, evangelicals strained to transform the world through fiction without themselves becoming worldly.[42]

Sunday School Libraries: The Usefulness of Socialization

Sunday school publications included not just one genre but a mix of doctrine, memoirs, fiction, periodicals, and hymns, all calculated to sanctify the world by connecting institutional and domestic sites of religious growth. Although a few scattered Sunday schools formed in the early nineteenth century, prior to the 1820s the schools lacked coordination and offered lessons taken primarily from the Bible and catechism. By midcentury, Sunday school texts formed a major component of religious publishing and a primary avenue for socializing the rising generations into evangelical culture. Nondenominational, denominational, and trade publishers all participated in the field with the result that the uses and meanings of Sunday school books proliferated. This diversity of publications reflected tensions deeply embedded in evangelical print culture between evangelical and denominational identity, religious and commercial value, and clerical and domestic models of piety. In balancing competing priorities, evangelicals continually renegotiated the boundaries of the cultural universe into which they socialized the young.[43]

The number of Sunday school texts increased dramatically during the nineteenth century. The ASSU, formed in 1824, listed 75 titles in its 1825 catalog; by 1863, that number had grown to 953. As early as 1830, the ASSU claimed to have sold 6 million volumes. Soon after the ASSU pioneered in the field, the ATS perceived the demand for Sunday school publications to be large enough to warrant its entrance into the market. At first, the ATS published only tracts for children, producing its first books in 1834. Imitating the London "toy book" trade, the ATS illustrated its volumes with woodcuts and covered them with brightly colored paper wrappers. By

1850, the ATS had printed over 1 million copies of 69 different books, as well as over 7 million copies of children's tracts, in English and several other languages. In addition, the ATS established an illustrated periodical, the *Child's Paper*, in 1852; the paper's subscription list grew from 250,000 in its first year to 348,000 in 1870. Each of the denominational houses also published books and periodicals for the Sunday schools. For instance, the *Presbyterian Sabbath School Visitor* had a distribution list of 54,000 in 1858. Three-fourths of the books published by the Presbyterian Board of Publication fell under the heading "Sabbath school" by 1870; cumulative sales of these books alone totaled approximately 11 million copies of 1,300 titles. In addition, trade houses, regardless of religious affiliation, also found Sunday school materials to be big business. Robert Carter & Brothers, the leader among trade houses in this field, listed 500 different books for children and the Sunday school in its 1875 catalog.[44]

Even though denominational publishers designed their books and periodicals for use by church members and affiliated Sunday schools, purchasers demonstrated looser denominational loyalty than publishers would have liked. The ABPS noted in 1870 that "forty or fifty different publishers" competed for patronage. The Methodist *Christian Advocate* (1845) reminded readers that the *Sunday School Advocate* was the official "organ of our Sunday School Union" and the "paper of the Church," implying that dedication to the Sunday School Union and church entailed subscription to the paper and that subscription rates had been less than desired. The *Christian Advocate* invited attention to the Sunday school organ from all who hoped to "exert an influence . . . for good," concluding its appeal with, "We beg you to take a personal interest in it." Whether on account of this and similar urging or by natural inclination, more than 200,000 Methodist families and Sunday schools had subscribed by 1860. Most other denominational publishers enjoyed less success in securing loyalty to their Sunday school publications. The AME Publication Department complained in 1884 that less than half of AME Sunday schools patronized the denomination's own materials.[45]

Evangelicals greeted the expanding market for Sunday school publications with mixed emotions; they felt encouraged by the abundance of religious print but apprehensive about the dangers of market corruption. The Southern Methodist *Sunday School Magazine* (1876) viewed the material quality of publications as greatly improved because "different church publishing houses vie with each other in the elegance of style and cheapness of cost." Yet, steadily growing market demand allowed booksellers to peddle such a large volume of wares that it became increasingly difficult for religious arbiters to regulate the contents. One AME writer claimed in 1862 that he had never seen a sizable urban Sunday school library that would not have been "enriched by having half its contents committed to the flames." A Baptist writer similarly characterized thousands of market offerings as "decidedly bad" and the "merest trash." Such critics accused publishers of failing to balance properly their identities as evangelicals and as book trades participants. The makers and sellers of books, as a "great company of un-ordained preachers," had a responsibility to influence children's spiritual growth. Yet, in pursuing financial profit, publishers reputedly failed to distinguish among worthy and unworthy texts. "O unscrupulous book-seller! . . . You ought not, for the sake of sales, to send out worthless or poisonous productions." Why did publishers put bad books in print? "Be-cause they expect to sell them," responded another critic, and "demand governs supply." Evangelicals worried that financial motives had lured even religious publishers into sending undifferentiated texts into the market.[46]

As in the wider evangelical canon, usefulness distinguished a good Sun-day school book from a bad one. A good book inclined the reader to love "The Book" more, while bad books made the Bible seem uninteresting, remote, or unpalatable. Books failed either by presenting "exciting stories" devoid of religious instruction or by teaching lessons in such an "utterly dull and heavy" style that no child could bear to read them. Rather than imitating unnaturally good characters in books, young readers would con-clude that such children were "destined to fill an early grave" and decide instead that they had "rather not be good, and live longer." Similarly, books failed to be of use to readers when they taught deceptive aphorisms, for example, that virtue inevitably leads to happiness when, in actual life, "ever since the days of Job the reward of merit has often been only blows." The usefulness of a text in fortifying young pilgrims determined relative value to evangelical commentators.[47]

In privileging usefulness over style, evangelicals informally classified Sunday school publications as religion rather than as literature. Indicative of this understanding, the ASSU established rules for its writers and substan-tively edited texts submitted for publication. The ASSU required that all texts be absolutely moral and religious, be graded to children's level of understanding, adhere to standards for style and content, be American in character, and avoid sectarianism. Even seminary professor Charles Hodge did not escape ASSU editing; for instance, the title of his book *The Narrow Way* was changed to *The Way of Life* (1841). Assuming that Sunday school texts were means rather than ends encouraged the fluidity of textual trans-mission. John Bunyan's allegory, *Pilgrim's Progress*, appeared in numerous

Figure 3.8. *The Singing Pilgrim* (1866) used hymns to teach Sabbath school children lessons based on Bunyan's allegory. (Used by permission of the University of Missouri–Kansas City Libraries, Kenneth J. LaBudde Department of Special Collections)

children's editions, including a version in *Words of One Syllable* (ca. 1870) and a modern sequel, *The Infant's Progress* (1821). *The Singing Pilgrim; Or, Pilgrim's Progress Illustrated in Song, for the Sabbath School, Church & Family* (1866) furnished hymns "illustrative of the same features of Christian experience" as those drawn by Bunyan (figure 3.8). Although evangelicals generally respected Bunyan's original as one of the best books of all time, they felt no qualms about altering the book to suit Sunday school instruction.[48]

Once texts were published, regulating purchasing decisions provided the surest protection against bad books. If Sunday schools ordered only the best books, the rest would remain unsold and thus incapable of exerting a harmful influence. Those who selected Sunday school books had a great responsibility not to allow "frivolous, eccentric, or godless bookmakers to preach to the children" but instead to mold children's character with pure gospel teaching. Yet local committees designated to select Sunday school libraries felt unable to distinguish among all the publications presented for sale. Often, complained critics, "ornamental bindings, pretty pictures, and cheap prices" constituted the chief merits of the books that unwary Sunday schools ordered. Some booksellers advised ordering more volumes than needed with the option of return after examination. Other publishers offered to select books for the purchaser, thereby controlling which titles and authors became most successful. The Presbyterian Board filled orders from "A SELECTED AND APPROVED STOCK," the suitability of which the board guaranteed. The trade house of Dodd & Mead hired specialists to read and grade all the books it sold, rating the overall quality of each book from A through D, rejecting C and D grade books as unsuitable for schools. One such critic analyzed 2,000 books over a three-year period, judging 263 as A grade, another 728 as B grade, and rejecting more than 1,000 books as not worth reading. Although not releasing the actual grade sheets, Dodd & Mead described sample evaluations: the aim of a book might be to "show the influence of a consistent Christian life," the style "stilted," the religious character "overdrawn," and the story "rather interesting." The grader dismissed some books for exhibiting "morbid" religious character and a larger number for failing to make spiritual teachings "sufficiently prominent." As in the broader evangelical print market, the twin forces of open competition and religious regulation directed the flow of Sunday school texts from writers and publishers to readers.[49]

Properly selected Sunday school libraries sanctified the world by extending Sabbath instruction into each day of the week, partially displacing the influences of clergy, church, and Sunday school in favor of family, home, and the books themselves. Evangelicals used publications to reinforce Sunday school lessons; at the same time, the texts defined a geographically expansive community that could potentially substitute for membership in a local Sunday school. The Southern Baptist *Kind Words for the Sunday School Children* (1866) retold Jesus' parable of the prodigal son in story form. At the end of the narrative, the article informed its readers that if they would like to learn more of this "beautiful story," they should get their "Testament and turn to the 15th chapter of Luke; and there you will find it. Ask your father to explain it all to you." Superadded to the biblical story, two mediating sources of interpretive authority were established by the text: the article's author and the child's parents, but no agent of the Sunday school or church. The paper's editor used the story as an incentive to coax its readers to further Bible study under the paper's tutelage by joining the "Try Society . . . a great big Bible class" consisting of 7,000 of the paper's readers "all reading the same chapter in the New Testament the same day" and all reading the editor's explanations of the chapters' meanings. The article suggested that Sunday school publications fulfilled the same function as school attendance.[50]

Just as certain Sunday school texts potentially competed with the schools they supported, so the publications simultaneously reinforced and presented an alternative to other church-building strategies, such as revivals of religion. Revivals assumed a crisislike model of justification and sanctification that set apart the time and place of the revival's occurrence as particularly suited to the reception of divine grace. By the 1820s, revivals had become routinized to the extent that in many communities, congregations anticipated them as annual events. Rather than emphasizing sporadic periods of heightened piety, Sunday school texts grew out of a more gradual understanding of the salvation process, which encouraged the sanctification of everyday times and places. Some books did focus on the moment of conversion, like *Our Battle-Cry: Immediate Conversion* (1875), but more often midcentury Sunday school texts envisioned a lifelong process of growth in grace. The Presbyterian Board published many such volumes, including *Emma Herbert; Or, Be Ye Perfect* (1863). Through repeated "trials and discouragements," Emma tries to, in the words of Philippians 3:14, "press toward the mark for the prize of the high calling of God in Christ Jesus." At the start of the story, Emma has already found "hope of salvation through Jesus' name" and begun using her "influence in bringing others to the same blessed Saviour." Still, she must pass through a steady stream of trials and disappointments in her "upward journey" as she continues to "press on till she is 'perfect as he is perfect'" (Matthew 5:48). The text assumes the importance of conversion but focuses more attention on the lifelong process of growth toward perfection in holiness. For Emma, this process occurs during everyday activities and interactions with family and friends and as she reads books borrowed from the Sunday school library.[51]

As the market for Sunday school publications expanded, styles and contents diversified. Sunday school libraries typically contained texts written both in didactic and narrative styles. Question books, related in form to the catechism, were a standard doctrinal tool for Sabbath instruction. Each lesson began with a passage from Scripture followed by explanations and questions for study and discussion. Prefaces recommended that readers memorize the Scriptures and then ask their own questions of their teacher and family to gain understanding. The *Berean Question Book* of 1875, part of a new international series of standardized, nondenominational studies, guided teachers and students successively through Old Testament history and the Gospel of John. To supplement question books, teachers and parents could also purchase collections of sermons addressed to children, such as Robert Boyd's *Food for the Lambs; Or, the Little Ones Invited to Jesus* (1865). Such books aided those "who have occasion to address children, and those who have not the time or do not feel qualified to prepare addresses of their own." Other texts gave lessons in a less formal style, for instance adopting the trope of a father offering "kind advice, and simple truths" while writing a letter or sitting by the domestic fireside. Still other books took the form of history, travel, or science. Sunday school teachers observed that children generally preferred highly illustrated, attractively bound fiction to more didactic volumes.[52]

The lines dividing Sunday school, religious, and miscellaneous genres blurred at the edges. A number of authors gained a reputation by writing books for trade publishers as well as for denominational and nondenominational societies. The Congregationalist professor and minister Jacob Abbott published with several houses, including the ATS and Harper & Brothers. Abbott wrote at least 180 books, most of them averaging 200 pages in length, in a variety of genres: history, biography, science, reading, arithmetic, and fiction. Subtitles directed some books to be used in the home or common school while indicating that others served the purposes of Sunday schools. Abbott resisted the kinds of distinctions we may be tempted to draw between evangelical and nonevangelical or sacred and secular texts. Some of his books aimed to "exert a direct religious influence" without being "exclusively of a religious character." Other works avoided "formal precepts and didactic instruction" altogether, relying instead upon the "influence of example" to provoke "sympathetic action" on the part of readers. Abbott's historical studies of figures such as Cyrus the Great and Julius Caesar were not explicitly religious in content yet received favorable reviews from a range of denominational papers. Abbott's publishing record defies any kind of rigid division between religious and nonreligious publications because, like a large segment of his readers, he envisioned all of his books as influencing children for good. Reflecting the tendency of Sunday

German Peasant Girl.

Figure 3.9.   Stories of Other Lands (1859) encouraged young readers to identify with Christian children living in other parts of the world, like this German peasant girl. (Courtesy of the American Antiquarian Society)

school books to sacralize everyday times and spaces, Abbott positioned the seat of religious growth not in the Sunday school room or church building but in the scenes of "happy domestic life" represented by "fire-side piety."[53]

Abbott's publications exemplify a broad-based assumption among evangelicals that writers, publishers, texts, and Sunday school teachers should all influence child readers in such a way as to promote holy action. By engaging children's interest, texts prepared them to receive instruction. *Child Life in Many Lands* (1871) intermingled "a large amount of information respecting many out-of-the-way portions of the globe" with the "most wholesome Christian counsel." *Tales from the Parsonage* (1846) similarly endeavored to "give interest to the lessons taught, by conveying them in the narrative style, and by illustrative characters." Authors advised children to identify with model characters, imitating their best qualities and avoiding their faults. *Stories of Other Lands* (1859) included full-color illustrations to assist children in identifying with individuals like Sophie, a German peasant girl (figure 3.9). In addition to expressing specific content, books emblematized the relationship between Sunday school teachers and students. "Teacher's Presents," given as rewards for Scripture memorization or good attendance, reminded children of their teachers' lessons and spurred future action. A copy of one such volume bears a typical inscription: "Presented to Ada Kinsell as a reward for missionary work in the Mt. Ayr S.S. April 9, 1871." As Sunday school teachers and books influenced child readers, young members of the priesthood of all believers could in turn influence others: "No one is too little to do good." Books reminded readers that even a "poor orphan girl" and "Crippled William" learned to use their influence to help others. Even as evangelicals continually redrew the boundaries of their print universe, Sunday school publications socialized young participants into a textually defined pilgrim community, the members of which hastened one another's heavenward progress.[54]

The canon of evangelical print artifacts illuminates an overlapping set of values and meanings: preserving the purity of the Word and adapting to a changing cultural milieu, balancing evangelical and denominational identity, integrating doctrine and experience, connecting religious and commercial value, and reconciling clerical and domestic models of piety. Adopting a conservative-progressive spirit, evangelicals from the time of Edmund Bunny entered the world of print in order to transform it. Nineteenth-century evangelicals considered diverse genres of canonical texts — including doctrine, memoirs, fiction, and Sunday school libraries — as functionally sacred because they were useful in particular ways. The influences of truth, example, imagination, and socialization provoked action that aided individual and communal progress along a heavenward journey. Lay and clerical writers, publishers, and readers negotiated shared ownership and regulation of texts that shaped a transgenerational, geographically expansive pilgrim community. The meanings of evangelical print culture, reflected in part by publishing practices and generic classifications, more fully emerge in chapter 4 through the interactions of readers and writers with this world of print.

4

Readers and Writers Navigate
the Currents of the Market

The "special danger" of the times, warned Yale president and Congregationalist minister Noah Porter in 1870, was that "so many books" were
cheaply available to the "mass of the community." Porter's concern reflected an age-old evangelical tension between the ideal of a priesthood of
all believers and the desire of a clerical elite, represented by Porter, to
regulate lay practices. Like most of his contemporaries, Porter assumed
that some form of external regulation inevitably shaped reading choices.
Porter worried about competition among sources of authority and that
those who were religious would lose out to those who were not. In an era of
rapid print market expansion, new, market-oriented elite, including authors, editors, publishers, booksellers, and reviewers, challenged the authority of an older religious establishment who felt increasingly anxious to
maintain the purity of the Word amid cultural change. Publishers and
booksellers could, warned Porter, advise potential purchasers only as to
which books were "popular," a quality that Porter considered of dubious
value. Distrusting the ability of the average reader to make prudent choices
without trustworthy guidance, Porter envisioned the mission of men like
himself as educating and reforming popular reading tastes. With this end in
view, he published an advice manual, *Books and Reading; Or, What Books
Shall I Read and How Shall I Read Them?* (1870), which aimed at mediating
between readers and the market. Porter argued that because books exerted
a powerful influence, both directly and indirectly, readers must learn how
to select from among alternatives even more carefully than they selected
their "friends and intimates."[1]

Porter worried as much about how readers approached texts as he did

about which books they read. Like many mid-nineteenth-century evangelicals, Porter believed that the Holy Spirit inspired readers as well as writers
of sacred texts. From this perspective, the processes by which individuals
read and wrote, as well as the words themselves, had to be sanctified in
order to achieve a redemptive influence. The danger, as Porter saw it, was
that market participation transformed reading and writing from useful,
sacred activities into mere entertainment. Porter's understanding of sacred
reading drew upon a theory of mental development that regarded the mind
as performing certain kinds of slow, steady work in order to grow, as it were,
real muscle. In this framework, the eagerness of readers and writers to enter
a time-sensitive print market corrupted slower, meditative textual practices
that were more conducive to mental and interrelated spiritual development. The "natural result of a profusion of books" is that in always seeking
"something new," "an active mind is in danger of knowing many things
superficially and nothing well, of being driven through one volume after
another with such breathless haste as to receive few clear impressions and
no lasting influences. *Passive* reading is the evil habit against which most
readers need to be guarded." Porter offered conventional advice about how
to maintain active, or intensive, reading practices; his "golden rule" was
always to "read with attention" and with an "earnest and reflecting spirit,"
having in mind "definite ends and purposes." As means to "*retain* what is
gathered from reading," he suggested repetition, review, and note-taking.
A similar evangelical advice manual, entitled *How to Read a Book in the Best
Way*, recommended that "one book," the Bible, should be "the first that is
read in the best way," that is, it should be read aloud and the reader should
stop often, reread, and write notes. The guide urged that a book worth any
attention at all deserved reading at least four times. All of this advice originates in the evangelical assumption that reading and writing should be
useful and therefore slow, repetitive, thoughtful, or, in sum, intensive processes rather than recreational pastimes. By the mid-nineteenth century,
the proliferation of cheap market alternatives had created unprecedented
tensions with this ideal of reading. Explicit efforts to regulate popular reading practices suggest a fear shared by many clergy and lay evangelicals that
individuals needed assistance in negotiating between the competing claims
of church and market.[2]

The boundaries of evangelical print culture expanded during the nineteenth century as readers and writers, partially guided by advice such as
Porter's, interacted with the canon to participate in a textually defined
community imagined as transcending space and time. At the moving inter-

section of the world of the text and the world of the reader, canonical texts transformed how readers experienced their lives and how they organized written records of their experiences. Through dialectical processes of sedimentation and innovation, advice literature alongside more informal rules embedded in the canon partially shaped the experiences of readers and writers while it allowed room for choices among interpretive conventions to create new meanings. I focus primarily on reading practices, but reading and writing are inextricably connected. Reading is one aspect of writing meaning, and writing reflects meanings that authors internalized as readers of other texts. Evangelicals viewed both practices as sacred activities, useful in promoting growth in holiness, rather than as merely recreational pursuits. The purpose of reading and writing, for evangelicals, was changed living. The biblical injunction "Be ye doers of the word, and not hearers only" (James 1:22) resonated throughout evangelical print culture. The high level of intertextuality that characterized this cultural universe blurred distinctions among writers, texts, and readers. Reading motivated writing, whether it was notes in margins, eclectic albums, diaries, memoirs, or bestselling novels. Such written records allow us to glimpse the practices of actual readers and to compare these practices with the portraits of readers idealized by prescriptive guides to proper reading.[3]

During the middle decades of the nineteenth century, older and newer reading strategies intermingled. An earlier generation of scholars interpreted this sea change as a "reading revolution," characterized by a transition from scarcity to abundance of printed texts that resulted in the replacement of intensive with extensive reading practices. More recent studies have demonstrated the ability of readers to select from among alternatives, moving between older and newer genres, steady sellers and recently popular titles, intensive and extensive reading styles, and evangelical and non-evangelical textual communities. Evangelical readers used this flexibility to balance their goals of purity and presence in the world. As the literary historian Cathy Davidson has noted, even novel reading could be an intensive pursuit, however extensive the list of titles read. What Davidson does not emphasize is that many of the same readers who selected novels because they were not tracts or histories also chose to read older evangelical genres as well as texts from sources as diverse as Catholicism, Unitarianism, and secular belles lettres for evangelical purposes. Readers who embraced the proliferation of market choices did not view any one genre as replacing other classes of texts that fulfilled related but distinct functions. Evangelical readers more often selected conventional than subversive texts and ways of

reading, using their market-given freedom to conform to communal narrative patterns that framed reading as a sacred process that produced growth
in holiness.[4]

Advice Literature

Midcentury evangelicals self-consciously retained traditional Christian
ideas of reading and writing as sacred activities while using the new resources of an expanding market. By the mid-nineteenth century, informally
designated cultural arbiters, including authors, editors, publishers, booksellers, and reviewers, shared authority with clergy to referee participation
in an evangelical textual community by offering readers explicit advice or
embedding in the canon implicit rules for textual usage. Evangelical rules
for reading assumed that canonical texts belonged to the entire Christian
community, that members of this community should uniformly use texts to
produce growth in holiness, and that achieving desired unity of purpose
required regulation. Advice literature accordingly prescribed reading programs and urged strategies such as prayer, memorization, and meditation
that defined reading as a sacred activity.

The genre of advice manuals responded to the problem of negotiating
among competing sources of authority that mediated between texts and
readers. As evangelical arbiters sought to regulate lay reading choices, they
worked against the structures of a book trade in which popular opinion and
the impersonal forces of supply and demand governed the flow of texts.
Evangelical author Caroline Fry articulated her understanding of the problem in her 1852 autobiography. Fry regretted that, as a child, her reading
had been indiscriminate since she had lacked "the smallest guidance or
restraint, or so much as advice upon what she had better read or not read."
She had access to the great supply of two circulating libraries to which her
father had subscriptions, but because she had "nothing else to choose them
by, the books had to be chosen by their names only." Although Fry did not
perceive her own character to have been damaged permanently — she had
been inclined naturally to healthful books — she warned incautious parents
against repeating the experiment. The *AME Church Review* (1891) similarly
warned parents that if they failed to select books for their children, "they
will make their own selections, or, what is worse, the 'trade' will select for
them." For African American patrons of the *AME Church Review*, the situation appeared doubly urgent since the titles that readers selected should
presumably advance both religious growth and social acceptance by white

evangelicals. For black and white readers alike, advice manuals like Porter's counteracted the corrupting influences of an unsanctified print market that threatened to lead unwary readers astray.[5]

Evangelicals believed that an expansive print market, if properly regulated, could promote heavenward progress. Yet the world of print was a dangerous place, a world that was becoming increasingly difficult to navigate safely. Alongside advice manuals, publishers' and booksellers' advertisements and critics' reviews guided readers' choices. According to self-appointed arbiters, the abundance and diversity of texts available at mid-century each had its own uses in promoting sanctified action. The option to choose from a variety of texts allowed for the targeting of works to narrowly defined reading audiences, depending on mood, age, gender, and stage of progress along the path toward heaven. In typical fashion, A. D. F. Randolph specified the age and gender of the audiences he deemed appropriate for each of Elizabeth Prentiss's volumes. Even as *Stepping Heavenward* best suited young "wives and mothers," advertisements described *Flower of the Family* as intended for girls from twelve to sixteen years of age; *The Percys* was for children ten to twelve; *Only a Dandelion* for children ten to fourteen; *Henry and Bessie* and *Little Threads* for children seven to ten (and for parents desirous of learning how to train "their little ones"); *Peterken and Gretchen* for children four to eight; "The Susy Books," *The Little Preacher*, and *The Story Lizzie Told* for children four to six. By directing the most relevant productions into the hands of individual readers, strategic marketing purportedly brought commerce into the service of religion.[6]

Like advertisements, book reviews carried by periodicals affected readers' expectations about the desirability of particular titles and editions. Even though reviews were apparently less biased than advertisements, publishers cut deals with critics and editors to "puff" titles. Remaining aloof from this common practice of the trades proved disadvantageous to publishers engaged in tight market competition. Early issues of the ATS's *Sabbath at Home*, first published in 1867, were exceptional in that the editors "formally noticed" every book received but only reviewed those they deemed appropriate to a religious magazine. The paper made passing reference to a new book entitled *Fonthill Recreations: The Mediterranean Islands; Sketches and Stories of their Scenery, Customs, History, Painters, &c.* The work was "a good book, but not one, which, from religious considerations, would claim an extended notice in this magazine." Refusal to review the book communicated to readers its lesser usefulness as compared with other publications. Within two years, however, the magazine's editors, concerned

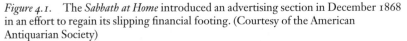

Figure 4.1.   The *Sabbath at Home* introduced an advertising section in December 1868 in an effort to regain its slipping financial footing. (Courtesy of the American Antiquarian Society)

about the paper's increasingly precarious financial status, began to include reviews and advertisements for a much wider array of publications as well as for nonliterary products (figure 4.1).[7]

Book reviews, like other religious genres, balanced denominational and evangelical concerns in shaping reading choices. The *Southern Methodist Pulpit* (1849) commended the new *Catalogue of the Presbyterian Board of Publication* as affording "great assistance to Methodists who are endeavoring to make for themselves valuable Christian libraries." Notwithstanding that a "large number of the books from that press are strongly Calvinistic," many others are of "practical value to Christians generally." Although affirming the overall quality of Presbyterian publications, the review made it clear that Calvinistic works were not among those the editors considered useful.[8]

Advice literature not only guided the selection of texts but also reinforced conventionalized ways of reading. Children's books prescribed rules for reading that were more often implicit in volumes targeted to older audi-

RULES FOR READING.

Read slowly.
Read thoughtfully.
Read understandingly.
Review what you read.
Read but few books, and those the best.
Read with a view to improvement rather than amusement.

Arthur receiving advice from his father about his reading.

See Youth's Penny Gazette, No. 6, 1850.

Figure 4.2. "Rules for Reading" regularly appeared in children's books and catalogs, such as *The Child's First Alphabet of Bible Names* (1827), at left, and *Valuable Books for Sunday School and Family Reading* (1850), at right. Evangelicals assumed that young readers, in particular, needed explicit advice about what and how to read. (Courtesy of the American Antiquarian Society)

ences who already assumed a common set of reading strategies. The Methodist *Sunday School Magazine* (1839) outlined typical "Rules for the Reading of the Bible." It should be read with prayer; diligently; patiently; attentively; with faith, obedience, self-application, and fervor; daily in regular course; with commentaries; and in a manner that charges the memory. Readers should exercise self-examination and meditation and converse often about what they have read. The ASSU likewise appended intensive "Rules for Reading" on the back covers of publications (figure 4.2): "Read slowly. Read thoughtfully. Read understandingly. Review what you read. Read but few books, and those the best. Read with a view to improvement rather than amusement." By reiterating such instructions, arbiters sought to make conventional reading strategies second nature to the rising generations.[9]

In writing children's literature, evangelicals embedded rules for reading in prefaces or authorial intrusions into the narrative line. Lydia Huntley Sigourney (1791–1865), of the Protestant Episcopal Church, was one of the most popular and prolific nineteenth-century authors, publishing 67

Figure 4.3. Nineteenth-century evangelicals presumed that the Word marked out "The Way to Happiness," as depicted in this undated lithograph published by J. Fisher of Boston. (Courtesy of the American Antiquarian Society)

books and more than 2,000 articles. Her children's book *How to Be Happy* (1833) offers a striking example of a text that self-consciously teaches reading as a tool to promote growth in holiness. Following each section of narrative, Sigourney asks her child-reader a set of questions, easily answerable by looking in the preceding paragraph; the 120-page book asks a daunting 482 such questions. The end of the book provides explicit instructions for its use. According to Sigourney's design, readers should study each section carefully, proceeding systematically until each is thoroughly memorized. Every morning the reader should review the section he or she would endeavor to practice that day and every evening recollect whether that practice was successful. This whole process should be repeated until the teaching of the book — "that the way to be happy is to be good, and to do good, and to make others good" — has been internalized (figure 4.3). The goal of this regimen is the reader's sanctification, or perfection, of character in preparation for heaven: "When you have thoroughly learned it, you will be ready to make greater advances in the science of being good and happy. Those who are made perfect in this science, are taken to heaven." The rules inscribed in Sigourney's text illuminate crucial attitudes underpinning evangelical efforts to regulate reading practices. By reading in the right way, and then using lessons learned to do good to others, idealized readers daily grew in holiness.[10]

Footprints on the Text: Marginalia, Albums, Diaries, and Memoirs

Advice literature offers a crucial perspective on evangelical cultural assumptions by articulating ideals of how reading should be conducted; it does not, however, answer the question of how readers actually read. As one nineteenth-century author admitted, "The effect of reading depends nearly as much on the disposition and taste of the reader, as on the character of the writer." As readers approached texts, they carried with them preconceptions that shaped their encounters, informed to varying degrees by previous textual experiences and by advice they may have internalized or rejected. Yet reading was a creative, dynamic activity rather than the absorption of predetermined meaning. Even as narrative conventions limited the options available to readers and writers, individual choices among interpretive possibilities continually refashioned evangelical print culture.[11]

Actual reading practices are exceedingly difficult to document. Although there is no way to enter into a full history of the responses of particular readers, certain evangelicals — especially educated, middle-class northeastern Congregationalists, Presbyterians, and Methodists — wrote about their reading practices. Such readers' self-reports illustrate some of the ways that evangelicals understood their relationships with other members of their textual community. Marginalia, albums, diaries, and memoirs all provide partial angles onto readers' interactions with the world of print. This evidence indicates that readers and writers saw their activities as means to give and receive influence calculated to promote individual and communal growth in holiness. Expressing a functionalist rather than an ontological view of sacred language, readers drew upon multiple genres and forms, considering that no one kind of text could replace the specific uses of another. Readers assumed an inevitable gap between signifiers and signified, which meant that no one linguistic act was sufficient to communicate religious truth. Rather, readers relied upon the successive approximations to the sacred made available by diverse market options. Even as market expansion encouraged individual choice, readers demonstrated their inclination to read substantially the same narratives repeatedly. Straddling older and more recent market patterns, readers engaged in a new kind of intensive reading. Evangelical readers reinforced conventional narrative patterns by discovering similar structures of meaning regardless of the titles or genres they selected.[12]

Marginalia recorded in specific copies of texts by individual readers offer one clue to reading practices, indicating the sources of interpretive authority that mediated between texts and readers. One such example is an 1845 copy of a Sunday school question book, written by Louisa Payson Hopkins, the daughter of the Congregationalist revival preacher Edward Payson and the older sister of the popular author Elizabeth Prentiss. The volume's reader completed her study of the book in the context of a Sunday school class in September 1857. Marginal notes suggest how this reader's practice was structured by rules embedded in the text itself, by oral cultural transmission, and by her situation in a local reading community. Marginal comments, recorded on nearly every page of the volume, added to the text information that was probably supplied orally by the reader's teacher, who, in turn, would have been summarizing what she had read in biblical reference books or teacher guides. Complementing, and perhaps competing with, the teacher's advice on how to read, the text itself embedded directions for its use: the child should read the Bible looking for answers to twenty or thirty specific questions listed at the end of each lesson. Comparing printed and oral instructions, readers supplemented the text with their own notes. In the context of the Sunday school meeting, students and teacher would have together discussed the meaning of the Bible passages studied and of the lessons taught in the book. The child's reading experience involved several levels of cultural interaction, bridging oral and printed sources of information and connecting a local Sunday school community with an implied textual community of others engaged in a shared interpretive task. Each mediating layer of explanation and direction oriented the reader to her text, shaping how and why she read and, consequently, what meaning she derived.[13]

Viewed alongside marginalia, literary albums give a different perspective on readers' experiences, clarifying the uses of texts in relational networks that crossed geographic and temporal boundaries. Throughout much of Britain and America, evangelicals shared textual practices that reflected an expectation that words convey sacred influences. In both countries, evangelicals used albums to collect original and selected writings that they wanted to remember and share with others. Yet to a greater degree in

Figure 4.4.   Album "Presented to Sarah A. Harding, Jan. 1st, 1837, by her mother."
(Courtesy of The Library Company of Philadelphia)

America than in Britain, the ritualized use of albums served as a surrogate
for community life as geographic dispersion disrupted local relationships
(figure 4.4). The practice of keeping an album or autograph book was especially prevalent among the young, mobile, and relatively educated. Upon
completing a term in school, one student might ask his classmates or teachers to transcribe a favorite selection of prose or verse or compose one for
the occasion. Albums reveal what certain evangelicals read and thought
worth recording for one another's edification and also indicate the importance of shared texts in the formation and preservation of personal relation-

ships that transmitted evangelical values across space and time. The sheer eclecticism of album notations suggests that evangelicals considered varied texts interesting and useful. Albumists extracted sermon notices and tidbits from religious periodicals, poems, and hymns written by British and American authors. Some texts, for instance, a poem on the substance of "True Happiness," made the rounds of albums signed everywhere from Massachusetts to New York to South Carolina. Reader-authors understood excerpted texts as functioning to influence the recipient's future steps, particularly when the author was an old one. Albumists demonstrated familiarity with old and new publications and an ability to move freely from one genre to another, drawing connections between texts and personal experiences.[14]

Diaries and memoirs reflect some readers' more systematic efforts to follow the prescriptions found in advice manuals by using reading programs to advance in holiness. Phoebe Palmer, a member of a Methodist Episcopal Church in New York and an internationally famed revivalist, gave the Bible first priority in her reading program. She endeavored (though, she admitted, not altogether successfully) to spend two hours, from four to six every morning, reading in the Old Testament and praying, a half hour in the Gospels each noon, and another hour in the Epistles every evening. Palmer also felt her faith strengthened and her soul "much blessed" by reading memoirs. The Methodist Nancy Dobbs, of Pennsylvania, likewise made a "systematic appointment of time" that incorporated Scripture study, prayer, and reading in Methodist literature. The Congregationalist Mandana Street Ferry Greenwood, of western Massachusetts, similarly viewed reading as a sacred process. She sought to maintain a "regular programme" of reading that made right use of time given by God. Greenwood's diary conveys her unabashed enjoyment of newspapers and popular periodicals like *Harper's Weekly* as well as her sustained efforts to allot a relatively greater proportion of time to reading the Bible and other more "solid" religious books. Martha Mellish of Woodstock, New York, also recorded reading experiences in her diary. For the year 1877, she commented on favorite texts and kept an orderly list of thirty-eight books completed, at least eleven of which she obtained through her Sunday school library. The Baptist A. W. Hilton kept a list of "Books Read throu and Noted" on topics such as "Habits of Devotion," "Baptism," "Mormonism," "Unitarianism," "Temperance," and "Congregational Singing." The Methodist Moses Taylor "loved the Scriptures and hymn-books; these were his constant companions." An anonymous Methodist man, writing his autobiography in 1850, lauded the usefulness of periodicals. The *Oberlin Evangelist* and Methodist

Christian Advocate convicted him of his "duty to strive to obtain" holiness; the more that he read, the greater his religious growth and the better he could influence others' growth by narrating his experiences.[15]

Some evangelicals, such as those just mentioned, kept scattered records of their reading experiences, tantalizing but not satisfying the historian of reading. Other individuals recorded their reading with much greater consistency and detail since they interpreted writing about reading as useful in stimulating individual and communal progress in holiness. The Congregationalist William Simonds (1822–59) of Massachusetts prized his reading journal as a help to his religious growth and as an asset to future readers. At an early age, Simonds read Richard Baxter's *Call to the Unconverted* (1657) and Jacob Abbott's *Young Christian* (1834) and soon after converted to Christianity. By his sixteenth year, Simonds kept a reading journal of "all that was valuable and interesting" to aid his sanctification. He considered that "*to grow in grace* is the duty of every Christian. . . . There are so many sins to subdue, so many temptations to assail, . . . that I find the Christian must ever be on the alert, lest he fall into sin, or at least make no progress in piety." Simonds kept track of how many evenings he spent reading and writing (about one night devoted to each weekly, in addition to Sundays), which texts occupied his attention, and how each contributed to his growth in holiness. Simonds conceived of the journal as helping him to "press forward . . . [to] strive to grow in grace every day." After his death in 1863, Simonds's biographer expressed a similar interpretation of the journal's function: "In these pages," explains the memoir, "he photographs his own consciousness, his own soul, for future reference and comparison. . . . It is pleasing and useful to see how the boy sets about improving his mind and sanctifying his heart." Writing, according to Simonds and his biographer, accurately conveys the influence of reading on the soul and preserves it in a permanent form; this process improves the mind and sanctifies the heart. The same benefit enjoyed by Simonds passed to others in the evangelical textual community through the publication of his memoir. The text promises not only to please the reader but also to be useful as a manual for the reader's improvement and sanctification.[16]

Long before the posthumous publication of his memoir, Simonds intended his writing to assist his textual community. Much as Lydia Sigourney advised her readers that doing good is the way to be happy, Simonds reminded himself: "Thus has God wisely connected duty and happiness. Let me strive, then, every day to become more holy . . . I must *do* good as well as *be* good; and I must labor to have those around me enjoy the same spiritual blessings that I do." Simonds understood his sanctification, and

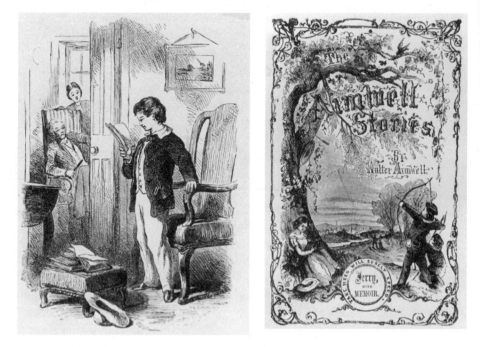

Figure 4.5.   William Simonds's *Unfinished Volume: Jerry; Or, The Sailor Boy Ashore* (1863). Using the pseudonym Walter Aimwell, Simonds, portrayed in the sketch at left above, wrote a seven-volume series of Sabbath school books designed to aid young boys in their journeys toward holiness. (Courtesy of the University of Missouri–Columbia)

consequent happiness, to depend upon his efforts to hasten the religious growth of other evangelical readers. Although Simonds had read numerous missionary memoirs, he did not think God had called him to imitate these exemplars directly by becoming a missionary. Rather, he perceived missions and authorship as parallel duties, through both of which the Christian might act as an example to influence others. As he reflected in his journal, "It may never be my privilege to give myself to the heathen and labor for their conversion to God, though I sincerely wish it might; but there are other ways in which I can help to do the work. . . . By my influence and example, I may be the means of promoting Christ's kingdom on earth." To this end, Simonds edited two religious weeklies, the *Christian Reflector* and *Saturday Rambler*, and, under the pseudonym Walter Aimwell, wrote a seven-volume series of Sunday school books for boys (figure 4.5). He modeled his first children's book, *The Pleasant Way* (1841), on *Pilgrim's Progress*; in it, Simonds sought to "illustrate, in a familiar and interesting manner, some of those virtues which constitute the character of the Pilgrim in the

Pleasant Way." Simonds connected the atemporal Christian narrative of pilgrimage with the everyday details of his young readers' lives. Aiding young boys' character formation through an interesting narrative, Simonds led boys into the pleasant way of daily growth in holiness. Simonds's adult reading audience shared his agenda; as a review in the Congregationalist *Boston Recorder* put it, *The Pleasant Way* guided the feet of its readers "in the narrow way to heaven." Simonds, and the textual community to which he belonged, envisioned reading and writing in strikingly similar terms: as means to encourage one's own and others' ongoing progress in holiness.[17]

As an expanding print market depersonalized communication among writers and readers, ritualized textual practices sustained readers' sense of personal connection with the authors whose books they read. Readers used texts to perform, or ritually enact, the grand narrative of the church's communal pilgrimage toward heaven by reciting, memorizing, and acting upon calls to holiness. The posthumously published diary of William Aitchison (1826–64), Presbyterian missionary to China, exhibits some of the ways that reading aided pilgrimage: by offering the individual a sense of membership in a Christian community, by influencing character formation through recitation and memorization, and by urging imitation of worthy models. Meditating on passages from books and hymns stimulated Aitchison's growth by connecting his individual experiences with the collective experiences of the evangelical community. In the middle of the Chinese landscape, familiar hymns reminded Aitchison that he belonged to a pilgrim community that transcended geographical divides. Repeated exposure to such texts solidified his identity as a member of the church universal. Aitchison also read a large number of memoirs; as he read, he compared his own character to those described to gain strength to press forward toward holiness. After reading the memoir of Harriet Winslow, he recorded his responsive prayer: "Oh, that I had her zeal, her love for immortal souls, her ardent desire to do good." Reading Edward Payson's *Memoir* (1827), Aitchison felt encouraged that the practice of reading could help him grow in grace, since Payson "estimated the progress he made in his studies by the progress he made in holiness." Aitchison frequently used his reading in making decisions. His resolve to become a missionary followed closely upon reading an article, "A Call to Personal Labor as a Foreign Missionary." After suffering the death of his wife and child, passages from the Episcopal archbishop Robert Leighton "struck . . . forcibly," reminding Aitchison that sufferings were part of God's plan for his growth in holiness. He prayed in response that even his "overwhelming afflictions" might "result in my sanctification and more entire consecration." Aitchison saw his reading as quintessentially useful, connecting his particular experiences with the universal pattern of life within a pilgrim community and providing him with models for emulation.[18]

Evangelical women readers answered the questions of what and how to read by following the same conventionalized formulas enacted by male readers such as Simonds and Aitchison. Elizabeth Prentiss understood reading and writing as sacred processes conducive to individual and communal growth in holiness. As a reader, Prentiss alternated between old and new genres, steady sellers and the most recent popular titles, intensive and extensive reading styles, evangelical and nonevangelical canons. She was familiar with the latest periodicals and books but preferred to have a "few books and to read them over and over." Prentiss felt a "peculiar love" for the Bible, which she read systematically and meditatively as many as four times through in the course of a year in addition to daily "dwelling" on brief verses. Even as Prentiss welcomed the expansion of the evangelical canon, the Bible remained at the center of her textual universe.[19]

Following in a religious tradition that dates back to the New Testament church, Prentiss believed that the Holy Spirit spoke through the Word as well as through human-authored words designated as sacred. She attributed personal qualities to favorite texts, which she viewed as repositories of the Holy Spirit's living presence and as faithful companions through her years of earthly pilgrimage. In 1835, Prentiss received as a gift a pocket-sized devotional guide published by the ATS, *Daily Food for Christians: Being a Promise, and Another Scriptural Portion, for Every Day in the Year; Together with the Verse of a Hymn* (1830). For at least the next thirty-six years, this book traveled with her constantly; she grew emotionally attached to it with an intensity similar to that which characterized her devotion "to Christian friends." Prentiss memorialized her perceived relationship with the book by composing a poem, which she inscribed in the time-worn volume:

> Precious companion! rendered dear
> By trial-hours of many a year,
> I love thee with a tenderness
> Which words have never yet defined.
> When tired and sad and comfortless,
> With aching heart and weary mind,
> How oft thy words of promise stealing.
> . . . .
> Have touched the heart with power of healing,
> And soothed the sharpest hour of woe.

Prentiss envisioned the book as a friend who remained with her in times of need to speak words of comfort and encouragement.[20]

Through her textual practices, Prentiss engaged in intimate, nearly audible dialogues with God and with other members of her textual community, some of whom had been dead for centuries. As the historian Leigh Eric Schmidt has demonstrated, many nineteenth-century Protestants felt drawn to Catholic devotional authors whose religious experiences emphasized the aural faculties. Prentiss developed a particularly intense relationship with the French Catholic François Fénelon (1651–1715). She kept her copy of "beloved" Fénelon's *Spiritual Progress* for over twenty-five years and "crowded" the text with "pencil-marks expressive of her sympathy and approval," some of them "very emphatic, underscoring or enclosing now a single word, now a phrase, anon a whole sentence or paragraph." Prentiss engaged actively in the reading process, conversing with her "friend," comparing his words with her own experience. She returned to the volume repeatedly because it influenced her progress along a heavenward pilgrimage:

> Oh wise and thoughtful words! oh counsel sweet,
> Guide in my wanderings, spurs unto my feet,
> How often you have met me on the way,
> And turned me from the path that led astray;
> Teaching that fault and folly, sin and fall,
> Need not the weary pilgrim's heart appall.

Prentiss developed an affectionate friendship with Fénelon and his writings as they guided her along the path toward heaven. She felt similarly about other steady sellers: she "reveled" in Bunyan's *Pilgrim's Progress*, which seemed "almost as much an inspiration as the Bible itself," and returned year after year to Thomas à Kempis's *Imitation of Christ* and to "good, wise, holy" Leighton's *Practical Commentary on the First Epistle of St. Peter* (1694). Prentiss communed with such texts, feeling herself deeply connected with their authors and with God as the Holy Spirit presumably indwelled the words she cherished.[21]

Although Leighton's 500-page commentary was densely theological, Prentiss did not generally "like to read sermons." Instead, she sought the "strengthening" food of Christian experience wherever she could find it, even culling the "cream" from authors outside the evangelical canon. She felt drawn to French Catholic devotional writer Madame Jeanne Marie Bouvier de la Mothe Guyon (1648–1717), an author widely read by nineteenth-century Protestants who craved Guyon's sense of God's holiness. As Prentiss's quest for Christian experience took her to nonevangelical authors, she read their writings more selectively and critically than texts clearly marked as evangelical. Although seeking to emulate Guyon's longing for holiness, Prentiss rejected the extreme self-mortification that kept Guyon feeling distant from God. Similarly, Prentiss approved the nineteenth-century British Roman Catholic Frederick Faber's "beautiful" hymns, even though his "shocking" reverence for Mary and the saints "pained" her. Faber "said some wonderful things among many weak and foolish ones"; Prentiss drew "a wee cross against" some of his "fine" sayings and ignored the rest. She also gleaned from French Catholic Madame Augustus Craven's *Sister's Story* (1868). Prentiss considered the volume a "nice Sunday book" because of the "cultivated, high-toned Christian character" exhibited as six family members died "beautiful, happy deaths" in the span of seven years. Given these virtues, Prentiss thought her friends "would not mind" the book's Catholicism. She also found "profitable" reading produced by Unitarian pens, such as Rev. A. P. Peabody's *Christian Consolation* (1847). Although Prentiss did "not like the cant of Unitarians any better than they like ours," she did like "what is elevating in any sect," and it did not "frighten" her to own a Unitarian book. Peabody's volume did not seem particularly Unitarian in theology, and it was "*full* of rich, holy experience." Prentiss thought that one of the book's sermons in particular, "Contingent Events and Providence," could influence a friend of hers for good since it touched on the woman's case "exactly." As she evaluated her reading options, Prentiss privileged Christian experience over doctrinal orthodoxy, learning from the experience and laying aside the objectionable theology. Rather than feeling constrained by nonevangelical rules for reading inscribed in the texts she encountered, she borrowed books from outside evangelicalism, reading in such a way as to make the texts useful for her own purposes.[22]

When feeling overwhelmed by her own daily struggles, Prentiss fled to the solace of hymns and memoirs that invoked a timeless Christian community. Imagining herself a member of the church universal moved Prentiss to action, empowering her to imitate pious exemplars and position her everyday experiences within an atemporal narrative framework as so many steps toward heaven. She loved hymns almost as much as the Bible, memorizing and reciting her favorites "many thousands of times." During her child-rearing years, she received comfort from singing through the whole of *Watts and Select Hymns* (1819) "as I marched night after night through my room, carrying a colicky baby." Prentiss also read David Brainerd's *Life* repeatedly; as she read, she compared her relationship with God to Brainerd's, "amid many doubts as to whether I ever loved the Lord at all, so different is my piety from that of this blessed and holy man." As she continued reading, she felt strengthened by the growing "influence of his life" on hers, which caused her increasingly to "long for his loose hold on earthly things." Henry Martyn's memoir (1819) gave Prentiss "new and peculiar desires to live wholly for the glory of God"; Susan Alibone's (1856) caused her to aspire after "so heavenly a temper!" Prentiss's own father's memoir encouraged her to persevere since he had "passed through far greater spiritual conflicts than will probably ever be mine." Encountering each text, she envisioned a personal relationship connecting the author or subject of the hymn or memoir with herself as fellow members of the church universal. Reading and recitation of such holy experiences spurred Prentiss to imitate Christian exemplars in her own daily pilgrimage toward heaven.[23]

Alongside her meditative devotional reading of steady sellers, Prentiss also read extensively among more recent texts, which she saw as useful because of, rather than despite, their recreational value. She enjoyed the "luxury" of reading the daily newspaper and regularly perused several religious periodicals, such as the *New York Observer*, the *Sabbath at Home*, and *Bibliotheca Sacra*. She also read fiction, poetry, and plays, including Stowe, Hawthorne, Dickens, Wordsworth, Tennyson, Longfellow, and Shakespeare. Interpretive frameworks that classify such authors as "secular" underestimate the role of the reader and his or her textual community in the creation of sacred meaning. Prentiss construed "harmless mirth" as valuable since it prepared the mind for a "return to Divine things with fresh zeal." She moved back and forth between genres and reading styles with ease, taking from each text and strategy what she considered useful.[24]

The Christian community that Prentiss imagined stretched outward to embrace Christians from every time and place who participated in the evangelical textual community and narrowed inward to focus on family and friends in her domestic sphere of influence. Reading a common body of printed texts with family and friends united the textual and local communities within a single frame of reference. During the long winter evenings, Prentiss read aloud by the domestic fireside, selecting passages that might "interest the whole family . . . for general edification." On other occasions, she quoted from favorite passages in the course of conversations or letters, using the authority of old authors to reinforce the counsel she herself gave. She once quoted from Leighton's commentary on 1 Peter 8 to give a friend "EMPHATIC warning" to stay alert during periods of spiritual prosperity since it is at these times that the "great Pirate" hoped to rob the "richest booty." When Prentiss encountered a volume of extraordinary usefulness, she purchased a second "lending copy" to share with her friends. She remarked of one such text: "It is not a great book, but I think it will be a useful one. It says we are all idolaters, and reminds me of my besetting sins in that direction." In addition to lending full-length books, Prentiss sustained a sense of community with distant friends by exchanging extracts from books, hymns, sermons, or periodicals, transcribed by hand and then recopied by both parties and shared with others. Prentiss saw herself as belonging to an expansive Christian community, unimpeded by the passage of time or by geographical dispersion, in which the exchange of texts facilitated one another's religious growth. In Prentiss's experience, growth in holiness occurred not only in church on Sunday under clerical supervision but also every day at home, guided by the examples of fellow pilgrims in her overlapping textual and local communities.[25]

Prentiss portrayed her writing, like her reading, as a powerful instrument to transform domestic experiences, especially painful ones, into sanctifying influences. As she suffered the deaths of two of her six children, chronic ill health, and daily domestic trials, Prentiss felt it a "relief to versify." Writing poetry sanctified sorrow by allowing Prentiss a medium in which to struggle with God, protesting her pain while reminding herself that God ordained suffering for her sanctification. Prentiss's poem "The Bitter Cup" alludes to Matthew 20:22, in which Jesus asks his disciples whether they can drink from his cup of suffering. The speaker knows intellectually that God offers a "bitter cup" for her healing. She wants to drink the cup "quickly" but sees that God wills for her to drink it "sip by sip." The poem describes the bitter "draught" vividly as "revolting to its dregs." The speaker holds the cup "with willing hands," yet asks that God "forgive the mortal shudder, mortal gasp / That proves me human, proves me not divine." The poem gives Prentiss and her readers emotional relief by acknowledging the extreme difficulty of submitting to God's will even as it defines God-ordained suffering as productive of holiness.[26]

In publishing her writings, Prentiss transformed her inward grief into healing balm for others. Prentiss wrote several books while mourning her children's deaths. In *Little Susy's Six Birthdays* (1853), Prentiss worked through the death of her son Eddy. The text warns child-readers that not all of them will live until their sixth birthdays. Just before her baby daughter Bessie's last illness, Prentiss had begun work on *Little Susy's Six Teachers* (1856). Prentiss completed the book soon after Bessie's death, explaining in her journal that to "divert my mind from such incessant brooding over my sorrows, I am writing a new book. . . . I trust it may do some little good." The story teaches that even little children may be sanctified through the help of their "teachers": the allegorical Mrs. Love, Miss Joy, Miss Faith, Mr. Ought, Mr. Pain, and Aunt Patience. Mr. Pain, an allegory for suffering, helps Susy most of all by preparing her for heaven through a protracted illness. In a telling scene, Susy's mother—a stand-in for Prentiss—explains that she has a Mr. Pain of her own. When the editor of a YMCA hymnal requested some poems on the eighteenth anniversary of Bessie's death, Prentiss was "exactly in the mood," wanting to spend the day "for others, not for myself." Writing for publication infused Prentiss's suffering with redemptive meaning, providing the means to help others in her textual community cope with suffering along the path toward heaven.[27]

Prentiss's awareness of the power of words to affect others caused her to estimate her publications as analogous to clerical sermons. Publishing seemed to Prentiss a "duty and privilege," for it was her avenue for "preaching," her means of exerting a sacred influence, thereby doing good to an extensive congregation of readers. As an evangelical woman restricted culturally to a domestic sphere, Prentiss could conceive of no other way by which to "reach so many minds and hearts." Only once did Prentiss attempt to write in the genre of doctrinal disputation; she wrote *Urbane and His Friends* (1874) to refute Higher Christian Life teachings that promised a shorter way to sanctification. The book was a market failure, leading Prentiss to return to a more indirect narrative voice in expressing theological views, as discussed in chapter 3. Much like Stowe, Prentiss configured her fiction as serving a moral purpose; she wrote of one such volume, *Flower of the Family* (1856): "I long to have it doing good. I never had such desires about anything in my life; and I never sat down to write without first praying that I might not be suffered to write anything that would do harm, and that, on the contrary, I might be taught to say what would do good. And it has been a great comfort to me that every word of praise I ever have received from others concerning it has been 'it will do good.'" Socially and religiously excluded from participating in formal theological discourse, Prentiss influenced other members of her textual community by preaching her doctrine of holiness through the medium of fiction.[28]

Although Prentiss longed to speak to many minds and hearts, she recognized the inherent limitations of writing for a mass market. She wrote as she read, with a sense of membership in overlapping textual and local communities. Prentiss valued correspondence with personal friends as a "tiny way to give pleasure or do good" by allowing God to speak through her to the particular cases of individuals. "Does He not speak through the living voice and the penning of that voice, as He does not do in the less unconstrained form of print? At any rate, I love to believe that He directs each word and look and tone; *inspires* it rather, I should say." Prentiss presumed that God inspired her to write letters to individual correspondents so that she could give more personalized counsel than she could in her books. Adopting language from *Pilgrim's Progress*, she encouraged one "young friend": "Let me assure you, as a fellow-traveler, that I have been on the road and know it well. . . . You will meet with hindrances and trials, but will fight quietly through." Whether writing for publication or writing letters to individuals, Prentiss viewed herself as a fellow pilgrim using words to spur others to keep traveling toward heaven.[29]

Like many of her contemporaries, Prentiss presented herself to friends and reading audiences as motivated to write entirely by religious concerns, while she participated in a financially remunerative print market. Authorship became a respected profession during the nineteenth century even as writers and publishers, fearful of being stigmatized by association with the market, continued to portray themselves as genteel amateurs. Evangelicals felt more wary of professional status than did their nonevangelical peers because professionalization challenged the notions that texts belonged to the Christian community rather than to their authors or publishers and that writing was a sacred process instead of a market-driven activity. Prentiss claimed that she never "gave a thought" to how she might make money, refused to make her books less "religious" to win a wider audience, hated writing serials, and never considered writing a profession. Yet Prentiss chafed at her neighbors' expectation that she join a local sewing society as a "farce" since she could earn thirty or forty times more for writing than for sewing and donate the money to charitable causes. Like many successful women authors, Prentiss did not write solely for charity but also contributed a significant share of her family income. Her books made it possible to escape a family debt and allowed for the purchase of a summer cottage. In furnishing this new home, Prentiss enthusiastically planned to "grab every check that comes in from magazine and elsewhere, and turn it into chairs and tables and beds and blankets!" She justified the expenditure to herself and any potential critics by describing her comfortable domestic space as better suited to heavenward progress than an unadorned home. As an evangelical and a book trades participant, Prentiss disavowed merely worldly ambitions even as she and her family enjoyed the financial fruits of her professional success.[30]

By denying agency in authorship, Prentiss depicted her writing process as sacred, set apart from market corruption. Like Stowe, Prentiss invoked the Protestant idea that the Holy Spirit could inspire human authors to write words that functioned as sacred texts. *Religious Poems* (1873) was a "sort of miracle" that emerged almost of itself "in one short month"; she "*never* meant to do it, but my will was taken away." Similarly, "every word" of *Stepping Heavenward* "was a prayer, and seemed to come of itself"; she never knew "how it was written," for all the while her "heart and hands" were full of maternal cares. Prentiss, like many women authors, urgently denied that she had shirked her domestic duties in order to write for the market. Portraying herself as obeying the miraculous influence of the Holy Spirit, Prentiss positioned her activities as a published author within a timeless stream of Christian activity.[31]

Prentiss nevertheless struggled in her identity as a book trades participant with the distinction between religious and literary texts that prevailed within the nineteenth-century print market. In a significant exchange of letters in the last year of her life, Prentiss voiced some of the tensions she had experienced as an evangelical woman author. J. Cleveland Cady (1837–1919), a well-known architect, read *Home at Greylock* (1876) and wrote to its author to express his high regard not only for the book's usefulness but also for its literary qualities. Prentiss responded that she felt gratified by the letter because she considered it the "most discriminating letter I ever received." But shortly "after the first rush of pleasure," she began to experience conflicting emotions. She battled "for two or three hours" against temptations from the "Evil One" to feel hurt and resentful that her works had not received literary attention. At last, she reminded Satan and herself that "I long ago *chose* to cast in my lot with the people of God, and so be off the line of human notice or applause, and that I was glad I had been enabled to do it, since literary ambition is unbecoming a Christian woman." Prentiss had not regretted her decision, "yet the human nature is not dead in me, and my instincts still crave the kind of recognition you have given me. I have had heaps of letters from all parts of this country, England, Scotland, Ireland, Germany, and Switzerland, about my books, till I have got sick and tired of them. And the reason I tired of them was, that in most cases there was no discrimination. People liked their religious character, and of course I wanted them to do so. But you appreciate and understand everything in Greylock." Prentiss had "steadily suppressed" natural literary ambition to avoid becoming "a sour, disappointed woman, seeing my best work unrecognized." Her feelings illustrate one difficulty of integrating the worlds of evangelicalism and of literature, an essentially secular sphere. Prentiss entered the print market to exert a distinctive kind of influence: to read and write religious rather than merely literary texts. Yet she felt tempted by literary success and experienced the limitation of using printed texts primarily to promote progress beyond rather than in the literary world.[32]

Readers and writers like Elizabeth Prentiss strove to balance their identities as evangelicals and as book trades participants in an era of rapid print market expansion. A lay priesthood and cultural arbiters negotiated the rules for involvement in a textually defined Christian community envisioned as transcending space and time. Maintaining a sense of writing and reading as sacred processes, evangelicals readily moved between old and new genres, steady sellers and recently popular titles, intensive and extensive reading styles, and evangelical and nonevangelical canons, all esteemed as functionally sacred. Guided by advice like Noah Porter's, readers employed a variety of strategies to retain purity and presence in the world of print: memorizing, reciting, taking notes, reading aloud, imitating examples, sharing texts with others, and writing their own texts to influence others. Through such practices, evangelicals living in local communities viewed themselves as intimately related to an invisible pilgrim community destined for sanctification. Part 2 examines how writers, publishers, and readers used particular forms and genres, such as periodicals and hymnals, to transmit and sustain evangelical print culture.

Part Two

The Uses of
Evangelical Print Culture

5

Earnestly Contending
for the Faith

"In these days when the press is resorted to by all parties and sects of men, when every section of our wide country has its advocates, and every sect and faction of the religious world has its Newspaper and Quarterly, . . . it is now absolutely necessary for all parties to use the press, if they intend to make progress to maintain their relative position in the world." So began the 1855 prospectus justifying a new bimonthly magazine, the *Missouri Presbyterian Recorder*, introduced by the New School Synod of Missouri for the price of fifty cents per year. The editors had long felt the want of a local paper to facilitate communication within the denomination and with the "world at large." Without their own periodical, New School Presbyterians had "suffered much misrepresentation which might have been promptly corrected, and we have had to sit quietly by and see the papers of other denominations, some of which delight to prophesy evil respecting us, and lose no opportunity of injuring us circulate among the members of our churches and gain advantages for themselves at our expense." The editors of the *Recorder* envisioned themselves as living in a world riddled with conflict among religious denominations. The way to overcome misrepresentations and evils published in other periodicals appeared perfectly clear to the *Recorder*'s editors: issue a new periodical to refute errors with pure gospel truth.[1]

The *Recorder* was but one of a great number of periodicals that ventured into the contentious print market of mid-nineteenth-century America for the avowed purpose of propagating evangelical truth and refuting religious errors, especially the errors of competing denominations. Merging their understanding of the perspicuity of Scripture with Scottish common sense philosophy, nineteenth-century evangelicals were confident that the average reader could, but did not always, discern and choose truth. From the perspective of the *Recorder's* New School editors, even Old School Presbyterians, who admittedly shared the same Confession of Faith and preached the "same great, fundamental doctrines of the Gospel with an equal degree of sincerity," erred in being unduly "sectarian, proselyting, and closely approximating in bigotry." Although affirming their determination to spread New School Presbyterianism to every spot not already occupied by "some good evangelical denomination," the *Recorder's* editors used the paper's columns to argue that their interpretation of gospel doctrines was purer than the alternatives that even good evangelical denominations represented.[2]

Periodicals like the *Recorder*, more than any other single form of print, exemplify evangelical efforts to transform the American print market. The term "periodical" refers not to any one literary genre but to a form of publication, often embracing multiple genres, issued serially at more or less regular intervals. Periodicity varies from daily to annual installments, each of which bears the same title but, usually at least, different contents. By virtue of their relatively low price, speed of production, and geographic range of distribution, nineteenth-century periodicals reflected and shaped the simultaneous intensification of denominational and evangelical identities and facilitated dialogue among religious and secular reading communities. In disseminating narratives of the Christian life extensively and repeatedly, periodicals fulfilled the criteria of two models of communication theorized by journalism scholar James Carey: transmission and ritual. Chapter 6 assesses how the periodical form served the ritual function of sustaining evangelical identity over time as members of the priesthood of all believers. The present chapter considers evangelical uses of periodicals in transmitting core cultural values across space by contending for religious truth.[3]

Although useful in many of the same ways as other forms of print, periodicals played a central role in promoting a core evangelical mandate: "Ye should earnestly contend for the faith which was once delivered unto the saints." This quotation from Jude 3 adorned the mastheads of countless nineteenth-century periodicals (figure 5.1). In their original context, Jude's words admonished Christians to guard against apostasy arising within the early church. Jude's counsel inspired nineteenth-century evangelical denominations to contend earnestly for the faith by engaging in doctrinal debates with one another as well as with those outside the bounds of evangelicalism. Since, in a corrupt world, no one apprehended gospel truth perfectly, correcting the doctrinal errors of others constituted a vehicle by means of which the members of competing denominations hoped to influ-

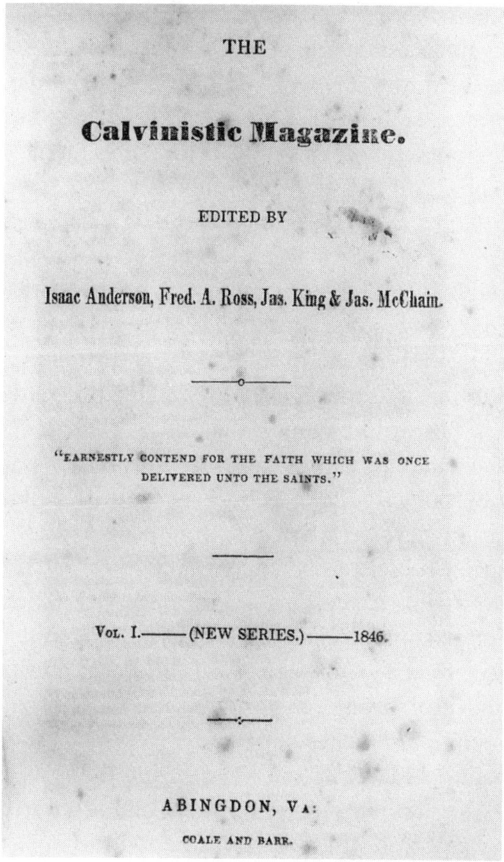

THE

Calvinistic Magazine.

EDITED BY

Isaac Anderson, Fred. A. Ross, Jas. King & Jas. McChain.

"EARNESTLY CONTEND FOR THE FAITH WHICH WAS ONCE
DELIVERED UNTO THE SAINTS."

VOL. I.——(NEW SERIES.)——1846.

ABINGDON, VA:

COALE AND BARR.

Figure 5.1.   The *Calvinistic Magazine* (1846). The mandate of Jude 3 framed countless nineteenth-century evangelical periodicals: "Earnestly contend for the faith which was once delivered unto the saints." (Courtesy of the American Antiquarian Society)

ence one another's religious growth. At the same time, gaining a hearing for the Word in a largely secular print market involved bending market strategies to religious purposes. Envisioning a widening range of narrative styles, packaging, and distribution tactics as functioning to convey sacred meanings, periodical editors contended against religious and secular competitors to win and keep an audience in the American print market.

The Rise of Religious Periodicals

Nineteenth-century American evangelicals considered periodicals an indispensable form of print through which to contend for the faith by efficiently broadcasting religious truth to geographically dispersed readers. The earliest news sheets appeared in Strasbourg, France, and Basel, Switzerland, in 1566. Eighteenth-century advances in printing and transportation technologies made it possible to transmit religious and secular news across greater distances more rapidly than ever before. During the Great Awakening, religious periodicals disseminated news of local revivals transatlantically in order to document and stimulate the revivals' spread. Around the same time, members of the rising middle classes in Europe and America began to demand regular communication concerning secular matters. The first American daily newspaper was published in 1783; the following year a new postal act encouraged the proliferation of periodicals by permitting their distribution through the mail. Most eighteenth-century newspapers circulated within narrowly circumscribed areas, though a few connected seaports on either side of the Atlantic. Apart from brief news sheets, prior to the 1790s only 100 periodicals, 14 of them explicitly religious, had commenced publication in America. Most of these papers had small readerships and short life spans; subscription lists averaged less than 500 names, and in most communities — the exceptions being coastal cities such as New York, Philadelphia, and Boston — just one or two periodicals circulated at any one time before 1800. By the 1830s, periodicals of every description, evangelical and nonevangelical, proliferated; subscription lists expanded, longevity increased, and cultural influence deepened.[4]

As denominational identities solidified during the first half of the nineteenth century, the periodical press reflected and promoted this development. Most eighteenth-century religious periodicals appealed to nondenominational audiences. Prior to 1800, only two out of thirty-four religious papers publicized their association with a particular religious group. Small subscription lists fostered ecumenical cooperation, especially in the South and West, since few periodicals could survive on any narrow party basis. Over the next half century, newspaper production cheapened, the establishment of periodical depots or warehouses made papers more readily available near urban areas, and denominational and sectional identities solidified. By 1830, 131 out of 193 publications, or 68 percent, openly declared their denominational affiliations. This ratio remained relatively stable throughout the antebellum period: 120 out of 185 religious periodicals cataloged by bibliographers from 1820 to 1852, or 65 percent, represented a specific denomination.[5]

The relative share of the periodicals market won by each denomination changed to correspond with the uneven growth of the various religious bodies. As of 1830, the five largest evangelical denominations published approximately 54 percent of the denomination-specific papers: Presbyterians counted twenty-one, Baptists eighteen, Congregationalists thirteen, Protestant Episcopalians ten, and Methodists nine. From 1820 to 1852, these same five groups laid claim to 71 percent of the total, a 17 percent increase relative to other denominations. The rankings among evangelical denominations simultaneously shifted: Methodists now sponsored twenty-seven papers, Baptists twenty-three, Presbyterians seventeen, Episcopalians fourteen, and Congregationalists four. The number of periodicals published by a denomination did not in every instance correlate with church membership, and some papers achieved more extensive circulations than did others. Nevertheless, the increasing number of denominational periodicals signaled a rising tide of denominationally based church growth.[6]

As the titles of periodicals more often identified the editor's religious affiliation, subscription to a church periodical became an act of expressing denominational loyalty. By the end of the 1840s, most religious denominations endorsed at least one periodical per state, many of them privately owned but issued in the name of the editor's denomination and unofficially adopted by an ecclesiastical body. In addition to papers supporting denominational interests in general, increasingly specialized periodicals gained readerships by focusing on printing sermons or missions or Sunday school news; by following doctrinal controversies; or by appealing to groups such as clergy, soldiers, juveniles, women, African Americans, or genteel literary aesthetes (figure 5.2). Not only did the growth of religious periodicals reflect emergent denominational identity, but, in the words of historian Nathan Hatch, they were also the "grand engine of a burgeoning religious culture, the primary means of promotion for, and bond of union within, competing religious groups." Periodicals became the medium of choice for promoting every old and new religious or moral cause.[7]

In an era of national expansion, denominational periodicals supplemented other church-building strategies such as preaching. "In this reading age," the ABPS reported in 1855, Baptists could no longer "depend entirely upon the pulpit to defend and propagate what we regard as the entire truth of God." The ABPS directed publications to Baptist households to remind church members of "why they are Baptists" and to the "community at large," hoping to persuade outsiders to join a Baptist church rather than another denomination. Especially in the West, where there was a shortage of Baptist clergy, periodicals constituted an informal mode of religious education that prepared people to welcome preachers once they arrived. A Baptist colporteur traveling through Indiana in 1866 urged the support of periodical literature so that the "minds of the people will be

PUBLISHED BY THE AMERICAN BAPTIST PUBLICATION SOCIETY.

VOLUME I.   JANUARY, 1881.   NUMBER I.

A STRANGE NEW YEAR'S DAY.

A STRANGE New Year's Day, indeed, it was for Charlie King. He had never spent one like it before, and was sincerely hoping he would never spend another like it as long as he lived.

This is the way it came about. Charlie King lived in a pleasant country town, not far from the great City of P——. His parents were not rich, but were in good circumstances; and Charlie, with his two brothers and a sister, had a very cheery and comfortable home. One would think, looking in upon this family of a winter's evening, when all were gathered round a table full of papers and books, and bright with the light of a student-lamp, that nothing was wanting to make their life delightful. If there was anybody in the world that ought to have been contented, that person was Charlie King.

But Charlie was not contented. He had somehow got hold of a book of adventures on the sea, and his imagination had been so inflamed by this book, that home seemed dry and tame, and he could think of nothing with pleasure but the life of a sailor. All the books he could find in the library, or borrow from his friends, which treated of the sea, he devoured with an ever-growing interest. He even dreamed at night of the sailor's life, and in his sleep was filled with longing to taste its freedom and joy.

Perhaps if he had spoken to his parents on the subject, they might have consented to his trying ocean life for a while, and might have secured some pleasant situation for him. But he was afraid that they would only laugh at him, and so determined that he would quietly slip off and find a place for himself. One autumn morning he put this resolution into effect. The thought of the pain he would give his mother, whom he tenderly loved, had long held him back; but now even this was swallowed up, and he made his way as quickly as he could

(HE STOOD WITH HIS ARM AROUND THE MAST, LOOKING LONGINGLY TOWARDS HOME.)

to the wharves of the great city, near by, where he knew a half dozen ships were preparing to sail.

As Providence would have it—for God meant to teach this boy a needed though hard lesson—Charlie found a place on a ship bound to the East Indies. The night after his engagement the ship started on her course. Charlie

Figure 5.2.   Our Young People (1881). Periodicals such as the ABPS's *Our Young People* appealed to specialized audiences, in this case Baptist juveniles. (Courtesy of the American Baptist Historical Society, American Baptist Archives Center, Valley Forge, Pa.)

moulded into Baptist faith" and thus be "prepared to receive the truth when it is preached." In the estimate of many like-minded evangelical clergy, the work of church-building required the concerted efforts of both the pulpit and the periodical press.[8]

The communications networks established by periodicals performed crucial functions in the formation, sustenance, and influence of competing religious institutions. Denominations that lacked centralized governing hierarchies, such as the Baptists, found periodicals especially important in helping individuals and churches to see themselves as belonging to a great denominational family, interested in one another's concerns. Kentucky's *Baptist Sentinel* (1869) articulated the goal of aiding "Christians in the great Baptist family to individual, earnest, systematic, and, on many subjects, concentrated effort to promote the cause of Christ." In addition to unifying individual denominations, periodicals also fueled church growth by accentuating differences among religious options. Members of an existing religious group founded their own periodical when they desired to distinguish themselves from other group members. With few exceptions, periodicals prepared the way for the emergence of new religious and moral causes, including the Seventh-Day Adventists, Jehovah's Witnesses, and Christian Scientists. Some of the smallest and least organized groups, such as Spiritualists, made highly effective use of the periodical press to maintain communication among scattered members. Whether old or new, well or poorly established, religious groups used periodicals to maintain identity as distinct from perceived competitors.[9]

The market for region-specific religious periodicals blossomed even as denominational and sectional identities solidified. Of the seventy locations sponsoring religious periodicals in 1830, over half were located west of the Alleghenies. Regional publications offered the distinct advantages of reaching their audiences quickly and cheaply and reflecting local sentiments. Sectional antagonisms slowed the formation of a truly national evangelical textual community. Northern and southern denominations split over slavery; westerners felt exploited by the East. Cincinnati emerged as a western publishing center for periodicals, as it was for other print forms. The Methodist *Western Christian Advocate*, published from 1834 to 1939 in Cincinnati, outstripped every religious and secular paper in the region by garnering 14,000 subscribers by 1840 and twice that number by 1860. In addition, the Methodist Western Book Concern issued editions of the *Advocate* in German and Swedish, designed to reach sizable immigrant communities. Reduction of postal rates and the extension of railroad and telegraph lines in the 1850s reshaped the balance between eastern and western publishers as a transcontinental communication network developed. By midcentury, northeastern papers traveled as far west as San Francisco and everywhere between nearly as quickly as could local organs. The *Missouri Presbyterian Recorder* (1855) aptly complained that "by means of railroads and telegraphs, eastern papers and eastern news reach us so soon, that it is vain to attempt to enter into competition with them, in a common field." Western papers increasingly focused their energies on local events in order to carve out a distinctive market niche. Wisconsin's *Presbyterial Reporter* (1852) presented a "multitude of facts and incidents, too local for publication a thousand miles away" but nonetheless essential to a "full history of the gospel's progress in the region—embracing the work of all denominations." As national communication lines solidified, western periodicals could compete against northeastern organs only by accentuating matters of regional rather than national interest and by endorsing some measure of interdenominational amity.[10]

With the intensification of sectional rivalries, the publishing of periodicals in the South, though never as robust as that in the North or West, expanded steadily from the 1830s through the Civil War. Sectional periodicals contributed to the split of the Methodist and Baptist denominations in 1844 and 1845 and of the Old and New School Presbyterians in 1857 and 1861 by reporting northern events that stirred up southern ire and by conveying to northerners southern comments on these events. Twenty-eight south Atlantic religious periodicals published in 1850 circulated 50,000 copies, roughly one subscriber for every ninety-six persons in the region. Baptists published twelve periodicals, with total circulation of 1,929; Catholics one periodical with 700 subscribers; Christians and Disciples three periodicals with 4,825 patrons; Episcopalians two periodicals with 775 subscribers; Methodists three periodicals with 2,400 subscribers; Presbyterians five periodicals with 1,300 subscribers; and two unclassified religious periodicals distributed 2,725 copies. Southern publishing peaked during the Civil War to compensate for the loss of northern periodicals, despite serious wartime disruptions from local fighting and paper shortages. Sixteen of the thirty-one southern religious periodicals issued in 1861 survived until 1865, during which period another twenty papers were added, twelve of which were still being published in 1865. Southern periodicals reflected and strengthened wartime resolve by justifying the conflict within a regionally specific evangelical narrative.[11]

Going on to Perfection

The relatively low price, speed of production, and range of distribution of the periodical form encouraged public discussion and debate among evangelicals of various denominations, if not always regions, calculated to heighten every Christian's knowledge of the truth. T. W. Haynes, editor of the *Carolina Baptist* (1845–46), alluded to a biblical passage often referenced by evangelical periodicals, Hebrews 6:1; he exhorted theological opponents to "go on to perfection" in understanding pure Bible doctrine until they should "come back to the truth as it is in Christ." Haynes viewed religious discussion as useful in purifying the church from error. In exposing what he considered the doctrinal errors of Campbellite (Disciples) periodicals, Haynes denied seeking to impair another religious group's "influence of good, rather we would strengthen the good that remains." Haynes described his Campbellite neighbors in warm language as "gentlemen whom we esteem and love. Of the rectitude of their intentions, we have no reason to doubt," though Haynes very much doubted the truth of Campbellite doctrines. Evangelicals like Haynes read periodicals published by other denominations cautiously, expecting to find debatable propositions alongside gems of gospel truth. Reading the latest publications of religious opponents kept evangelicals apprised of potential heresies as each arose in order to be better equipped to refute error and reinforce doctrinal truth.[12]

The periodical form, by making it easy to print correspondence between parties, stimulated public dialogue among members of different religious groups who interacted infrequently or inharmoniously on a personal level. Voicing his own doctrinal interpretations in every issue of the *Carolina Baptist*, Haynes also welcomed responses from correspondents "of all denominations," provided that their articles breathed a "kind spirit." One writer, dubbed "Nathaniel" and labeled a Pedobaptist by Baptists like Haynes, responded to the editorial invitation in 1845. Nathaniel regretted that most Christians read only periodicals sponsored by their own sect rather than seeking to "understand each other better" so as "more nearly to approximate each other" in perfect knowledge of biblical doctrine. Debating controverted points openly, Nathaniel believed, would enable evangelicals to form an "undivided front" to advance "Christ's spiritual kingdom." Haynes approved Nathaniel's opinion, informing his readers that they would be "edified by continuance of his contributions." Encouraged by the tone of Nathaniel's letter, Haynes invited any Pedobaptist minister to debate in the columns of his paper, asking for the return favor that the exchange be republished in some Pedobaptist journal. Before Christians of various denominations could unite against their common opponents, they had to discuss their differences with one another. Voicing a sentiment similar to those expressed by Haynes and Nathaniel, Rev. John M. Brown, editor of the AME *Repository of Religion and Literature, and of Science and Art* (1862), believed that "men ought to understand each other before they unite in any enterprise," since all Christians are "labourers together with God" (1 Corinthians 3:9). By opening a forum for communication among religious groups, periodicals promoted dialogue that could potentially provide a foundation for Christian unity.[13]

The editors of evangelical periodicals distinguished between controversy for the sake of controversy, which they unanimously opposed, and debate necessary to arrive at a common understanding of biblical truth. In the view of Ellison Grisham of Florida, correspondent to the *Southern Baptist Messenger* (1857), discussions among brethren helped all parties if "conducted in good spirit"; when one "should make a blunder," another could undertake to correct him. Not every published exchange exemplified the good spirit Grisham envisioned. Maryland's Baptist *True Union* (1860) warned the editors of other papers that they jeopardized their "own eternal interests" when they failed to debate in a spirit of "meekness and gentleness" (2 Corinthians 10:1). The Presbyterian *Southern Christian Sentinel* (1841) of South Carolina differentiated helpful discussion from damaging controversy. Dialogue managed in a right spirit served a vital role in the "discovery of valuable truth" and the "extinction of pernicious error." Although it was proper to dispense with controversy in matters of small importance, given the "admitted evils with which it is too frequently intermingled," it was essential to speak for truth in matters of "first-rate magnitude." In such instances, " 'Get thee behind me, Satan' [Matthew 16:23], should be the indignant reply to all who would dissuade us from using every necessary and scriptural method of coming at the truth." The African American *Baptist Preacher* (1886) of Texas also contrasted doctrinal truth and mere controversy; the editor denied intending to publish offensive disputations, but should the truth itself, rather than a contentious spirit, be the source of offense, "then I shall not be sorry, but go right on with my message." Although rejecting the love of controversy, evangelicals perceived debates carried out through periodicals as well suited to defending religious truth.[14]

The tone of discussions in evangelical periodicals varied tremendously depending on region, year, denomination, and the specific writers and papers considered. Some periodicals, although affirming the importance of contending for the faith against unevangelical onslaughts, rejected the legitimacy of disputes among Christians. Pennsylvania's antisectarian *Christian Union, and Religious Review* (1853) balanced two epigraphs as themes for the paper: "Earnestly contend . . ." and "Keep the unity of the Spirit in the bond of peace" (Ephesians 4:3). The periodical advocated the "UNION OF ALL CHRISTIANS on the broad and immutable basis of—The Bible, the whole Bible and nothing but the Bible" but said nothing about the possibility that Christians might interpret the Bible differently from one another. The paper's editors hoped that a return to biblical purity could quell the religious dissension that abounded from the 1840s through the 1860s, a period in which denominational consolidation and sectional antagonisms intensified doctrinal disagreements.[15]

Regional temperaments contributed to the diversity of attitudes toward religious contention. Northeastern periodicals, like the *Christian Union*, generally expressed less of the venom apparent in some southern and western papers, but in every region there were geographic and denominational variations. Relationships among Methodists and Presbyterians were, for instance, more harmonious in eastern Virginia than in western Virginia and eastern Tennessee. Charles Deems, of Richmond's *Southern Methodist Pulpit* (1849), congratulated Presbyterians in eastern Virginia on their great "Christian love towards their Methodist brethren" shown for some years past and insisted that "some of our dearest Christian friends are Presbyterians." In stark contrast, the New School Presbyterian *Calvinistic Magazine*, published in Rogersville, Tennessee, from 1827 to 1831 and revived in Abingdon, Virginia, from 1846 to 1850, devoted its columns almost exclusively to contending for the faith against Methodism, Arminianism, Deism, Infidelity, Roman Catholicism, Unitarianism, and Universalism. The magazine aimed particularly to refute the "slanders and disabuse" of Methodists who had long taken advantage of a "clear field to abuse and misrepresent Presbyterians, and to decoy into their own church the members of Presbyterian churches and families." Soon after the periodical's arrival in Virginia, the Methodist Russell Reneau founded the *Arminian Magazine* "for the purpose of hurling back the assaults of the notorious *Calvinistic Magazine*." The two papers regularly swapped volleys of religious fire with each other and also entered into disputes with other editors through periodical exchanges. The August 1846 issue of the *Calvinistic Magazine*, in typical fashion, used sixteen of thirty-two pages to rebut an editorial in the *Methodist Episcopalian* that reviewed an article in the Congregationalist *Home Missionary* on the topic of "Methodist Admissions to the Church." The series of articles debated which denomination's admission policies most effectively encouraged religious growth after conversion. The editors of the *Calvinistic Magazine* accused the Methodist editor of knowingly presenting false and slanderous accusations — as well as adopting bad grammar. The Presbyterian article revealed the "flame of Methodism" in its "proselyting arts" to lure Presbyterian children into joining their churches at emotional camp meetings. Having "got religion" under such circumstances, Methodist converts *"fall from grace*, and become two-fold more the children of hell" (Matthew 23:15). Whatever Christian love eastern Presbyterians and Methodists shared, controversies raged fiercely along the Virginia-Tennessee border.[16]

As with regional differences, denominational emphases impacted relative concern with religious controversy. Baptists concluded that certain doctrines and practices (notably adult baptism by immersion) were worth fighting for more often than did Methodists, who generally resisted allowing such disputes to interfere with the business of soul-winning. As in the Landmark disputes of the 1850s–70s, discussed in chapter 1, Baptists not only debated other denominations but also split from other Baptists along urban-rural, southeastern-southwestern, and settled-frontier lines, with rural southwestern frontier areas being more inclined to controversy. By the 1830s, no evangelical denomination published more periodicals in the South than did the Baptists, even though Methodists surpassed Baptists for church membership until the 1890s. John Waller, editor of Kentucky's *Western Baptist Review* (1846), explained the Baptist penchant for controversy by warning that " 'false teachers and damnable heresies' [2 Peter 2:1], 'seducing spirits and doctrines of devils' [1 Timothy 4:1], must be strenuously opposed. However lamentable and baneful the influence of religious warfare, peace must not be purchased at the expense of truth." Like many evangelicals, Waller distinguished between worldly and godly disputation: "Controversy is seldom promotive of godliness; contention, never. Yet, the disciple of Jesus must frequently grasp the 'sword of the Spirit' [Ephesians 6:17] and 'contend earnestly for the faith which was once delivered unto the saints' [Jude 3]." Waller did not hesitate to take up his sword to combat the forces of religious error.[17]

Intermixed with denominational concerns, the temperaments of periodical editors shaped the tone of religious discussion. Announcing an editorial policy of refusing "all personal controversy, unless forced upon us," Waller apparently felt forced into controversy repeatedly. In objecting to the "superciliousness" and "patronizing" tone of the Georgia Baptist *Christian Index*'s editorial notice of the *Review*, Waller resorted to personal attack: "We acknowledge our fault in commenting so severely upon the article of the *Index*. Surely we ought to feel ashamed, when a brother so *remarkable* for placidity of tone and temper as the editor of *Christian Index*, administers a reproof for *hard words!*" With comparable sarcasm, Waller "respectfully informed" the editor of the *Presbyterian Herald* that "we cannot enter into any controversy with him" since he is "altogether too formidable an adversary for us. The very countenance of such an opponent would drive us from the field. We would rather encounter the rugged Russian bear, the armed rhinoceros, or the Hyrean tiger!" Two months later, Waller could not resist adopting a more biting tone in accusing his Presbyterian opponent of exhibiting the "venom and virulence of personal abuse and billingsgate worthy only of the most reckless and dirty political prints." Apparently oblivious to any similarity between such a characterization and his own remarks, Waller claimed to "smile with supreme contempt upon the abortive effusions of witlings and the impotent maledictions of Lilliputian bigots." As Waller's rhetoric suggests, the public debates encouraged by the periodical form made it difficult for some evangelicals to disentangle doctrinal contention from more personal animosity.[18]

Although leading religious spokespersons such as Dwight L. Moody and Henry Ward Beecher shunned religious controversies by the 1870s, other evangelicals maintained the central importance of contending for pure Bible doctrine. Kentucky's *Baptist Sentinel* (1869–71) emphatically denied that "one doctrine is as good as another." One of the paper's correspondents, W. E. Paxton of Louisiana, affirmed sentiments shared by his fellow subscribers to the paper, that the foremost perils confronting the church were latitudinarianism and liberalism. The former error involved the "general and indefinite statement of doctrine which avoids collision with any particular view, and accommodates itself to the views of all." The second error was more dangerous than the first, "for whilst latitudinarianism would nullify the utterance of religious conviction, liberalism, clothed in the stolen habiliments of a broad charity, strikes at the root of all conviction by stifling all preference for one form of doctrine above another." Responding to pleas for Christian union that abounded in the 1870s, the *Sentinel's* editors explained that "if all the professed followers of Christ were truly such, union would be both desirable and attainable; but while this is not the case, it will be better for the people of God, that divisions should continue." Although acknowledging that "some Baptists will be lost; and . . . some who are not Baptists will be saved," the *Sentinel's* editors and correspondents felt confident in their interpretation of biblical truth and committed to ensuring its preservation.[19]

Contending against Religious and Secular Alternatives

Evangelical periodicals contended against religious and secular candidates for patronage both by debating doctrine and by making publications attractive to potential readers. As the journalism historian David Nord has noted, the marketplace of ideas was literal as well as metaphorical. Quantifying evangelical success in winning a share of the American periodicals market is problematic for the same reasons that it is difficult to calculate evangelical influence in the print market as a whole: the absence of comprehensive data and the impossibility of disentangling religious from secular meanings. It is necessary to piece together data from incomplete historical surveys, census records, and self-promoting claims by the periodicals themselves. From 1730 to 1830, 590 religious periodicals commenced publication, 75 percent of which folded within four years or less. By 1830, just 193 papers remained in circulation; continual additions and failures left 191 religious periodicals surviving in 1850 and approximately 171 in 1860. A minority of the religious papers enjoyed considerable longevity: 152 lasted for at least 5 years, and 27 lived more than 100 years. Contextualizing these figures relative to the trade press, there were perhaps 5,000–6,000 periodicals founded during the first quarter of the nineteenth century, 4,000–5,000 in the second quarter, 2,500 from 1850 to 1865, and 4,300 in the 1870s, with a total circulation of 10.5 million, or enough to reach one in three Americans. The average life expectancy for any paper ranged somewhere from two to four years, with the longevity of papers increasing slightly as the century progressed. As of 1850, there were roughly 600 periodicals in print, nearly one-third of which claimed a religious affiliation.[20]

Religious and secular publications cannot, however, be quite so neatly categorized because the boundaries dividing the religious from the secular were permeable. Both evangelical and nonevangelical editors regularly exchanged copies of their papers through the mail in order to keep abreast of what other editors were publishing and to facilitate the reprinting of articles from other papers. Exchanges encouraged cross-fertilization among periodicals as secular newspapers consistently borrowed religious materials and as religious periodicals likewise included secular news. When the Presbyterian John Holt Rice established the *Virginia Evangelical and Literary Magazine* in 1818, he placed the term "literary" in the title to indicate the appropriateness of articles on agriculture, inland navigation, roads, and schools in a religious publication. Rice voiced a characteristically evangelical conviction that "learning and philosophy are handmaids to religion." Despite the assumption of many cultural analysts that the inclusion of "secular" matters in religious publications reveals secularization, evangelical papers printed secular articles because editors and readers wanted religion to govern every aspect of life. Indeed, evangelicals understood texts classed by scholars as secular to function in conveying sacred meanings.[21]

Given the ease with which evangelicals blurred the religious and the secular in their own calculations of influence, quantification must allow for a certain fuzziness of categories. Of the 485 periodicals that bibliographer Orville Roorbach cataloged for 1820 to 1852, 49 percent might be classed under the general headings of religious, denominational, or moral reform — 237 as compared with 248 apparently secular titles. Some of the religious titles occupy an ambiguous location between evangelical and secular interests, for example a "religious and literary" magazine and papers devoted to moral reform causes such as temperance (35) and antislavery

(13). Evangelical readers likely subscribed to some of the secular works pertaining to literature (97), agriculture (26), medicine (25), and education (12). Of the secular papers, only two were explicitly antireligious in their leanings, one classed by Roorbach as rationalist, the other as infidel. In any particular locality, people often subscribed to a mixture of religious and secular titles. For the year 1831–32, the Jacksonville, Illinois, post office kept detailed records of periodical subscriptions. Of the 133 periodicals recorded, 42 of them, or 32 percent, had a distinctly religious affiliation. The Methodist *Christian Advocate* had more than twice the number of subscribers, 58, as any other paper, religious or secular. The number of subscribers to religious periodicals totaled 212, compared with 261 patrons of all the secular papers; in other words, subscriptions to religious papers accounted for 45 percent of the total. Quantification of distribution lists in other localities similarly indicates that religious publications enjoyed a substantial share of the antebellum periodicals market.[22]

Comparing the subscription lists of the most successful religious and secular periodicals reveals a pattern in which religious titles led the way until midcentury when certain secular papers caught up with religious innovators. Evaluating relative circulation is fraught with difficulty since there are few sources to draw upon besides the self-promoting claims of the papers themselves. In 1829, the Methodist *Christian Advocate* and the nondenominational *American National Preacher* attested to 20,000 and 25,000 subscribers respectively, the highest numbers then recorded by any periodical in the world. No secular paper could, in 1829, boast a circulation higher than 4,500. In 1830, total subscriptions for religious periodicals reached an estimated 400,000. By midcentury, the religious share of the periodicals market arguably declined. Historian Frank Luther Mott has estimated that from 1850 to 1865, thirteen periodicals had subscription lists of over 100,000. Among the most successful papers, *Harper's New Monthly* averaged 110,000 subscribers, *Harper's Weekly* counted 120,000, *Godey's Lady's Book* 150,000, *Frank Leslie's Illustrated* 164,000, and, leading the pack, the *New York Ledger* was "rumored" to have 400,000 subscribers. If these numbers can be trusted, by midcentury evangelical periodicals no longer enjoyed unrivaled ascendancy, but neither did secular papers carry the day. Not only did the ATS's *American Messenger* have one of the largest readerships, 200,000, but the ATS *Child's Paper* (not mentioned by Mott) catered to 290,000 patrons. Complicating such comparisons, subscription lists tell only part of the story, since one copy of any given periodical often had several readers, including not only family members but also neighbors and distant friends who used the postal system to share news. In addition, information read by one community member traveled by word of mouth to others who could not or did not care to read.[23]

After midcentury, the share of the periodicals market claimed by evangelical trade publishers exceeded the proportion suggested by the juxtaposition of individual religious and secular subscription lists. Some trade publishers issued periodicals that attracted both religious and secular readers, strategically developing families of papers, each member of which filled a specific market niche. The Methodist Harper brothers held fast to their goal of publishing only "interesting, instructive, and moral" publications that nonetheless won both religious and nonreligious audiences. In establishing separate weekly and monthly papers, the Harpers judged that they could appeal to different segments of the market, thus extending their reach. Rather than evaluating individual subscription lists, one might instead view Harper & Brothers' overall share of the market as the sum of its subscription lists, adding together not only the monthly (founded 1850) and weekly (founded 1857) papers but also *Harper's Bazaar* (founded 1867) and *Harper's Young People* (founded 1879). Trade publishers like Harper expanded evangelical inroads to the national print market even after highly successful secular publishers stepped up their efforts to win readers.[24]

Families of denominational periodicals similarly augmented evangelical influence even after midcentury. By 1860, the Methodist Book Concern published eight official, regional papers in the "*Christian Advocate* family" as well as German and Swedish editions, a quarterly review, a literary magazine, a missionary paper, a women's magazine, and four Sunday school papers. All of these periodicals shared a common agenda: "the spread of what *we* believe to be the genuine doctrines of the gospel, and true vital godliness and scriptural holiness." Since each paper approached this goal somewhat differently, advertisements proclaimed that "many of our people" found it advantageous to subscribe to the entire "family." The total weekly circulation of all the official Methodist papers exceeded 400,000 throughout the 1860s, a figure that brings the Methodist family into the ranks of the most successful periodicals. Other denominations similarly published entire families of publications. The Presbyterian Board estimated in 1875 a distribution list of 35,000 for the *Presbyterian at Work* and, for its Sunday school papers, 100,000 for the *Presbyterian Sabbath School Visitor*, 22,000 for the *Sunbeam*, and 210,000 for the *Westminster Lesson Leaf*. Adding in the *Presbyterian Monthly Record, Golden Texts,* and the *Annual Report,* the board calculated an annual circulation of nearly 4.9 million copies of its periodical publications. Mott estimated that each of the major evangelical denominations sponsored from twenty-five to fifty periodicals between 1850 and 1865, many of which endured longer than the overall average of two to four years.[25]

Alongside growth in evangelical trade and denominational publishing, nondenominational periodicals also continued to gain strength after midcentury. The ATS introduced the *American Tract Magazine* in 1825, selling 3,000 copies of its first issue. The paper's circulation grew at a moderate pace, reaching 8,000 copies by 1842. In 1843, the ATS replaced the magazine with a new monthly, the *American Messenger*. This paper's more varied contents, including religious news, "brief evangelical narratives," and articles "for the young and the family circle," all for the low subscription price of twenty-five cents annually, immediately attracted a wide audience; circulation soared to 30,000 by the end of 1844. In 1847, the society established a German language edition, the *Botschafter*, which promptly sold 10,000 copies. By 1848, just five years after the *Messenger*'s founding, its circulation had grown to 100,000. In 1852, the *Messenger*'s distribution list neared 200,000, and the ATS started a new *Child's Paper*, illustrated with engravings, which gained 250,000 monthly subscribers within its first year. By midcentury, the *Messenger* and *Child's Paper*, viewed independently, had two of the largest readerships of any periodical in the world. Subscription rates for all the ATS periodicals grew steadily, even during the Civil War, when increasing production costs and decreasing demand were driving other papers out of business. In 1865, the *Messenger*'s circulation peaked at 200,000; at the same time, the ATS sent out 43,000 copies of the *Botschafter* and 290,000 copies of the *Child's Paper* for an aggregate monthly distribution of 533,000 copies. By 1870, the *Messenger*'s circulation had decreased somewhat to 170,250, but other publications in the ATS family compensated for this deficit; total monthly issuance reached an all-time high of 556,000 copies. After 1870, distribution lists for all the ATS periodicals diminished, reflecting a realignment of religious alliances. By 1890, only 33,000 copies of the *Messenger* circulated monthly; aggregate distribution of all the papers fell to 139,000. Yet for much of the nineteenth century, the overall subscription rates achieved by ATS publications surpassed every rival, whether secular or religious.[26]

Contending with Market Constraints

The statistical data point to an overall tendency for denominational, nondenominational, and evangelical trade houses to publish multiple periodicals and for a few of these to flourish, even as the vast majority quickly faded into oblivion. This pattern raises the questions of why some periodicals succeeded while others failed, why religious periodicals fared as well as they did relative to the secular press, and why most religious papers fared no better than they did. Evangelical periodicals shared some constraints in common with other religious and secular publishing endeavors. In addition, evangelical papers built in elements of their own restriction while enjoying certain advantages relative to other classes of publication.

Most editors, evangelical and nonevangelical, struggled to sustain adequate subscription lists or find sufficient original material, given the limitations of an immature periodicals market. Observers frequently noted the abundance of papers competing for a relatively small number of potential subscribers. In the evaluation of one correspondent to Georgia's *Southern Baptist Messenger* (1861), "There are [*sic*] such a flood of newspapers, secular and religious, that even the most desirable sheet has but a slim chance of patronage." The periodicals best able to compete for customers were those with the most capital to invest in features such as illustrations. From 1853 to 1865, *Harper's New Monthly* printed 10,000 engravings, which cost $300,000. Not many publishers could afford such an outlay of funds. In addition to their constant hunger for subscribers, editors also had difficulty attracting enough contributors. Few periodicals paid authors anything before the 1820s, and the fees generally remained quite small until the 1840s. Moreover, most papers published articles anonymously until the 1840s–50s. This practice, along with the editorial liberties it allowed, discouraged authors from remaining loyal to any particular periodical.[27]

Compounding limitations shared with secular papers, religious periodicals battled against additional, self-imposed constraints. Most evangelical editors were clergymen who were neither qualified for the business of running a newspaper by training nor motivated to pursue professional goals. As sole or joint proprietors, many minister-editors funded their papers from personal resources, hoping (often in vain) to sell enough copies to repay themselves. Secular papers endorsing political positions, by contrast, frequently secured government assistance. The Methodist *Christian Advocate* (1890) justified its annual subscription rate of $2.70 by noting additional disadvantages that evangelical papers faced; for instance, religious periodicals could not be sold as cheaply as "vicious newspapers" because the cost of production correlated with the number of copies sold, and sensational articles attracted the largest audiences. The costs of evangelical periodicals were also higher, the *Advocate* insisted, since "Christian literature is published on Christian principles by paying living prices for labor and material, and excluding low advertisements." Although few publishers kept adequate financial records to confirm the first part of the *Advocate*'s assertion, there is evidence that evangelical publishers were selective in their choice of advertisements. As the development of national markets encouraged businesses to seek venues for nationwide advertising, evangelical periodicals opened their columns, but only in a limited fashion, to accommodate this new financial opportunity. Religious periodicals almost never printed advertisements on the front page, as was common in secular papers, and evangelical editors rigidly excluded advertisements for presumed vices such as liquor, tobacco, theatrical performances, horse races, and, in most cases, patent medicines. The *Advocate* "considerably increased" its advertising department by 1849 but continued to limit the number and selection through the end of the century in order to keep the notices from becoming "obnoxious." Those advertisements the *Advocate* accepted did not generate sufficient revenue to prevent price increases.[28]

Denominational periodicals, because of their intrinsically restricted market appeal, required high levels of institutional support in order to flourish. The Methodist Episcopal Church officially sponsored several periodicals that achieved some of the most extensive subscription lists. The General Conference not only authorized but also required all ministers to act as agents for all official Methodist publications. Periodicals affiliated with other denominations appealed to ministers for aid but lacked the official endorsement necessary to secure compliance. The Presbyterian *Evangelical Repository* (1842) called upon the "ministers of our church especially" to "exert their influence to increase the number of subscribers." Without a centralized denominational enforcement mechanism, not only did ministers provide weak support but also periodicals affiliated with the same denomination often competed against one another. W. C. Buck, editor of the *Baptist Banner and Western Pioneer* (1842), complained of the "unconquerable inclination among the people to multiply newspapers." Competition among Baptist periodicals, from Buck's self-interested perspective, exerted a "pernicious influence upon the Baptist cause in America, and particularly in the West," because of the pecuniary losses experienced by established papers when readers switched to another periodical or ceased paying their former subscriptions. Since denominational papers had a limited number of potential patrons from which to draw, intradenominational rivalries often had disastrous financial effects.[29]

Like papers of every class, denominational periodicals could be initiated with relatively little outlay, but long-term sustenance proved much more difficult. As with the Baptists, AME periodicals faced competitors that sprang up from within their own denomination. Meetings of the AME General Conference for years granted approval to denominational papers without giving exclusive authority to any one periodical as *the* church organ. Two AME papers ambitious for a national audience clashed in the 1860s amid sectional controversies: the *Christian Recorder* of Philadelphia and the more refined *Repository of Religion and Literature, and of Science and Art* of Baltimore, which gained its following primarily in Maryland, Indiana, and Missouri. The *Recorder* repeatedly published accusations that the *Repository* was stealing its readers; the latter paper's editor, Rev. John M. Brown, denied the "strong and bungling" charges, insisting that the papers must "work harmoniously together" or, like Abraham and Lot, divide their areas of patronage (Genesis 13:9). The *Repository* folded in 1863, but other competitors continued to surface. The AME *Church Review* (1891), sanctioned by the General Conference to supply the want of a denominational quarterly, spoke harshly of wealthy black men with editorial ambitions who initiated local papers. Such entrepreneurs made arrogant claims that " 'they have come to stay,' but like mushrooms they spring up and die in a night; and thus a good deal of the support that should go to sustain our newspapers is drawn away by these local 'come-to-stays' " of the "fungi" class. Complaints such as these indicate that it was fairly easy to start a paper but much more difficult to sustain it without unified institutional support.[30]

Denominational periodicals struggled because church members did not necessarily constitute a ready pool of paying customers. Indeed, evangelical readers generally demonstrated much looser denominational allegiances than editors wanted, a situation reflected by constant editorial pleas for support of church papers. The *Methodist Quarterly Review* (1856) represented itself as "almost indispensable" to "members of the Methodist Episcopal Church." An advertisement urged that "it would be well if many of them who are now spending their money for light and trifling trash— injurious and pernicious at that—would discontinue such publications and send a dollar for this." Periodicals sponsored by other denominations regularly made parallel appeals. Bishop Henry McNeal Turner was elected manager of the AME Publication Department in 1876. Within four years, his aggressive lobbying for support of the *Christian Recorder*, the "authorized organ" of the church, raised the number of paid subscriptions from 2,000 to 3,000, just over half the 5,400 copies that circulated weekly. The remaining copies went to exchanges with other editors, to the "illustrious roll" of those who subscribed on behalf of congregations at greatly reduced rates, and to those who simply did not bother to pay for their copies of the paper. Turner complained in 1880 that, based on church membership statistics, the *Christian Recorder* should have had 25,000 paying subscribers. The leaders of other denominations made similar calculations based on church membership and were likewise disappointed. The problem, according to the AME Publication Department (1882), was not that church members failed to take any periodical but that they chose competitors rather than patronizing "our own house." Compounding the problem of low circulation rates, pastors and church members failed to pay for their subscriptions. The black American Baptist Missionary Convention claimed that two-thirds of its periodicals' debts represented money owed by defaulting subscribers. Although legislation nominally gave periodical publishers the right to collect past dues, consistent complaints by papers of every affiliation suggest that laws were rarely enforced. Without the assistance of the "whole church," denominational periodicals could not survive. Some of the papers that did endure were subsidized by donations, including the AME *Christian Recorder* and the *Methodist Quarterly Review.*[31]

Presence in the World of Print

Contending for the faith in the American print market inevitably required periodical proprietors and editors to negotiate between their identities as evangelicals and as book trades participants, a dynamic more fully explored in chapter 2. Over time, evangelical editors increasingly recognized that effective competition with other secular or religious papers meant using market strategies to attract an audience. From the 1840s to the 1860s, evangelicals became progressively more comfortable with blending religious and commercial agendas in an effort to balance purity and presence in the world of print.

Evangelical editors addressing their readers in the 1830s and 1840s explicitly denied that their papers were financial ventures. T. W. Haynes of the *Carolina Baptist* (1845) insisted that pastors "will receive as much benefit from [the paper's] circulation among the families of his hearers as the Editor, whose services are given freely, *without money and without price*, up till the subscription list shall be nearly doubled." Haynes identified himself as a disinterested bearer of the gospel by alluding to Isaiah 55:1: "Ho, every one that thirsteth, come ye to the waters, and he that hath no money; come ye, buy, and eat; yea, come, buy wine and milk without money and without price." Haynes promised to preach the Word through his paper, not mere words printed for the sake of worldly wealth. The Methodist *Christian Advocate* (1845) similarly assured ministers that profit did not accrue to the publishers but to the "souls of your people, and to the superannuated preachers" and their widows and orphans, whom the paper's financial income supported. Disclaiming financial motivations, editors affirmed their own purity from worldly corruption and the sacredness of the texts they offered for sale.[32]

By the 1860s, editorial language increasingly embraced market terminology in a bid to contend against religious and secular alternatives. Two advertisements appearing in the nondenominational *Mothers' Journal and Family Visitant*, in 1841 and 1860, illustrate this cultural transition. The earlier promotional adopted language designed primarily to appeal to evangelical readers concerned with domestic piety: "Every mother, who duly appreciates the responsibilities which rest upon her in training a soul for eternity, will gladly welcome this work to her fireside, if it be presented to her notice." Twenty years later, the same magazine asked to be selected over other options not only because of its religious content but also because it exhibited a "much finer and higher style of steel plate, than are to be found in any other Dollar Magazine. They are equal to the very best engravings of the most fashionable and costly monthlies." The advertisement reflects a shift in evangelical discourse intended to match the simultaneous maturation of refined literary culture in the secular market. The editors of *Mothers' Journal* appealed to women readers accustomed to selecting from among market offerings that excelled in material presentation and literary style as well as in religious sensibilities. Indeed, as an examination of hymn language will confirm, by midcentury some evangelicals considered a text's sacred influence to be augmented by the adoption of a finer and higher style, which provided a more appropriate repository for the Holy Spirit's indwelling presence.[33]

No class of publication more fully exemplified the refinement of the secular literary market than the annuals that proliferated in the trade lists in the 1840s and 1850s. Advertisements typically portrayed these finely bound and elaborately illustrated volumes as suitable for display in the middle-class Victorian parlor. As in so many other fields of publishing, evangelicals contended for a share of the annuals market. *The Sacred Annual: A Gift for All Seasons* (1851) suggests the permeability of religious and literary culture and illuminates one way that evangelicals entered the literary world in order to transform it. The word "sacred" in the volume's title differentiated it from merely literary publications. A preface, written by the *Sacred Annual*'s minister-editor, Rev. H. Hastings Weld of Philadelphia, articulated a characteristically evangelical aim: to use a popular cultural medium as a vehicle for religious truth. This annual sought to make "art subservient to the advancement of piety; to ennoble as well as to amuse the mind." Implicitly, other annuals stopped short of true value by settling for mere amusement. The practical usefulness of the *Sacred Annual* marked it as a

Figure 5.3. "Evening Sacrifice," *Sacred Annual* (1851). The *Sacred Annual* avowedly used beautiful articles and illustrations to heighten the influence of evangelical truth. (Courtesy of the American Antiquarian Society)

distinctively evangelical text. It is "for no useless purpose" that the "eye delights in pleasant things." God created the "love of the beautiful," not as an end in itself, but as an avenue through which the "truth should enter into our hearts" (figure 5.3). Alluding to Philippians 4:8, Weld argued in a manner parallel to Wesley and Edwards that God designed all that is beautiful to direct the mind to "worship of the Holy." But the "treachery of art" and of the press, unleavened by the gospel, perverted beauty into a "disguise for immorality and vice" by masking the "unworthiness of their themes." The *Sacred Annual*, by employing the same means as used by the opponents of truth, aimed to "restore the Beautiful to its true ministry." The material embodiment of the volume — its fine "embellishments, and typographical and general execution" — would, Weld hoped, inspire "love at first sight" among potential readers. Once the annual's external appearance caught readers' attention, its contents could potentially lead them to religious truth. Lighter articles accompanied more severe sermons and essays so as to reach even the minds of the young through their imagination. In adopting a popular cultural medium and recasting its purpose, the *Sacred Annual* purportedly brought literature into the service of religion.[34]

Despite efforts to embrace refined literary sensibilities, denominational periodicals often failed when they attempted head-to-head competition with more market-oriented religious or secular papers. Many editors of denominational periodicals initially resisted publishing fiction, one of the most desired genres among general reading audiences as well as among increasing numbers of evangelicals. The Methodist Book Concern created the *National Magazine* in 1852 as a substitute for *Harper's New Monthly*, established in 1850. The *National* claimed to present all the attractions of *Harper's*, minus the "morbid appeals to the passions" found in fiction. Even as *Harper's* prospered, the *National* was discontinued in 1858 "for want of support." The Methodist Western Book Concern attempted a different strategy in sponsoring the *Ladies' Repository, and Gatherings of the West* in 1841 as a less worldly alternative to *Godey's Lady's Book*, founded in 1830. The *Repository* aimed "to entertain as well as to instruct" without becoming the "vehicle of silly jests and sickening tales." In its first decade, the *Repository* attracted a subscription list of 40,000, primarily among Methodist readers. To give the paper a "wider scope," in 1855 the editors introduced two steel plate engravings with each issue. Fiction appeared in 1853, in serialized form by 1873. The paper's title also broadened in 1876: *The National Repository, Devoted to General and Religious Literature, Criticism and Art*. The effort to enter "the world of letters as a friendly competitor for a place among the great literary monthlies of the day" proved disastrous. The publishers' final statement in December 1880 admitted that the bid for worldly attention had resulted in "a rapid decline in circulation." The paper's earlier success had depended "upon being wisely, if need be, solely, adapted to the field of Methodism." This example suggests that evangelical periodicals could enjoy substantial success by appealing to a clearly defined audience of church adherents. Efforts to extend this readership did not always result in new subscribers but rather discouraged those who wanted a denominational paper instead of less religious market options.[35]

By the 1860s, editors who refrained from entering more refined literary markets nevertheless felt comfortable in envisioning a range of market strategies as functionally sacred because they were useful in contending for the Word in the world. The Methodist *Christian Advocate* expressed this new sensibility as staying "up to the age." From 1860 forward, the *Advocate* more often included articles on commerce and the produce market and expanded its advertising department. Simultaneously, the editors of denominational and nondenominational papers more frequently acknowledged the usefulness of seeking financial as well as spiritual profit. The *Advocate* (1860) argued that clerical support of church periodicals would not only "spread holiness . . . *over the world*" but also present ministers with the "opportunity for replenishing your libraries and of filling your pockets." In a similarly practical vein, West Virginia's *Baptist Record* (1870) recognized that printing is "a business, as well as an art—that it must be made profitable to be continued." Contending for a hearing in the world required, first of all, maintaining periodicals on a solid financial basis. Since editors could not count on denominational loyalties to secure subscriptions, religious periodicals began to adopt a strategy long practiced by trade publishers: offering premiums to current subscribers for convincing their neighbors to take the paper. In typical fashion, the AME *Repository of Religion and Literature, and of Science and Art* (1862) promised anyone who would send in the names of twenty new purchasers a free year's subscription to the paper and a steel engraving of AME founder Bishop Richard Allen. Periodical editors conceived of themselves as sanctifying market strategies that functioned to maintain an evangelical presence in the print market.[36]

During the last two decades of the nineteenth century, evangelicals continued to experience tension between their religious and market identities. Success in the periodicals market intensified feelings of failure expressed by evangelicals committed to purity. In its 1886 annual report, the ABPS distinguished between its own periodicals, directed toward the "spiritual profit" of readers, and the mere merchandise of other avowedly religious publishers, produced simply for the sake of financial profits. The AME *Church Review* (1891) similarly denounced the tendency of evangelical editors to reduce publishing to a "business . . . carried on with a single view to dollars and cents. This throws upon the market much of that class of literature which is positively hurtful." As religious publishers resorted to beautiful bindings and the unsparing use of "loud and attractive colors," the contents presumably suffered for lack of similarly meticulous attention. In their efforts to transform the world using the tools of a largely secular market, evangelical editors strained to avoid compromising purity.[37]

Nineteenth-century evangelicals privileged the periodical form in their most earnest efforts to "contend for the faith which was once delivered unto the saints." The relatively low price, speed of production, and geographic range of distribution of periodicals facilitated discussion and debate across denominational and regional lines. Evangelicals used periodicals like the *Missouri Presbyterian Recorder* to overcome the errors of religious opponents by persuasively arguing on behalf of pure gospel truth. Appropriating diverse market strategies to compete against secular and religious alternatives, periodicals disseminated evangelical influences across an American cultural milieu. In the process, editors and readers renegotiated the boundaries separating evangelical from denominational loyalties and sacred from secular meanings. The communication networks established by periodicals functioned both to transmit evangelical and denominational values across space and to sustain collective identities over time. Chapter 6 resumes the story of the cultural work performed by periodicals, focusing on the ritual power of communication to intensify evangelical identification as members of the priesthood of all believers.

6

Priesthood of
All Believers

P. West of Dansville, New York, wrote a letter to the editor of Georgia's
Old School *Southern Baptist Messenger* in April 1861. Voicing conventional
diffidence, West insisted that he felt his "incompetency to write anything
worthy of public notice." West nevertheless wrote because he had "derived
so much pleasure and satisfaction from reading the soul-cheering communications from the dear saints hitherto published in the *Messenger*, and
which has given much assurance that they were led through the same experiences of hopes and fears, temptations and triumphs that I have been
through, I have many times felt as though I would like to contribute to
their joy, if I could do so by any manifestation of sympathy." The correspondence columns of the *Messenger* represented for West a medium
through which Christians encouraged one another by communicating
shared experiences.[1]

As an Old School Baptist, West felt personally responsible to support the
Messenger's editor, William Beebe, as well as other subscribers to the paper.
West "recognized the importance of holding up your hands in the work of
publishing pure Bible doctrine among those who truly love our Lord Jesus
Christ, and for sustaining this medium of correspondence between the
members of Christ's body." West urged other readers to write more fre-
quently so that Beebe would have material to publish and bade them to
canvass for more subscribers so that the journal would be assured of making
ends meet financially. In envisioning himself as holding up Beebe's hands,
West alluded to the language of Exodus 17:11. In the biblical account,
Moses enabled the Israelites to win a lengthy battle by holding the rod of
God above the Israelite army. When Moses' arms drooped from exhaus-

tion, Aaron and Hur — a priest and a layman — held up their leader's hands. The allusion casts the editor in the role of Moses, West in the place of Hur, Baptist clergy in the position of Aaron, and the periodical's other readers as representatives of the Israelite army. The comparison illustrates West's understanding of the priesthood of all believers: the success of the periodical and its mission depended on subscribers to hold up their editor's hands and fight the battle for pure Bible doctrine by winning a share of the American print market.[2]

Warfare imagery seemed appropriate to West not only because the states of the Union were even then choosing sides for mortal combat but also because a more momentous spiritual battle was raging. Only the "despised few" joined the Old School Baptists in defending the absolute sovereignty of God and inability of humankind in salvation against the "opposing influences" of the doctrines of free will and human ability. Even other Baptists, not of the Old School, supported such causes as missions, clerical education, and Sunday schools, all of which rested upon ill-founded confidence in human ability. "This being the case, how important that each one strives in his place to speak comfortably to brethren in affliction, to cheer and encourage each other in the way, and endeavor to promote the interests of Zion by cultivating acquaintance and mutual good feeling and fellowship." Frequent communication spurred an embattled community to keep on striving against the forces that opposed true doctrine. West testified that it was a "source of great encouragement to me when I read the communication of some brother or sister. . . . I experience a fellowship of brotherhood that I feel belongs not to this world. When brethren write of the precious Saviour, and give him all the glory of the salvation of sinners, it is satisfying to me." West did not need or want to learn anything new from his reading of the *Messenger*'s correspondence columns, but he craved to hear his convictions confirmed by the repeated testimony of others who shared his understanding of the Christian life.[3]

In corresponding with the *Messenger*, West participated in a textual community that supplemented and potentially replaced relationships in a local church. Other correspondents to the *Messenger* likewise viewed themselves as taking part in a textually defined community through their acts of reading and writing the journal's columns. Texan Thomas Whitely wrote to the *Messenger* in 1857 because he sensed the importance of Christians speaking encouragement to one another. Whitely alluded to two Bible passages, Malachi 3:16 and Hebrews 10:25, to affirm that "they that feared the Lord spake often one to another" and forsook not assembling together "as the manner of some is." Although both sections of the Bible that Whitely cited assumed membership in a local congregation, he applied the injunctions to the textual community constructed by the *Messenger's* correspondence columns. Whitely admittedly did not attend a local church. Similarly, Ellison Grisham of Florida, also writing in 1857, considered it "good for children of God to speak often one to another." Rather than turning to his pastor or fellow church members for spiritual counsel, he appealed to the brethren and sisters who wrote in the *Messenger*, those from the extreme North, East, and South who could explain "disputed points of Scripture." For Whitely and Grisham, as for West, relationships within their textual community surpassed or replaced local church fellowship.[4]

The correspondence columns of the *Southern Baptist Messenger* suggest the ritual power of communication networks sustained by nineteenth-century evangelical periodicals. By conveying the same body of texts at roughly the same time to readers dispersed geographically, periodicals functioned as a surrogate for patterns of local community life that physical mobility and religious or social dissension had disrupted. Periodicals facilitated a cultural transition in which the locus of Christian community — particularly in the mobile, religiously fragmented society of nineteenth-century America — simultaneously broadened outward to embrace scattered individuals who read the same texts and narrowed inward to the domestic fireside (figure 6.1). Noting the shared linguistic roots of the terms "commonness," "communion," "community," and "communication," journalism scholar James Carey defines a ritual view of communication as the ongoing representation of shared beliefs in order to sustain an interpretive community over time. Rather than providing novel information, communication networks so employed regularly portray and confirm a particular vision of the world already assumed by its participants. Readers and writers engage in a dramatic confrontation between opposing forces — such as pure and corrupt Bible doctrine — and, even when the act of communicating does not change the outcome of this conflict, they feel satisfied by rehearsing a familiar explanation of how things are in the world.[5]

Nineteenth-century evangelical periodicals reinforced authors', editors', and readers' sense of identity as members of the priesthood of all believers. As the language used by the *Messenger's* correspondents suggests, participation in a textually defined community simultaneously strengthened denominational allegiances and individuals' sense of belonging within the church universal. Unlike democratic political sentiments, the evangelical premise that all Christians are priests has less to do with power sharing

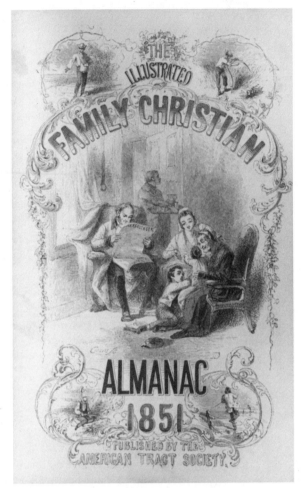

Figure 6.1.   Illustrated Family Christian Almanac (1851). Evangelical periodicals, read by
families like the one portrayed in this scene, linked textual and domestic models of
community participation. (Courtesy of the American Antiquarian Society)

than with the idea that both clergy and laity exercise influence to mediate
between the sacred Word and profane world. Conflicting interpretations of
how best to exert this influence often led to contention among and even
within denominations, as explored in chapter 5. At the same time, the
notion of a shared priesthood heightened evangelicals' sense of belonging
within a heavenbound community that, to a degree, moderated disagreements among Christians. Periodicals played a particular role in reinforcing
the priesthood ideal because of features distinctive to the form: regular

publication schedules, formats that facilitated widespread participation in shaping the evangelical canon, and simultaneous dispersion of the same ideas among geographically scattered readerships.[6]

The Ritual Significance of Regular Communication

The qualities of periodicals as words, objects, and commodities made the form useful in sustaining collective identity as the priesthood of all believers by giving scattered readers regular installments of evangelical communications. The practice of habitually sharing the latest news reaffirmed long-established ideas about how the world works. Reading extensively among current periodicals intensified the claims of underlying narrative structures that frequently reappeared in slightly varied forms. Periodicals solidified readers' sense of community by keeping them coming back for more of the same at predetermined intervals, since by definition one issue was out of date once the next appeared.

The regularity and geographic reach of periodicals marked the passage of time and provided spatial coordinates for community involvement. Nineteenth-century readers expected to know something about the style, contents, intended audience, and uses of a periodical based on its frequency of publication, whether annual, quarterly, monthly, weekly, or daily. Evangelicals produced almost every class of periodical except the daily newspaper, which most editors considered better suited to secular news than religious intelligence. Publications of each periodicity invited readers at relatively predictable intervals (despite frequent delays in printing or delivery) to view themselves as members of a textual community governed by the rules of sacred time and space.[7]

Annual publications functioned as milestones commemorating how the church had redeemed the time during the preceding year. Most denominational and nondenominational societies issued annual reports quantifying the group's recent progress. Such reports typically consisted of 50 to 100 pages of meeting notes, summaries, and statistics from each department of the sponsoring agency's operations. Annual reports appealed to a quite narrow, primarily clerical, audience and almost never reaped financial profits for their publishers. Lay Christians uninterested in all the details of the reports could hear summaries from the pulpit or read abstracts reprinted in one of the monthly magazines. Literary annuals, written in more refined styles and priced, at several dollars apiece, for wealthier audiences, preserved tributes to the progress of such Christian programs as missions, Sunday schools, and elevating literature. Catering to different audiences, both annual reports and literary annuals blended the timeliness of periodicals with the durable physical form of books to serve as keepsakes reminding Christian readers of where they had come from and where they were headed as a community of saints.[8]

Quarterly reviews marked the passing seasons, keeping readers apprised more frequently than annuals of the weighty issues facing the church. Some of the heavier reviews appealed to clergy concerned about pressing theological questions. The price for a year's subscription could run as high as five dollars, too much for the average reader to venture. Other reviews, like the *Presbyterial Reporter* (1852), called upon a larger segment of the church to follow the leading issues of the day by printing them in a form more "cheap and convenient than a book," as little as twenty-five cents a year for four sixteen-page installments. One of the most circulated reviews, the *Methodist Magazine and Quarterly Review* (1830), printed articles of "wide and permanent interest," each of which averaged 10 to 30 pages in length, for a total of 100 to 200 pages per volume. Each issue began with an extended memoir, followed by theological and practical sermons, articles, and in-depth book reviews on matters of doctrine, church government, missions, and Sunday schools, with occasional attention to topics in science and history. At the end of each year, the Methodist Book Concern, like other presses, collected its issues into a bound volume, numbering the pages consecutively as for a book.[9]

Monthly publications offered a still broader spectrum of readers frequent points of contact and more eclectic materials than did the bulkier and costlier quarterlies and annuals. The line dividing quarterlies from monthlies was not entirely clear, a fact suggested by the shifting periodicity and title of the *Methodist Magazine* (1818–28), *Methodist Magazine and Quarterly Review* (1830–40), *Methodist Quarterly Review* (1841–84), and *Methodist Review* (1885–present), published at monthly, quarterly, and bimonthly intervals. As a general rule, monthlies included shorter articles adapted to more diverse reading preferences and consequently gained larger subscription lists than did quarterlies. The editors of Virginia's *Calvinistic Magazine* (1846) advertised the monthly as occupying a cultural space in between that of the quarterly and the weekly. The magazine's prospectus boasted advantages above the "heavy quarterly publications," which were not "works for all members of the Church," while it professed to avoid the pitfalls of the dailies and weeklies, which "make slight impressions, and are not preserved." The *Calvinistic Magazine* claimed to present readable narratives that would exert a lasting influence, since "our people" want a "magazine every month, which they can take up again and again, and which will be a book for the reading of their children, in years to come." The substantial contents and material form of the magazine avowedly contributed to both its timeliness and its permanent value. The *Calvinistic Magazine* ran 32 pages, but other monthlies varied in size and price, usually falling somewhere between the 8-page Methodist *Missionary Advocate* issued for one dollar per year, and the 144-page, two-column *Harper's New Monthly*, which sold for three dollars. At either end of the range, monthly magazines offered readers frequent samplings of the diversity of texts that made up the evangelical canon.[10]

Weekly miscellanies, which surpassed monthlies for extent of circulation by the 1830s, promised to help readers regularly position their week-by-week experiences within an evangelical narrative frame. The Methodist *Christian Advocate*, initiated in 1826, grew from four to sixteen pages by 1890. The *Advocate* printed matters of "miscellaneous interest of weekly occurrence," including brief religious narratives and "lighter" articles, most of which were one or a few paragraphs long. Topics varied from the transcendent to the quotidian, such as revival and missionary intelligence; doctrine and practice; the Sabbath; Sunday schools; dueling; temperance; general news; brief memoirs; poetry; book notices; items for children, youth, and ladies; history and natural science; and, from the 1860s forward, advertisements and articles on commerce, agriculture, and the law. The *Advocate*, like other weeklies, urged evangelicals to envision their weekly life cycles within an evangelical explanatory framework.[11]

The frequency and ubiquity of weeklies, by infusing sacred influences into everyday times and spaces, made the form useful to a lay priesthood that mediated between the Word and the world. A weekly publication schedule punctuated the passage of time by the Genesis model of six days of work followed by a Sabbath rest. Evangelical periodicals — never themselves issued on a Sunday — explicitly upheld the uniqueness of the Sabbath while extending Sabbath influences beyond Sunday church services. The Methodist *Christian Advocate* (1850) devoted a regular column to the Sabbath's special claims, often reminding readers that " 'God blessed the seventh day, and sanctified it' [Genesis 2:3] — that is, he set it apart . . . from the other days of the week from secular to sacred purposes." The AME *Christian Recorder* (1865) similarly referred to the Sabbath as the "best day of the seven" because it was the only day "exclusively devoted to the concerns of eternity." An evangelical priesthood retreated from worldly concerns on the Sabbath but used periodicals to carry sacred influences to the most ordinary places throughout the week. The ABPS argued in 1870 that periodicals could play a special role in sanctifying the world since they "dwell with the people who have received them; they will travel with them; they will tell the story over and over again in the kitchen, the chamber, the closet, the shop, the railway car, the steamboat, — everywhere." Conveyed by the periodical press, the sacred Word and functionally sacred words penetrated every space on every day of the week. The sanctifying influences of religious periodicals even conquered those readers who would never have consented to attend a church service, stealing over them in "moments of calmness and reflection." In those situations when a preacher would have awakened hostility, the press penetrated "walls of prejudice." Evangelical weeklies regularly affirmed the uniquely sacred status of the Sabbath while transporting Sabbath influences into weekday living.[12]

Although evangelicals generally did not publish daily newspapers, secular dailies printed religious news as a marketing device that inadvertently strengthened evangelicals' sense of community. During the Revival of 1857–58, religion captivated secular newspaper editors. Several of the nation's most important dailies, including the *New York Tribune*, *Boston Post*, and *Charleston Daily Courier*, sold papers by broadcasting news of the revival; these reports intensified the revival as participants felt themselves, in the words of Kathryn Long, "part of a widespread, simultaneous religious event." The feature of the revival that most often attracted public notice was the popularity of noon urban prayer meetings, which spilled beyond church buildings to large auditoriums in the heart of downtown commercial districts, attended by thousands of businessmen in the middle of the workday. Although clergy and women both played important roles in the revival, it seemed most newsworthy to reporters that religion had permeated the lay, male world of business, claiming these everyday spaces and times as sacred.[13]

As an evangelical priesthood used periodicals of every frequency and provenance to sanctify their worlds, their sense of Christian community both pushed outward to embrace everyone who read the same texts and narrowed inward to a domestic center. Rev. Franklin Wilson, editor of Maryland's Baptist *True Union* (1860), regarded the periodical "as *our* pulpit," effective as a "fireside messenger of light, and truth, and love" to everyone who read the paper. The *Texas Baptist* (1855) adopted similar domestic imagery in asserting that distribution of the paper would make families everywhere "most happy as they gather around the domestic hearth, and derive rich intellectual and religious nutriment from this paper." By portraying the domestic fireside as a fulcrum for spiritual growth, editors depicted themselves as extending sacred influences to every home their papers reached.[14]

Periodicals suited a broader cultural transition in which evangelicals North and South deemphasized local church communities and centered more religious practices in the home by midcentury. Reflecting this tendency, the ATS published the *Sabbath at Home* from 1867 to 1870, a paper modeled on the widely circulated London Religious Tract Society's *Sunday at Home*. ATS editors equated home and the Sabbath as the "two precious spots of Eden, left unblighted by the curse . . . sacred enclosures of time and space on this blighted earth!" The editors likewise described the family as a "hallowed circle" where spiritual growth occurred: "A mighty process is constantly going forward which tends to blessedness and life, to usefulness and glory, that eternity alone can measure, or to their opposite." Families must therefore give careful attention to "the kind of topics of conversation, the kind of books read, the kind of visitors entertained." Toward this end, the *Sabbath at Home* asked for a "place on the Sunday-evening table. What would a family be without its Sunday evening," an oasis of "quiet, happy, instructive hours"? As more families spent their Sabbath evenings at home rather than at church, the ATS sought to infuse the domestic setting with evangelical influences. The periodical linked the family circle with a larger textual community, the members of which ideally read the same magazine at the same time every Sabbath evening.[15]

As periodicals reflected and promoted the displacement of religious practices from Sabbath church services to texts read by the domestic fireside, certain evangelicals resisted efforts to reconfigure religious meanings separate from church institutions. The Boston-issued *Sabbath at Home* made its way into the center of a thorny religious and social conflict over the meanings of Sabbath reading that raged during the 1860s and 1870s. From 1859 to 1872, many of Boston's evangelicals joined forces with non-evangelical Sabbatarians to campaign aggressively, ultimately unsuccessfully, to block the opening of the Boston Public Library on Sunday afternoons and evenings. By the early 1870s, public libraries had opened on Sundays in cities around the country, making it easier for working-class Americans to select from among religious and nonreligious texts for Sunday reading. In the view of some critics of the *Sabbath at Home*, the ATS had, in publishing the magazine, unwittingly aligned themselves with the cultural forces that threatened to desacralize the Sabbath by encouraging the reading of extrabiblical and even immoral texts on Sundays. One of the magazine's correspondents, a Presbyterian minister, felt deeply troubled by the foundational premise of the paper. This writer complained in 1867 that the magazine was replacing Bible reading with popular literature, thereby compromising the sacredness of the Sabbath and the Bible: "The book for the Sabbath is the *Bible*. But this magazine-reading and these Sunday school story-books are just crowding the Bible in our families into the background; and therefore I lamented that you published under the name you did. It was as much as saying to the world, 'Here is your profitable Sunday reading. We learned men and spiritual guides stamp it with our approbation.'" The periodical's editors printed the letter, along with a justification of the course taken: "God forbid that we should crowd the Bible into the background! . . . Even our 'Bible Recreations' alone have already greatly *promoted* the study of the Bible on the Sabbath." Indeed, "if on the Lord's Day we 'crowd' anything, it is more likely that it will be the secular magazine, the semi-religious paper, and the trashy story-book. The way to hold the Bible and religious truth in their true rank, is to keep watch of the tendencies in literature, and occupy the whole field for Christ." As an array of religious and nonreligious texts became more readily available for Sunday reading, an evangelical priesthood debated among themselves how best to occupy the whole field for Christ by infusing the world with sacred influences.[16]

The Ebb and Flow of Textual Transmission

The departmentalized format of periodical publications reinforced notions of the priesthood of all believers by inviting participation by editors, authors, and readers in shaping a fluid canon of evangelical texts. Religious and secular periodicals alike attracted and retained a loyal readership by balancing predictability and anticipation. Subscribers wanted to receive a recognizable product and yet one that offered something new with every issue. Each installment accordingly presented new material in a regular format. Most periodicals were rigidly organized into topical departments such that readers did not need to read cover to cover as they might a book. Instead, readers could expect to find the same kinds of articles in the same place at each perusal. One or more departments promised something for every potential reader. Although particular departments shifted over time, in a typical religious weekly folio the first page featured articles of religious, historical, and literary interest. The second page contained editorials; correspondence; and local, national, and international religious news pertaining to revivals, church growth, missions, and Sunday schools. The third and fourth pages introduced more miscellaneous subjects, including foreign and domestic news; market and agricultural reports; obituaries; poetry; special sections for the family, parents, ladies, youth, and children; and possibly some advertisements. Those departments the editors deemed most important or as appealing to the largest segment of readers appeared first, with departments of narrower or more ephemeral interest positioned from front to back in descending order of esteemed significance.[17]

Departmentalization heightened editorial and reader propensities to contextualize articles within the narrative frameworks of evangelicalism. David Nord has described two kinds of reader responses to religious periodicals as "cueing" and "linking." Cueing happens when an article reminds a reader of a Bible passage or elicits a conventional religious response. Linking occurs when readers make sense of one article by relating it to others to form a coherent pattern of meaning. Departmentalization stimulated both categories of response by orienting readers to interpret individual texts in the context of other articles appearing in the same department in past and future issues. The themes and tone of articles printed in any given department remained relatively consistent from one issue to the next, even as the specific contents varied. The complete set of departments printed within a periodical formed a curriculum of topics that the editors considered essential to the well-informed Christian family. In contrast to secular newspapers that were inherently arbitrary in the juxtaposition of articles connected primarily by calendrical coincidence, the editors of religious papers concerned themselves less with comprehensive coverage of the news and more with the selection and placement of the texts they deemed appropriate to the purposes of each department. Many of the articles published in evangelical papers were not news at all but serialized reprints or abstracts from evangelical steady sellers and selections from other religious and secular periodicals. Even the latest news, for instance, reports of recent revivals in a particular locality, made most sense as readers linked this intelligence with all the other reports of revivals, missions, and other aspects of church growth that they repeatedly read about in various departments of the paper. Both the continuity of articles within specific departments and the diversity of departments within the paper as a whole encouraged readers to view separate items within the context of a larger narrative structure that explained the world and the Christian's place within it.[18]

Editorial organization of texts by department rather than by literary genre loosened the control of authors over their texts by defining genre in functional instead of literary terms. Framing devices like tables of contents, titles, and subject headings interpreted texts from multiple genres as functionally sacred because they were useful in particular circumstances. The nondenominational monthly *Beauty of Holiness* organized articles under headings such as "Meditation," "Family Worship," and "Sabbath Miscellany." These headings introduced texts by when and how readers should use them rather than according to formal qualities. The same magazine customarily positioned within each department a spectrum of literary genres of older and newer derivation, including abstracts from John Bunyan's *Pilgrim's Progress*, David Brainerd's *Life*, Robert Leighton's doctrinal writings, Henry Martyn's *Memoir*, Thomas Chalmers's sermons, Charles Deems's hymns, and Harriet Beecher Stowe's letters. By positioning diverse genres within the paper's consistently departmentalized format, the editors instructed readers to privilege the uses of texts above their formal qualities or original contexts.[19]

Serialization complicated negotiations among authors, editors, and readers in the ongoing construction of the evangelical canon. Serials invited dialogue while an author might still be composing installments for future issues. Readers influenced the narrative by registering their reactions to the text in letters to the editor. Authors potentially lost control over their stories as readers and editors added their input to the evolving text. Harriet Beecher Stowe noted the responses of her readers as she was composing *Uncle Tom's Cabin*, first published serially in the *National Era* from 1851 to 1852. In a lesser known but equally revealing incident, Elizabeth Prentiss wrote and published *Pemaquid* serially in 1877 for the *Christian at Work*. While she was writing, Prentiss received conflicting advice about how to develop one of her characters, Juliet. Prentiss told a friend that her husband had "made me cut out" what she herself considered the best part of the character because he "*loathes* so to read about bad people." Prentiss's editor, Mr. Hallock, offered his own advice, having received "hundreds of letters daily" from a primarily female readership of the story. These readers, Hallock advised, wanted to hear more about Juliet and more about the marriage of another character, Ruth. Hallock urged Prentiss to heed her readers' preferences rather than her husband's or even his own, since "what do we men know about such things, anyhow?" In response to her textual community, Prentiss added another chapter to the story. In many similar situations, male and female editors and readers negotiated with authors in augmenting the evangelical canon.[20]

Editors reshaped the canon by juxtaposing divergent texts in order to reinforce theological positions that sometimes differed from those of the selected authors. The Baptist *Western Christian* for 28 June 1845, included extracts from Congregationalist revival-preacher Edward Payson and Unitarian William Ellery Channing. Payson's text described the "strange reluctance with which impenitent men yield" to gospel invitations: "Reason with them, they will not be convinced. . . . In vain have prophets prophesied."

Embracing the Calvinist doctrine of double predestination, Payson assumed that many of the impenitent were hopelessly reprobate, regardless of missionary efforts. Two pages later, the editors inserted a quotation from Channing, to the effect that parents could exert the "noblest influence" on their children's character. In contrast to Payson, Channing did not assume that the sinfulness of human nature hindered efforts to influence spiritual growth. In the columns of the *Western Christian*, the theological tenets of the two texts merged as the editor wielded both to reinforce the periodical's missionary agenda, proclaimed in large print on the paper's masthead: "Go Ye into all the World and Preach the Gospel to Every Creature" (Mark 16:15). The *Western Christian* used both Payson's and Channing's writings to confirm a Baptist interpretation of the evangelical mandate. Periodicals affiliated with other denominations similarly wielded a range of texts to promote particular versions of the evangelical canon.[21]

Editors continually reconfigured the canon through a practice prevalent in the secular as well as the religious press: exchanging papers and reprinting selected items. The same articles went "the rounds" of multiple periodicals, reappearing in the organs of other denominations and in distant regions. Especially for editors who lacked an adequate pool of contributors, exchanges provided new sources of quality material to print. The Methodist *Southern Lady's Companion* (1848) was typical in preferring original articles to selections of equal value and the "good selection" over the "inferior original." Since editors generally neglected to pay authors or other papers for selections, copying articles was also economical; according to an estimate by the AME *Christian Recorder* (1868), selections cost a fifth the price of originals. Even though a federal copyright law was passed in 1790 and strengthened in 1831, few periodicals copyrighted their materials until *Graham's* and *Godey's* began the practice in 1845, and an international copyright law did not pass until 1891. Evangelicals, presuming the shared ownership of texts by the Christian community, were relatively slow to follow suit by copyrighting their materials. Some evangelicals continued to debate the legitimacy of copyright through the end of the century.[22]

Periodical exchanges encouraged cross-fertilization between evangelical and nonevangelical reading communities. The *Beauty of Holiness* (1855) regularly copied texts from *Frederick Douglass' Paper*, even though the latter did not have an evangelical affiliation. Sharing a commitment to the antislavery cause constituted a sufficient basis for cooperation. AME member Frances Ellen Watkins Harper wrote one of the poems printed in *Frederick Douglass' Paper* in 1855; the *Beauty of Holiness* reprinted the poem, which elaborates on Psalm 68:31, shortly thereafter:

> Yes, Ethiopia yet shall stretch
> Her bleeding hands abroad;
> Her cry of agony shall reach
> The burning throne of God.

Harper's membership in both African American and evangelical communities enabled her to address audiences that partially overlapped.[23]

Readers worked with editors to select articles reprinted from other publications. The practice of selectively reprinting texts from steady sellers and recent issues of other periodicals contributed to the sedimentation of the evangelical canon as readers and editors repeatedly privileged similar texts. Juxtaposing older and newer texts also established rules for legitimate innovation by marking the more recent selections as appropriate additions to the canon. In seeking an extensive readership, editors tried to include something for everyone, provided that no selection strayed too far from values already shared by the paper's anticipated readership. Hoping to win and keep their audience's attention, editors opted for shorter over longer articles, usually representing a variety of topics and genres. Editors called upon readers for assistance in culling materials from other sources by requesting contributors to excerpt passages from longer texts and submit them for reprinting. The *Western Presbyterian* (1864) urged readers to look for useful texts pasted or summarized in their scrapbooks. The *Sabbath at Home* (1867) asked readers to draw "their pencils around choice paragraphs" so as to share these passages "with their friends" through the magazine. Reader input to periodical contents privileged certain portions of the evangelical canon as particularly useful. One reader's judgment of which paragraphs were choice, confirmed by the paper's editor, led other readers to privilege the same passages over other sections that, given the original, different readers might have instead selected for themselves. Periodical contributors joined with editors in arbitrating between authors and readers, continually redrawing the boundaries of the evangelical canon.[24]

Lay Participation and Clerical Regulation

Alexis de Tocqueville, the best-known foreign critic of antebellum American culture, articulated a theory to explain the abundance of periodicals that cluttered the American landscape by the 1830s: "Newspapers do not multiply simply because they are cheap, but according to the more or less frequent need felt by a great number of people to communicate with one another and to act together." As was so often the case when Tocqueville rendered judgment, he astutely diagnosed the usefulness of American periodicals in strengthening participatory communication networks. Periodicals dissolved geographic and temporal barriers to community by dropping, in Tocqueville's words, "the same thought into a thousand minds at the same moment." The geographic reach and speed of periodical distribution made the form useful to evangelical clergy concerned with both encouraging and regulating lay involvement in denominational and evangelical communication networks.[25]

Editors helped readers to see themselves as belonging to the priesthood of all believers by endorsing active lay support of denominational periodicals. The AME *Repository of Religion and Literature, and of Science and Art* (1863) asked all AME church members to "sustain *your* own cause" by subscribing and canvassing for the paper. The *Western Presbyterian* (1864) invited both pastors and laity "living in different sections of the country" to mail reports of "general religious intelligence and local news" in order to aid Presbyterians living in various regions to feel more connected with one another. The *Baptist Layman* (1894) similarly requested its readers "to drop us a postal card giving any church news," including notes on baptisms, building repairs, protracted meetings, and lectures. Subscribing to periodicals and sharing local news involved lay readers in promoting conversation among scattered churches and individuals.[26]

Even as clerical editors solicited readers' contributions, they regulated published communications. The Methodist *Christian Advocate* (1840; 1870) called for "sensible, well written articles" by lay correspondents. "But," the editors clarified, "let it be distinctly understood, that, in giving this general invitation, we do not send out a request to unskillful and inexperienced writers to try their hand in the way of a written composition." Every article would be "subject to examination, and rejection or adoption, as the editors may think fit" and, if adopted, "subject to revision and occasional abridgement." Editors presumed that texts printed in periodicals belonged to the entire textual community rather than to specific authors; consequently, editors felt no inhibition in altering texts to make them more useful. Often only a single sentence seemed suitable for publication. On the other hand, one word "printed and published in thousands of copies," if ill chosen, could influence souls to "wander from the good and right way." The *Advocate*'s editors saw themselves as arbitrating between authors and readers. They felt "accountable, not only to men, but to God" for watching "with a jealous eye" over the "purity and peace of the Church" and the "present and eternal welfare of thousands of individuals" who read their paper. For "what is the business of the editors but to read, examine, and judge whether an article is, or is not, respectable in its literature, sound in its theology, wholesome in its tendency, and proper, all things considered, to be given the public?" Clerical editors positioned themselves as mediators among lay participants in a textually defined community.[27]

The regulatory impulse of clerical editors stemmed from their view of publishing as an extension of their ministerial duties. Most editors of denominational papers were either ordained ministers or elders in local congregations. The editor of the AME *Christian Recorder* (1886), portraying himself as acting in a pastoral capacity, advised correspondents to write with questions about sermons printed in the paper or concerning any other subject. Similarly, the editor of the Methodist *Christian Advocate* (1890) offered to answer any query. One correspondent wanted to know the biblical reference for a text cited by his minister. The editor responded that his inquirer could not find the verse because an ill-informed preacher had mistakenly quoted an extrabiblical text as Scripture! In this and similar instances, clerical editors presented themselves as religious experts, supplementing and at times correcting the views of lay correspondents or the pastoral counsel given by local ministers. Even as such minister-editors bolstered their own authority, they also taught lay readers to become more critical and demanding of their religious leaders and less dependent on any one minister for information.[28]

In soliciting correspondence from lay readers, clerical editors depicted themselves as cultivating pastoral relationships with geographically expansive congregations. Rev. Henry Keeling of the Virginia *Baptist Preacher* (1844), the most successful denominational periodical to specialize in printing sermons, worried that local congregations did not always enjoy a relationship of "intimate friendship and confidence" with their preachers. Addressing his "Beloved Patrons and Readers" in 1857, Keeling claimed to "feel towards you as a pastor does towards his people." He informed his congregation of readers that "by your subscription to the paper, you in a manner place yourselves in our parish — take a pew in our church — set before us on your seat, while we preach the gospel to you." Keeling conceived of relationships within his metaphorical congregation as more intimate than those most preachers established with their flocks. Keeling made pastoral visits by responding to correspondents who wrote to him expressing "something of the personal, individual effects" of his ministry. In reprinting sermons, Keeling preached "not from the pulpit, as you might sit away off some twenty or sixty feet — but at your fireside, in your own parlor face to face, as friend with friend or brother with brother." Keeling's rhetorical style of conversational address offered an alternative to Sunday morning preaching. According to Keeling's model of the pastoral relation, a preacher stimulated religious growth by speaking as a friend to others in his textual community, the members of which sat imaginatively gathered around the domestic fireside. Evangelical periodicals, because of the speed with which they permitted communication among scattered church adherents, facilitated both lay involvement and clerical regulation of the evangelical textual community.[29]

Evangelical Women and the Priesthood of All Believers

Evangelical assumptions about the priesthood of all believers opened some room for participation in a textually defined community by members of politically disempowered groups such as women and African Americans. Editors requested women and men to contribute to correspondence columns or send in choice extracts for reprinting. One of the *Southern Baptist Messenger's* (1859) male correspondents, Abel Phelps, welcomed "precious fruits" from the minds and pens of his "brothers and sisters." Women comprised a substantial and growing segment of the authors who regularly wrote for periodicals. By 1860, most periodicals had discontinued the long-standing practice of anonymous publication. Signed articles revealed the gender and, in an increasing number of cases, the professional status of contributing authors. Magazines usually included departments that many nineteenth-century Americans associated with women's sphere, embracing articles addressed to ladies, mothers, parents, families, youth, and children. Periodicals targeted to women constituted a notable exception to the rule that most editors were clergymen. Perhaps sixty to ninety specialized women's periodicals were published from 1850 to 1865, or roughly 2 to 4 percent of the total, and many of these papers had unordained female editors. Sarah Josepha Hale (1788–1879), a high church Episcopalian, was one of the first and most popular editors of women's periodicals that embodied refined literary sensibilities. Editing the *Ladies' Magazine*, founded in 1828, and its successor, *Godey's Lady's Book*, until 1877, Hale developed a national reputation. Some of America's best-known literary figures, women and men, contributed poetry, fiction, and moral essays to *Godey's*, where the articles appeared accompanied by high-fashion illustrations.[30]

Evangelicals published women's papers modeled after *Godey's* but designed to instruct women to prefer articles more evangelical in content and style. Mrs. S. R. Ford, editor of the *Baptist Family Visitant* (1857), urged women readers to exchange the "light" literature of popular magazines for the "beautiful and good" articles, fact stories, and essays that she published

gentile

in her paper. Indeed, critics like Ford often faulted women readers for pretensions to gentility that gave them a taste for superficial eloquence lacking in real culture or piety. Ford's husband edited an analogue to the *Visitant*, the *Christian Repository*, but did not articulate a similar agenda for the reform of men's reading habits. S. H. Ford assumed that his male readers would already desire "critical, exegetical, and theological essays" and histories. The Fords' expectations about their readers reflected beliefs widespread among nineteenth-century evangelicals that different kinds of religious reading suited men and women and that women readers required closer oversight than men did.[31]

Evangelical periodicals invited women to actualize the priesthood of all believers by writing articles for other women. Caroline Hiscox, a Baptist minister's wife and editor of New York's nondenominational *Mothers' Journal* (1860), saw her magazine as a medium through which mothers could influence one another's progress in holiness by sharing their experiences. The "thousands of mothers who read the *Journal*, could briefly narrate some circumstance in their own experience, or in their observation of the history of others, which would be of interest and profit to thousands of our readers." As with the memoirs discussed in chapter 3, Christian experience rather than theological training or social status qualified women to influence other readers of the *Journal*. Hiscox asked mothers to relate anecdotes illustrating such themes as the benefits of religious reading in the family and the importance of good domestic government, local examples of revivals or religious destitution, and the good effects or great need for Sunday schools. Adopting a regulatory stance parallel to that assumed by male editors, Hiscox advised her potential contributors that if their submissions were "not exactly in shape for printing," she would arrange them properly. Women editors such as Hiscox both supported and guided the activity of other women in geographically expansive, gender-segregated communication networks.[32]

Periodicals edited by and for women fostered a sense of community involvement that promised to alleviate the domestic isolation that many nineteenth-century women experienced. Hiscox described the *Mothers' Journal* in relational language as a "valuable household friend and companion" and a "helper to all families." The conversational space of the *Journal*'s correspondence columns provided an alternative to more formal sermonic or literary discourse over which men usually presided. Through the paper's correspondence columns, "many of our readers would be brought into close and friendly contact with each other as well as with us. . . . Let us hear from many more, in different parts of the country. We wish to talk freely

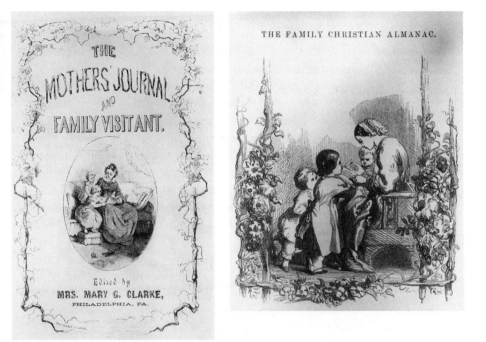

Figure 6.2.   The *Mothers' Journal and Family Visitant* (1856) and the *Family Christian Almanac* (1869). Periodicals designated for the family circle encouraged mothers, who were surrounded by children but isolated from adult companionship, to exert a moral influence at home. (Courtesy of the American Antiquarian Society)

with them on these subjects, as we should if we could sit down in their homes with them for an hour, and converse without restraint." Conventional language compared correspondence in the journal's columns with conversations transacted in more personal domestic settings, spaces designated by middle-class Americans as suited to women's moral influence (figure 6.2). Hiscox and others like her offered participants in a women's community of print relief from domestic and religious isolation.[33]

African American Uses of Textual Community

The textual community imagined by white evangelicals allowed slimmer room for participation by African Americans than by white women. Periodicals edited by both northern and southern whites did occasionally report the progress of the church among blacks, often promoting racist ideas in the process. The northern *Beauty of Holiness* (1856) reviewed a sermon delivered by an African American preacher amid similar reviews of white ministers, patronizingly though appreciatively characterizing the black minister's address as "eloquent." As Christine Heyrman has argued, the predilection of southern whites for celebrating black spirituality stemmed from deeply negative assumptions about the natural abilities of blacks unaided by supernatural assistance. With typical condescension, the Methodist *Southern Lady's Companion* (1848) printed a fictional narrative of a Methodist slave named "Old Cato" to demonstrate the slave's influence on the conversion of his masters and implicitly to condone a slave system that permitted such influence to occur. Old Cato consistently prayed for his young master George and finally succeeded in bringing him to a Methodist camp meeting. At the meeting, a black preacher, with stereotyped "African eloquence" and deference toward whites, addressed the congregation on the text "Come unto me, all ye that labour and are heavy laden, and I will give you rest," taken from Matthew 11:28 — a passage that some whites used to justify slave labor. George experienced a religious conversion at the meeting because of the prayers of Old Cato. As a result, George's parents disowned him, and he became a Methodist preacher. Twenty-five years later, George's preaching became the instrument of his aged parents' conversion, the long-delayed result of Old Cato's fervent prayers. The meanings of the story were certainly complex: rebuking the racism and servitude of the "cold and icy regions of the frigid north" and reinforcing the slave system, although acknowledging black evangelicals as "brothers in the Lord Jesus Christ." Despite white affirmation of black membership in the priesthood of all believers, white control of evangelical communication media in many instances nullified recognition of a shared spiritual status.[34]

As with women's specialty periodicals, black evangelicals carved out the largest space for written expression through periodicals owned, edited, and targeted primarily to African Americans. A free black Presbyterian minister, Rev. Samuel Cornish, along with another free black, John Russwurm, founded the first African American newspaper, *Freedom's Journal*, in 1827, in protest against the refusal of white editors to allow black evangelicals to print articles in their papers. The AME *Christian Recorder* was the first enduring periodical owned and edited by African Americans, beginning operations in 1848 and remaining in continuous publication until the present day (figure 6.3). Although the *Recorder* seldom counted more than 5,000 subscribers at any one time, the periodical exerted an influence well beyond these numbers since families shared copies of the paper and relayed its intelligence by word of mouth. As of 1886, black Baptists edited and published fourteen religious periodicals; most of these papers had short life spans, but as one perished others rose to replace it.[35]

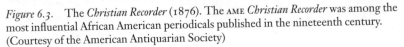

Figure 6.3. The *Christian Recorder* (1876). The AME *Christian Recorder* was among the most influential African American periodicals published in the nineteenth century. (Courtesy of the American Antiquarian Society)

An explosive failure at interracial cooperation in 1890 further stimulated African American Baptist publishing. ABPS director Benjamin Griffith invited three prominent black Baptist ministers, William J. Simmons, Emmanuel K. Love, and William H. Brooks, to publish doctrinal articles in the society's Sunday school periodical, the *Baptist Teacher*. Southern whites, warning that the proposal would encourage "wickedly ambitious" blacks, pressured Griffith to withdraw the offer and then seceded from the ABPS anyway to form a rival society. Despite ABPS efforts to appease southern blacks by hiring more African American agents and printing doctrinal texts written by blacks in other venues, the incident contributed to the founding of the black separatist National Baptist Convention in 1895 and the National Baptist Publishing Board in 1896.[36]

In consequence of ongoing white oppression and racism, the periodicals published by black evangelicals served a community defined in both social and religious terms. One of the earliest black newspapers, the *Colored American* (1837), printed "lessons of instruction on religion and morals, lessons on industry and economy — until our entire people are of one heart and of one mind, in all the means of their *salvation, both temporal and spiritual*." The editors viewed temporal and spiritual progress toward salvation as inseparable given the social conditions of black Christians in the present world. The aspirations of black middle-class editors for respectability induced them to reject vernacular forms of expression when they spoke in public venues. Periodicals such as the AME *Repository of Religion and Literature, and of Science and Art*, published from 1858 until 1863, and the AME *Church Review*, published from 1884 to the present, refuted white stereotypes and aided the social ascendancy of blacks by exhibiting intellectual refinement.

African American periodicals, like many of the black-edited hymnals discussed in chapter 7, subordinated vernacular linguistic traditions in order to express a refined aesthetic calculated to win black acceptance within the white evangelical mainstream.[37]

Black evangelical editors urged a lay priesthood to demonstrate their achievements to critical white observers by supporting the black periodical press. The *Anglo-African Magazine*, published from 1859 to 1865, portrayed itself as meeting the need for an "independent voice" to represent the views of black evangelicals. In order to "assert and maintain their rank as men among men," African American publishers, editors, and contributors had to "speak for themselves; no outside tongues, however gifted with eloquence, can tell their story." The AME *Repository of Religion and Literature, and of Science and Art* (1862) similarly made the case for publications produced entirely by "colored men and women." The textual community created by the periodical press provided a space for black evangelicals to narrate their experiences and attainments, unmediated by white editorial interventions.[38]

The task of sustaining black periodicals required clergy and laity alike to subscribe to (and pay for) papers edited by blacks in preference to others and to contribute articles for publication. The Baptist *African Expositor* (1880) asked all black "ministers, Sabbath and public school teachers, and friends generally" to support the paper: "Its life depends upon you." The AME *Christian Recorder* (1854) called for lay readers, including the "self-taught and the self-educated," to discuss the most important religious questions: "Come, clergy and laity, come friends, one and all . . . let us hear what you have to say upon these great questions" of establishing the "Redeemer's kingdom upon the earth." The *Recorder* offered "the people" means to communicate their thoughts "to the church and the world," including the world inhabited by white evangelicals. Periodicals, the American National Baptist Convention noted in 1887, could fall into the hands of those "not of our way of thinking." Even the black woman preacher could gain an audience: "Here she can command the attention of thousands. She can thunder from the editor's chair and make the people hear." The *Recorder* (1862) likewise acted as a "silent, but most efficient missionary," going "where the colored preacher or teacher is seldom, if ever, heard of, much less, suffered to speak," even entering the parlors of white "ladies and gentlemen." Unable to gain a hearing among most whites in local communities even after emancipation, African Americans used the periodical press to demonstrate their abilities to participate in evangelical print culture.[39]

Like P. West of the Old School *Southern Baptist Messenger*, many evangelicals used periodicals ritually to envision themselves as active participants in the priesthood of all believers. Linking domestic and textual models of community, periodicals intensified both denominational and evangelical identities. Regular publication schedules, by positioning ordinary times and spaces within a sacred narrative framework, aided a lay priesthood in mediating between the Word and the world. The departmentalized format of periodicals invited the input of clergy, authors, editors, and readers in shaping a fluid canon of texts that reinforced evangelical narrative structures. By minimizing geographic and temporal barriers to community, periodicals strengthened both lay involvement and clerical regulation of extensive communication networks. Members of politically disempowered groups such as women and African Americans adapted the priesthood ideal to carve out space for public expression in a textually defined evangelical community. As evangelicals used periodicals to contend for the faith and to act as the priesthood of all believers, they transmitted and sustained a distinctive print culture across space and over time. Even as evangelicals used periodicals to enter the world of the American print market, they looked to other classes of texts for help in traveling through the world without succumbing to its corruption. Hymnals, the subject of chapters 7 and 8, aided evangelicals in this effort to sanctify their world while journeying as a unified pilgrim community.

7

Singing with the Spirit
and the Understanding

William Aitchison, of the Presbyterian mission to China, lay on his death-bed. Some of his fellow travelers to Zion, missionaries from other de-nominations, visited him for the last time in 1864. Aitchison used the cher-ished opportunity for their mutual benefit in the way he best knew how: he exhorted his visitors to make their "calling and election sure." To encour-age them in journeying toward Zion, and to reaffirm his own membership in their pilgrim community, Aitchison requested that they sing together some of his favorite hymns: "All Hail the Power of Jesus' Name," "When I Can Read My Title Clear," and "There Is a Land of Pure Delight." As his friends sang, Aitchison "attempted to join with his feeble faltering voice." The group paused from time to time for him to repeat from memory "such passages as he was still able to recollect." The singers, fortified to persevere in their own pilgrimage by the corporate rehearsal of "exceeding great and precious promises," dismissed Aitchison to "rest from earth's toilsome strife, / till God shall wake me to endless life."[1]

In countless situations such as this, nineteenth-century evangelicals used hymns to solidify their membership in a pilgrim community traveling from this world toward the holiness of heaven. By 1892, British and American publishers had introduced an estimated 40,000 English-language hymns and reprinted many of them in hundreds of different collections used across denominational lines. The hymn-writing impulse transcended national and linguistic boundaries. During the nineteenth century alone, publishers sponsored approximately 400,000 Christian hymns, the great majority of them evangelical in theme and tone, in 200 different languages. This chap-ter asks how evangelicals used hymns to sanctify the world of nineteenth-century America as they traveled to a better world. Chapter 8 considers the roles played by hymnal editors, compilers, and translators in shaping hymn texts for the purpose of unifying the pilgrim community.[2]

Hymns occupied a privileged position in the evangelical canon because of their presumed effectiveness in interfacing biblical doctrine with Christian experience, thereby linking the Word with the world. In the language of Brian Stock, hymns offered "procedural knowledge," a script that taught singers how to connect theology with their own attitudes and behavior. By drawing out the "inner meaning and spiritual application of Scripture," hymns, in the evaluation of nineteenth-century evangelicals, made doctrine more practical than could biblical commentaries or sermons. Evangelicals viewed hymns as expressing "the uttered testimony of the whole brotherhood" of Christians more richly than "the best teachings of any single Christian man." Hymns stimulated religious devotion and functioned as a "guardian of a sound faith," preserving theology against "doctrinal aberration" and "spiritual declension." Even clergy acknowledged that hymns could be more influential in shaping morals than "a thousand tracts and sermons" or "vast tomes of theology." Some hymnal editors introduced their collections with a quotation from the Anglican George Herbert: "A verse may find him who a sermon flies." Accordingly, ministers began and ended sermons with hymn singing, quoted from hymns while preaching, and even wrote hymns to reinforce sermon messages. Evangelicals used hymns during Sunday church services, at midweek interdenominational prayer and praise meetings, in private devotions and family worship, and at camp meetings, revivals, and gospel-song services. Children memorized hymns before they could read, and the aged recited hymns on their deathbeds.[3]

Hymns functioned in evangelical print culture as one of several overlapping genres of texts that influenced progress along a heavenward journey. Evangelicals saw hymns as one "department of Christian literature," intimately connected with other branches of publishing. Many of the same authors and editors published texts in multiple genres and forms, for instance, writing hymns, contributing to periodicals, and composing novels or memoirs. When Harriet Beecher Stowe realized the success of *Uncle Tom's Cabin*, she felt a "wonderful consciousness of God's presence" and responded by writing a hymn: "Still, Still with Thee, When Purple Morning Breaketh," published in 1855.[4]

The frequency with which other classes of texts referenced hymns or embedded hymns within their own narrative structures suggests the genre's centrality to evangelical textual practices. Periodicals testified that hymns resulted in conversions and growth in grace, and they recommended hymns appropriate for settings such as private devotions or social meetings. Novels incorporated hymns in dialogue between characters. Whenever the protagonist in Elizabeth Prentiss's *Stepping Heavenward* found that her own words failed her, she quoted lines from favorite hymns. In conversing with a dying, unconverted friend named Amelia, Katy wanted to "ask her if, when earthly refuge failed her, she could not find shelter in the love of Christ. But I have what is, I fear, a morbid terror of seeking the confidence of others." Rather than lose the opportunity to influence Amelia on account of her timidity, Katy repeated "two lines from a hymn of which I am very fond: 'O Saviour, whose mercy, severe in its kindness, / Hath chastened my wanderings, and guided my way.'" Katy used the hymn to urge Amelia to interpret her sickness as a severe but merciful warning from God to cease wandering from the way of salvation. Memoirs, such as William Aitchison's, used hymns to document the language of the dying soul and thus urge forward the feet of a pilgrim community and allure others to begin traveling toward heaven.[5]

Although sharing characteristics with other evangelical genres, hymns functioned in distinctive ways to infuse the world with sacred influences. The hymns canonized by nineteenth-century evangelicals were poems sung or read in worship of God that were remarkably nonspecific as to time, place, or circumstance of composition, instead expressing sentiments that any Christian could affirm. Unlike temporal narratives such as those found in novels, memoirs, or periodicals in which a sequence of events produces a different situation at the end than at the beginning, hymns articulated atemporal narrative structures that merged separate events into an overall explanatory pattern. Evangelicals used hymns to rehearse a universalizing framework that sanctified everyday life experiences as significant within a larger story of God's redemptive purposes for the world. Writing, reading, and singing hymns extended the reach of the evangelical textual community to embrace every event when people used hymns: on Sundays and weekdays, at church and at home, from early childhood to the deathbed, in all moments and places of experience. Hymns acquired ritual significance as evangelicals intoned them in the context of relationships with others in their textual and local communities to order daily experiences and formulate connections between embedded narratives and the details of everyday life. By repeatedly performing hymn narratives, evangelicals reenacted the story of divine redemption and intensified that story's authority to infuse the world of nineteenth-century America with sacred influences.[6]

As evangelicals used hymns to sanctify the world, they struggled to rec-

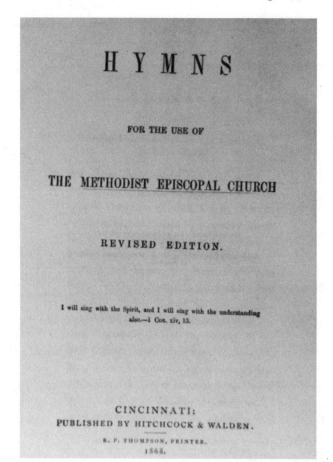

Figure 7.1. *Hymns for the Use of the Methodist Episcopal Church* (1868). The title pages of many nineteenth-century evangelical hymnals quoted 1 Corinthians 14:15: "I will sing with the spirit, and I will sing with the understanding also." (Used by permission of the University of Missouri–Kansas City Libraries, Kenneth J. LaBudde Department of Special Collections)

oncile overlapping alternatives for how to understand and wield sacred language. In contexts as diverse as church services, private devotions, and camp meetings, evangelicals envisioned themselves as modeling their use of hymns after Paul's example: "I will sing with the spirit, and I will sing with the understanding also." This verse, 1 Corinthians 14:15, more frequently adorned the title pages of nineteenth-century hymn collections than did any other epigraph (figure 7.1). For midcentury evangelicals, the effort to balance the spirit and the understanding brought competing aesthetics of sacred language into tension: ontologically and functionally sacred words, oral and literate expression, African and European traditions, and vernacular and refined styles. Evangelical print culture embraced and partially reconciled all of these alternatives as a pilgrim community strained after purity and presence in the world while traveling home toward heaven.

The Rise of Congregational Hymn Singing

Mid-nineteenth-century evangelicals understood congregational hymn singing as bringing Christians as close to heaven as they could come on earth. Social worship foreshadowed the heavenly worship of the church universal because it combined the "separate devotion of each particular person present, with the sense of Christian brotherhood, binding them all together." Such an exalted view of corporate hymn singing had not always characterized evangelicalism; rather, the ideal emerged through a lengthy struggle to preserve the uniquely sacred status of the Word while defining a widening range of words as functioning to convey sacred influences.[7]

The history of hymns in the Judeo-Christian tradition began with practices prescribed in the Hebrew canon. The third division of the Scriptures, the Writings, includes a collection of 150 texts named *Tehillim*, a term that can be translated as psalms, hymns, or songs of praise. Early Jewish worship involved psalm singing, accompanied by musical instruments, in thanksgiving and praise to God. At the time of Christ, choirs led complex rituals of temple worship, designating particular songs for each day of the week and special occasions. The New Testament depicts continuity between Jewish worship traditions and those of the early Christian church. Following Jesus' final meal with his disciples, the group sang a hymn together. Paul's letter to the Colossians taught Christians how to use hymns to experience the living Word after the resurrection: "Let the *word* of Christ dwell in you richly in all wisdom; teaching and admonishing one another in psalms and hymns and spiritual songs, singing with grace in your hearts to the Lord." The early church used the word of Christ, expressed through psalms, hymns, and spiritual songs, to strengthen their community after Jesus had departed from the world.[8]

Christian churches continued to sing selections from the Psalms, as well as hymns composed by extrabiblical authors, up until the Reformation. Martin Luther wrote new hymns in his efforts to reform the church. Luther's followers in Germany developed an extensive hymn writing and singing tradition. John Calvin, by contrast, encouraged the singing of metrical translations of the Psalms to simple one-line melodies but worried that extrabiblical hymns might introduce heresy into the church. Calvin insisted that the Bible alone should provide the basis for congregational worship, as for every other church practice. Luther and Calvin agreed that the Holy Spirit was present in a special way to illuminate the Word when Christians read the Bible as opposed to any other text. But Calvin more sharply differentiated between the sacred Word and profane words, even when Christians employed the latter to worship God. Calvin's distinction between sacred and profane language influenced both the Church of England and dissenters, who consequently restricted congregational worship to recitation of the Psalms.[9]

During the seventeenth century, the boundary separating the Word from words softened as members of a lay priesthood shaped their own worship practices. English Protestants, especially dissenters from the established church, wrote increasingly complex metrical paraphrases of the Psalms. The paraphrasers modified the wording of translations from the Hebrew, using poetic language to incline singers' affections heavenward. British publishers introduced more than 300 different Psalm versions during the seventeenth and eighteenth centuries, primarily for use in private devotions and social gatherings and only secondarily for chanting or singing during congregational worship. The very first book printed in the American colonies was the *Bay Psalm Book*, published in Cambridge, Massachusetts, in 1640. Two Irishmen, Nahum Tate, a playwright, and Nicholas Brady, an Anglican vicar, composed the most popular psalmbook in Britain and its colonies, *A New Version of the Psalms of David: Fitted to the Tunes Used in Churches* (1696).[10]

The nonconformist minister Isaac Watts (1674–1748) went a step beyond writing Psalm paraphrases by composing hymns designed to be sung in church. Watts published a nondenominational collection, *Hymns and Spiritual Songs*, in 1707. The hymns gained such popularity among diverse congregations, even in America, that when the Deist Benjamin Franklin opened his printing shop, Watts's was the first book he produced, in 1729. By the middle of the nineteenth century, publishers had distributed nearly 650 editions of Watts in Britain and America, and Watts's hymns had made their way into most collections, regardless of the compiler's denominational affiliation.[11]

During the religious revivals of the mid-eighteenth century, hymns gained increasing prominence in congregational worship. Charles Wesley and John Wesley wrote thousands of hymns for use in Methodist meetings, many of which attained extensive circulation throughout the transatlantic revivals. John Wesley published his first hymnbook, a nondenominational

Collection of Psalms and Hymns, in 1736–37 while traveling in Georgia. Of the seventy hymns included in the volume, Watts wrote more than a third, and John or Charles Wesley wrote or translated the remainder. As evangelical denominations expanded during the nineteenth century, use of extra-biblical hymns in worship grew correspondingly. During the Second Great Awakening, the Congregationalist minister Joshua Leavitt published *The Christian Lyre* (1831) for use in Charles Finney's revival meetings. Unlike the majority of previous collections, the *Lyre* positioned texts and tunes side by side instead of in separate volumes in order to make congregational singing easier.[12]

By introducing hymns into church services, evangelicals descending from the Calvinist wing of the Reformation, beginning with the Psalm paraphrasers and more decisively with Watts, moved from an ontological to a functional view of sacred language. Watts argued that, in certain respects, hymns surpassed the Psalms because of their usefulness in expressing the New Testament gospel. The Presbyterian minister James Murray, in an 1869 sermon on "Christian Hymnology," attributed to hymns a functionally sacred status. Murray, intent upon preserving the unique reputation of the Bible as the Word of God, distinguished sharply between an "inspired psalmody" and an "uninspired Christian hymnology." Even Psalm versions differed fundamentally from the Bible, since compilers added "human measure and human rhyme" to "such compositions as *God gave them*." Denying that the Holy Spirit inspired hymns in the same way as the Bible, Murray argued that the usefulness of hymns in moving the "soul to heavenly communion" nevertheless marked them with a "seal of divine approval" as, in a sense, sacred or heavenly.[13]

Murray understood sacred language in a twofold sense: as embracing the Word inspired by the Holy Spirit and a wider range of words through which the Holy Spirit acted to infuse the world with sacred influences. Because hymns grew out of their authors' interactions with the "living Word of God," hymn language conveyed the "spirit of God." The uninspired hymn carried the "Spirit of inspiration in it and which exhales from it" to sanctify its surroundings. The Methodist George Stevenson, writing in 1883, likewise positioned hymns as "merely human compositions" that yet possessed "something like inspiration." Hymns seemed to Stevenson closely akin to inspired Scripture since they moved Christians to encounter the living Word through worship. For Stevenson as for Murray, hymns passed a functional, though not an ontological, test for sacred language by carrying the sanctifying influences of the Holy Spirit into the world of human experience.[14]

Devotional Hymn Writing, Reading, and Memorization

As with the textual interactions explored in chapter 4, evangelicals worried as much about sanctifying the processes of hymn usage as they did about the words themselves. For evangelicals who wrote, read, and memorized hymns in the context of private devotions, ritualized textual practices sustained a sense of personal connection among participants in an increasingly impersonal print market. Because "some soul has lived" them, hymns offered "warm encouragement to devotion" in others by awakening "religious feeling" and stirring "kindred emotions." Hymn writers influenced others in their textual community by putting into words their own encounters with the living Word. The process of hymn composition connected religious feelings with appropriate linguistic representations since hymnists adopted diction and poetic structures that aptly captured their experiences.[15]

As hymnal publishing became a "branch of popular literature" grossing millions of dollars by the late nineteenth century, evangelicals feared that the market could desanctify the language of hymnody. Viewing hymn writing as a devotional activity mediated by the Holy Spirit, evangelicals wondered whether language could still convey a sacred influence when words flowed rapidly, without time for prayer or meditation. Rather than growing out of authors' sanctified religious feelings, so deep that they had to be written, critics warned that hymns were increasingly made "to order" for market-conscious publishers. As one minister cautioned, "Too many hymn-books have been made with the market as well as the church in view." Such books were merely "wares to sell" rather than repositories of the author's encounter with the living Word.[16]

Hymnists responded to their critics by representing themselves as resisting market pressures to truncate the writing process. The defenses that successful hymn writers felt called upon to make illuminate evangelical assumptions about how hymn writing should be conducted in order to convey a sacred influence. Fanny Crosby (1820–1915), the Methodist author of over 8,000 published hymns — the highest number attributed to any single writer — often created hymn texts to match melodies played for her while her publishers literally sat waiting for the product (figure 7.2). In her 1906 autobiography, Crosby denied that financial motivations had compromised the processes by which she composed hymns. Although blind almost from birth, Crosby insisted that rather than writing to earn money, she had donated her royalties (which never amounted to more than a dollar or two per hymn) to "worthy causes." Crosby defended herself by claiming that even though she had written a great number of hymns, she wrote all of

Figure 7.2. Fanny Crosby (ca. 1895). Although blind almost from birth, Crosby was the most prolific published hymn writer of all time. (Courtesy of the University of Missouri–Columbia)

them in a sanctified manner. Her "most enduring hymns" were "born in the silences of the soul, and nothing must be allowed to intrude while they are being framed into language." She often wrote "during the long night watches, when the distractions of the day could not interfere with the rapid flow of thought." Crosby attested that some of her hymns had been "dictated by the blessed Holy Spirit" and that others resulted from "deep meditation." Even in writing hymns to assigned melodies, the compositions "seemed to express the experience" of the tune writer as well as to reflect her own experience. Crosby framed her writing as a sacred activity through which the Holy Spirit flowed to influence those who used her hymns.[17]

Evangelicals who read or sang hymns during private devotions, like those who wrote hymns, ritually participated in a textual community through which hymns conveyed sacred influences. By meditating slowly and repeatedly on hymns sung at other times in company with others, individuals prepared for personal engagement in the worship of the gathered congregation by taking the words "more closely to the heart" and internalizing a shared cultural vocabulary. For the individual unable to enjoy fellowship with a local congregation, hymns compensated for physical isolation by invoking an imagined pilgrim community. Alone in the East African wilderness, Anglican bishop James Hannington could often be heard singing "some old familiar . . . Christian hymn" of "peace, perfect peace." Participation in a textually constituted community through hymn singing allowed Hannington to experience a reassuring spiritual connection with other Christians who cherished the same hymns.[18]

Private devotional reading coupled individuals' sense of membership in an expansive textual community with a narrower domestic locus for the practice of piety. "In the hour of secret prayer," hymns sanctified the most mundane times and spaces as sacred. Used at the beginning of devotions, hymns functioned to "banish intruding worldly thoughts, and lift the soul out of its dull round of earthly care," composing the mind for "communion with God." Hymns sharply distinguished between the profane and sacred worlds, transporting the reader from one to the other, regardless of physical location. At the same time, hymns integrated every "earthly care" into a sacred framework: "Ten minutes spent each day in reading the hymn-book . . . spread a blessed influence over all the hours and engagements of the day." Used alongside congregational hymnals, the special devotional "manual for the closet" included hymns of a "more personal and individual character" with longer lines and a more "reflective tone of thought" than those most people considered suitable for congregational singing. From such devotional volumes, individuals selected hymns adapted to "particular circumstances or periods of life and to peculiar states of feeling." Such hymns incorporated individual experiences within the same framework that structured participation in the church universal.[19]

Like devotional reading, memorization wove hymns into the texture of everyday experience, since memorized words could presumably infuse any time or place with sacred influences. Evangelicals understood memorization to aid the personal appropriation of hymn texts, the internalization of "holy words we have thus made our own." Memorized hymns could be recited when printed texts were unavailable or unusable, such as during a "time of sickness, when an enfeebled mind in an enfeebled body will long for some expression of its faith and love, which it cannot frame for itself."

Through the "cumulative power of repetition," the language of hymnody became embedded in evangelicals' cultural vocabulary, so much so that hymn phrases were "frequently heard in prayer, testimony, and exhortation." Memorized hymns shaped Christians' "daily and most sacred feelings . . . interweaving them in the very fabric of their spiritual nature." Memorization facilitated the process by which evangelicals used hymns to interpret their ordinary experiences within a sacred narrative system.[20]

Evangelicals used hymn memorization to socialize the rising generations in evangelical values and vocabulary, thus "forming the Church of the future." From before the age of reading, hymns became a part of children's lives. Hymns held great "doctrinal usefulness" because they impressed children with "dogmatic teaching" in a pleasing form. Evangelicals believed that hymns memorized in childhood could "inform the memory and impress the heart," exerting a "permanent influence" that even shaped the "language and aspirations of declining age." Sunday school publications accordingly taught the importance of memorization. In Elizabeth Prentiss's *Little Susy's Little Servants* (1856), Susy's mother helps her to memorize a hymn, and then mother and daughter sit singing together. Another Sunday school book, *The Freed Boy in Alabama* (1869), described the "freed Boy" Tom as having memorized all the verses to "Jesus Loves Me." Tom, although portrayed in a patronizing manner typical of the genre, crosses racial, class, and gender barriers to teach the hymn to his employer's daughter, "Miss Lillie," as he testifies to her that he himself loves "the Lord Jesus."[21]

Alongside fictional narratives that depicted characters memorizing hymns, periodicals printed hymns with explicit instructions for readers to memorize the selected texts. The Methodist *Youth's Magazine* (1839) presented a brief biographical sketch of the hymnist "Good Bishop Ken," informing readers that Bishop Thomas Ken began his morning by singing with "holy feelings": "Awake, my soul, and with the sun thy daily course of duty run," which prepared him to live "through the day" in the same holy manner as he began it. The article advised that "it would be well for us to learn by heart" Bishop Ken's hymn, using it as a catalyst to sanctify the remainder of the day. Evangelicals used hymn memorization to teach the rising generations how to infuse their world with sacred influences.[22]

Alternative Aesthetics of the Sacred

Evangelicals who privileged hymns did not all agree about which cultural values to instill in the next generations. Two models of functionally sacred language coexisted within evangelicalism at midcentury. Both aesthetics had their roots in the revivals of the Great Awakening and, in the context of nineteenth-century cultural dialogues, offered alternatives to New England romantic conceptions of literature. For American proponents of romanticism such as Emerson, divine inspiration and truth were symbolic rather than literal. Although they at times blended elevated and folk styles, romantics tended to equate poetic and religious speech, arguing that poetry worked directly on the feelings to make people virtuous. For evangelicals, God literally inspired Scripture through the Holy Spirit; truth was uniform and ascertainable. One evangelical aesthetic interpreted the ideas articulated by John Wesley and Jonathan Edwards in the eighteenth century to argue that the poetic beauty of hymns acted on the human affections to instill truth experientially into the heart. James Murray represented this more refined view when he claimed that there were "many cases in which spirit is not independent of form, and the hymn is one of them." God himself had "so constituted the soul of man that hymns having high merit as lyrical poetry affect it most powerfully." Mere "rhymed prose" could not affect the soul in the same way as poems possessing "lyrical excellence." Evangelicals like Murray defined their identity in relation to romanticism by voicing a common esteem for the poetic diction and structure of hymn language; poetry, because of its beauty, provided an avenue to access divine inspiration. Yet, the evangelicals insisted, poetry could not be equated with revelation; God providentially used poetic language to convey the Holy Spirit's influence, but poetry was not itself sacred.[23]

A second, more vernacular, aesthetic diverged more sharply from romantic ideals of literature. This model grew out of the interdenominational, interracial camp meeting with its folk emphasis on heartfelt words stripped free of the encumbrance of artificially poetic speech. Advocates of both evangelical aesthetics distanced themselves from romanticism and literature by pointing out fundamental differences in assumptions about the nature and purpose of religious language. For evangelicals, language had functional value because, as a conduit for the Holy Spirit, it sanctified daily experience. Evangelicals debated among themselves which forms of linguistic and corresponding musical expression were most useful as channels for sacred influence and whether clergy or laity should judge the relative usefulness of particular hymn and tune styles. These cultural divisions did not, however, constitute immutable hierarchies as much as partial and provisional efforts to understand the nature of the sacred. In the lives of particular individuals and congregations, styles overlapped and shifted over time.[24]

Proponents of refined hymnody, especially highly educated clerical leaders of urban, middle-class congregations, took it upon themselves both to select poetic texts and to instruct congregations in singing methods that they considered suited to sacred language. Clerical efforts to cultivate congregational musical abilities began as early as 1715 among New England congregations that restricted their singing to the psalms, unaccompanied by musical instruments. During the revivals of the Great Awakening, at the same time that clergy introduced hymns into worship, they also established informal singing schools to provide congregations with basic musical instruction. Prior to the nineteenth century, when books became more available and literacy rates increased, it was rare for every attendee at a church or revival service to own a personal copy of a common hymnal. Instead, congregations "lined out" hymns: a song leader or minister read or sang from a psalmbook or hymnbook line by line, and the congregation sang back the text in unison to a tune of the same meter that the leader selected.[25]

Since few congregations received adequate musical training, the tunes sung by individuals often strayed from that set by the song leader. To remedy this situation, singing instructors William Little and William Smith introduced the first "shaped-note" tune book, *The Easy Instructor* (1802). Shaped notes consisted of standard musical notation in which the heads of the notes, instead of all being round, were fashioned into triangles, circles, squares, and diamonds. Rather than learning notes by their position on the staff, singers only had to learn the shapes (figure 7.3). Equipped with type specially adapted to the purpose, Cincinnati became the capital of shaped-note publishing. The South Carolina Baptist "Singin' Billy" Walker (1809–75), author of *The Southern Harmony* (1835), traveled across frontier areas using shaped notes to hold singing schools, which consisted of one or two evenings a week of instruction in reading music and four-part harmony, conducted over the period of a month or two. In the first half of the nineteenth century, hymns sung to shaped-note versions of popular folk tunes swept across southern and western frontier congregations who had minimal access to more formal musical instruction.[26]

During the nineteenth century, the rift between more and less refined linguistic and musical practices widened, and urban congregations, by then familiar with the best European classical traditions and adept at reading sheet music, derided shaped-note singing as backward by comparison. Urban clergy introduced musical instruments, especially organs, and trained choirs, some of them paid, to lead or replace congregational singing. Choir music, in the words of one proponent, was "designed to be *impressive* on the heart of the worshipper rather than directly *expressive* of his devout feelings." Even among the advocates of refinement, conflict brewed over

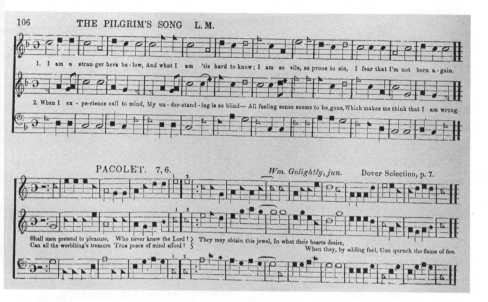

Figure 7.3. "Singin' Billy" Walker's *Southern Harmony* (1854). Shaped notes made it easier for the musically untrained to sing a tune. (Courtesy of the University of Missouri–Kansas City)

heightening musical standards. The Second Congregational Church of Cambridgeport, Massachusetts, voted in 1848 to dispense with its choir on the grounds that insistence on a "powerful organ" and the "setting apart of a few to perform the service of the many" had changed a house of worship into a "place of godless fashion and heartless mummery." James Murray cut to the heart of the issue when he warned that refined poetic language and music suited to the elevated "tastes of the few" could not by themselves produce a sacred influence unless these grew out of "hearts filled with the Spirit." On the one hand, beautiful poetry and music served as channels for the powerful operation of the Holy Spirit on the human affections. On the other hand, fashion as an end in itself threatened to replace the laity's heartfelt worship. If sacred music were to be "of any worth in the sight of God and for the soul of man," then spirit and form must correspond.[27]

Clergy, who acquired refined sensibilities through educational acculturation, often felt frustrated by the more vernacular preferences of their congregations. Evangelical notions of the priesthood of all believers implied both the importance of lay empowerment and, simultaneously, the need for expert regulation. Since hymns ideally expressed heartfelt worship, congregational singing seemed to many evangelicals the unique province of the Christian laity, articulating the "people's theology, their commentary, their experience." Indeed, the "best practical test" of a hymn was that it be "proven in actual use to be truly effective." Hymns "universally known, sung, and loved" that were both "very popular and unquestionably useful" justified themselves by their usefulness. Nevertheless, clerical arbiters such as James Murray considered it their role "to educate the Christian popular heart in the very best and highest forms of devotional experience." Murray worried about "catering to the popular taste, rather than standards of worship"; he distrusted the laity's ability to distinguish between the popular and the useful. Other clergy, like the Congregationalist minister J. W. Dadmun, had more confidence in lay judgment: "It is true that a great deal of *trash* is thrown into the market, but the good taste of the people will select the good and throw the bad away, — the thing will regulate itself." Implicit in Murray and Dadmun's debate were two contests: between vernacular and refined sensibilities and between lay and clerical authority to judge the usefulness of commonly recognized hymns.[28]

Tensions between clerical and lay preferences played themselves out in congregational singing practices. Despite the pleas of cultivated ministers, hymnody belonged at least as much to oral as to literary culture. Hymns learned through oral transmission processes often circulated for twenty-five years or more, evolving all the while, before becoming embedded in standard hymn collections. Regardless of their intentions, clergy could not fully regulate the writing and singing of such hymns by individuals and congregations who felt themselves inspired by the living Word, the Holy Spirit. The Methodist minister S. W. Christophers, writing in 1874, regretted the "oral rhyme" tradition that had "always been afloat among Methodists." In congregational usage, alongside the singing of Wesley's hymns, "now and then some zealous, though uncultured, brother or sister has been known to start up under rhyming inspiration and set all like-minded fellow-worshippers a-singing at the poet's dictation. Many a ditty never submitted to an 'editor' has become more popular in its oral form than it would have been as shut up in print." Christophers had little regard for the poetic quality of improvised ditties popular among Methodist congregations, yet he acknowledged the power of the oral song tradition to stimulate fervent worship.[29]

Christophers's dilemma evokes a conflict between orality and literacy as standards for evaluating poetic discourse. Christophers felt drawn to elevated diction, believing beautiful words a conduit for the Holy Spirit's presence. Yet he could not deny that for many lay practitioners, uncultivated yet heartfelt oral expression fulfilled the same purpose of bringing Christians into contact with God's Spirit. Another way to frame this prob-

CAMP-MEETING

Figure 7.4. "Camp-Meeting," lithograph by Hugh Bridport, after Alexander Rider (ca. 1829). In the expressive space of the camp meeting, hymn singing could not be constrained by printed words or tunes. (Courtesy of The Library of Congress)

lem is as a conflict over the meanings of poetry; evangelicals disagreed as to whether diction and form made language poetic or whether instead the poetry, or beauty, of language consisted in how well it reflected religious experience. Christophers was not alone in voicing ambivalence toward vernacular worship styles. In the opinion of Presbyterian minister W. T. Eva, many of the hymns "in common use" and most approved by congregations possessed a "literary and poetic character . . . so inferior that if they were found in the papers, cultivated people would not read them." The unease expressed by Christophers and Eva points to larger debates within evangelicalism over the meanings of orality and literacy, lay and clerical authority, and vernacular and refined sensibilities.[30]

Nowhere did these alternatives interact more creatively than in the camp meeting. Evangelical aesthetics of the sacred overlapped and competed, bringing together African- and European-influenced vernacular and refined linguistic traditions. Despite the proliferation of books designed for revivals and social meetings, many who attended the meetings did not have books. Some singers were illiterate, others found books a hindrance to oral practices, and books helped no one when singing extended late into the night (figure 7.4). Hymns transmitted through books, and perhaps memorized by many of those present, blended with the spontaneous productions of the meeting itself. Singers shortened favorite hymns and added choruses, some of which were composed at the time and set to folk tunes and written down only later. "Alas! and Did My Saviour Bleed," written by Isaac Watts in the eighteenth century, ranked thirteenth among hymns most often reprinted in nineteenth-century hymnals. This hymn was also a camp meeting favorite. Out of a sample of 200 revival songbooks, the hymn, often in abbreviated form, appeared seventy times, paired with seventeen different choruses. One version began with the original Watts:

> Alas! and did my Saviour bleed,
> And did my Sov'reign die?
> Would he devote that sacred head
> For such a worm as I?

Following this stanza, a chorus elaborated on the hymn theme:

> O the Lamb, the loving Lamb,
> The Lamb on Calvary,
> The Lamb that was slain, Yet lives again,
> To intercede for me.

Repetition of the word "Lamb" four times aided memorization of the chorus and reinforced the central idea that individuals could appropriate Christ's sacrifice. Not only could one hymn be paired with several choruses but also the choruses traveled across hymns. Couplets from one hymn might be mixed with another, a chorus added, and a substantially new song created. The choruses popular among camp meeting participants can be traced to African worship traditions through the songs' condensed meanings, repeated musical phrases, improvisational words and melodies, call-and-response structures, and multiple rhythms.[31]

The practice of combining hymns and choruses illuminates some of the dynamic exchanges that connected white and black evangelicals in the camp meeting context. Evidence of white influence on black singing comes from the texts of spirituals, recorded later, that adopted phrases and lines from hymns written by white authors. Similarly, wandering choruses and spiritual songs embodying African traditions printed in revival hymnbooks provide a glimpse at how influence flowed from black to white camp meeting attendees. *The Golden Harp* (1857) recorded several hymns, written in dialect, that the Methodist compiler G. W. Henry attributed to African American singers. In "Negroes Song,"

> Negro walk de Golden Street,
> Cast his crown at Jesu feet,
> And sing de happy song.
> Oh! dat will be joyful.

Henry's transcription suggests that white auditors, whatever subtleties of black spirituals they missed, recognized black anticipation of arrival in heaven. "The Old Ship of Zion" appeared in *The Golden Harp* with the subtitle "Negro hymn" and the acknowledgment "altered by John Stamp." This attribution indicates that a white editor appropriated a text composed by African Americans for use by white evangelicals. The call-and-response structure of the chorus supports this interpretation:

> Can you tell me what ship is a going for to sail?
> Oh, glory, hallelujah.
> Yes, the old ship of Zion. Hallelujah.
> Can you tell me what is her captain's name?
> King Jesus is her captain. Hallelujah.
> Can you tell me what is her compass and chart?
> God's word and holy spirit. Hallelujah.

This chorus, similar in theme and form to numerous other camp meeting refrains, might have been appended to any standard hymn of a loosely related subject.[32]

The rigid boundaries that normally separated races, genders, age groups, and refined and vernacular styles loosened in the liminal space of the camp meeting. The rules of sacred time temporarily overcame the rules of everyday social interaction as whites and blacks ritually enacted a narrative structure in which all Christians were members of the family of God or pilgrims journeying together toward Canaan. Not everyone embraced the implications of such blurred social distinctions. John Fanning Watson complained in the *Methodist Error* (1819) of the "growing evil" of white evangelicals singing hymns adapted to "*merry* airs" that were "composed and first sung by the illiterate *blacks* of the society." The phrasing of Watson's lament — that white evangelicals borrowed from "illiterate" blacks — points to several reasons many white evangelicals resisted the cultural exchanges that the camp meeting setting encouraged. Part of Watson's resistance was certainly racial, but Watson felt troubled not only because whites were learning from blacks but because the blacks were, he assumed, illiterate. At stake was a spiritual and social hierarchy that privileged whites over blacks in part because of whites' presumed monopoly over literacy. For whites like Watson, camp meeting innovations threatened to invert the relationship between literary refinement and uncultivated though heartfelt expression.[33]

Black and White Uses of the Spirit and the Understanding

African American evangelicals experienced the tensions between aesthetics of the sacred with particular acuteness. Black singers borrowed a subset of the psalms and hymns sung by whites and adapted them to African worship traditions such as verbal and musical improvisation, call and response, the ring shout, and the rhythmic cadences of hand clapping and foot stomping. Pavel Svin'in, a Russian visitor to AME founder Richard Allen's Bethel Church in 1811, observed antiphonal singing patterns: "At the end of every psalm, the entire congregation, men and women alike, sang verses in a loud, shrill monotone. This lasted about half an hour. When the preacher ceased reading, all turned toward the door, fell on their knees, bowed their heads to the ground and set up an agonizing, heart-rending moaning. Afterwards, the minister resumed the reading of the psalter and when he had finished sat down on a chair; then all rose and began chanting psalms in chorus, the men and women alternating, a procedure which lasted some twenty minutes." In the evaluation of Eileen Southern, the congregation's choral response to the psalms and the alternation between men and women were distinctive features of African-influenced black worship. Blacks and whites used shared religious texts in profoundly different ways that stemmed from divergent group histories, social conditions, and community settings.[34]

As blacks withdrew from interracial congregations late in the eighteenth century, they struggled to harmonize African traditions and European standards of respectability. Richard Allen, instead of retaining the official Methodist hymnal for use at the separatist Bethel Church, published his own: *A Collection of Hymns and Spiritual Songs from Various Authors* (1801). The volume contained fifty-four hymns, most of which Allen borrowed from the Methodist hymnbook, simplifying the selected texts. Allen also added a number of camp meeting spiritual songs and choruses, some of which he likely wrote himself. In contrast, the AME hymnal of 1818, compiled by Richard Allen and Daniel Coker, veered sharply in the direction of refined sensibilities. Of the 314 hymns in the collection, only 15 of the camp meeting songs remained from the 1801 edition. The 1837 revision removed virtually every vestige of distinction from the hymnal of the white-dominated Methodist Episcopal Church. Not until the publication of the

1876 hymnal revision did African-American–authored hymns and choruses again appear in the collection. Finally, in the words of the collection's editor, Bishop Henry McNeal Turner, "The old hymns gave way to the new, and the children of freedom sang a new song from their own Church Book." The publication histories of the AMEZ, Colored Methodist Episcopal, African Episcopal, and National Baptist hymnals all proceeded along similar lines; only in the 1890s did African-American–authored hymns appear in any of these collections.[35]

Editorial decisions reflected a deep cultural rift over the spiritual and social purposes of hymnody. The preface to the 1858 hymnal of the AMEZ Church suggests the issues at stake: "In submitting this to you, we would recommend the laity to be more prudent, in their social prayer-meetings and similar exercises, by avoiding that irregularity in the singing which destroys the harmony that should exist in this part of Divine worship. We are commanded to *sing in the spirit and with the understanding*: by strictly observing this precept, we cannot but be blessed under its influence." The phrasing and tone of the preface hints at disputes between clerical and lay and refined and vernacular views of sacred language. The biblical allusion, in this context, served to distance African Americans from the stigma of illiteracy by demonstrating that blacks, like whites, could sing with understanding.[36]

Formally educated, middle-class urban black clergy saw the refinement of worship as an avenue for gaining social acceptance by bourgeois white evangelicals. Conversely, any association with the illiteracy of slavery seemed to such arbiters a barrier to African Americans' acceptance within mainstream white culture. Allen began the AME Church's move toward respectability in the antebellum period. Pressures to conform to white middle-class standards of decorum only intensified after emancipation. Daniel Alexander Payne, sixth bishop of the AME Church from 1852 until his death in 1893, spearheaded the drive for musical reform, introducing European classical instrumental music and choirs into church worship beginning in the 1840s and banishing such activities as dancing, trances, and ring shouts. Elias Camp Morris played a similar role as president of the black National Baptist Convention from 1895 through 1920. On the whole, Baptist churches remained more open to expressive worship than did Methodist churches, which is one of the reasons Baptists surpassed Methodists for the largest black membership by the 1890s, a trend that has continued to the present. As the historian Michael Harris has observed, assimilationists such as Payne and Morris worked with white missionaries and against black traditionalists to mold black church culture after the image of refined white churches. By the turn of the twentieth century, more expressive worship had been pushed to the margins of mainstream denominations, finding a home in new Holiness and Pentecostal churches.[37]

The pre-emancipation spiritual songs figured prominently in postbellum battles over the cultural meanings of vernacular worship traditions. White evangelicals rather than blacks took the lead in efforts to preserve the old spirituals, once prominent in camp meetings. Ambivalent about their own move toward refinement, cultivated whites felt attracted to the "heart religion" of black oral culture, feeling something missing in white "book religion." The publication of *Slave Songs of the United States* (1867) represented the first of numerous efforts on the part of white evangelicals to collect and transcribe African American spirituals. White editors had some sense of the inherent difficulty of transmitting oral tradition through print and admitted that paper and types could "convey but a faint shadow of the original," which "cannot be reproduced on paper." Most of the white cultural mediators who did the transcribing were neither trained in musical composition nor deeply familiar with black folk traditions. Written in the more "dignified" form of white hymns, the spirituals were greatly simplified and lost much of the dynamism of oral participation. Most blacks resisted the transcription efforts, both because they wanted to distance themselves from songs that they considered emblems of slavery and because they resented the transformation of deeply emotional expressions into "art" approved by white audiences. Parallel to publication efforts, in the 1870s white evangelicals sponsored "Jubilee Singers" from Fisk, Hampton, and other black schools to introduce their songs to white audiences through performances across the United States and Europe. The Jubilee Singers only reluctantly agreed to the venture, principally in order to raise money for their schools. Resistant blacks recognized that white evangelicals had their own reasons for wanting to preserve black vernacular traditions: to work out their nostalgia for lost folk ways by mediating the transmission of the spirituals and repositioning them in the more refined cultural contexts of print and performance.[38]

White appropriations of black spiritual traditions produced among white evangelicals a shift away from denominationally controlled decorous worship practices. In the 1870s, the nondenominational gospel-song meetings that emerged out of the international revivals of Dwight L. Moody and his song leader, Ira Sankey, drew from African-influenced camp meeting spiritual-song traditions. In the United States, the revivals were primarily northern, urban phenomena, but gospel music also appealed to rural churches in the South and West whose members favored vernacular styles.

Figure 7.5.   This illustrated 1876 edition presented Philip Bliss's gospel song "Hold the Fort" for use by more refined audiences. (Courtesy of The Library Company of Philadelphia)

As an aid to the revivals, Sankey published a thin pamphlet of *Sacred Songs and Solos* in 1873. Encouraged by its success, Sankey and Philip Bliss published a much larger book, *Gospel Hymns and Sacred Songs*, in 1875; the collection grew to six volumes by 1891 and sold over 50 million copies by the end of the nineteenth century. More than 1,500 different gospel songbooks appeared during the final quarter of the nineteenth century, most of them published by three trade houses: Biglow & Main Company of New York and Chicago, John J. Hood Company of Philadelphia, and John Church Company of Cincinnati.[39]

The nondenominational nature of the Moody-Sankey meetings and songsters reflected the revivalists' frustration with the refinement of denominational church services and hymnals and their desire to restore vernacular worship in order to disperse sanctifying influences more broadly.

Gospel hymns, in Sankey's opinion, were more useful than "standard church hymns" because their popularity facilitated conversions and growth in grace. As an example, Annie Hawks contributed "I Need Thee Every Hour" (1872) to the *Gospel Hymns* collection:

> I need Thee ev'ry hour,
> Most gracious Lord;
> No tender voice like Thine
> Can peace afford.
> [Refrain:] I need Thee, oh! I need Thee;
> Ev'ry hour I need Thee;
> O bless me now, my Saviour!
> I come to Thee.

The song employed everyday language, repetition and direct address, and a catchy melody — all of these devices the heirs of African American spirituals and camp meeting religious styles — to represent a deeply personal relationship between the singer and her Savior. Despite the generally acknowledged usefulness of gospel hymns in stimulating religious growth, many church leaders continued to resist vernacular styles, preferring literary elevation. Clerical critics denounced gospel hymns as "fifth class poetry" and "dyspeptic-producing pabulum" strong enough "to turn the spiritual stomach." Yet the songs only became more and more popular, even among even refined congregations (figure 7.5). Through such ongoing confrontations between vernacular and refined sensibilities, African and European traditions, oral and print cultures, and clerical and lay control, hymnody became an increasingly powerful means for evangelicals to use the Word to meet the needs of every hour.[40]

As evangelicals used hymns in Sunday worship, midweek meetings, private devotions, camp meetings, and gospel-song services, they sanctified the world by redefining daily life experiences within the framework of redemption history. In seeking to sing with the spirit and the understanding, evangelicals accommodated diverse possibilities for how to view sacred language and for who should control its uses. Like William Aitchison, who began and ended his earthly pilgrimage singing the songs of Zion, many evangelicals found hymns useful in infusing the present world with heavenly influences. Hymns seemed so useful that some evangelicals — editors, compilers, and translators — took it upon themselves to frame, select, and alter the hymns they included in printed collections in order to unify the pilgrim community and aid its heavenward progress. The following chapter takes up the story of how these hymnal shapers multiplied the meanings of hymnody.

8

Unifying the
Pilgrim Community

John Wesley and Augustus Toplady could not agree. Despite their common passion for evangelical truth, the two men bitterly disputed doctrines characteristic of their respective denominations. In the course of debates printed in England's periodical press, the Calvinist Toplady wrote the hymn "Rock of Ages" as part of an article in the *Gospel Magazine* (1776) to refute the Wesleyan doctrine of entire sanctification. Wesley averred that justified Christians could attain a degree of holiness in this world such that they ceased to commit intentionally sinful acts. Toplady rebutted that Christians "never, in the present life, *rise* to the mark of legal sanctity," and that to the contrary, "our *Sins* multiply with every second." Toplady introduced "Rock of Ages" to reinforce his argument, supplying the explanatory heading: "*A living and dying* PRAYER *for the* HOLIEST BELIEVER *in the World.*" In Toplady's view, even the holiest Christian remained desperately corrupted by sin. Ironically, nineteenth-century evangelicals of every denomination — including Methodists — appropriated Toplady's hymn to promote Christian unity, a quality seen as necessary to the holiness of the church universal. Evangelicals considered hymns, because of their usefulness in evoking experiences shared by all Christians, as specially suited to disseminating a corporate model of pilgrimage. In positioning hymn texts within published collections, hymnal editors, compilers, and translators muted theological disputes for the purpose of unifying the textual community that the hymn canon helped to define.[1]

The publication history of Toplady's "Rock of Ages" illustrates how hymnbook editors, compilers, and translators acted as cultural arbiters by framing, selecting, and altering hymns to encourage evangelical unity on denominational terms. Early Methodist collections omitted the hymn altogether. "Rock of Ages" first appeared in the 1830 supplement to the Methodist hymnal in a significantly modified form that approximated a version written by the Anglican Thomas Cotterill in 1815. Editors of the *Hymnal of the Methodist Episcopal Church* (1878) expressed concern for Christian unity by incorporating hymns written by non-Methodists, such as Toplady, while erasing textual evidence of theologies inconsistent with Methodism. The editors positioned hymns within the Methodist theological system by silently altering or omitting troubling stanzas and by appending headings that taught Methodist doctrine. Comparing Toplady's original with the version that appeared in the 1878 Methodist hymnal (which had evolved somewhat from both Cotterill's and the 1830 rendition) indicates how editorial decisions recast doctrine without appearing controversial.[2]

Augustus Toplady (1776):

1. Rock of Ages, cleft for me,
Let me hide myself in Thee!
Let the Water and the Blood,
From thy riven Side which flow'd
Be of Sin the double Cure,
Cleanse me from its Guilt and Pow'r.

2. Not the labors of my hands
Can fulfill thy Law's demands:
Could my zeal no respite know,
Could my tears for ever flow,
All for Sin could not atone:
Thou must save, and thou alone!

3. Nothing in my hand I bring;
Simply to thy Cross I cling;
Naked, come to Thee for Dress,
Helpless, look to Thee for grace;
Foul, I to the fountain fly:
Wash me, Saviour, or I die!

4. While I draw this fleeting breath,
When my eye-strings break in death,
When I soar to worlds unknown,
See Thee on Thy judgment throne:
Rock of Ages, cleft for me,
Let me hide myself in Thee.

Methodist *Hymnal* (1878):

1. Rock of Ages, cleft for me,
Let me hide myself in thee;
Let the water and the blood,
From thy wounded side which flowed,
Be of sin the double cure,
Save from wrath and make me pure.

2. Could my tears forever flow,
Could my zeal no languor know,
These for sin could not atone;
Thou must save, and thou alone.
In my hand no price I bring;
Simply to thy cross I cling.

3. While I draw this fleeting breath,
When my eyes shall close in death,
When I rise to worlds unknown,
And behold thee on thy throne,
Rock of ages, cleft for me,
Let me hide myself in thee.

The Methodist version transformed the hymn's theology from a statement denying the possibility of entire sanctification to a prayer for its attainment. Three exclamatory statements expressed Toplady's urgent sense of unrighteousness: "Let me hide myself in Thee!," "Thou must save, and thou alone!," and "Wash me, Saviour, or I die!" The intensity of the hymn's pleas for Christ's grace diminished in the Methodist version, which omitted all exclamation marks. More directly, the last line of the first stanza, "Cleanse me from its Guilt and Pow'r," became "Save from wrath and make me pure." Both lines refer to the "double cure" of justification and sanctification, but the second version implies that purity from sin is possible in this life. The second and third stanzas merged in the Methodist version. The revision left out the couplet "Not the labors of my hands / Can fulfill thy Law's demands," lines that assert human inability to live a righteous life. The hymn similarly modified absolute statements of human helplessness and divine sovereignty — "*All* for Sin could not atone," "*Nothing* in my hand I bring," and "See Thee on Thy *judgment* throne" — attenuating the claims to read, "*These* for sin could not atone," "In my hand *no price* I bring," "And behold thee on thy throne." The revision omitted another four lines that emphasize the extent of human sin and helplessness:

> Naked, come to Thee for Dress,
> Helpless, look to Thee for grace;
> Foul, I to the fountain fly:
> Wash me, Saviour, or I die!

The text in the Methodist hymnal appended the signature "Augustus Toplady, alt.," but this admission of alteration did little to evoke the extent of changes made.

The Methodist hymnal struck its final blow by organizing Toplady's text according to Wesleyan doctrine. The editors chose not to place the hymn in the section "The Christian — Sanctification and Growth," even though Toplady intended the hymn to address the subjects of sanctification and growth in grace. Instead, the hymn appeared in the section "The Sinner — Repentance," thereby implying that the sin-consciousness that still pervades the hymn pertains to the beginning stages of the Christian life rather than to the mature Christian's experience. Hymnal compilers encouraged a corporate sense of Christian pilgrimage by including hymns from a range of sources, manipulating texts to reinforce the editors' theology. The appropriation process elided significant theological differences to indicate perceived, if not actual, evangelical unity.[3]

The practices involved in hymnal publishing illuminate denominational divisions and countervailing efforts to unify evangelical print culture. Marketed to large, diverse audiences wider than church members, hymnals sustained a timeless, placeless textual community defined by an informal hymn canon. As denominations consolidated in the first half of the nineteenth century, clergy shared authority with a lay priesthood of editors, compilers, and translators who reconfigured the canon through their choices in framing, selecting, and altering hymns. These cultural mediators obscured denominational differences in order to promote Christians' corporate pilgrimage through the world.

Cultural Mediators: Editors, Compilers, and Translators

The example of "Rock of Ages" demonstrates the importance of the people who edited hymn texts, compiled hymnals, and, when necessary, translated hymns written in languages other than English for shaping the cultural meanings of hymns to nineteenth-century American evangelicals. Not only clergy but also lay men and women and whites and blacks from every section of the country introduced a growing variety of hymnals into the print market. Disavowing the mantle of authorship, these hymnal shapers remained nearly transparent, all the while silently framing, selecting, and altering hymns popularized through printed collections. Hymnal compilers avoided close reader scrutiny by denying professional ambition, insisting rather that they collected hymns during leisure hours as a "profitable study and a delightful pastime." Despite such conventional disclaimers, which reflected discomfort with the rising tide of professional authorship, editors acted as self-appointed cultural arbiters, instructing the average hymnal user in which hymns to sing or read, and in what manner, to pursue a heavenward journey.[4]

As in other fields of the evangelical print market, John Wesley set a precedent for the level and kinds of influence a hymnal editor could exert in framing the meanings of hymn texts. In compiling his first hymnbook, *Collection of Psalms and Hymns* (1737), Wesley organized the volume into three sections: hymns for Sundays, hymns for Wednesdays or Fridays, and hymns for Saturdays. The Sunday hymns focused on praise; the Wednesday or Friday hymns on humiliation, repentance, and prayer; and the Saturday hymns on adoration of God as Creator of the universe. Each day's hymns commemorated a different stage in sacred history, encompassing creation, sin, redemption, and worship. By a simple organizational act, Wesley instructed his readers in using hymns to cycle through sacred time during the course of each week. Simultaneously, Wesley taught his understanding of the Christian textual community. Assuming that hymns belonged to the church rather than to their particular authors, Wesley borrowed more than a third of his hymns from his contemporary Isaac Watts, freely altering their language to reflect a deeper sense of Christ's grace and love than that expressed by the Calvinistic Watts. Wesley's editorial decisions not only helped readers to find desired hymns quickly and easily but also reinforced their sense of membership in a textually defined community wider than any one denomination.[5]

By the nineteenth century, most denominations had begun to incorporate hymns in congregational worship. Despite Wesley's precedent, most early collections were loosely organized at best. This all changed with the publication of the Anglican John Keble's innovative *Christian Year* in 1827, first in London and then in New York, which sold more than half a million copies by the end of the century and significantly influenced hymnal publishing in Britain and America. Keble renewed Anglican interest in the *Book of Common Prayer* (1549) and in arranging hymns for the liturgical purpose of measuring sacred time by the annual cycle of fasts and festivals in the church calendar. Although Keble himself was a leader in the decisively antievangelical Tractarian movement, evangelicals adapted lessons from Keble to their own purposes. Keble's *Christian Year*, like Wesley's *Collection* before it, became a model for evangelicals who desired to use hymns systematically to position daily life within the narrative structure of sacred pilgrimage.[6]

Nineteenth-century compilers framed their volumes with "pre-texts" — prefatory information in titles, frontispiece quotations, and prefaces — that oriented readers to their texts through usage instructions. *The Wesleyan Psalmist; Or, Songs of Canaan* (1842) identified the book's Methodist affiliation by its title while attesting that its songs could be sung by Canaan-bound pilgrims of any denomination. A subtitle further explained the volume's intended uses: *A Collection of Hymns and Tunes Designed to be Used at Camp-Meetings, and at Class and Prayer Meetings, and Other Occasions of Social Devotion.* The editor indicated the usefulness of the volume during any occasion when Christians gathered for social worship while implicitly denying an intention to supplant the official Methodist hymnal already in use during Sunday worship services. The editor next identified himself: "Compiled by M. L. Scudder, of the New-England Conference." Scudder portrayed himself as a compiler rather than as an author with independent responsibility. He also cast himself as a representative of the Methodist Episcopal Church, even though the book lacked denominational sponsorship as a "regular church Hymn-Book." Scudder implied, moreover, that the hymns and tunes in his volume might coincide particularly well with New England tastes. Finally, he alluded to 1 Corinthians 14:15, the same verse that prefaced many similar collections: "Sing with the Spirit and with the Understanding also." Scudder hoped not only to regulate hymn choices but also to teach congregations how to sing, using the spirit and the understanding to avoid what he considered the extremes of unspiritual repetition and uncontrolled emotion. Through a few bare phrases, Scudder invited his readers and singers to greet the volume as a useful compendium of hymns, appropriate for Methodists as well as other Christians.[7]

The editorial presence in hymn collections materialized most clearly in the preface. Addresses to the "Christian public" invoked a relationship between the editor and readers in an evangelical textual community. Compilers cast themselves as helping other Christian pilgrims find their "way to heaven by these songs." The language of pilgrimage conveyed an expectation that readers would consider hymns useful throughout the salvation process: in entering the path to salvation at the moment of conversion and then as an aid to traveling through "every stage of progress in the divine life" during the lifelong journey toward sanctification. Editors promised a "practical method of advance" along the "highway of holiness" and "pools of refreshing" to encourage pilgrims wearied by the journey. Hymns prepared Christians for heaven, a place characterized by "endless song," by moving "the soul to heavenly communion" and "evoking the most spiritual and deepest worship of God." Prefaces redolent with allusions to pilgrimage and heaven prepared singers to view themselves as members of a pilgrim community who used hymns to travel heavenward.[8]

Selling the Songs of the Church

Elaborating on the doctrine of the incarnation, nineteenth-century evangelicals assumed that both the Word and functionally sacred words transformed the world when incarnated in human cultures. In a manner analogous to the way in which the living Word entered a human body in the person of Jesus Christ, editors and compilers embodied sacred hymn texts within printed artifacts that they marketed commercially. In both instances, sacred influences presumably remained pure while becoming more present in the world. The hymn canon took form as compilers positioned isolated texts within a larger narrative pattern evoked by all the hymns included in published volumes. At the same time, innovative marketing strategies expanded the size and diversity of audiences that hymns addressed. Clerical and lay arbiters balanced denominational and evangelical priorities to shape a hymn canon that represented their sense of membership in the church universal. In many instances, the textual community defined by the hymn canon provided a more harmonious alternative to the local congregation. Editors invited hymnal users to see their lives as typical, conforming to the same patterns that had guided generations of Christians before them and that unified Christians around the world in their own time. Hymnals helped individuals to participate in the church universal by making an interpretive connection between the temporal realities of hymn authors, editors, and singers who all understood their lives as meaningful in terms of a shared narrative framework.[9]

Advances in printing technology solidified the hymn canon and increased the variety of hymnals available for purchase. Before the widespread adoption of stereotyping in the 1820s, each new hymnal edition included a different selection of hymns, the wording of which shifted from one printing to the next. Stereotyping, by preserving exact typesetting for use in multiple editions, standardized hymn selection and froze hymn texts. Improvements in printing, binding, and paper production simultaneously made it cheaper and easier for publishers to manufacture editions varying in size, binding, and quality. Advertisements for the 1878 Methodist *Hymnal* offered purchasers a choice from among thirty-six versions of the same hymn collection, ranging in price from forty cents to six dollars, depending on whether the volume came with or without music, in large or small formatting, or with cloth or morocco binding.[10]

The proliferation of hymnal editions extended the influence of canonical hymns to purchasers drawn from multiple denominational and social groups. Hymn collections ranged from broadsides carrying two or three hymns, designed for one-time use at a special meeting, to hardbound volumes embracing over a thousand hymns, intended for decades-long exclusive use. At one end of the social and economic spectrum, elegant giftbooks priced at several dollars apiece were suited for display in the Victorian parlor. An 1858 edition of the Anglican Catherine Winkworth's *Lyra Germanica* was well adapted to this purpose (figure 8.1). The book is large and substantial, measuring 11 by 7½ by 1½ inches; the morocco binding is heavily gilt, the text replete with full-page illustrations. One copy of the volume is inscribed "To Harriet F. Wheeler, On Her Wedding Day, with her Pastor's love, Nov. 13, 1861." Alongside elegant giftbooks, advertisements promoted "remarkably cheap" pamphlets that sold for a few cents each, a price "so low as to put them within reach of the poorest." By fashioning hymn texts into material artifacts and marketing them as commodities, evangelical publishers attracted a numerous, undifferentiated audience that was broader than evangelical church members.[11]

Improved craftsmanship of both elegant and cheap hymnal editions enhanced the presumed usefulness of hymns to potential consumers. Adver-

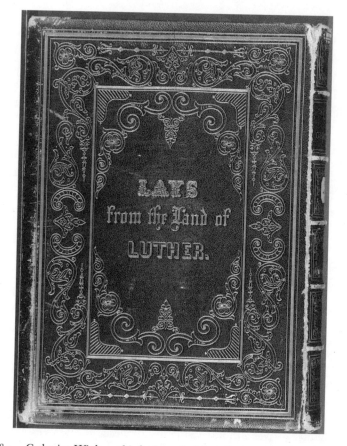

Figure 8.1.   Catherine Winkworth's finely crafted *Lyra Germanica*, or *Lays from the Land of Luther*, of 1858 was suited for display in the middle-class Victorian parlor. (Courtesy of the President and Fellows of Harvard College)

tisements and prefaces that endorsed volumes as "printed from clear type on fine paper, in convenient form" and "much better executed" than other hymnbooks suggest some of the characteristics valued by anticipated purchasers. The *Old School or Primitive Baptist Hymn Book* (1860) boasted its elegant style and availability in both red and blue bindings. Advertisements for even the least expensive hymn collections denied the use of "poor type and poorer paper" and appealed to buyers' desire to obtain "rich, cheap treasure." High-quality binding, paper, and gilt edges made a hymnal more durable so as to last for many years, just as clear type made the texts of hymns easier to read, thus "suitable for weak eyes." Even consumers who purchased attractive hymnals for aesthetic or social reasons could, argued hopeful evangelicals, fall under the spiritual influence of the hymns they encountered.[12]

Hymnals and Denomination Building

A torrent of hymnal publishing accompanied and accelerated the processes of denominational consolidation well underway by the 1840s. Following the pioneering ventures of eighteenth-century writers such as Watts and the Wesleys, British and American compilers introduced an increasing number and variety of hymnals calculated to serve denominational as well as more broadly evangelical purposes. Those denominations with formal ecclesiastical hierarchies earliest regulated the hymnals used by affiliated churches. By the second quarter of the nineteenth century, advances in printing technology and competition among churches had convinced most denominations of the need to oversee the growing body of hymnody used in congregational worship.[13]

Denominational leaders learned by experience that in the absence of clerical regulation, a lay priesthood of all believers could and would introduce hymnals of their own that might or might not correspond with denominational purposes. To govern congregational singing, the Methodist Book Concern became the first American denominational publisher to sponsor an official hymn collection. The Book Concern imported *A Pocket Hymn-Book* (1781) from England and printed an American edition in 1789. In 1808 the pioneering Bishop Francis Asbury oversaw the publication of the first American Methodist collection: *A Selection of Hymns from Various Authors: Designed as a Supplement to the Methodist Pocket Hymn-Book*. When lay Methodists began to issue their own unofficial Methodist collections, such as *The Wesleyan Harp* (1834), the General Conference in 1836 prohibited the use of such books during Sunday worship services. The preface to the 1836 Methodist hymnal urged, moreover: "We must, therefore, earnestly entreat you, if you have any respect for the authority of the Conference, or of us, or any regard for the prosperity of the Church of which you are members and friends, to purchase no Hymnbooks but what are published by our own Agents, and signed with the names of your Bishops." The AME hymnal published in 1837, cued by the Methodist precaution, included an almost identical plea. Methodist leaders, earlier than most other clergy, recognized the need to regulate hymnal publishing in order to guard against doctrinal heresy and promote denominational unity.[14]

Clergy focused their regulatory measures on hymnals used in Sunday services, settings that they viewed as crucial opportunities to impart denominational teachings. Like the Methodists, the Protestant Episcopal General Convention closely monitored church hymnody. In 1789 the denomination's publishing board issued an edition of the *Bay Psalm Book*, which added a supplement of 27 hymns. Hymnody became increasingly important to the denomination as the century progressed; by 1874, the *Hymnal According to the Use of the Protestant Episcopal Church in the United States of America* embraced 300 hymns. Only in 1861 did some dioceses begin to admit the use of a few supplemental collections, chiefly the Anglican bestseller *Hymns Ancient and Modern* (1861). The convention allowed the use of other books only in midweek services, which church leaders informally designated as suitable for cultivating lay piety.[15]

Denominations with looser ecclesiastical hierarchies experienced more difficulty in achieving a uniform hymnody. The Presbyterian Church adopted its first official hymnal in 1828. After splitting into Old and New School branches in 1837, each side chose its own collection. The New School Publication Committee sponsored *The Church Psalmist* (1843), and the Old School Board of Publication "approved and authorized" a *Book of Psalms and Hymns* (1843) "to be used in all our Churches." Yet neither publication board had the authority to enforce its selections on Presbyterian congregations. The New School Committee complained in 1863 that, unlike other denominations, the Presbyterians had countenanced the publication of "multitudinous discordant hymn-books . . . gotten up on private responsibility, without the endorsement of the Church, and expressing simply the taste of the compiler—books which may be filled with heresy as well as bad poetry." The complaint reflected two related concerns, over doctrinal content and linguistic expression suited to the purposes of worship. Indeed, as chapter 7 argues, disagreements over hymn selection arose among clergy and laity as refined and vernacular aesthetics of the sacred competed. Once the northern branches of the Old and New School Presbyterian Church had reunited in 1870, denominational leaders reiterated earlier appeals for centralized regulation of church hymnody. The reorganized General Assembly of the Presbyterian Board argued in 1871 that the "psalmody of the Church should have most careful official and authoritative supervision to secure freedom from doctrinal error, and adaptation to the purposes of worship." Implicitly, denominational leaders believed themselves better qualified than lay practitioners to determine which doctrinal and formal elements constituted sacred language. The board regretted that individual congregations had up until that time "felt themselves at liberty" to adopt any book they pleased. Although denominational leaders advocated voluntary action to forward moral and social reform causes, the close connection between hymnody and the Word made voluntarism in this area seem an "irresponsible course." The board accordingly commissioned a new, official *Presbyterian Hymnal*, published in 1874. In regulating denominational hymnody, Presbyterian leaders struggled to control a lay priesthood that was determined to publish and purchase books on their own initiative.[16]

Denominations governed on the congregational level proceeded still more slowly and haltingly in coordinating worship practices of affiliated churches. Congregationalist leaders made exceptionally few efforts to guide hymnal selection for the denomination as a whole. The Mohegan Indian Samson Occom, a Congregationalist missionary to other Native Americans, wrote one of the first American hymnbooks, an explicitly nondenominational volume: *A Choice Collection of Hymns and Spiritual Songs, Intended for the Edification of Sincere Christians of All Denominations* (1774). Congregational churches chose from among a number of collections, including Nathan Strong's *Hartford Selection* (1799), Samuel Worcester's edition of *Watts and Select Hymns* (1819), Asahel Nettleton's *Village Hymns for Social Worship* (1824), Joshua Leavitt's *Christian Lyre* (1830–31), and Henry Ward Beecher's *Plymouth Collection* (1855). Congregational churches in many, but not all, instances adopted books compiled by Congregationalists. Yet no denominational organ designated a particular volume as the authoritative collection.[17]

For locally governed denominations, regional preferences complicated the problem of securing denominational uniformity in hymn singing practices. As chapter 7 discusses at length, tastes in hymnody and corresponding aesthetics of the sacred varied geographically and socially. Southern, western, and rural congregations generally preferred more vernacular styles, and northern, urban congregations favored more refined linguistic expression, although the boundaries between the folksy and the formal were fluid in both settings. Congregationalist churches remained concentrated in New England, but Baptist churches dotted the national landscape. At least forty-two unofficial Baptist hymnals, representing diverse regional preferences, appeared from 1766 to 1843. William Buck, a Regular Baptist missionary to Virginia, Kentucky, Mississippi, Alabama, and Texas, worried that "nearly every Protestant denomination has a collection that accords with their own peculiar tenets. The Baptists have *many* such, and this redundancy has become so great as to destroy any approach towards uniformity." While living in Kentucky, Buck published his own volume, titled *The Baptist Hymn Book* (1842), to "give to our denomination 'A BAPTIST HYMN BOOK' — one which the denomination at large will adopt." Within two years, Buck sold 10,000 copies in the Mississippi Valley, but the hymnal failed to gain nationwide acceptance. Even in neighboring southern and western states, other unofficial collections, like the *Baptist Psalmody* (1850), soon competed with Buck's volume for congregational adoption. In the North, the ABPS worked with the Boston trade house of Gould, Kendall, & Lincoln to issue *The Psalmist* (1843), intending the volume to serve "as the standard Baptist hymnal." Reflecting on the hymnal's influence in 1845, the ABPS concluded that it had done "more to produce uniformity in the use of hymn-books, and correct the taste of the churches, than its projectors ever anticipated." Despite ABPS optimism, other hymnals competed with *The Psalmist*, including a "Baptist edition" of the Congregationalist Henry Ward Beecher's *Plymouth Collection*. Regardless of the intentions of Baptist leaders such as Buck and the ABPS to oversee denominational hymnody, individuals and congregations expressed their own tastes in compiling hymnals and choosing from among market options.[18]

Despite the limitations of denominational efforts to regulate church hymnody, the publication of denominational hymnals played a critical role in the formation and sustenance of an informal hymn canon. Presented by denominational committees as comprehensive repositories of all useful hymns, denominational volumes in large measure defined the canon of hymns in circulation. According to one contemporary estimate, as of 1878 denominational collections included an average of 1,266 different hymns. Compilers gathered hymns on each subject they considered useful and that fitted the tastes of committee members drawn from various regions. The *Presbyterian Hymnal* (1874) was typical in incorporating hymns indexed as suitable for "Invitation to Worship," "Adoration," the "Sacraments," "Prayer Meetings," "Family Worship," "Dedications," "National Commemoration," "Private Meditation," and "Devotion." In addition to marking hymns as appropriate to particular occasions, denominational hymnals systematically addressed every doctrine of the church and each stage of Christian pilgrimage. The Methodist *Hymnal* (1878) began with hymns marking the daily and weekly cycles of "Morning" and "Evening" devotions and "Sabbath" worship. The book then proceeded through the doctrines of "God," "Christ," the "Holy Spirit," the "Scriptures," the "Sinner," the "Christian," the "Church," and "Time" and "Eternity." Organizational headings taught singers to interpret even unpleasant or banal life experiences such as "Trial" and "Suffering" as experiences that contributed to the spiritual phases of "Justification," "Regeneration," "Adoption," "Consecration," "Entire Sanctification," and "Christian Growth." By accounting for diverse experiences within an overarching theological framework, denominational compilers demarcated an extensive yet limited body of texts from which singers might draw.[19]

The size and consequent expense of denominational hymnals slowed changes to the hymn canon. The per-unit cost of such collections averaged roughly one to two dollars. When a denominational publishing board officially sponsored a new edition, church leaders urged the members of every cooperating congregation to purchase copies. Due to the substantial sum invested in church hymnals, the General Conference of the Methodist Episcopal Church felt reluctant to revise its book more frequently than once in sixteen years. The influence of hymns included in denominational collections became more deeply entrenched as congregations selected texts from a single edition for decades.[20]

Conservative compilation and revision processes dispersed a common body of hymns geographically and preserved substantially the same hymns from one edition to the next. The Methodist Episcopal revision committee of 1878 consisted of fifteen members representing the middle, eastern, and western sections of the country, all of whom had to agree on each hymn chosen. The committee read every hymn aloud, often several times, discussing the texts stanza by stanza and sometimes line by line. The committee affirmed that "every excellent hymn must be retained, and that no good hymn should be ejected except to make room for a better; also that hymns that were universally known, sung, and loved, even if they could not endure the rigid application of sound rules of criticism, could not be disturbed." The committee adopted not only those hymns that met clerically defined standards of criticism but also those approved by congregations. Similarly, a committee of the Methodist Episcopal Church, South, meeting in 1886 to revise an edition in use for the past forty years, required a two-thirds vote to omit an existing hymn or to admit a new hymn. As a result of such conservative criteria, the contents of denominational hymnals changed little between editions.[21]

The same editorial processes that solidified a single denomination's hymnody diminished the perceived distance separating evangelical denominations. Revision committees typically examined the hymnals published by other denominations as well as their own, incorporating what they considered the best hymns from every source. The Presbyterian committee for the 1874 hymnal included those hymns and tunes "approved by the judgment of all evangelical Christians, as expressed by the selection of them by the compilers of their standard books." The committee approved only one "untried" hymn among its 1,006 selections.[22]

As a result of frequent borrowing, the contents of hymnals sponsored by different denominations overlapped substantially. According to a database compiled by the historian Stephen Marini, out of a sample of fifty-nine denominational hymnals published from 1830 to 1890, 136 titles appeared in twenty-five or more of the collections. My analysis of themes, scriptural references, and narrative patterns reveals consistency across hymn texts in the various collections. Marini has, moreover, noted the relative absence of hymns addressing topics that generated interdenominational controversy, such as ecclesiology, missions, Communion, baptism, the Bible, the Godhead, and the Last Judgment. At the same time, Marini has observed the repetition of themes representing a "core of consensus beliefs," including the atonement, invitation, salvation, sanctification, witness, perseverance, death, and heaven. Indeed, it is in many instances difficult to discern the affiliation of an official denominational hymnal by any means other than the book's title and publisher. The breadth of subject matter, expense, and conservative selection processes involved in the making of denominational hymnals sustained a unity wider than the denomination itself, disseminating a common body of hymnody to multiple generations of congregations across diverse regional and denominational affiliations.[23]

By the 1840s, most sizable denominations had sponsored at least one official hymn collection with the goal of regulating the hymns sung during Sunday services. Yet only the Methodists and Episcopalians strictly prohibited the use of competing collections, and no denomination fully controlled the books used in midweek or extrainstitutional religious services. In the absence of tighter denominational oversight, individuals acted in an expansive print market to publish hymnals that often worked at tangent to denominational purposes. The innovative work of supplementary collections accompanied and qualified the sedimentation of the hymn canon accomplished by denominational hymnals.[24]

Supplementing the Hymn Canon

Both clergy and laity followed the example set by Watts and the Wesleys in privately sponsoring their own compilations to supplement the hymn canon. An evangelical priesthood of all believers produced and purchased what the Anglican compiler Sir Roundell Palmer called, with some skepticism, a "great and constantly increasing multitude of hymn-books intended for congregational use." Expressing greater confidence in lay initiative, the Southern Methodists Rev. Atticus Haygood and R. M. McIntosh endorsed the proliferation of unofficial hymn collections; that "pastors and people desire such supplementary books is made manifest by their buying and using them." Hymnal supplements, as compilers referred to the volumes, denied competing with the "authorized church hymnal," which, the collections urged, should still be used in official church services and "always have the pre-eminence." The preface to one such supplement described the volume as a companion to other books, a helper in promoting "devotion and culture." Another preface claimed paradoxically that the book was "not designed to supersede books already introduced, but rather to be used in connection with them; yet its contents are sufficiently varied and full to meet the wants of congregations that have not been previously supplied, or that desire a change." Although not intended to compete with other books, the volume purportedly could do so effectively.[25]

In contrast to denominational hymnals that preserved the continuity of the hymn canon, supplemental collections augmented and refashioned the canon to adjust to a changing world. Hymn supplements ranged from "pocket-sized" to midsized collections that treated topics underaddressed by denominational hymnals, such as private devotions, revivals, and regional and interdenominational religious practices. Individual compilers acted more rapidly than denominational committees who had to build consensus. Because many supplements aimed to serve narrowly defined purposes — such as use in a revival or temperance meeting — the books tended to be smaller, less expensive, and more quickly tailored to changing tastes in hymns and music. The nondenominational *New Revival Melodies* (1860), for example, offered the "*cream* of modern social hymns and tunes" for the "remarkably cheap price" of fifteen cents per copy. The word-only edition of *Gospel Temperance Songs* (1879) sold at the bulk rate of 100 copies for three dollars. The limited objectives, speed of production, and relatively low price of supplements made them adaptable to the changing needs of hymnal users.[26]

Pocket-sized supplements, suited to the mobility of nineteenth-century society, made it easier for individuals to carry hymns with them everywhere they went, on weekdays as well as on Sundays. As an advertisement for one "pocket-companion" boasted, "One can take this neat little volume in his pocket when going to meeting, and thus have the benefit of it at home and abroad." *Social Hymns: Original and Selected* (1865), by Horace Lorenzo Hastings, is a pocket book measuring 5 inches long by 3 inches wide and less than half an inch thick that encompasses 284 hymns. By contrast, the *Presbyterian Hymnal* of 1874 is more than twice the size, measuring 9 by 6 ¼ by 1 ¼ inches and embracing 1,006 hymns (figure 8.2). Hastings told his readers that he had selected most of the hymns from a more extensive collection, to which he added a few original compositions. The volume's

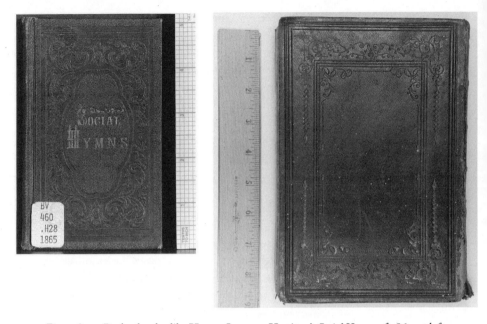

Figure 8.2. Pocket books, like Horace Lorenzo Hastings's *Social Hymns* of 1865, at left, could be carried around much more conveniently than denominational compendiums, such as the *Presbyterian Hymnal* of 1874, at right. (Courtesy of the President and Fellows of Harvard College, and used by permission of the University of Missouri–Kansas City Libraries, Kenneth J. LaBudde Department of Special Collections)

portability recommended it "as a matter of convenience" above bulky alternatives. The volume transported the influence of a subset of the hymn canon wherever its owner carried it.[27]

Midsized supplements reshaped the canon by privileging certain hymns as more useful than others. Asa Hull's *Pilgrim's Harp: A Choice Collection of Sacred Music, Adapted to All Occasions of Social and Family Worship, and a Convenient Hand-book for Church Choirs* (1869) furnished "in the most compact form, and at the lowest possible price, a Hand-Book of Sacred Song which shall amply meet all ordinary demands of Social Worship and Congregational Singing." Hull, like other individual compilers, claimed that his collection, half as large as most denominational hymnals, succeeded better in gathering together in a manageable compass the "cream of the sanctified Christian thought of the ages." Compilers such as Hull likewise asserted that their volumes — more effectively than pocketbooks — presented a sufficient variety of hymns to appeal to diverse tastes and "avoid repetition, and all sorts of getting into ruts." At the same time, and in contrast to heftier denominational hymnals, the compact size encouraged singing the same hymns "so long and so often" that the words became familiar, their truths fixed in the minds and hearts of the church. Supplements like Hull's functioned to narrow the portion of canonical hymns most circulated among evangelical singers.[28]

Although denominational hymnals excluded texts ill-suited to congregational singing, certain supplements invoked a more inclusive textual community by offering intensely personal hymns appropriate for individual reading or singing during private devotions. Winkworth's *Lyra Germanica* (1855) translated a series of long, meditative devotional poems that interpreted individual experience in terms of seasons in the Christian's "Inner Life." Organizational headings denoted texts as useful to individual Christians in particular circumstances, such as those struggling "Under a Heavy Private Cross or Bereavement," against "The Weakness and Restlessness of Sin," and in "Preparation for Death." Headings connected readers with other members of a textually defined community by suggesting that other Christians had used the same hymns to overcome conflicts like those the reader confronted. Another devotional volume, *Christ in Song* (1870), compiled by the German Reformed theologian Philip Schaff, helped readers to interpret stages in their own lives in relation to the life of Christ. The first cycle of hymns directed readers to meditate on each stage in Christ's life: "Advent," "Incarnation," "Passion," "Resurrection." The second cycle of hymns interpreted the Christian's life in relation to the life of Christ: "Christ our Refuge and Strength," "Love and Gratitude to Christ," "For Ever with Christ." Such devotional volumes added hymns to the canon that aided Christians of every denomination in interpreting seasons in their inner lives as corresponding to a pattern of spiritual pilgrimage that all Christians followed.[29]

In contrast to devotional volumes that guided meditation on particular spiritual seasons, revival hymnbooks addressed a nondenominational religious community by moving singers through a common sequence of stages in the Christian life. Editors arranged hymns to trace steps of "Warning" and "Inviting" the impenitent; leading the convicted in "Penitence" and "Supplication" toward "Conversion," "Bible Reading," "Baptism," "Social Worship," "Work," and observing the "Sabbath"; experiencing "Comfort," "Joy," "Praise," and "Thanksgiving"; overcoming "Trials" and "Backsliding"; toward "Restoration," "Revival," "Death," and "Judgment," all the way to heaven. By singing through the cycle of hymns, the ideal singer followed in the wake of a unified stream of Christian pilgrims who had similarly moved stage by stage toward salvation.[30]

As denominational regulation of official hymn collections tightened by midcentury, evangelicals used supplemental volumes to express a broader range of hymn preferences than those accommodated by church leaders. Supplements included hymns and tunes not in the "regular Hymn book," appealing, for instance, to regional tastes overlooked by collections designed for use nationwide. John Wyeth's *Repository of Sacred Music* (Pennsylvania, 1813) and Ananias Davison's *Supplement to the Kentucky Harmony* (Virginia, 1820) were two of the earliest regional collections. South Carolina native "Singin' Billy" Walker's *Southern Harmony* attained such extensive acceptance throughout the South that it sold 600,000 copies between 1835 and 1860.[31]

Supplements designed for use in nondenominational meetings promoted a sense of Christian unity that transcended denominational allegiances. Supplements differentiated between those hymns suitable for denominationally governed Sunday church services and for nondenominational settings, such as revivals, camp and protracted meetings, and social, prayer, praise, missionary, and temperance song services. Christians of different denominations living in Charleston, South Carolina, in 1846 came together weekly at a Union Prayer Meeting. Participants selected hymns that evoked Christian unity, such as

> Blest be the tie that binds
> Our hearts in Christian love;
> The fellowship of kindred minds
> Is like to that above.

Hymns sung in community gatherings alleviated denominational rivalries by emphasizing experiences shared by all Christians. The ATS's *Hymns for Social Worship* (1840), among many similar collections, gained acceptance at meetings like that held in Charleston. The volume contained 549 hymns "adapted for use in neighborhood and other Social Meetings, embracing individuals under the various operations of the Holy Spirit; and by Christians of different denominations." The ATS supplement provided an alternative to collections designed for any one denomination. Although encouraging nondenominational worship services, the ATS avoided publishing hymnals for use in Sunday services. The denominational identities of ATS members precluded their sponsorship of a hymnal that competed with denominational collections. By informally designating Sunday services for denominational purposes and midweek gatherings for interdenominational cooperation, evangelicals simultaneously reinforced goals in tension with one another.[32]

The boundaries separating officially sponsored and supplemental hym-

nals, clerical and lay arbitration, and denominational and evangelical purposes all were permeable, and crossover occurred constantly. Supplements
published throughout the nineteenth century included standard church
hymns, such as Isaac Watts's "Alas! and Did My Saviour Bleed" and Charles
Wesley's "Jesus, Lover of My Soul." Likewise, denominational hymnals,
increasingly as the nineteenth century progressed, embraced hymns orig-
inally designated for extrainstitutional usage. *The Service of Song, for Baptist
Churches* (1876) presented both standard selections and hymns and tunes
"of the more popular and stirring kind," such as the gospel song "I Need
Thee Every Hour." The hymn was first sung at the National Baptist Sunday School Convention, held in Cincinnati in 1872, but congregations soon
began to sing the hymn during Sunday worship. Congregations did not
rigidly distinguish among hymns appropriate to one setting or another, and
purchasers generally preferred books useful for multiple occasions. As the
number and variety of hymn collections proliferated, the hymn canon expanded while remaining sufficiently coherent to facilitate dialogue among
evangelicals across denominational and regional divides.[33]

The Significance of Hymn Selection

The hymns that constituted the evangelical canon elaborated a complex,
meaningful pattern of significance understood by evangelical editors, compilers, and translators as interfacing the biblical narrative with experiences
shared by all Christians. Even the most comprehensive volumes did not
include more than a fortieth of the English-language hymns written by
midcentury. Inevitably then, someone had to choose which hymns to select
or omit in each published collection. In forging an informal canon of evangelical hymn texts, compilers sought out hymns that they considered useful
in aiding Christian pilgrimage.

Most authors who wrote on the subject articulated three basic criteria
for a useful hymn, that is, one that balanced purity and presence in the
world. First of all, a hymn originated with its author's encounter with
"inspired truth." Consequently, the "spirit of the hymn — its aroma, its
indescribable tone — must come from the Word of God." Second, hymns
connected the Word with the Christian's life in the present world. Hymns
reflected the "truths of that Word concreting themselves in Christian experience and life." Finally, hymns corresponded to experiences shared by all
Christians. In marked contrast to periodical literature, hymns purportedly
offered refreshment and rest from the divisions of the Christian world. The
language embodied sound doctrine without being "too didactic" or contro-

versial. Rather than expressing "sectarian peculiarities," hymns formed a special bond of Christian unity.[34]

Evangelicals coded the terms "old" and "new" to define an informal canon of hymns that used the timeless Word to unify the pilgrim community as it traveled through the changing world of human experience. The nondenominational *Songs of the Christian Creed and Life: Selected from Eighteen Centuries* (1876) exhibited "the complexion of all the Christian centuries" by juxtaposing old and new hymns "without partiality, from almost all the Churches, and almost all the Centuries." Likewise, the Methodist *Hymnal* (1878) worked to "revere the past, appropriate all that is good in the present, and joyfully anticipate the future." By embracing old and new texts, each such hymnbook provided a portable version of the hymn canon.[35]

The juxtaposition of old and new texts evoked a timeless, unified Christian community that contrasted with many local communities, which religious and social dissension had fragmented. In an effort to restore a lost sense of Christian unity, compilers and translators turned to the ancient and medieval Catholic Church and to early modern German and British Protestantism for resources. Coinciding with the literary refinement of evangelical print culture discussed in chapter 7, translations from the Latin and German proliferated, culminating in the publication of *Hymns Ancient and Modern*, first in England in 1861, then in America in 1866. The hymnal immediately gained unprecedented popularity, selling more than 25 million copies during the nineteenth century. Of the collection's 273 hymns, translators adapted 132 texts from Latin and 10 from German, reprinted 119 texts from eighteenth-century English hymnists, and included 12 new English compositions. The old hymns won their place in new collections because they had "consoled thousands of God's faithful servants in all kinds of circumstances, almost from the days of the Apostles to our own." Nineteenth-century evangelicals considered such hymns "dear" since they reflected the unity of a timeless pilgrim community.[36]

Amid social instability and denominational competition, the translation impulse eased anxieties about rapid change and conflicting claims to authority. In contrast to the "eager enterprise and noisy self-assertion" of modern times, quiet hymns offered welcome respite and comfort to weary pilgrims. "Saints of other days had so much more quiet illumination, rested in the Lord more perfectly, and told their mysterious secret in numbers at once nobler and sweeter, than modern Christians." The old hymns, moreover, presumably grew out of religious feelings rather than being made to order for the market. Insisting that the "old is better," translators sought to restore the "intensity of devotion to the person of Christ" and the "individuality of the relation between the Redeemer and his disciples" apparently lost by most nineteenth-century hymnists. For example, the Congregationalist minister Ray Palmer translated a Latin devotional hymn of unknown origin:

> I give my heart to Thee,
> O Jesus most desired!
> And heart for heart the gift shall be,
> For Thou my soul hast fired:
> . . . .
> I would love Thee as Thou lov'st me,
> O Jesus most desired!

The hymnist voiced a desire for Jesus more intense than any worldly longing. Winkworth translated a hymn from the German Catholic Angelus Silesius (1657) that similarly expressed its author's single-minded pursuit of heaven.

> Thou Holiest Love, whom most I love,
> Who art my long'd-for only bliss,
> . . . .
> I give Thee thanks that Thou didst die
> To win eternal life for me,
> To bring salvation from on high;
> Oh draw me up through love to Thee!

The hymnist longed for Jesus to draw him from life on earth toward the bliss of eternal life in heaven. Translators used such meditative devotional texts to calm the unrest that characterized the industrializing, market-driven world of nineteenth-century British and American society.[37]

Seeking an antidote to modern religious controversies, translators claimed that shared experiences transcended doctrinal and denominational divisions among Christians. Translators hoped to "exhibit that oneness of evangelical faith, and that Christian union in the great characteristic and essential elements of our holy religion, which enables us to acknowledge our brotherhood with these simple-minded, cultivated, and sanctified men." Impressed by the piety of their earlier brethren, translators purportedly could "make little account of the fact that they may have believed something which I cannot believe, and may have used a ritual and liturgy which I disapprove." The unity that so amazed translators derived in part from their own decisions to elide theological differences. As one compiler admitted, translated hymns often bore the "doctrinal sense according to the wish of the translator." Evangelicals who borrowed Catholic hymns omitted references to saints and altered lines that implied the efficacy of works or the sacraments in salvation. Translators mediated between hymn writers and readers, since hymnal users could not generally compare the original text with the new version. Although some translators acknowledged producing imitations rather than strict translations, most others said little about their rationales in rendering texts in particular ways.[38]

Even more often than turning to Catholic or German hymns for inspiration, nineteenth-century American compilers preferred eighteenth-century British texts to newer American compositions. Editors argued that the old British hymns were "so full of Bible truth, Christian experience, and sacred associations" that they served better than modern texts to "refresh, and vitalize, and sanctify God's people, and to direct and win sinners to Christ and heaven." Out of 5,014 hymns printed in five denominational hymnals, the *Methodist Episcopal Hymnbook* (1849), the *Baptist Hymn Book* (1871), the *Presbyterian Hymnal* (1874), the *Episcopal Hymnal* (1871), and the loosely Congregationalist *Plymouth Collection* (1855), American authors contributed 616 hymns, or just 12 percent of the total. Eighteenth-century British hymnists wrote most of the remaining selections.[39]

American evangelicals used the old British texts to invoke a pattern of nondenominational Christian fellowship that they perceived as characterizing this earlier era better than their own. Scholars have identified the hymns printed most frequently in a cross section of American hymnals published from 1830 to 1890. The thirty most reprinted hymns all appeared in at least thirty-nine, or two-thirds, of the fifty-nine collections examined. Of these hymns, Isaac Watts wrote ten and Charles Wesley five; other eighteenth-century English authors wrote twelve; an eighteenth-century Welshman wrote one; one was translated from the Latin of Saint Augustine; a nineteenth-century Englishman wrote the final selection. The hymnists represented a variety of denominations. Presbyterian and Independent nonconformists wrote a total of fourteen of the hymns, Methodists six, Baptists four, Moravians two, and members of the established churches in England and Wales another two; one hymn originated in the pre-Reformation church and one in an unknown communion. The American evangelical hymn canon, to a greater extent than the evangelical canon as a whole, remained anchored in a constellation of eighteenth-century British texts that presumably reflected experiences shared by Christians of every denomination.[40]

American compilers favored those British hymns that reiterated narratives of pilgrimage from the sin of this world to the holiness of heaven. The British Methodist (later Moravian) John Cennick's "Children of the Heav'nly King" (1742) ranked as the thirteenth most frequently reprinted hymn in collections published from 1830 to 1890. The Methodist *Hymnal* (1878) added a subtitle, "The Pilgrims' Song," to highlight the theme of corporate pilgrimage.

> We are traveling home to God,
> In the way our fathers trod;
> They are happy now, and we
> Soon their happiness shall see.
> . . . .
> Lift your eyes, ye sons of light;
> Zion's city is in sight;
> There our endless home shall be,
> There our Lord we soon shall see.

The singing congregation encouraged one another to keep traveling home to God by recalling the journey that previous generations had undertaken and by anticipating arrival in heaven.[41]

Throughout the body of texts that Americans gleaned from eighteenth-century British hymnists, verbal metaphors define the Christian life as pursuing a journey, fighting a battle, and running a race. Traveling through the present world seemed so difficult that Christians needed the support of God and fellow pilgrims to attain their goal. Hymn narratives culminate with Christians' arrival in heaven, a land of rest, home, and eternal day, where one united church will forever worship God. Although some hymns, like Cennick's, frame life in terms of a literal journey, others focus on the spiritual journey of Christians struggling against sin and longing for growth in holiness, or sanctification. "Love Divine, All Love Excelling," written by Charles Wesley in 1747, ranked sixteenth for number of occurrences in nineteenth-century hymnals.[42]

> 1. Love divine, all love excelling,
> Joy of heaven, to earth come down!
> Fix in us thy humble dwelling;
> All thy faithful mercies crown.
> Jesus, thou art all compassion,
> Pure, unbounded love thou art;
> Visit us with thy salvation;
> Enter every trembling heart.

2. Breathe, O breathe thy loving Spirit
Into every troubled breast!
Let us all in thee inherit,
Let us find that second rest.
Take away our bent to sinning;
Alpha and Omega be;
End of faith, as its beginning,
Set our hearts at liberty.

3. Come, almighty to deliver,
Let us all thy life receive;
Suddenly return, and never,
Never more thy temples leave:
Thee we would be always blessing,
Serve thee as thy hosts above,
Pray, and praise thee without ceasing,
Glory in thy perfect love.

4. Finish then thy new creation;
Pure and spotless let us be;
Let us see thy great salvation,
Perfectly restored in thee:
Changed from glory into glory,
Till in heaven we take our place,
Till we cast our crowns before thee,
Lost in wonder, love, and praise.

Wesley's hymn traces the pilgrim community's journey through each stage, from the beginning of faith to its end in perfect heavenly worship. The first stanza addresses Jesus as the source of love and asks for his presence in the heart of every Christian. The second stanza appeals to the Holy Spirit to take away the bent to sinning, freeing hearts from the power of sin. The third stanza envisions the possibility of pure worship on earth as in heaven, in enjoyment of perfect love. The final stanza anticipates continual growth in purity; Christians change from glory into glory as the Father perfects the new creation.

"Love Divine," like most of its companion hymns, helps singers to interpret their lives as sacred pilgrimage by connecting biblical passages to Christian experience. The Methodist *Hymnal* of 1878 indexes the hymn's scriptural allusions: Malachi 3:1 (prophecy of Jesus' arrival in his temple) — stanza 1, line 2, and stanza 3, line 4; Matthew 14:14 (Jesus' compassion) —

stanza 1, line 5; 2 Corinthians 3:18 (the Holy Spirit transforms Christians from one degree of glory to another) — stanza 2, lines 1 and 2, and stanza 4, line 5; Revelation 4:10 (crowns cast down in worship) — stanza 4, line 7; Revelation 21:5 (God makes all things new) — stanza 4, line 1; and Revelation 21:6 (God is Alpha and Omega) — stanza 2, line 6. Biblical references offer Christians assurance at each stage of their journey as they experience trembling hearts, feel bound by their bent to sinning, bless God, and finally lose themselves in wonder, love, and praise. "Love Divine" weaves the Word into a narrative of Christian progress through this world toward heaven.

Hymnal editors applied the timeless narrative of Christian pilgrimage to the world of nineteenth-century America by coupling older hymns with newer compositions, those "many PRECIOUS GEMS" that had recently become familiar by frequent use. The evangelical hymn canon included both the "good old STANDARD HYMNS" and "MODERN FAVORITES," thereby preserving the "old time spirit, with the culture of modern times superadded." An unofficial Methodist camp meeting songbook, *The Golden Harp* (1857), presented almost fifty eighteenth-century British hymns, which carried "the gray hairs of more than a century." The book balanced these old hymns with more than twice as many new camp meeting songs and choruses, such as "The Gospel Steamer":

> Yes, We'll land on Canaan's Shore;
> Oh, He'll land us on the shore;
> Yes, We'll land on Canaan sure,
> And be safe forever more.

The repetitive diction, rhyme, narrative structure, and heavenward focus reflected the timeless theme of Christian pilgrimage adapted to vernacular camp meeting traditions. The book's organization made no distinction between old and new songs but placed them side by side, suggesting their equal membership in an implied evangelical canon.[43]

Hymnals embraced newer hymns originating outside evangelicalism if the texts bore marks of membership in the evangelical canon. "Nearer My God to Thee" (1841) by the Unitarian Sarah Adams was a favorite among nineteenth-century evangelicals, ranking number eighty-one out of those hymns most often reprinted. Although some evangelicals resisted the hymn because it lacked Trinitarian theology, others considered it evangelical on account of its usefulness in promoting Christian pilgrimage: it "deeply moved" the singer to strain after heavenly communion. The hymn gained authority as an evangelical text when compilers juxtaposed it with more explicitly Christ-centered selections. Taken together, the body of hymns chosen by nineteenth-century editors encouraged Christian unity in traveling from this world toward the holiness of heaven.[44]

Alterations and Questions of Authorship and Copyright

The hymn canon, like the larger evangelical canon, was open, fluid, conditionally authoritative, and functionally sacred. Assuming that hymns belonged to the entire Christian community, editors felt considerable freedom to alter texts to make them more useful in achieving Christian unity. As one editor put it, "A Hymn, whether original, or translated, ought, the moment it is published, to become the common property of Christendom; the author retaining no private right in it whatever." Because hymns played a special role in expressing shared Christian experience, editors considered hymns, more than any other genre, open to appropriation by participants in the evangelical textual community.[45]

The practice of altering hymn texts written by other authors emerged simultaneously with the blossoming of hymnody in the eighteenth century. Even though John Wesley altered the hymns of his contemporaries, he objected when George Whitefield, Augustus Toplady, and others meddled with his hymns. Alterations obscured but could not eliminate theological and aesthetic divides that persisted within evangelicalism. Nineteenth-century editors considering potential hymn alterations grappled with a tension between two of their core ideas about hymnody: that the Christian community shared hymn ownership and that hymn writing was a sacred process influenced by the Holy Spirit. If a hymn grew out of an author's encounter with the living Word, editors risked diluting sacred language by tampering with the hymn's original words. At the same time, editors felt themselves responsible for guarding against theological and linguistic corruption to which a lay priesthood of hymn authors and singers remained vulnerable.[46]

In altering hymns written by others, editors presumed a right to mediate relationships between authors and readers in a textually defined community. Because hymns powerfully connected the living Word with the realm of human experience, editors felt particularly concerned with hymns' doctrinal content. Editors accordingly revised even single words or phrases that they considered theologically misleading. Wilson Thompson, an elder in a Regular Baptist Church, compiled *A Baptist Hymn-Book* (1844). He "varied the language of the authors, in many hymns, avoiding such terms as I believed unsound, and only calculated to give a false impression to the mind." Thompson changed the word "Canaan" to "heaven," "Sabbath" to "Lord's day," and "dying love" to "eternal love." He insisted that he changed the terms only to better express what the authors "intended them to mean." Where Thompson considered hymn diction flawed, he replaced whole phrases with "words of ideas instead of tiresome and unmeaning repetition." Only in those instances in which Thompson conceived of himself as making a "material change in the doctrinal import" did he affix his own name alongside the original author's. Even when editors, like Thompson, acknowledged altering hymn texts, they almost never presented the original alongside the alteration. Interested readers would have had to find another hymnal to make the comparison, assuming they could find an edition that did not introduce other emendations.[47]

Throughout the antebellum period, editors from most denominations readily altered hymn texts while straining to avoid mutilating sacred language. William Francis, compiler of *A Collection of Psalms and Hymns for Christian Worship* (1835), an avowedly nondenominational hymnbook, exercised a somewhat more restricted level of editorial intervention than did Thompson. Francis consistently retained words such as "Canaan," "Zion," and "Israel," considering these terms the "peculiar and appropriate diction and imagery of sacred poetry." He claimed to reprint the old hymns in a purer form than did other books, excluding those that, for doctrinal reasons, needed a "great deal of alteration." In the hymns he selected, Francis "freely omitted such verses, however, as I did not approve." Depicting himself as preserving the sacred language of hymnody, Francis nevertheless reshaped the hymn canon by including and excluding complete hymns and isolated stanzas.[48]

Besides altering or omitting texts, editors regulated hymn doctrine by adding stanzas. The 1858 Regular Baptist *Psalms and Hymns* appended a sixth verse to Sarah Adams's "Nearer My God to Thee." That verse, written by the English Independent minister Arthur Russell in 1851, transformed a Unitarian hymn into a Trinitarian doctrinal statement:

> Christ alone beareth me,
> Where Thou dost shine;
> Joint heir He maketh me
> Of the divine.
> In Christ my soul shall be
> Nearest, my God, to Thee,
> Nearest to thee!

Other stanzas brought singers nearer to God, but only Christ brought them nearest. The new stanza revised the hymn's doctrinal import to make it more explicitly evangelical.[49]

By the 1860s, as an expanding print market threatened to depersonalize relationships between writers and readers, evangelicals turned their attention to history and biography, as discussed in chapter 3, to restore intimacy among participants in a textually defined community. Writing in 1869, the Presbyterian minister James Murray voiced a widely held view that "the personal histories of all hymn-writers should be most deeply studied if we would have their hymns affect us most profoundly." Singers felt better able to understand the meanings of hymn language when they could identify with the experiences that led authors to compose their texts. Christians gained encouragement not only from the hymns themselves but also from the insights hymns offered into experiences that readers shared with hymn authors. The reader enjoyed "an hour's pleasant communion with the spirit of Christian hymns, or with the mind and hearts of those who wrote them." Hymns forged a bond of connection among participants in the evangelical textual community, regardless of the time or place in which hymns were written or read.[50]

Evangelicals commonly referred to the 1860s as a hymnological decade since never before had hymns been "so widely studied, so generally and so deeply loved" by Christians. In an era when Civil War was shattering physical communities and ideals of national union, hymnody aided American Christians in viewing themselves as interrelated members of a unified textual community. Numerous volumes narrated the stories of particular hymns and their authors, the circumstances under which hymnists had composed their texts, and testimonies of hymns' usefulness in the lives of singers and readers. One such volume bore the descriptive title *Illustrated History of Hymns and Their Authors: Facts and Incidents of the Origin, Authors, Sentiments and Singing of Hymns, Which, with a Synopsis, Embrace Interesting Items Relating to Over Eight Hundred Hymn-Writers, with Many Portraits and Other Illustrations* (1876). The volume promised to augment the usefulness of hymns by presenting information about particular texts, authors, and circumstances of composition and usage. The inclusion of portraits alongside biographical details helped readers envision themselves as related to the authors of favorite hymns (figure 8.3).[51]

Increased attention to relationships among hymn writers and readers caused evangelicals to revisit their assumptions about the nature of authorship and, by implication, the legitimacy of copyright. As chapter 6 notes, federal copyright laws had existed since 1790, but few American authors

Figure 8.3. These portraits of hymnists Lady Huntingdon and Charles Wesley from the *Illustrated History of Hymns and Their Authors* (1876) helped evangelical readers envision hymn writers as fellow members of a textual community. (Courtesy of the University of Missouri–Columbia)

copyrighted their materials before the 1840s. Given evangelicals' emphasis on the shared ownership of hymns, anonymous authorship was a more common practice for hymns than for any other genre. Most antebellum hymnbooks omitted the names of all hymn authors, and few compilers claimed copyrights. By midcentury, historical study had reinforced evangelicals' sense of membership in a timeless, placeless Christian community. Yet this same process also worked against the anonymity of authorship, the disregard of copyrights, and the malleability of texts. Hymnals published from the 1860s forward usually included the names and dates of authors and the years of hymn composition, while by contrast earlier collections had generally presented hymns as autonomous texts. At the same time, increasing numbers of hymn collections added warnings against the violation of copyrights. More compilers began to copyright their selections, although complaints about the "pernicious habit" of unauthorized borrowing as late as the 1890s suggest that, in practice, many evangelicals retained their earlier assumptions about shared ownership of hymns regardless of copyrights.[52]

As evangelicals associated hymns with individual authors, editorial liberties diminished. Hymnal editors from a spectrum of denominations objected to the "unwarrantable liberties" taken by other editors, whom they accused of mutilating hymns by "substituting words, and even whole stanzas of their own" to the detriment of more excellent originals. In rejecting editorial liberties, evangelicals emphasized the genesis of hymn language in an author's sacred experiences. Since words presumably conveyed the Holy Spirit's influence, a growing proportion of editors concluded that changing an author's language diminished a hymn's effect on its readers.[53]

After midcentury, editors who resisted altering original hymn language continued to affect textual transmission in two significant ways: by returning texts in common usage to earlier forms and by introducing avowedly insubstantial changes in wording. The committee for revising the Methodist *Hymnal* in 1878 argued that every hymnist ought to be allowed "to express his own thoughts in his own way." The hymnal returned texts to their original form when possible, omitting those texts that had grown "so altered and mutilated that it was deemed dishonest to make their authors responsible." Nevertheless, the committee introduced new changes in phrasing, arguing that since the revisions better reflected original meaning, they would have been "approved by none more heartily than by the authors themselves." In seeking to preserve the substance of hymnists' experiences, editors nevertheless continued to intervene between authors and singers in ways that reconfigured the canon of hymns in common usage.[54]

Nineteenth-century hymnals disseminated an informal canon of hymns that quieted religious dissension and sustained evangelicals' sense of membership in a pilgrim community traveling through this world toward heaven. Clerical and lay cultural arbiters, including editors, compilers, and translators, erased textual evidence of denominational disputes through their active involvement in framing, selecting, and altering the body of hymns most often read and sung by evangelicals. The publication of hymn texts in varied denominational and supplemental collections increased the power of hymns to incarnate the Word in the world of human experience. Editorial mediation could not eliminate doctrinal disagreements, such as those that spawned the publication and appropriation of Augustus Toplady's "Rock of Ages," but the negotiations made by lay and clerical editors could and did intensify evangelicals' sense of unity as members of a timeless, placeless church universal. As individuals and congregations used hymnals alongside other genres and forms to participate in a textually defined community, their practices shaped the world of evangelical print culture.

The Word in the World
of Twenty-first-Century
American Culture

"For the first time in the history of our annual hardcover bestseller charts," announced *Publishers Weekly* in 2002, "the #1 fiction and #1 nonfiction title come from Christian publishers." *Desecration: Antichrist Takes the Throne*, the eighth end-times novel in the *Left Behind* series, and Bruce Wilkinson's *Prayer of Jabez*, a devotional aid, sold 2.9 million and 8 million copies respectively. Tim F. LaHaye and Jerry B. Jenkins's 1995 novel, *Left Behind*, its soon-to-be eleven sequels, and over a dozen related titles have together sold over 50 million copies; the final title in the series is scheduled for release in the summer of 2004. The novelists' agent, Alive Communications, has authorized offshoot children's books, audio and graphic editions, apparel, and a movie that hit mainstream theaters in 2001 — although it has refused contracts for other accessory products and has criticized the movie's coproducer, Cloud Ten Pictures, for releasing a board game. In a similar vein, the *New York Times* reported that religious titles accounted for four of the ten best-selling *Idiot's Guides* for 2001. Annual sales of Christian books and accessories (like candles, action figures, key chains, coffee mugs, bookmarks, neckties, Christmas ornaments, Bible covers, and computer screen savers) have soared to $4 billion, up from $1 billion in 1980.[1]

Contemporary evangelical authors and publishers — more aggressively than their nineteenth-century precursors — seek and generally find an outlet for their wares by participating in the distribution networks of the general book trades. Evangelicals, like their nonevangelical peers, exploit the vast markets served by internet vendors such as Amazon.com, mammoth bookstore chains like Borders and Barnes & Noble, and all-purpose retailers, including Wal-Mart, Costco, and Sam's Club. Yet, as in earlier centuries, market participation forces evangelicals, in the words of one top publishing executive, to weigh "ministry versus margin." S. Rickly Christian, founder and president of Alive Communications, the largest religious literary agency in America, suggests the difficulty of balancing purity of the Word and presence in the world of print by asking, "Does having a book in Wal-Mart really matter to God?"[2]

The print market has changed dramatically between the nineteenth and twenty-first centuries, yet the cultural negotiations of an earlier era have important implications for understanding ongoing ties between religion and the media. From 1789 to 1880, evangelical print culture expanded and diversified as book trades participants used the Word and printed words to sustain their sense of membership in a pilgrim community traveling through the world while working to sanctify the changing milieu of nineteenth-century America. Evangelicals' struggle to balance purity and presence indicates the need to revise scholarly interpretations that unduly privilege emotional conversion as the apex of evangelical experience or that reduce the significance of religious publishing to secularization and American cultural declension. Adopting a conservative-progressive spirit, evangelicals used texts to reinforce a sacred story of communal growth in holiness while strategically adapting narrative and marketing strategies to the shifting currents of American culture. As evangelicals forged an informal canon and interacted within a textually defined community, individuals positioned everyday, worldly relationships and events within an otherworldly or sacred framework of meaning and cultivated a sense of personal responsibility to influence others for good.

As nineteenth-century evangelicals developed a functionalist understanding of sacred language, the test of usefulness allowed writers, publishers, and readers substantial freedom to view a widening range of textual practices, evangelical and nonevangelical resources, and religious and market strategies as exerting a sanctifying influence. The same individuals pursued religious and financial profit, read sermons and novels, and juxtaposed the daily news with translations of medieval Latin hymns, all without experiencing the strain of incongruity. Strains there were, nevertheless, as evangelicals balanced their goals of contending for the faith, acting as a priesthood of all believers, sanctifying the present world, and uniting as the church universal. Nineteenth-century evangelicals held in tension but could never fully reconcile overlapping alternatives: evangelical and denominational identity, clerical and lay authority, local and textual communities, domestic and institutional sites for religious growth, conservative and radical views of race and gender, print and oral modes of expression, and refined and vernacular aesthetics of the sacred.

Evangelicals succeeded in their objectives to the extent that they struggled to maneuver between the extremes of purity and presence. As writers, publishers, and readers avoided the poles of conformity and irrelevance to their cultural surroundings, conflicts and contradictions inevitably accompanied this balancing act. Evangelicals could never hope fully to succeed in transforming the world because their sense of identity depended upon setting themselves apart as a pilgrim community traveling through this world toward heaven.

Twenty-first-century interpreters of religion and the media can perhaps gain some perspective from knowing that worries about confusing ministry and margin are scarcely new. Ever since the jeremiads of the seventeenth century, Americans have been exceptionally articulate about their own failings relative to previous generations. Some level of cultural criticism has often provided a potent antidote to complacency. Yet history also reveals that American declension narratives can easily become self-consuming, siphoning energy toward attempts to recapture a nonexistent past rather than focusing attention on efforts to shape the future. The story of nineteenth-century evangelical print culture resists both cynicism and nostalgia by recalling a period marked by successive appropriations, uncertainties, and negotiations among alternatives.[3]

As Americans find their stride in the twenty-first century, the world—once again—looks more complex than ever. Scholars have only begun to assess the implications of the newest communications revolution that has virtually dissolved temporal and geographic divides. Yet community, many critics lament, has never appeared more elusive. The domestic fireside, once envisioned as the center of community life, seems assaulted from within and without. In an era of globalization, it is no longer possible to view American print culture as relatively insulated. Amid the explosion of books, newspapers, radio, television, film, and internet media, words—printed, spoken, and digitized—influence cultures in America and around the world. Impersonal entities such as Google and CNN make all kinds of information immediately accessible to people everywhere, encouraging extensive browsing as well as a new kind of intensive reading as the click of a mouse button offers endless replays of text, sound, and images.[4]

In this communications age, religious uses of the media perplex many cultural critics. The televangelism scandals of the 1980s left numerous Americans ready to suspect any religious use of mass media as disingenuous.

Yet today's evangelicals, who like their predecessors see language as the lever that moves the moral world, have not slackened their pace in communicating with each other and the world. Some steady sellers have persisted from earlier centuries, but other words that once presumably functioned to convey sacred meanings today seem — even to evangelicals — out of step with contemporary cultural currents. Many churches have, for instance, exchanged hymns sung to organ and choir accompaniment for newer songs led by rock bands strumming electric guitars and pounding drums. Evangelical critics of the "new" music who nostalgically lament losing the "old" hymns forget that their forebears similarly resisted hymns as unscriptural innovations that compromised with popular culture. The evangelical canon, which has always blended the old and the new, encompasses a shifting assortment of textual forms. Many religious groups service internet sites that invite readers to learn more about local religious communities and that sustain new kinds of textual communities of scattered individuals sharing intelligence and mutual support. Film series such as VeggieTales (in which animated vegetables teach moral lessons), including the 2002 theater release *Jonah* and offshoot web sites and accessory products, join Sunday school publications in socializing young children into evangelical culture. The most influential evangelical leader of the twentieth century, Billy Graham, has in the last decades of his long and relatively unblemished career used television, radio, and the internet to communicate his message to millions of listeners.[5]

Public opinion polls demonstrate that evangelicalism remains prominent in the American cultural landscape even as religious and nonreligious options for the moral life proliferate. Denominational labels, once moderately useful in defining the contours of evangelical culture, fail to suggest the diversity that exists among Protestants. Rather than identifying denominational variations in the twenty-first-century evangelical narrative, I find it more descriptive to classify contemporary Protestant attitudes toward the Word and world as "confessional," "charismatic," and "progressive." Confessional churches emphasize faithfulness to the printed Word, charismatic churches open their ears to hear from the living Word, and progressive churches cultivate responsiveness to the world. Both confessional and charismatic Protestants see themselves as evangelicals but disagree about the means by which the Word transforms the world. Other religious bodies, such as Mormons, Jehovah's Witnesses, and Muslims, have grown dramatically in America and internationally as each group articulates its own model of the relationship between the Word and the world. Nonreligious story structures likewise compete with the evangelical narrative. Disavowing the need for intervention by a creative, incarnate, or judging Word, scientific naturalism tells the story that an undesigned material world is all there is. Political correctness is charitable toward all stories of how things are in the world, excepting those that assert the priority of one view of the Word over any other. Postmodernism — itself a narrative — asserts that all narratives are human efforts to create meaning in an otherwise meaningless world. As has been the case throughout American history, religious and secular alternatives for meaning intermingle, rather than one being swallowed by another.[6]

In the wake of events since 11 September 2001, more people have contemplated the relationship between religion and American culture than ever before, lustily singing "God Bless America" while expressing anxiety about the claims of so-called fundamentalists who want their interpretation of the Word to influence the world. As communication networks that have developed since the nineteenth century continue to facilitate dialogue within and among religious groups and the world, there is the potential for words to reduce misunderstandings or to intensify disputes, to strengthen or to fragment communities, and to achieve or to block the acknowledgment of differences that is essential to cooperative ventures. The standard for measuring success established by nineteenth-century evangelicals is illuminating. Will twenty-first-century religious uses of the media balance purity and presence or instead flow toward one or another extreme?

NOTES

Abbreviations

The following abbreviations are used throughout the notes and bibliography.

AAS	American Antiquarian Society, Worcester, Massachusetts
ABPS	American Baptist Publication Society
ABS	American Bible Society
AME	African Methodist Episcopal
AMEZ	African Methodist Episcopal Zion
ASSU	American Sunday School Union
ATS	American Tract Society
CBP	Congregational Board of Publication
GPE	General Protestant Episcopal
MEC	Methodist Episcopal Church
MECS	Methodist Episcopal Church, South
MSSS	Massachusetts Sabbath-School Society
PBP	Presbyterian Board of Publication
PBPSSW	Presbyterian Board of Publication and Sabbath-School Work
PESPEK	Protestant Episcopal Society for the Promotion of Evangelical Knowledge
PPC	Presbyterian Publication Committee
RTS	Religious Tract Society
SPCK	Society for Promoting Christian Knowledge
SSU	Sunday-School Union

Introduction

1. John L. Waller, "Introduction to Volume 5," *Western Baptist Review* 5 (June 1850): 3.

2. Gen. 1:1–3; John 1:1–3, 1:14, 16:7–14; 2 Tim. 3:16 (all references are to the King James Version); J. Green, *Interlinear Bible*, 835, 925; Unger, *Bible Dictionary*, 583, 620–22.

3. Unger, *Bible Dictionary*, 493; J. Green, *Interlinear Bible*, 767, 785; Mark 1:1, 16:15; Gamble, *Books and Readers*, 152.

4. Ahlstrom, *Religious History*, 70–83; J. Smith, *Dictionary of Religion*, 349; Calvin, *Institutes*, 502–3.

5. Knott, *Sword of the Spirit*, 76, 96; Johns, *Nature of the Book*, 331; Eisenstein, *Printing Press*, 303, 329, 368, 374, 424–25; John Foxe, *The Acts and Monuments of John Foxe*, ed. Stephen Reed Catley (London: R. B. Seeley & W. Burnside, 1837–41), 3:720, qtd. in Gilmont, "Protestant Reformations," 213; Stout and Hatch,

"Religious Press," 1; Gutjahr, *American Bible*, 92; D. Hall, *Worlds of Wonder*, 27. Walsham, *Providence in Early Modern England*, 54–55, notes that early Protestants felt misgivings about the usefulness of printing.

6. Damrosh, *God's Plot*, 5; Greengrass, *European Reformation*, 242; Richard Baxter, *The Saints' Everlasting Rest . . .* , (London: Thomas Underhill & Francis Tyton, 1650), 211–12, and *The Practical Works* (London: Thomas Parkhurst, Jonathan Robinson, & John Lawrence, 1707), 1:xxi, qtd. in Knott, *Sword of the Spirit*, 6–7, 27, 62–65, 76; Eisenstein, *Printing Press*, 700; Johns, *Nature of the Book*, 31, 91, 424.

7. Gutjahr, *American Bible*, 110; D. Hall, *Cultures of Print*, 5–7, 152; Brodhead, *Cultures of Letters*, 9; Levine, *Highbrow/Lowbrow*, 3; Rubin, *Making of Middle/Brow Culture*, 17; Buell, *New England Literary Culture*, 57; Cmiel, *Democratic Eloquence*, 12, 37, 58, 74–75; Bushman, *Refinement of America*, xiii, xix.

8. Reardon, *Religious Thought in the Reformation*, 62, 168; Knott, *Sword of the Spirit*, 18, 35; Frei, *Eclipse of Biblical Narrative*, 19–22; Pelikan, *Christian Tradition*, 208–10, 343–44.

9. Archibald Alexander Hodge and B. B. Warfield, "Inspiration," *Presbyterian Review* 2 (Apr. 1881): 237, qtd. in Marsden, *Fundamentalism*, 14, 26, 113; Bendroth, *Fundamentalism and Gender*, 3–8, 33–35; Gura, *Wisdom of Words*, 7; Buell, *New England Literary Culture*, 167–68.

10. Gutjahr, *American Bible*, 3; McDannell, *Material Christianity*, 5; Ong, *Presence of the Word*, 11–13, 273; Eisenstein, *Printing Press*, 49, 57; D. Hall, *Worlds of Wonder*, 24, 30.

11. C. Campbell, *Romantic Ethic*, 49.

12. Niebuhr's *Christ and Culture* is the classic articulation of the possible stances of Christianity toward culture; nineteenth-century evangelicals most closely approximated the position of "Christ transforming culture." E. Morgan, *Puritan Dilemma*, 3, similarly argues that Puritans sought to live in the world and "lend a hand in shaping it."

13. D. Hall, *Worlds of Wonder*, 49.

14. Pelikan, *Christian Tradition*, 343–44; Greengrass, *European Reformation*, 223; Tracy, *Analogical Imagination*, 276–77. Damrosh, *God's Plot*, 2, and Frei, *Eclipse of Biblical Narrative*, 152, trace a lost sense of coherence in biblical narrative.

15. Geertz, *Interpretation of Cultures*, 5, 24.

16. D. Hall, *Worlds of Wonder*, 18; Fish, *Is There a Text*, 199; Tracy, *Analogical Imagination*, 313.

17. Johnson, *Reading "Piers Plowman,"* 10–17; Knott, *Sword of the Spirit*, 142–49; Dieter et al., *Five Views on Sanctification*, 51, 57, 72, 158.

18. Ricoeur, *Figuring the Sacred*, 239–41; Damrosh, *God's Plot*, 10; Johnson, *Reading "Piers Plowman,"* 18.

19. Brumberg, *Mission for Life*, x, 34; D. Hall, *Lived Religion*, xi; Ortner, "Theory in Anthropology since the Sixties," 127, 152–53; Hannah Arendt, *The Human Condition* (Chicago: University of Chicago Press, 1958), qtd. in Ricoeur, *Figuring the Sacred*, 240; Hendler, *Public Sentiments*, 10–12, 35, 115.

20. Davidson, *Revolution and the Word*, 57–60; Gilmore, *Reading Becomes a Necessity*, 5, 49, 121; Boylan, *Sunday School*, 71; Daniel Calhoun, *Intelligence of a People*, 130–31; Zboray, *Fictive People*, 83, 90.

21. Genovese, *Roll, Jordon, Roll*, 239, 252–55; Hutton, *Early Black Press*, 10;

Mathews, *Religion in the Old South*, 185–86, 209, 220, 248; J. Campbell, *Songs of Zion*, 39, 55; Harvey, *Redeeming the South*, 28.

22. Ricoeur, *Figuring the Sacred*, 240; Ong, *Orality and Literacy*, 133; Johnson, *Reading "Piers Plowman,"* 17; Fish, *Is There a Text*, 11, 199; Geertz, *Interpretation of Cultures*, 17; Machor, *Readers in History*, vii, xi.

23. Ricoeur, *Figuring the Sacred*, 237, 243–44; Nischan, *Lutherans and Calvinists*, 144–49; L. Schmidt, *Holy Fairs*, 69; Frei, *Eclipse of Biblical Narrative*, 24–25; D. Hall, *Worlds of Wonder*, 70, 237, 245.

24. D. Hall, *Worlds of Wonder*, 11; Zboray, *Fictive People*, 80; Lindbeck, *Nature of Doctrine*, 18.

25. Zboray, *Fictive People*, 77–79, 111; Long and Ferrie, "Labour Mobility"; Mathews, *Religion in the Old South*, 13, 54; Calhoon, *Evangelicals and Conservatives*, 13, 111.

26. Carey, *Communication as Culture*, 15–21, 43; Nord, *Communities of Journalism*, 2; Zboray, *Fictive People*, 119–21; L. Schmidt, *Hearing Things*, 47.

27. Mathews, *Religion in the Old South*, 244–45; Calhoon, *Evangelicals and Conservatives*, 154. For examples of scholarly concern over institutional growth, see Finke and Stark, *Churching of America*, 42, and Schneider, *Way of the Cross*, 207. Carwardine, " 'Antinomians' and 'Arminians,' " 286–91, notes the ability of Methodists to embrace religious convictions and market opportunities simultaneously.

28. Mathews, *Religion in the Old South*, 100–101; Calhoon, *Evangelicals and Conservatives*, 111–12; Schneider, *Way of the Cross*, 207; Heyrman, *Southern Cross*, 159–60; McDannell, *Christian Home*, xi; McCrossen, *Holy Day, Holiday*, 16.

29. Anderson, *Imagined Communities*, 6; Watt, *Cheap Print*, 332.

30. C. Smith, *Christian America?*, 11.

31. Pilkington, *Methodist Publishing House*, 500–501; Steinberg, *Printing*, 137–45; Tebbel, *Book Publishing*, 186, 206, 257; Exman, *House of Harper*, 9, 149–50; Gutjahr, *American Bible*, 166–73.

32. Dwight L. Moody, *Moody's Latest Sermons* (Chicago: Bible Institute Colportage Association, 1900), 27–28, qtd. in Marsden, *Fundamentalism*, 22–38, 72–75.

33. For exemplary studies of the later period, see, for instance, Marsden, *Fundamentalism*; Wacker, *Heaven Below*; and Harvey, *Redeeming the South*.

34. For examples of scholarship on America's ties to evangelicalism, see Handy, *Christian America*; Noll, Marsden, and Hatch, *Search for Christian America*; and Carnes, "Bush's Moment."

35. McDannell, *Christian Home*, 105.

36. For definitions of evangelicalism, see, for instance, Conkin, *Uneasy Center*, xii–xiii, 65, 114–15, 294; Hatch, *Democratization*, 3; and Brumberg, *Mission for Life*, x–xi.

37. Hedrick, *Harriet Beecher Stowe*, 144–49, 278–84; McLoughlin, *Henry Ward Beecher*, 49; Hewitt, *Regeneration and Morality*; Gura, *Wisdom of Words*, 8, 53–67.

38. D. Hall, *Lived Religion*, xi; Gunther (Brown), "Spiritual Pilgrimage of Rachel Stearns," 578, 582–83.

39. For examples of the secularization thesis, see Douglas, *Feminization*, 68; Reynolds, *Faith in Fiction*, 197; Sellers, *Market Revolution*, 212–16; R. Moore, *Selling God*, 10; Gutjahr, *American Bible*, 3; and Lehuu, *Carnival on the Page*, 159.

40. Brumberg, *Mission for Life*, 255.

41. Scholarship similarly dissatisfied with secularization narratives includes L. Schmidt, *Consumer Rites*, 197; Brumberg, *Mission for Life*, 216; Grimsted, "Books and Culture," 191; McCrossen, *Holy Day, Holiday*, 16; and McDannell, *Material Christianity*, 4.

42. Noll, *America's God*, 13; Hatch, *Democratization*, 3.

Chapter One

1. K. M'Clellan, *Two Christmas Gifts*, 3–4. Students of nineteenth-century religious fiction will immediately think of a similar passage in Warner, *Wide, Wide World*, 29–31, in which the protagonist, Ellen, selects a Bible from a dazzling array of various styles, sizes, and bindings. For a discussion of Warner, see MacDonald, *Christian's Children*, 46–58.

2. K. M'Clellan, *Two Christmas Gifts*, 131. Scholars continually struggle with the meanings of a commercial print market in which Bibles and other religious books were bought and sold and given as holiday gifts. L. Schmidt offers one of the most sophisticated analyses of the commingling of sacred and secular meanings of giftbooks and Christmas gift-giving rituals in *Consumer Rites*, 9, 108, 116–17, 182, 197. Howsam, "Nineteenth-Century Bible Society," 131, points to possible religious meanings of commodification by demonstrating that the British and Foreign Bible Society (unlike the ABS) resisted giving away "free" Bibles because doing so severed gift-giving from the context of reciprocal relationships; the BFBS sold Bibles even to the indigent in an effort to restore reciprocity. C. Campbell, *Romantic Ethic*, 89–92, suggests that window-shopping (like Johnny's) for holiday gifts generated a sense of longing that created wants for new commodities, which might or might not have been religious.

3. Lehuu, *Carnival on the Page*, 76–86, interprets the treatment of Bibles and other giftbooks as objects and commodities in terms of secularization. McDannell, *Material Christianity*, 86–87, distinguishes between texts as objects and commodities, finding the latter status more problematic than the former.

4. K. M'Clellan, *Two Christmas Gifts*, 9, 10, 17, 23.

5. Ibid., 23–27.

6. Ibid., 25, 130.

7. Marsden, *Religion and American Culture*, 17–20; Ahlstrom, *Religious History*, 84–95.

8. Marsden, *Religion and American Culture*, 21–27; Ahlstrom, *Religious History*, 90–98, 218.

9. Richey, "Denominations and Denominationalism," 83–86; J. Wesley, "The Character of a Methodist," 245; Ahlstrom, *Religious History*, 381; O'Brien, "Transatlantic Community of Saints," 813–17.

10. J. Smith, *Dictionary of Religion*, 349–50; O'Brien, "Eighteenth-Century Publishing," 44; Durden, "Study of the First Evangelical Magazines," 259–61; "General Fisk's Address," *Centennial*, 63–69; Pilkington, *Methodist Publishing House*, 87; Hatch, *Democratization*, 142.

11. Ahlstrom, *Religious History*, 390–97; J. Smith, *Dictionary of Religion*, 350.

12. Noll, *History of Christianity*, 144; Noll, *America's God*, 56, 174; Butler, *Awash in a Sea of Faith*, 257–68; Baird, *Religion in America*, 206.

13. L. Beecher, *Autobiography*, 1:252–53. Mathews, *Religion in the Old South*, 57, notes that southern evangelical churches never depended on state support.

14. Butler, *Awash in a Sea of Faith*, 167, 221–23; L. Schmidt, *Holy Fairs*, xii, 59; Frey and Wood, *Come Shouting to Zion*, 118–19; Marini, *Radical Sects*, 38–40; Mathews, *Religion in the Old South*, 132; Sweet, *Religion*, 150; Schneider, *Way of the Cross*, xxvi; T. Smith, *Revivalism and Social Reform*, 39–42; W. Cross, *Burned-Over District*, 7, 214–15; Walters, *American Reformers*, 129–35; Boylan, *Sunday School*, 48, 71; Baird, *Religion in America*, 156.

15. Noll, *History of Christianity*, 163, 220; Hatch, *Democratization*, 3–4; Gaustad and Barlow, *New Historical Atlas*, 79, 98–100, 131, 136, 178, 219, 226; Belcher, "History of the Baptists," 63. One difficulty in assessing church growth statistics is that each denomination had its own criteria for church membership (and these criteria changed over time). Moreover, the statistics say nothing about the number of regular church attendees or about the quality of members' or attendees' religious experiences. In addition, because denominations for the most part kept their own records, it is not possible in all cases to make direct comparisons between the kinds of information recorded by one group relative to another.

16. Bangs, "History of the Methodist Episcopal Church," 360–68; Summers, "History of the Methodist Episcopal Church, South," 383; Sweet, *Religion*, 57, 119; Sweet, *Methodism in American History*, 313; Hatch, *Democratization*, 157; Gaustad and Barlow, *New Historical Atlas*, 69–73, 221; Finke and Stark, "How the Upstart Sects Won America," 31; Noll, *History of Christianity*, 153; Ahlstrom, *Religious History*, 381; Albaugh, *Religious Periodicals*, xix; Rupp, *Religious Denominations*, 10–11; Harvey, *Redeeming the South*, 70; Frey and Wood, *Come Shouting to Zion*, 149; J. Campbell, *Songs of Zion*, 62–63.

17. Mathews, *Religion in the Old South*, 133–34; Noll, *America's God*, 176, 244–47; Harvey, *Redeeming the South*, 88–90; Carwardine, "'Antinomians' and 'Arminians,'" 296.

18. *Home Missionary* (1827), qtd. in Finke and Stark, *Churching of America*, 65; W. Cross, *Burned-Over District*, 48.

19. J. Lee, *Life and Religious Experience*, 39, 41, 44; Cartwright, *Autobiography*, 338–39; Simonds, *Unfinished Volume*, 89, 103, 165, 198.

20. Walters, *American Reformers*, 278; L. Thompson, "Printing and Publishing Activities," 84; Baird, *Religion in America*, 267.

21. J. P. Durbin and T. Merritt, "Prices of Sunday School Books," *Christian Advocate* 7 (8 Mar. 1833): 3; George Peck, rev. of Methodist Book Concern, *Descriptive Catalogue*, *Methodist Quarterly Review*, 3d ser., 9 (Apr. 1850): 281; Bangs, "History of the Methodist Episcopal Church," 367–79; I. M. Allen, "Summary of History of Baptist General Tract Society," *United States Baptist Annual Register and Almanac* (1833): 15; "Dr. Buckley's Address," *Centennial*, 70; Pilkington, *Methodist Publishing House*, 192–96; Mathews, *Religion in the Old South*, 31–34; Gutjahr, *American Bible*, 100–109.

22. Walters, *American Reformers*, 25–33; Noll, *History of Christianity*, 215, 307; Marsden, *Fundamentalism*, 12.

23. Turner and Turner, *Image and Pilgrimage in Christian Culture*, 249–51; C. Bell, *Ritual Theory, Ritual Practice*, 81–83, 134; Wosh, *Spreading the Word*, 84–88; Baird, *Religion in America*, 220, 251; Fish, *Is There a Text*, 173. Mathews, *Reli-*

gion in the Old South, 132–32, and Noll, *America's God*, 5, unlike Conkin, *American Originals*, 1–56, do class Disciples as evangelicals. Hatch, *Democratization*, 71.

24. Baird, *Religion in America*, 612; Albaugh, *Religious Periodicals*, xix–xx.

25. Hatch, *Democratization*, 3–4, 125; Conkin, *American Originals*, 118–35, 147, 237–53; D. Morgan, *Protestants and Pictures*, 163; Hatch, *Democratization*, 125–27; Cather and Milmine, *Mary Baker G. Eddy*, 176, 312–13; Gill, *Mary Baker Eddy*, 325–30; Braude, *Radical Spirits*, 26–27, 41; Madison, *Jewish Publishing*, 6–28, 74.

26. Ong, *Presence of the Word*, 276; McDannell, *Christian Home*, 64–70, 86–96; Cavanaugh, *Catholic Book Publishing*, i–ii, 8, 33, 41, 122–25; McDannell, "Catholic Women Fiction Writers," 386, 396–99; Ryan, "Inventing Catholicism," 67, 160, 190–96; Gutjahr, *American Bible*, 23.

27. White, *Roman Catholic Worship*, 56; McDannell, *Christian Home*, 75, 86–89, 96–107; McDannell, "Catholic Women Fiction Writers," 402; Cavanaugh, *Catholic Book Publishing*, ii.

28. Madden, *Bodies of Life*, 1–6, 26–27; Ong, *Presence of the Word*, 262–86; Bauman, *Let Your Words Be Few*, 21–42; Conkin, *American Originals*, 167–73; Hansen, *Mormonism*, xv–xvi, 1–7, 21.

29. Hansen, *Mormonism*, 29, 37, 198.

30. Mathews, *Religion in the Old South*, 134, 242. Generalizations about social status should not be taken too far; for instance, Wacker, *Heaven Below*, 197–216, argues that, at least by 1910, few Pentecostal heirs of the nineteenth-century Holiness movement were nearly as marginalized as stereotypes suggest.

31. Buell, *New England Literary Culture*, 39, 47, 185; Gura, *Wisdom of Words*, 3–7; C. Campbell, *Romantic Ethic*, 187.

32. Marsden, *Fundamentalism*, 113; Brumberg, *Mission for Life*, xi.

33. Marsden, *Fundamentalism*, 22–25; Gura, *Wisdom of Words*, 7–8, 53–67.

Chapter Two

1. Thomas Coke, *Extracts of the Journals of the Rev. Dr. Coke's Five Visits to America* (London, 1789), 144, qtd. in Pilkington, *Methodist Publishing House*, 45.

2. Ricoeur, *Figuring the Sacred*, 240;

3. Johns, *Nature of the Book*, 153; Secord, *Victorian Sensation*, 33, 48–54, 119–22; Steinberg, *Printing*, 137–45; Tebbel, *Book Publishing*, 206, 217–21, 508; Gutjahr, *American Bible*, 12–14; Winship, *American Literary Publishing*, 12; Exman, *House of Harper*, 37; Brumberg, *Mission for Life*, 140; Zboray, *Fictive People*, 58, 144; "Literature," *Christian Diadem* (1852): 183.

4. Tebbel, *Book Publishing*, 217–21; Amory and Hall, *History of the Book*, 118, 511; Buell, *New England Literary Culture*, 57.

5. Zboray, *Fictive People*, 55, 66, 77; Albaugh, *Religious Periodicals*, xi–xiii; Stout and Hatch, "Religious Press," 22; Holland, "Religious Periodicals in the Development of Nashville," 636; Thomas, "Who Makes the Text?" 104–13; Tebbel, *Book Publishing*, 203–7, 325, 382, 474–80.

6. "Reading," *Methodist Quarterly Review*, 3d ser., 6 (Jan. 1846): 83–84, 87; Walsham, *Providence in Early Modern England*, 54; Secord, *Victorian Sensation*, 51–54; Physician, *Confessions and Experience of a Novel Reader*, 26–27; N. Porter, *Books and Reading*, 5–9; T. T. Eaton, "Our Distinctive Principles as Baptists, and our Litera-

ture Necessary to a True and Complete Evangelism . . . ," *Michigan Christian Herald* 8 (17 June 1880): "Herald Pulpit" section, 2.

7. C. Moore, *What to Read, and How to Read*, 10; *Christian Herald* (1823), qtd. in Hatch, *Democratization*, 142; ATS, "Home Evangelization," in *Confessions and Experience of a Novel Reader*, by A Physician, 73–76; E. H., "The Press," *Christian Diadem* (1852): 61.

8. Amory and Hall, *History of the Book*, 511. Figures for the earlier period are based on information cataloged in the North American Imprints Program on-line, machine-readable database of the AAS. I did not include captivity narratives or poems as religious texts, although many of them included religious content. For the later period, the nineteenth-century bibliographer Orville Roorbach compiled a catalog of more than 25,000 titles published in the United States between 1820 and 1852, *Bibliotheca Americana*, with supplements that covered 1852 to 1855 and 1855 to 1858. I derived percentages for 1852–55 by analyzing a random sample of all titles listed by Roorbach starting with the letter "D." *Annual Report of the ATS* (1847): 18. I calculated circulation based on ATS reports dating from 1826 to 1890; here, as in many similar instances, we must rely upon statistics kept by publishers themselves. Self-interested reporting is possible, although there is no reason to distrust the general accuracy of these figures.

9. Tebbel, *Book Publishing*, 217, 222, 553; Westerhoff, *McGuffey and His Readers*, 74–104. For an interpretation of genre diversity as symptomatic of secularization, see Zboray, *Fictive People*, 142.

10. Tebbel, *Book Publishing*, 224, 542–43; Mott, *Golden Multitudes*, 122–24; Zboray, *Fictive People*, 142.

11. Noll, *History of Christianity*, 227; Gutjahr, *American Bible*, 9–37; E. H., "The Press," *Christian Diadem* (1852): 63; Tebbel, *Book Publishing*, 221, 508; Zboray, *Fictive People*, 142–46; Nord, "Evangelical Origins," 83–84. I based these estimates on a linear interpolation of the figures $12.5 million total sales in 1850 and $16 million total sales in 1856 to reach a figure of $15.4 million for 1855. I assume an average trade book price of $1. The ABS reported 901,400 volumes sold for $346,811.57; the ATS counted 961,863 volumes sold for $413,173; the ASSU reported receipts of $248,605; and I have estimated 578,151 volumes sold, assuming prices comparable to the ATS average of forty-three cents per book. Society publications accounted for $1,008,589 out of $15,400,000 total sales (6.6 percent) and 2,441,414 books produced out of 15,400,000 total (15.9 percent). There are too many gaps in the data (e.g., diversity of book prices and gratuitous distribution) to view my estimates as more than ballpark figures.

12. Tebbel, *Book Publishing*, 213, 229–30; Winship, *Ticknor and Fields*, 1, 13; Gilreath, "American Book Distribution," 144–64; speech by Rev. Albert Barnes, in *Remarks on the Publication Cause*, 10–14.

13. Tebbel, *Book Publishing*, 516–18; Pilkington, *Methodist Publishing House*, 352; Carwardine, "Trauma in Methodism," 196, 205–10; "Address by M. D. C. Crawford, D.D.," "Address by George S. Chadbourne, D.D.," "Prayer by J. M. Reid, D.D.," "Address by Bishop Cyrus D. Foss, D.D., L.L.D.," "General Fisk's Address," "Dr. Buckley's Address," *Centennial*, 25–78.

14. "Address by Dr. Hunt," *Centennial*, 49–52.

15. *Christian Advocate* 23 (1 Oct. 1848): 161, qtd. in Pilkington, *Methodist Pub-*

lishing House, 364–66, 459–60; George Peck, rev. of *Descriptive Catalogue, Methodist Quarterly Review,* 3d ser., 9 (Apr. 1850): 281; "Prices of Sunday School Books," *Christian Advocate* 7 (8 Mar. 1833): 3.

16. *Southwestern Christian Advocate* (10 Nov. 1843): 9, and "Manuscript Report of Publications Committee of Baltimore Conference to that Conference, 1844," South Carolina Conference Historical Society, Wofford College, qtd. in Pilkington, *Methodist Publishing House,* 286.

17. "Dr. Buckley's Address," *Centennial,* 76; Pilkington, *Methodist Publishing House,* 87–107; Cavalier, "Wesley's Reading as a Means of Grace," 1, 7.

18. "Dr. Buckley's Address," *Centennial,* 71–76.

19. *Descriptive Catalogue of the Books Published by the Congregational Board of Publication,* 3–6.

20. Ibid.

21. *Annual Report[s] of the Congregational Board* (1855): 11, (1859): 6–13; Steinberg, *Printing,* 138–39; Johns, *Nature of the Book,* 31, 91; Winship, *Ticknor and Fields,* 13.

22. *Christian Recorder* 9 (28 Jan. 1871): 1; Arnett, "Quadrennial Report," *Budget* (1884): 99–108. The AME Publication Department also struggled against the obstacles posed by the racism of white book market participants and by the lower economic and literary opportunities attained by AME church members.

23. Tebbel, *Book Publishing,* 213; speeches by Rev. Albert Barnes and Rev. Dr. Spear, in *Remarks on the Publication Cause,* 10–13, 20.

24. "Reading," *Methodist Quarterly Review,* 3d ser., 6 (Jan. 1846): 83–87; speeches by Rev. Dr. Darling, Rev. Mr. Bird, and Rev. H. Johnson, in *Remarks on the Publication Cause,* 8, 16, 17.

25. Cooke, *Gospel in Christ,* 6; C. W. Andrews, *Apology,* 7, 15, 40; A. Lee, *True Nature of the Kingdom of God,* 23; Ryle, *The Cross,* 16; Easturn, *Moderation of the Protestant Episcopal Church,* 27; Rice, *History of the Presbyterian Board,* 4; Gaustad and Barlow, *New Historical Atlas,* 136.

26. Speeches by Rev. Dr. Darling, Rev. Dr. Skinner, and Rev. Albert Barnes, in *Remarks on the Publication Cause,* 4–6, 3, 10.

27. Rice, *History of the Presbyterian Board,* 59–61.

28. William Jones, *The Jubilee Memorial of the Religious Tract Society: Containing a Record of Its Origin, Proceedings, and Results* (London: RTS, 1850), 147–48, qtd. in Secord, *Victorian Sensation,* 321–23; Nord, "Benevolent Capital," 147–48.

29. *Catalogue of the Juvenile, Sunday-School, and Family Library;* Baird, *Religion in America,* 267; J. Cross, *Five Years in the Alleghenies,* 203.

30. ASSU advertisement, in *Little Bill at the Pump,* back; ASSU advertisement, in *Influence; Or, The Little Silk-Winder,* back; ASSU advertisement, in *Ellen; Or, The Disinterested Girl,* back; Boylan, *Sunday School,* 48.

31. Watt, *Cheap Print,* 253–72; Amory and Hall, *History of the Book,* 387; Walsham, *Providence in Early Modern England,* 43; J. Cross, *Five Years in the Alleghenies,* 5–10, 162, 201–3.

32. Donald and Palmer, "Toward a Western Literature," 413–28; ATS, circular letters, 1 Aug. 1857, 31 May 1866, photocopies in Book Trades Collection, AAS.

33. Nord, "Systematic Benevolence," 239–52; Nord, "Benevolent Capital," 148–62; Nord, "Free Grace, Free Books, Free Riders," 243.

34. "Publications of the American Tract Society," in *Memoir of Wilberforce Richmond*, by Richmond, back; Cmiel, *Democratic Eloquence*, 17.

35. Nord, "Systematic Benevolence," 249–54; ATS, "To Evangelical Christians, and Especially to the Society's Colporteurs, Superintendents, and General Agents, and to Editors of the Religious Press in the Northern, Middle, Western, and North-Western States," 23 July 1857, ATS Broadsides, AAS; ATS, "Home Evangelization," in *Confessions and Experience of a Novel Reader*, by A Physician, 73–76; ATS, circular letters, 1 Aug. 1857, 31 May 1866, photocopies in Book Trades Collection, AAS. Colportage has roots in the practices of seventeenth-century itinerant booksellers, called pedlars or chapmen in Britain and colporteurs in France. Howsam, "Nineteenth-Century Bible Society," 129.

36. In the messy world of lived experience, the boundaries between evangelical and nonevangelical trade publishers were unclear. Not every publisher who belonged to an evangelical church expressed a uniform, unchanging level of commitment to using publishing for evangelical purposes. It is, moreover, impossible for the historian to recover the exact motives of any publisher (or writer or reader).

37. Stout and Hatch, "Religious Press," 24–25. Ticknor & Fields provides an example of a publishing house that lacked denominational ties; "religious titles" accounted for between 1.7 and 9.4 percent of the publisher's sales between 1840 and 1859. Winship, *American Literary Publishing*, 77–78; *Bookmakers*, 29, 34, 36, 40, 51, 83, 102; Bussy, *Philadelphia's Publishers and Printers*, 24, 39–46; Tebbel, *Book Publishing*, 389–404; Pilkington, *Methodist Publishing House*, 88; advertisement, in *Kept from Idols*, by Denison, back; advertisement, in *Tom Bently; Or, The Story of a Prodigal*, back; C. Davis, *Little Apple Blossom*, i; Headley, *New Series of Question Books*, i; *Seasonable Supply*, i; R. Clark, *New Serial Question Books*, i; *Charlie Scott; Or, There's Time Enough*, i.

38. *Bookmakers*, 70, 96, 104; *Catalogue of Books Published* (Carter); *Baptist Banner and Western Pioneer* 12 (2 Oct. 1845): 1; *United States Baptist Annual Register and Almanac* (1833): 20; *Almanac and Baptist Register* (1851); "Standard, Religious, and Miscellaneous," *Mississippi Baptist* 1 (17 Sept. 1857): 3; *Western Presbyterian* 1 (15 Jan. 1864): 48.

39. *Bookmakers*, 74–75; Pilkington, *Methodist Publishing House*, 651–52; Tebbel, *Book Publishing*, 339–42; Exman, *House of Harper*, 133.

40. "Illustrated Works Published by Henry Hoyt, 1870," in *Tom Bently; Or, The Story of a Prodigal*, back.

41. Ibid.; L. Schmidt, *Consumer Rites*, 116–17, 182; Lehuu, *Carnival on the Page*, 79–86; Bushman, *Refinement of America*, 283–84; Cmiel, *Democratic Eloquence*, 12–13, 96.

42. *Bookmakers*, 29, 34–36, 74–75, 40, 51, 83, 102; Bussy, *Philadelphia's Publishers and Printers*, 24, 39–46; advertisement, in *Education*, by H. Schmidt, back; Tebbel, *Book Publishing*, 283–94; *Appleton's Library Manual*; F. Turner, *John Henry Newman*, 1–7; Chew, *Fruit among the Leaves*, 3–51.

43. "Christmas Greetings," *Christmas Catalogue*, 795; L. Schmidt, *Consumer Rites*, 121–80.

44. *Illustrated Catalogue*, n.p.

45. Ibid.; Cmiel, *Democratic Eloquence*, 12.

46. *Illustrated Catalogue*, n.p.; McDannell, *Material Christianity*, 93–94; Ollier, *Doré Gallery*, iii.

47. J. Harper, statement to friend, and Harper & Bros., 1830 advertisement, qtd. in Exman, *House of Harper*, 9–11; Tebbel, *Book Publishing*, 88, 94, 270.

48. Exman, *House of Harper*, 18; Steinberg, *Printing*, 138; Tebbel, *Book Publishing*, 214, 229–30; Casper, *Constructing American Lives*, 79. Trade sales died out soon after the establishment of the American Book-Trade Union in 1874.

49. Tebbel, *Book Publishing*, 222, 253, 270–79; Mott, *American Magazines*, 2:3, 10, 11, 28, 31, 192, 383; Exman, *House of Harper*, 34–35, 69–70, 79–80, 92; *Book-makers*, 1; Greenwood, diary (4–5 Oct. 1857, 4 Nov. 1857, 24 Mar. 1858), AAS; *Valuable Standard Works* (1842); *Valuable Works* (1850); Wosh, *Spreading the Word*, 19–20; McDannell, *Material Christianity*, 89.

50. Exman, *House of Harper*, 150; Gutjahr, *American Bible*, 166–73.

51. Francis C. Blanchard, *The Life of Charles Albert Blanchard: Retold by His Wife* (New York: Fleming H. Revell, 1932), 65, 73, qtd. in Marsden, *Fundamentalism*, 31.

Chapter Three

1. Gillett, *Life Lessons in the School of Christian Duty*, 298–302.

2. Buell, *New England Literary Culture*, 16–17; D. Hall, *Worlds of Wonder*, 245; D. Hall, "Readers and Writers in Early New England," 118; Cavallo and Chartier, *History of Reading*, 31; Johnson, *Reading "Piers Plowman*," 26; Brumberg, *Mission for Life*, 50.

3. D. Hall, "Readers and Writers in Early New England," 118.

4. "A Word to Preachers," *Christian Advocate* 35 (5 Jan. 1860): 2; "Holiday Gift-Books," *Christmas Catalogue*, 796–803.

5. Gamble, *Books and Readers*, 152; Jude 3; Cmiel, *Democratic Eloquence*, 58, 81; Daniel Calhoun, *Intelligence of a People*, 210, 261–62, 288; Hatch, *Democratization*, 133–38; Searle, diary (8 Jan. 1809), Houghton Library, Harvard University; advertisement, in *Catalogue*, by Schneider, n.p.; advertisement, in *Lessons on the Book of Proverbs*, by Hopkins, n.p.; Coleman, *Casket of Pulpit Thought*; Harris, *Rise of Gospel Blues*, 4–9.

6. "Tribute by A. D. F. Randolph," *Robert Carter: His Life and Work*, 61; Tebbel, *Book Publishing*, 328–33; "Valuable Standard Works Published by Harper," in *On the Improvement of Society*, by Dick, back; *Price List* (Scribner); Abbott and Conant, *Dictionary of Religious Knowledge*, iii; Rev. John Hall, "Sabbath-School Books: How to Get and How to Use Them," *Sunday-School Annual* (1874): n.p.

7. "The Power of a Tract," James Willard Willmarth Papers, American Baptist Historical Society; Rice, *History of the Presbyterian Board*, 29; *Annual Report of the ATS* (1853): 17; "Tracts Written by Rev. G. S. Baily," in *Jennie and Her Mother*, by Rayne, back.

8. Frei, *Eclipse of Biblical Narrative*, 18, 87, 143–45; Marsden, *Fundamentalism*, 26; Mears, *From Exile to Overthrow*, 37.

9. Hare, *Epitome*; Bacon, *Christian Comforter*; M. S. B., *Temperance Lyre*; Sellers, *Market Revolution*, 264.

10. Advertisement, in *Letters to Little Children*, by Their Father, back; *American Tract Magazine* (New York) 15 (Mar. 1841): back.

11. Ziff, "Upon What Pre-Text?," 297–302; D. Hall, "Literacies," 3; Johnson, *Reading "Piers Plowman,"* 5, 18; preface to *Treatise on Religious Affections*, by Edwards, ii; preface to *Alarm to Unconverted Sinners*, by Alleine, ii.

12. Rev. of *The Baptist Library*, by Sommers and Williams, *Western Baptist Review* 2 (Mar. 1847): 238; rev. of *The Baptist Library*, by Sommers and Williams, *Western Christian* 1 (28 June 1845): 2; "Libraries," *Annual Report of the . . . ABPS* (1870): 63; rev. of *The Calvinistic Family Library*, *Christian Magazine of the South* 9 (Sept. 1851): 282; "Sunday School Libraries Expressly Prepared for the Use of Sunday Schools in the Methodist Episcopal Church, South," *Sunday School Magazine* 6 (May 1876): 161.

13. Loughlin, *Telling God's Story*, 218; Casper, *Constructing American Lives*, 2, 33; Roorbach, *Bibliotheca Americana*, 51–60. I based this estimate on a random sample of titles that begin with the letter "D" published by trade houses between 1852 and 1855; the ratio of biographical texts published by evangelical houses was even higher.

14. For more on character, see Halttunen, *Confidence Men and Painted Women*, 4; Casper, *Constructing American Lives*, 6; Rubin, *Making of Middle/Brow Culture*, 2–3; Augst, "Business of Reading," 269–71; "Payson — His Life and Works," *Mothers' Magazine* 17 (1849): 158–59; and "Editor's Table," *Beauty of Holiness* 6 (Dec. 1855): 382.

15. Edwards, *Account of the Life of the Late Reverend Mr. David Brainerd*; Leighton, *Whole Works of Robert Leighton*; A. Cummings, *Memoir of the Rev. Edward Payson*; Sargent, *Memoir of the Rev. Henry Martyn*; H. Rogers, *Short Account of the Experience*; Wayland, *Memoir of the Life and Labors of the Rev. Adoniram Judson*; "Payson — His Life and Works," *Mothers' Magazine* 17 (1849): 158–59; L. Smith, *Heroes and Martyrs*.

16. A. Green, *Life of the Rev. Dandridge F. Davis*, 21, 39; M. Robinson, *Sketch of the Life of Truman Pratt*, 13; J. Webb, *Memoir of Miss Charity Richards*, vi.

17. I. Parsons, *Memoir of Amelia S. Chapman*, 36; Wells, *Saved by Grace*, 4, 9, 99–100; Burns, *Death Bed Triumphs*, 3, 5; Hedrick, *Harriet Beecher Stowe*, 278; Fisher, *Hard Facts*, 87–127.

18. Egliseau, *Lizzie Ferguson*, 168–70; "Lives of Pious Children," *Christian Recorder* 1 (4 Jan. 1862): 4.

19. Rev. of *Spicy Breezes from Minnesota Prairies*, by B. Smith, *Annual Report of the . . . ABPS* (1886): back; G. Thompson, *Thompson in Africa*, 4; Woods, *Memoir of Mrs. Harriet Newell*; Cott, *Bonds of Womanhood*, 41; Stuart, *Lives of Mrs. Ann H. Judson and Mrs. Sarah B. Judson*, iii; Tracey, *Myra*, iii.

20. "Life and Times of Bishop Hedding," *Methodist Quarterly Review*, 4th ser., 7 (Oct. 1855): 590; "Revival of Religion," *Methodist Magazine* (Baltimore) 1 (Aug. 1855): 178; "Letter about Pearsall Smith's 'Fall from Grace,' Written to Owner of Broadlands" (15 Jan. 1876?), Mt. Temple Collection, Gebbie Archives and Special Collections, Wheaton College.

21. David Calhoun, "David Brainerd," 49; Pettit, intro. to *The Life of David Brainerd*, by Jonathan Edwards, 3–9, 80–83; Conforti, *Jonathan Edwards*, 63–86;

J. Wesley, *Extract of the Life of the Late Rev. David Brainerd*; Styles, *Life of David Brainerd*, vii–viii; D. Hall, "Literacies," 2; Brantley, "Common Ground of Wesley and Edwards," 274–75.

22. Heyrman, *Southern Cross*, 219; I. Warren, *Sisters*, iii; H. Moore, *Life of Mrs. Mary Fletcher*, 8–9, 43–63, 98–129, 249–315; Taves, *Fits, Trances, and Visions*, 84–86; C. Brown, "Prophetic Daughter."

23. William M. Wightman, *The Life of William Capers, D.D.* (Nashville: Southern Methodist Publishing House, 1858), 124–28, and James Jenkins, *Experience, Labours, and Sufferings of Reverend James Jenkins of the South Carolina Conference* (Columbia, S.C.: State Commercial Printing, 1842), 120–21, qtd. in Heyrman, *Southern Cross*, 224–25.

24. A number of scholars have observed evangelicals' turn toward fiction, in most instances interpreting the trend as indicating secularization, for example, Sellers, *Market Revolution*, 372–75; Douglas, *Feminization*, 5–10, 62, 68, 115, 347–49; R. Moore, *Selling God*, 6, 10, 17; and O'Connor, *Religion in the American Novel*, 1. Davidson, *Revolution and the Word*, 70–73, interprets novel reading as contributing to women's educational and social liberation. Brumberg, *Mission for Life*, 216, views evangelical adoption of fiction less as declension than as reluctant "expropriation of secular trends after initial resistance — absorption when the deluge seems inevitable."

25. Charles Andrews, *Religious Novels*, 6, 8, 25.

26. Physician, *Confessions and Experience of a Novel Reader*, 11, 13.

27. E. H., "The Press," *Christian Diadem* (1852): 62; "Reading," *Methodist Quarterly Review*, 3d ser., 6 (Jan. 1846): 73; Physician, *Confessions and Experience of a Novel Reader*, 20, 22, 38.

28. "Bad Books," *Our Young People* 6 (Jan 1881): 2; *Three Darlings*, 76; "The Need of Pure Literature," *AME Church Review* 8 (Oct. 1891): 229–30.

29. N. Porter, *Books and Reading*, 11, 48, 76, 111, 125, 195, 231–33; L. Stevenson, *Scholarly Means to Evangelical Ends*, 48; Brodhead, *Cultures of Letters*, 160–61; Reynolds, *Faith in Fiction*, 72–73; Tompkins, *Sensational Designs*, xi.

30. E. A. Park, "Intellect and Feelings," *Bibliotheca Sacra* 7, no. 27 (July 1850): 533–69, qtd. in Cecil, *Theological Development*, 81–108; C. Stowe, *Life of Harriet Beecher Stowe*, 33–35; H. Stowe, *Uncle Tom's Cabin*, xx, xxvi. There is a large literature on sentimentalism, including Hendler, *Public Sentiments*, 64, 145, 209, 279, 289; Tompkins, *Sensational Designs*, 124–25; Baym, *Woman's Fiction*, 15, 17, 27; and Fisher, *Hard Facts*, 87–127.

31. Caroline Ticknor, *Hawthorne and His Publisher* (Boston: Houghton Mifflin, 1913), 141, qtd. in Mott, *American Magazines*, 2:173; Buell, *New England Literary Culture*, 57; Reynolds, *Faith in Fiction*, 72–73, 94; Showalter, *Literature of Their Own*, 22; B. Epstein, *Politics of Domesticity*, 55, 87.

32. Lewis, *Blackwell Dictionary of Evangelical Biography*, 901; Hammack, *Dictionary of Women in Church History*, 120; Malone, *Dictionary of American Biography*, 15:189; G. Prentiss, *Life and Letters*, 391; Winslow, "Elizabeth Prentiss," 3:95–96. I thank Jeremy Huggins for bringing to my attention six little-known books by Prentiss.

33. G. Prentiss, *Life and Letters*, 183, 266, 273, 339; A. Cummings, *Memoir of the Rev. Edward Payson*, 4, 33, 51, 81, 88; Malone, *Dictionary of American Biography*,

14:333; Hambrick-Stowe, *Practice of Piety*, 68–90; C. Brown, "Domestic Nurture Versus Clerical Crisis." Payson did strive to grow in holiness after his own conversion, but Prentiss, more than Payson, viewed the entire salvation process as gradual.

34. Bercovitch, *Puritan Origins*, 9; Zboray, *Fictive People*, 149; E. Prentiss, *Stepping Heavenward*, 4, 32–39, 50–52, 103, 140–41, 158.

35. E. Prentiss, *Stepping Heavenward*, 51–53.

36. Ibid., 39, 170; G. Prentiss, *Life and Letters*, 396, 404; Hedrick, *Harriet Beecher Stowe*, 278; Fisher, *Hard Facts*, 93, 97.

37. E. Prentiss, *Stepping Heavenward*, 34, 136, 141–42.

38. Ibid., 121–24.

39. Ibid., 56, 183, 206; G. Prentiss, *Life and Letters*, 63.

40. E. Prentiss, *Stepping Heavenward*, 206; Tompkins, *Sensational Designs*, 126–28; Baym, *Woman's Fiction*, 15.

41. E. Prentiss, *Stepping Heavenward*, 38, 135, 140, 193; G. Prentiss, *Life and Letters*, 435, 516. Scholars have noted a similar connection between self-denial, self-fulfillment, and empowerment in Stowe's fiction. See, for instance, Hedrick, *Harriet Beecher Stowe*, 9, and Buell, "Calvinism Romanticized," 271.

42. G. Prentiss, *Life and Letters*, 282; advertisement, in E. Prentiss, *Aunt Jane's Hero*, back.

43. Boylan, *Sunday School*, 3–10, 48, 68–78; Kaestle, *Pillars of the Republic*, 44–47.

44. Tebbel, *Book Publishing*, 515, 531–39, 651; *Annual Report of the ATS* (1853): 23, (1870): 20; Rice, *History of the Presbyterian Board*, 4, 27–29, 42, 186. Sabbath-school sales for the Presbyterian Board are based on the board's estimate that its overall output was 15 million copies of 1,720 titles.

45. "Premiums for Sunday School Books," *Annual Report of the . . . ABPS* (1870): 58; "The *Sunday School Advocate,*" *Christian Advocate* 19 (16 Apr. 1845): 2; Sweet, *Methodism in American History*, 334; Arnett, "Quadrennial Report," *Budget* (1884): 99.

46. "Our Sunday School Interests," *Sunday School Magazine* 6 (May 1876): 135; "The Library," *Christian Recorder* 1 (11 Jan. 1862): 1; "Premiums for Sunday School Books," *Annual Report of the . . . ABPS* (1870): 58; C. S. Robinson, D.D., "The Clamor about Books," and J. Hall, "Sabbath-School Books," *Sunday-School Annual* (1874): n.p.

47. J. Hall, "Sabbath-School Books," and L. Abbott, "Sabbath-School Libraries," *Sunday-School Annual* (1874): n.p.; "The Library," *Christian Recorder* 1 (11 Jan. 1862): 1; A Mother, "The Children of Books," *Sunday School Magazine* 6 (May 1876): 132.

48. Tebbel, *Book Publishing*, 531; Noll, *Charles Hodge*, 47; advertisement, in *Catalogue*, by Schneider, n.p.; Godolphin, *Pilgrim's Progress in Words of One Syllable*; Sherwood, *Infant's Progress*; Phillips, *Singing Pilgrim*, iii; D. Hall, "Literacies," 2, 6; Johnson, *Reading "Piers Plowman,"* 7, 26, 129; MacDonald, *Christian's Children*, 35–40.

49. "A Word to Pastors, Superintendents, Librarians, and Library Committees, about the Selection of Sunday-School Libraries," *Annual Report of the . . . ABPS* (1870): 58; *Numerical Ordering Catalogue of the . . . PBP*; Our Reader, "Sunday

School Books," and L. Abbott, "Sabbath-School Libraries," *Sunday-School Annual* (1874): n.p.; D. Hall, *Cultures of Print*, 1, 5.

50. "The Try Society," *Kind Words* 1 (Sept. 1866): 4; Anderson, *Imagined Communities*, 6, 35.

51. Mathews, *Religion in the Old South*, 245; Calhoon, *Evangelicals and Conservatives*, 154; Boylan, *Sunday School*, 90, 131, 144, 149; "Publications of Nelson & Philipps," in *Berean Question Book*, back; *Emma Herbert*, 178.

52. Boylan, *Sunday School*, 50, 76; *Berean Question Book*; Boyd, *Food for the Lambs*; advertisement, in *Jennie and Her Mother*, by Rayne, 13, 21; epigraph to *Letters to Little Children*, by Their Father; "Premiums for Sunday School Books," *Annual Report of the . . . ABPS* (1886): 34.

53. Tebbel, *Book Publishing*, 515; "Notice," in *Fire-Side Piety*, by J. Abbott, 9; J. Abbott, *Mary Erskine*, v–vi; Harper & Bros., "Valuable Works," in *Malleville*, by J. Abbott, back; MacLeod, *Children's Fiction and American Culture*, 10. Boylan, *Sunday School*, 3, interprets moral instruction as promoting values conducive to capitalism and respectability.

54. "Choice Illustrated Books for Children," in *Evenings with the Children*, by Ramsey, back; Strong, *Child Life in Many Lands*; A. Stevens, *Tales from the Parsonage*; inscription, in *Mary and Frank*, AAS; Theolinda, *Vail Family*, 15, 17; *Influence; Or, The Little Silk-Winder*, 14, 58; advertisement, in *Catalogue*, by Schneider, n.p.

Chapter Four

1. N. Porter, *Books and Reading*, 7–8, 33; L. Stevenson, *Scholarly Means to Evangelical Ends*, 42; R. Brown, *Knowledge Is Power*, 243; D. Hall, *Cultures of Print*, 1, 5. Grimsted, "Books and Culture," 203, regrets that scholars have shared Porter's dismissive evaluation of "popular" texts.

2. Faculty of Yale College, "Original Papers in Relation to a Course of Liberal Education," *American Journal of Science and Arts* 15 (1829): 302–05; N. Porter, *Books and Reading*, 5–9, 29, 31, 33, 34, 41, 45, 47; Philes, *How to Read a Book*, 23. Similar advice literature abounded from the 1840s through the 1870s, for instance, "The Manner of Reading," *Carolina Baptist* 1 (Dec. 1845): 73; "Manner of Reading the Scriptures," *Sabbath School Visiter* 8 (1840): 209; Potter, "Preliminary Observations," xx, xxvii; and C. Moore, *What to Read, and How to Read*, 10–11.

3. Ricoeur, *Figuring the Sacred*, 240; Johnson, *Reading "Piers Plowman*," 17; Brumberg, *Mission for Life*, 34, 34; Cavallo and Chartier, *History of Reading*, 31; James 1:22; Ong, *Orality and Literacy*, 133.

4. Wittmann, "Was There a Reading Revolution," 285–99; D. Hall, *Cultures of Print*, 162, 184–85; Gilmore, *Reading Becomes a Necessity*, 348; Lehuu, *Carnival on the Page*, 18–19; Bakhtin, "Epic and Novel," 37–39; Davidson, *Revolution and the Word*, 72–73, 262. For the argument that readers did choose subversive styles, see Reynolds, *Beneath the American Renaissance*, 7–10.

5. Fry, *Christ Our Example*, 23–24; "The Need of Pure Literature," *AME Church Review* 8 (Oct. 1891): 229–30; Hall and Reilly, "Practices of Reading," 379; Hatch, *Democratization*, 3–9; Harvey, *Redeeming the South*, 243–44.

6. Machor, *Readers in History*, xv; advertisement, in *Aunt Jane's Hero*, by E. Prentiss, back.

7. Exman, *House of Harper*, 46; "Book Notices," *Sabbath at Home* 1 (Jan. 1867): 64; "Sabbath at Home Advertiser," *Sabbath at Home* 1 (Dec. 1868): 64.

8. "Literary Notices," *Southern Methodist Pulpit* 2 (1849–50): 367.

9. "Rules for the Reading of the Bible," *Sunday School Magazine* 8 (1839): 53; *Child's First Alphabet*, back.

10. Sigourney, *How to Be Happy*, 116–18; MacLeod, *Children's Fiction and American Culture*, 31.

11. Potter, "Preliminary Observations," x. Numerous scholars have begun to assess the interplay among readers and the forces that shaped readers' encounters with texts in the creation of meaning; for example, Cavallo and Chartier, *History of Reading*; Machor, *Readers in History*; Fish, *Is There a Text*; Johnson, *Reading "Piers Plowman"*; Davidson, *Revolution and the Word*; Amory and Hall, *History of the Book*; and Casper, *Constructing American Lives*.

12. Rabinowitz, *Spiritual Self*, iii; Damrosh, *God's Plot*, 5; Gura, *Wisdom of Words*, 53–67; R. Brown, *Knowledge Is Power*, 277; Davidson, *Revolution and the Word*, 73.

13. Marginalia, in *Lessons on the Book of Proverbs*, by Hopkins, Widener Library, Harvard University.

14. Zboray, *Fictive People*, 119–21; Long and Ferrie, "Labour Mobility." See, for example, unpublished albums by Margaret S. Taft (1838), Helen M. Everest (1847), Ezra S. Williams (n.d.), H. W. Londey (1845–52), and Sarah E. Webb (1841–43), AAS, and Sarah A. Harding (1837) and Edna May (6 Sept. 1862–21 Feb. 1864), Library Company.

15. P. Palmer, *Way of Holiness*, 83, 123, 170; "Obituary Notices," *Christian Advocate* 39 (1 Jan. 1864): 6; Greenwood, diary (4–5 Oct. 1857, 4 Nov. 1857, 24 Mar. 1858), AAS; Mellish, diary (1877), AAS; Amos William Hilton Papers (30 Sept. 1882), American Baptist Historical Society; "Moses Taylor," *Christian Advocate* 45 (6 Jan. 1870): 2; "Christian Experience," *Christian Advocate* 25 (10 Jan. 1850): 1.

16. Simonds, *Unfinished Volume*, 80–89, 97–99, 103–9, 136–37, 152–72.

17. Ibid., 192, 138, 143, 147, 152, 157, 161, 103–4, 165, 173.

18. Bush, *Five Years in China*, 15, 17, 55.

19. Lehuu, *Carnival on the Page*, 11, argues that "gender represented a critical line of distinction in the reading public," whereas Zboray, *Fictive People*, 167–69, questions the notion that nineteenth-century men's and women's reading practices differed significantly. G. Prentiss, *Life and Letters*, 35, 39, 309.

20. G. Prentiss, *Life and Letters*, 259, 370.

21. L. Schmidt, *Hearing Things*, 40, 52–53; Wittmann, "Was There a Reading Revolution," 296; G. Prentiss, *Life and Letters*, 5–8, 26, 52–58, 68, 94, 244, 254, 293–98, 311–13, 320, 338, 365, 432, 462, 471, 482, 561.

22. G. Prentiss, *Life and Letters*, 114, 142, 191, 240, 245, 267, 293, 308, 320, 334–39, 352, 418–20, 432, 454, 561; L. Schmidt, *Hearing Things*, 10, 52, 168.

23. G. Prentiss, *Life and Letters*, 27, 43–46, 50, 68, 151–52, 215–16, 221, 296–98, 340, 344–52, 369, 396, 411, 418, 422, 432–33, 527; Bishop, *Isaac Watts's Hymns*, xviii, 307; Hitchcock and Sadie, *New Grove Dictionary*, 445.

24. G. Prentiss, *Life and Letters*, 28, 41, 128, 306, 332, 420; E. Prentiss, *Home at*

Greylock, 179; E. Prentiss, *Stepping Heavenward*, 123. D. Hall, *Cultures of Print*, 181–82, notes the ease with which religious readers moved back and forth among texts and reading strategies, whereas Zboray, *Fictive People*, 147, interprets the juxtaposition of diverse genres as evidence of secularization.

25. G. Prentiss, *Life and Letters*, 41, 79, 145, 152, 254, 281, 297, 365, 388, 390; E. Prentiss, *Stepping Heavenward*, 205.

26. G. Prentiss, *Life and Letters*, 297; E. Prentiss, *Religious Poems*, 22.

27. G. Prentiss, *Life and Letters*, 132–45; E. Prentiss, *Little Susy's Six Birthdays*, iv; E. Prentiss, *Little Susy's Six Teachers*, 4–6, 25, 93–102.

28. G. Prentiss, *Life and Letters*, 141, 255, 391, 419, 427–40, 450; H. Stowe, *Uncle Tom's Cabin*, xx, xxvi.

29. G. Prentiss, *Life and Letters*, 299, 312, 377.

30. Buell, *New England Literary Culture*, 54–60; Coultrap-McQuin, *Doing Literary Business*, 13–28, 194; Brodhead, *Cultures of Letters*, 76–77; G. Prentiss, *Life and Letters*, 234–44, 296, 388, 459.

31. Johnson, *Reading "Piers Plowman,"* 187–89; G. Prentiss, *Life and Letters*, 281, 426.

32. G. Prentiss, *Life and Letters*, 486–89.

Chapter Five

1. "Prospectus," *Missouri Presbyterian Recorder* 1 (Jan. 1855): back.

2. Marsden, *Fundamentalism*, 16; Nord, *Communities of Journalism*, 6; "Old and New School," *Missouri Presbyterian Recorder* 1 (Jan. 1855): 69.

3. Price and Smith, *Periodical Literature*, 9; Lehuu, *Carnival on the Page*, 79; Carey, *Communication as Culture*, 15–21.

4. Steinberg, *Printing*, 122; O'Brien, "Eighteenth-Century Publishing," 44; Durden, "Study of the First Evangelical Magazines," 259–61; Carey, *Communication as Culture*, 21; Price and Smith, *Periodical Literature*, 4; Mott, *American Magazines*, 1:24; Albaugh, *Religious Periodicals*, xi–xiii.

5. Stroupe, *Religious Press*, 10–11; Norton, *Religious Newspapers*, 3; Humphrey, "Religious Newspapers," 105; Albaugh, *Religious Periodicals*, xvi–xviii; Zboray, *Fictive People*, 32–34; Roorbach, *Bibliotheca Americana*, 644–52; Sweet, *Religion*, 184–85.

6. Albaugh, *Religious Periodicals*, xvi–xviii; Roorbach, *Bibliotheca Americana*, 644–52; Stroupe, *Religious Press*, 13.

7. Stroupe, *Religious Press*, 11, 17; Humphrey, "Religious Newspapers," 106; Sweet, *Religion*, 184–85; Albaugh, *Religious Periodicals*, xx; Hatch, *Democratization*, 126.

8. "Address by Rev. D. B. Cheney of Philadelphia," *Annual Report of the . . . ABPS* (1855): 54; Daniel Calhoun, *Intelligence of a People*, 51; "Indiana Colporteur," *Annual Report of the . . . ABPS* (1866): 36.

9. "Editorial Department," *Baptist Sentinel* 1 (Nov. 1869): 35; Albaugh, *Religious Periodicals*, xix–xx; Hatch, *Democratization*, 126; Stroupe, *Religious Press*, 10; D. Morgan, *Protestants and Pictures*, 163.

10. Albaugh, *Religious Periodicals*, xiii; Sutton, *Western Book Trade*, 46, 65–67, 150, 162; Norton, *Religious Newspapers*, 10, 15; Zboray, *Fictive People*, 65–66; Baldasty, *Commercialization of News*, 42; Hatch, *Democratization*, 144; "Prospectus,"

Missouri Presbyterian Recorder 1 (Jan. 1855): back; advertisement, *Presbyterial Reporter* 1 (July 1852): back.

11. Stroupe, *Religious Press*, 19, 26, 33; Gaustad and Barlow, *New Historical Atlas*, 136; Tebbel, *Book Publishing*, 474.

12. "A Disciple," *Carolina Baptist* 1 (Apr. 1846): 188.

13. "A Proposition," "Reply to Above Letter by Nathaniel," *Carolina Baptist* 1 (Oct. 1845): 39–40; "The Laborers of God," *Repository of Religion and Literature* 4 (Jan. 1862): 14.

14. "Correspondence," *Southern Baptist Messenger* 7 (1 Feb. 1857): 19; *True Union* 11 (13 Dec. 1860): 2; "Discussion — or Controversy," *Southern Christian Sentinel* n.s., 1 (May 1841): 7; "Baptism," *Baptist Preacher* 2 (May 1886): 2.

15. *Christian Union, and Religious Review* 3 (Mar. 1853): 1.

16. "Religious Intelligence," *Southern Methodist Pulpit* 2 (1849–50): 123, 215; *Calvinistic Magazine* 3 (Jan. 1848): 1, and *Arminian Magazine* 1 (Jan. 1848): 18, qtd. in Stroupe, *Religious Press*, 19; "Editorial: *Methodist Episcopalian,*" *Calvinistic Magazine*, n.s., 1 (Aug. 1846): 170–85.

17. Mathews, *Religion in the Old South*, 31–34; Stroupe, *Religious Press*, 13; Harvey, *Redeeming the South*, 30; "Exposition of Hebrews 6:4–6," *Western Baptist Review* 1 (July 1846): 51. Knott, *Sword of the Spirit*, notes the power of the warfare metaphor in the writings of seventeenth-century English Puritans.

18. Rev. of *Christian Mirror*, *Western Baptist Review* 1 (July 1846): 275–76; "Walter Scott, of the Protestant Unionist," *Western Baptist Review* 3 (Mar. 1848): 272; rev. of *Christian Index*, *Western Baptist Review* 2 (Sept. 1846): 32; rev. of *Christian Index* and *Presbyterian Herald*, *Western Baptist Review* 2 (Nov. 1846): 112, 113; rev. of *The Presbyterian Herald*, *Western Baptist Review* 2 (Jan. 1847): 151.

19. Marsden, *Fundamentalism*, 22, 33; "Mere Denominationalism," *Baptist Sentinel* 1 (Nov. 1869): 42–43; Paxton, "Perils of the Church," *Baptist Sentinel* 1 (Apr. 1870): 248–56; "Editorial Department," *Baptist Sentinel* 2 (Dec. 1871): 564–67.

20. Nord, *Communities of Journalism*, 7; Albaugh, *Religious Periodicals*, xi–xiii; Mott, *American Magazines*, 1:120, 341, 370, 2:4; Sellers, *Market Revolution*, 370; Price and Smith, *Periodical Literature*, 4.

21. Albaugh, *Religious Periodicals*, xvi; Norton, *Religious Newspapers*, 2; John Holt Rice, "Introduction," *Virginia Evangelical and Literary Magazine* 1 (Jan. 1818): 2–8, qtd. in Stroupe, *Religious Press*, 7.

22. Roorbach, *Bibliotheca Americana*, 644–52; Frank J. Heinl, "Newspapers and Periodicals in the Lincoln-Douglas Country, 1831–32," *Journal of the Illinois State Historical Society* 32 (Oct. 1930): 271–438, qtd. in Sweet, *Religion*, 186.

23. Nord, "Evangelical Origins," 69; Albaugh, *Religious Periodicals*, xi–xvi; Baird, *Religion in America*, 171; Mott, *American Magazines*, 1:581, 2:10–11, 28, 39; 356, 475; Tebbel, *Book Publishing*, 279; Angell, *Bishop Henry McNeal Turner*, 5.

24. Exman, *House of Harper*, 11, 69–80, 121.

25. Rev. of *Christian Spectator*, *Methodist Magazine*, n.s., 1 (Jan. 1830): 114; "Our Periodicals," *Christian Advocate* 45 (6 Jan. 1870): 5; Sweet, *Methodism in American History*, 290, 334; Sweet, *Religion*, 185–88; Hatch, *Democratization*, 126; *Annual Report of the PBP* (1875): 12, back; Mott, *American Magazines*, 2:62, 1:300.

26. *Annual Report of the ATS* (1826): 12, (1842): 14, (1847): 18, (1853): 23; Tebbel, *Book Publishing*, 474; Marsden, *Fundamentalism*, 22, 33.

27. P. West, "Correspondence," *Southern Baptist Messenger* 11 (1 May 1861): 18; Tebbel, *Book Publishing*, 394; Mott, *American Magazines*, 1:197, 503–4, 2:192; Exman, *House of Harper*, 70–92, 122.

28. Norton, *Religious Newspapers*, 21–28; Baldasty, *Commercialization of News*, 25, 53, 59; Mott, *American Magazines*, 1:34, 2:13–14, 31, 266; *Christian Advocate* 45 (2 Jan. 1890): 3; advertisement, *Christian Advocate* 25 (7 Jan. 1850): 2.

29. *Christian Advocate* 15 (19 Aug. 1840): 2–3; advertisement, *Evangelical Repository* 1 (Jan. 1842): 1; "Religious Newspapers in the West," *Baptist Banner and Western Pioneer* 9 (26 May 1842): 5.

30. *Repository of Religion and Literature* 4 (Oct. 1862): 199; "The Negro Press in Critique," *AME Church Review* 8 (Oct. 1891): 214.

31. Advertisement, *Methodist Quarterly Review* 2 (June 1856): 349; Angell, *Bishop Henry McNeal Turner*, 123, 127; "To Our Subscribers," *Christian Recorder* 1 (11 July 1855): 126; "Second Annual Report of the Business Manager of the Publication Department," *Budget* (1882): 43; "Third Annual Report of the Business Manager of the Publication Department," *Budget* (1883): 1, 8; *Annual Meeting of the Consolidated American Baptist Missionary Convention* (1872): 11–13; "Newspaper Laws," *Christian Recorder* 9 (28 Jan. 1871): 1.

32. "To Ministers," *Carolina Baptist* 1 (Sept. 1845): 20 (emphasis added); rev. of *Sunday School Advocate*, *Christian Advocate* 19 (16 Apr. 1845): 2.

33. *Mothers' Monthly Journal* 6 (Sept. 1841): cover; "Editor's Miscellany," *Mothers' Journal and Family Visitant* 25 (Jan. 1860): 38; see also "Engravings of the Recorder," *Missouri Presbyterian Recorder* 1 (Jan. 1855): 119, and advertisement for *Ladies' Repository*, *Christian Advocate* 39 (7 Jan. 1864): 5; Brodhead, *Cultures of Letters*, 9, 160–61; Rubin, *Making of Middle/Brow Culture*, 2, 17; and Bushman, *Refinement of America*, 322.

34. *Sacred Annual* (1851): 3–4; Mott, *American Magazines*, 1:421, 2:192; L. Schmidt, *Consumer Rites*, 116–17, 182; Lehuu, *Carnival on the Page*, 85–86; Bushman, *Refinement of America*, 283–84; Halttunen, *Confidence Men and Painted Women*, 4–5.

35. *Ladies' Repository* 1 (Jan. 1841): 1, *National Repository* 1 (Jan. 1877): 1, and *National Repository* 8 (Dec. 1880): 1, qtd. in Mott, *American Magazines*, 2:31, 301–5.

36. "A Word to Preachers," *Christian Advocate* 35 (5 Jan. 1860): 2; "Commercial Matters," "Money Market," "Produce Market," *Christian Advocate* 39 (7 Jan. 1864): 8; "Excuses," *Baptist Record* 2 (4 May 1870): 2; "Publishers' Open Letter to their Patrons," *Repository of Religion and Literature* 4 (Oct. 1862): 220.

37. *Annual Report of the . . . ABPS* (1886): 12; "The Need of Pure Literature," *AME Church Review* 8 (Oct. 1891): 229–30; Rubin, *Making of Middle/Brow Culture*, 18.

Chapter Six

1. "Correspondence," *Southern Baptist Messenger* 11 (1 May 1861): 18.
2. Ibid.
3. Ibid.; Stroupe, *Religious Press*, 15.
4. "Correspondence," *Southern Baptist Messenger* 7 (1 Feb. 1857): 19; Nord, *Communities of Journalism*, 6–7.

5. Zboray, *Fictive People*, 79–80, 119–26; Carey, *Communication as Culture*, 15–21, 43; C. Bell, *Ritual Theory, Ritual Practice*, 81–83, 134.

6. Hatch, *Democratization*, 9–10; D. Morgan, *Protestants and Pictures*, 20.

7. Mott, *American Magazines*, 2:75; Reilly and Hall, "Modalities of Reading," 404.

8. "Abstract of the Fifteenth Annual Report," *American Tract Magazine* 15 (June 1840): 67; L. Schmidt, *Consumer Rites*, 116–17, 182; Lehuu, *Carnival on the Page*, 79–86; Bushman, *Refinement of America*, 283–84.

9. Mott, *American Magazines*, 1:513; advertisement, *Presbyterial Reporter* 1 (July 1852): cover; "Prospectus," *Methodist Magazine*, n.s., 1 (Jan. 1830): 1–2.

10. Mott, *American Magazines*, 1:299; "Prospectus," *Calvinistic Magazine*, n.s. 1 (Jan. 1846): 1; *Missionary Advocate* 10 (May 1854): 1; Exman, *House of Harper*, 69–70.

11. Stroupe, *Religious Press*, 11; Pilkington, *Methodist Publishing House*, 201, 455; "Prospectus," *Methodist Magazine*, n.s., 1 (Jan. 1830): 1–2; "Commercial Matters," "Money Market," "Produce Market," *Christian Advocate* 39 (7 Jan. 1864): 8; "Editorial," *Christian Advocate* 65 (2 Jan. 1890): 1.

12. "Sanctification, or Christian Perfection: In What it Consists," *Christian Advocate* 25 (17 Jan. 1850): 1; "But One Sabbath in the Week," *Christian Recorder* 5 (8 Apr. 1865): 3; "Sixty-Three Thousand Good Books at Work," *Annual Report of the . . . ABPS* (1870): 21; "Address of N. N. Wood, D.D.," *Annual Report of the . . . ABPS* (1855): 59.

13. K. Long, *Revival of 1857–58*, 27, 36–36, 71.

14. "To Our Readers," *True Union* 4 (6 Jan. 1853): 2; "A Word About Papers," *Texas Baptist* 5 (17 Oct. 1855): 41.

15. Mathews, *Religion in the Old South*, 100–101; Calhoon, *Evangelicals and Conservatives*, 111–12; Schneider, *Way of the Cross*, 207; Heyrman, *Southern Cross*, 159–60; McDannell, *Christian Home*, xi; McCrossen, *Holy Day, Holiday*, 16; "The Sabbath at Home," *Sabbath at Home* 1 (Jan. 1867): 1–2; "The Editor to His Readers," *Sabbath at Home* 4 (Oct. 1870): 666.

16. "Sabbath Evening," *Sabbath at Home* 1 (July 1867): 445–46; McCrossen, *Holy Day, Holiday*, 58–64.

17. Brodhead, *Cultures of Letters*, 78; Norton, *Religious Newspapers*, 4.

18. Nord, *Communities of Journalism*, 253–54; Anderson, *Imagined Communities*, 33; D. Hall, *Worlds of Wonder*, 18, 70; Loughlin, *Telling God's Story*, 19–20; Tracy, *Analogical Imagination*, 275.

19. "The Fruit of the Spirit," *Beauty of Holiness* 5 (Jan. 1855): 1; "Meditation," *Beauty of Holiness* 5 (Feb. 1855): 35; "Anything but This," "Hymn," *Beauty of Holiness* 5 (Mar. 1855): 79, 88; "To One in the Slough of Adversity," *Beauty of Holiness* 5 (Aug. 1855): 227; "Family Worship," "Sabbath Miscellany," "Editor's Table," *Beauty of Holiness* 6 (Sept. 1855): 56, 57, 63, 64; "But Grow in Grace," *Beauty of Holiness* 7 (Jan. 1856): 5.

20. S. Smith, "Serialization," 71, 74; G. Prentiss, *Life and Letters*, 483–84.

21. "Strange Reluctance," "A Great Work," *Western Christian* 1 (28 June 1845): 1, 3.

22. "The New Volume," *Southern Lady's Companion* 1 (Feb. 1848): 24; "Editorial News," *Christian Recorder*, n.s., 8 (8 Aug. 1868): 78; Tebbel, *Book Publishing*,

139, 558; Mott, *American Magazines*, 1:503; J. Neale, *Hymns, Chiefly Mediaeval*, ix; Hugg, *On Wings of Song*, iii.

23. Francis Ellen Watkins [Harper], "Ethiopia," *Beauty of Holiness* 5 (July 1855): 202. Psalm 68:31 reads "Ethiopia shall soon stretch out her hands unto God"; the AME *Christian Recorder* adopted the same verse as an epigraph for its masthead.

24. Ricoeur, *Figuring the Sacred*, 240; "Our Next Number," *Western Presbyterian* 1 (15 Jan. 1864): 39–40; *Sabbath at Home* 1 (Mar. 1867): 189.

25. Alexis de Tocqueville, *Democracy in America*, ed. J. P. Mayer (New York: Doubleday Anchor, 1969), 518–20, qtd. in Nord, *Communities of Journalism*, 7; Zboray, *Fictive People*, 119, 126; Alexis de Tocqueville, *Democracy in America*, trans. Henry Reeve, 2 vols. (New York: Oxford University Press, 1959), 2:111, qtd. in Hatch, *Democratization*, 145.

26. "Our Duty to Aid Ourselves and to Support Our Literature," *Repository of Religion and Literature* 5 (Jan. 1863): 21; "Our Next Number," *Western Presbyterian* 1 (15 Jan. 1864): 39–40; "Mississippi. Baptist News, Notes, and Comments," *Baptist Layman* 4 (1 July 1894): 1.

27. "The New Volume," *Christian Advocate* 15 (19 Aug. 1840): 3; "A Word to Our Correspondents," *Christian Advocate* 45 (6 Jan. 1870): 4.

28. Norton, *Religious Newspapers*, 26; "Questions Asked Mr. Editor," *Christian Recorder* 24 (18 Mar. 1886): 1; "Answers to Inquiries," *Christian Advocate* 65 (2 Jan. 1890): 5.

29. Stroupe, *Religious Press*, 18; "Editorial Note," *Baptist Preacher* 3 (June 1844): 104; "Editor's Annual Address," *Baptist Preacher*, n.s., 16 (Jan. 1857): 23; Daniel Calhoun, *Intelligence of a People*, 52.

30. "Correspondence," *Southern Baptist Messenger* 9 (15 Jan. 1859): 11; Bennett, "Not Just Filler," 203; Buell, *New England Literary Culture*, 54–60; Coultrap-McQuin, *Doing Literary Business*, 2, 10, 194; Brodhead, *Cultures of Letters*, 76–77; Mott, *American Magazines*, 1:348–54, 503, 580–94, 2:11, 56–59, 306–11.

31. Rev. of *The Christian Repository and Family Visitant*, *Mississippi Baptist* 1 (17 Sept. 1857): 3; Lehuu, *Carnival on the Page*, 30, 102. Zboray, *Fictive People*, 167–69, questions the gendered nature of nineteenth-century reading patterns.

32. "Free Talk with Our Friends," *Mothers' Journal and Family Visitant* 25 (Jan. 1860): 33; Cmiel, *Democratic Eloquence*, 132–34.

33. "Free Talk with Our Friends," "Editor's Miscellany," *Mothers' Journal and Family Visitant* 25 (Jan. 1860): 33, 37–38; Cott, *Bonds of Womanhood*, 5, 138.

34. "Indiana Department," *Baptist Banner and Western Pioneer* 9 (26 May 1842): 3; Gabler-Hover, "North-South Reconciliation Theme," 247; "African Christian Eloquence," *Beauty of Holiness* 7 (May 1856): 125; Heyrman, *Southern Cross*, 219; Rev. C. B. Parsons, "A Tract: Who Knows But He Will," *Southern Lady's Companion* 1 (Sept. 1848): 131–39.

35. Tripp, "Origins of the Black Press," 94–95; Wright, *Bishops*, 32; Angell, *Bishop Henry McNeal Turner*, 5; Rev. J. R. Yungstor, *American National Baptist Convention* (1886): 67.

36. Harvey, *Redeeming the South*, 70–72.

37. J. Campbell, *Songs of Zion*, 55; "Proposals and Plan of a Newspaper of Color," *Colored American* 4 Mar. 1837, qtd. in Tripp, "Origins of the Black Press," 95 (emphasis added); Angell, *Bishop Henry McNeal Turner*, 125.

38. "Apology," *Anglo-African Magazine* 1 (Jan. 1859): 1; Danky, *African-American Newspapers and Periodicals*, 44; "Editor's Repository," *Repository of Religion and Literature* 4 (Jan. 1862): 20.

39. Editorial, *African Expositor* 3 (Oct. 1880): 2; "Our Expectation," "A Word to the Preachers," *Christian Recorder* 1 (13 July 1854): 62; "The Printing Press," and Prof. Mary V. Cook, "Woman's Place in the Work of the Denomination," *American National Baptist Convention* (1887): 11, 51; "A Word to the Subscribers," *Christian Recorder*, n.s., 1 (4 Jan. 1862): 2.

Chapter Seven

1. Bush, *Five Years in China*, 147, 271, 274. The hymns requested by Aitchison were some of the most popular among nineteenth-century evangelicals, according to Marini, "Hymnody Database," ranking numbers 4, 8, and 13 out of the hymns most frequently reprinted from 1830 to 1890. For the 1830–90 time period, Marini examined a total of 59 hymn collections by a range of denominational and independent authors and ranked the 300 most frequently reprinted titles. See also Marini, "Hymnody as History," 273–306. Aitchison wrote the last hymn couplet cited.

2. Julian, *Dictionary of Hymnology*, 332–38, 655.

3. Brian Stock, *Listening for the Text: On the Uses of the Past* (Baltimore: Johns Hopkins University Press, 1990), 146, qtd. in Sizer, *Gospel Hymns*, 20, 25, 141; R. Palmer, "Remarks on Hymnody," v; H. Beecher, *Revival Hymns*, iv; J. O. Murray, *Christian Hymnology*, 21, 35; E. H. Sears, epigraph to *Hymn Lover*, by Horder; A. E. C., *Hymns and Their Stories*, viii; Kynaston, *Occasional Hymns*, v; "Psalms and Hymns," Presbyterian Historical Society.

4. Burrage, *Baptist Hymn Writers*, v; Rogal, *Sisters of Sacred Song*, 70; Hart, *Hymns in Human Experience*, 161.

5. "Methodists and Music," *Methodist Quarterly Review* 48 (July 1865): 359–68; E. Prentiss, *Stepping Heavenward*, 135.

6. Southern, *Music of Black Americans*, 39; Bradley, *Abide with Me*, 57; Ong, *Orality and Literacy*, 147; Damrosh, *God's Plot*, 10; D. Hall, *Worlds of Wonder*, 18, 70, 237, 245; Loughlin, *Telling God's Story*, 19–20; Tracy, *Analogical Imagination*, 275; Anderson, *Imagined Communities*, 35; Turner and Turner, *Image and Pilgrimage in Christian Culture*, 249–51; C. Bell, *Ritual Theory, Ritual Practice*, 81–83, 134.

7. R. Palmer, "Remarks on Hymnody," vi.

8. Unger, *Bible Dictionary*, 1,048; Sadie, *Dictionary of Music and Musicians*, 13:36–37; Brawley, *English Hymn*, 14; Mark 14:26; Col. 3:16 (emphasis added).

9. Burrage, *Baptist Hymn Writers*, 1; Brawley, *English Hymn*, 35; Miller, *Singers and Songs*, 43; Eva and Barr, *Hymns of Human Composition*, 3; Frei, *Eclipse of Biblical Narrative*, 21; Knott, *Sword of the Spirit*, 4, 18; Greengrass, *European Reformation*, 236–37.

10. Foote, *American Hymnody*, 3, 28, 29, 36, 73–79, 146–56, 202; Bird, "American Hymnody," 57; Julian, *Dictionary of Hymnology*, 333.

11. Bishop, *Isaac Watts's Hymns*, ix–xxii, 307; Reeves, *Hymn as Literature*, 11.

12. Bird, "American Hymnody," 57; Julian, *Dictionary of Hymnology*, 332–38, 655; Sallee, *Evangelistic Hymnody*, 13, 44; Foote, *American Hymnody*, 146.

13. Routley, *Hymns and Human Life*, 63; J. O. Murray, *Christian Hymnology*, 16–17; Eva and Barr, *Hymns of Human Composition*, 12.

14. J. O. Murray, *Christian Hymnology*, 20; G. Stevenson, *Methodist Hymn Book*, 3, 9.

15. J. O. Murray, *Christian Hymnology*, 22; Christophers, *Epworth Singers*, 340; Havergal, *Old Hundredth*, vii.

16. R. Palmer, *Book of Praise*, v; J. Warren, *O for a Thousand Tongues*, 119; Bradley, *Abide with Me*, 57, 100; *Short Commentary*, iv; J. O. Murray, *Christian Hymnology*, 37.

17. Crosby, *Memories*, 127, 166–69; Ruffin, *Fanny Crosby*, 7, 129.

18. G. Smith, *Eminent Christian Workers*, 365, 383–84; Biggs, *English Hymnology*, 83.

19. J. O. Murray, *Christian Hymnology*, 28–30; Parker, *Psalmody of the Church*, 254; Mills, *Horae Germanicae*, iii; Winkworth, *Lyra Germanica: Second Series*, v, xi.

20. Snepp, *Songs of Grace and Glory*, xi; J. O. Murray, *Christian Hymnology*, 31; Routley, *Church Music and Theology*, 26; Miller, *Singers and Songs*, v.

21. Hurlbut and Ford, *Imperial Songs for Sunday Schools*, iii; Biggs, *English Hymnology*, 61; G. Stevenson, *Methodist Hymn Book*, 54; E. O. P., *Gleams of Interest*, iii; E. Prentiss, *Little Susy's Little Servants*, 18; A. Mitchell, *Freed Boy in Alabama*, 52–54.

22. "From *The Boys' Scrap Book*, A Work Lately Published by the American Sunday School Union," *Youth's Magazine* 1 (Mar. 1839): 393–94.

23. C. Campbell, *Romantic Ethic*, 187; Gura, *Wisdom of Words*, 6–11, 31, 53; Buell, *New England Literary Culture*, 47; Cmiel, *Democratic Eloquence*, 94–95; McLoughlin, *American Evangelicals*, 19, 128; Brantley, "Common Ground of Wesley and Edwards," 274–75; Marsden, *Fundamentalism*, 113; Bushman, *Refinement of America*, 313–52; J. O. Murray, *Christian Hymnology*, 20–22, 36.

24. Bealle, *Public Worship, Private Faith*, 16; Harris, *Rise of Gospel Blues*, 3–4, 9, 102, 110; Harvey, *Redeeming the South*, 78, 124; Routley, *Church Music and Theology*, 177; Foote, *American Hymnody*, 264; Jackson, *White and Negro Spirituals*, 66; Southern, *Music of Black Americans*, 39, 96; D. Epstein, *Sinful Tunes and Spirituals*, 199; Bruce, *And They All Sang Hallelujah*, 5, 60; Spencer, *Sing a New Song*, 196; Hatch, *Democratization*, 25, 128, 152, 157; Levine, *Black Culture and Black Consciousness*, 20–21; D. Hall, *Cultures of Print*, 5.

25. Foote, *American Hymnody*, 73–75; McCue, *Music in American Society*, 62, 65; Breed, *History and Use of Hymns*, 302.

26. Bealle, *Public Worship, Private Faith*, 1, 32; Bean, intro. to *Missouri Harmony*, by Allen D. Carden, vii; Harvey, *Redeeming the South*, 98; McCue, *Music in American Society*, 69.

27. Harvey, *Redeeming the South*, 97–101; Harris, *Rise of Gospel Blues*, 7; J. Campbell, *Songs of Zion*, 41; Finke and Stark, *Churching of America*, 160; McLoughlin, *American Evangelicals*, 186; Burt, *Pastor's Selection*, 4; Fitz, *Congregational Singing Book*, iii; J. O. Murray, *Christian Hymnology*, 4, 40.

28. H. Beecher, *Revival Hymns*, iv; Hutchins, *Annotations of the Hymnal*, iii; Towner, *Hymns New and Old*, iii; Committee to the Bishops, *Revision*, 14–16; J. O. Murray, *Christian Hymnology*, 37; Dadmun, *Musical String of Pearls*, iii.

29. Breed, *History and Use of Hymns*, 84; Foote, *American Hymnody*, 263. Hobbs,

"I Sing for I Cannot Be Silent," 23–26, argues that evangelical culture, post-1870, was "anti-print," viewing the printed word as "a mode inferior to oral expression." Christophers, *Epworth Singers*, 12.

30. Eva and Barr, *Hymns of Human Composition*, 3.

31. Harvey, *Redeeming the South*, 124; Lorenz, *Glory Hallelujah*, 52–54, 106; Bruce, *And They All Sang Hallelujah*, 90–92; Peters, *Lyrics of the Afro-American Spiritual*, xvi; Jackson, *White and Negro Spirituals*, 83–86; Southern, *Music of Black Americans*, 190.

32. D. Epstein, *Sinful Tunes and Spirituals*, 199; Work, *American Negro Songs*, 8; G. Henry, *Golden Harp*, 10, 63, 71.

33. Stearns, diary (25 Jan. 1835, 1 Nov. 1835, 15. Oct. 1834), Schlesinger Library, Harvard University; Gunther (Brown), "Spiritual Pilgrimage of Rachel Stearns," 580; John Fanning Watson, *Methodist Error* (Trenton, N.J., 1819), qtd. in Southern, *Music of Black Americans*, 78.

34. Harris, *Rise of Gospel Blues*, 3, 110; Taves, *Fits, Trances, and Visions*, 80–81; Avraham Yarmolinsky, *Picturesque United States of America, 1811, 1812, 1813, Being a Memoir on Paul Svinin . . .* (New York, W. E. Rudge, 1930), 20, qtd. in Southern, *Music of Black Americans*, 79; J. Campbell, *Songs of Zion*, 41; Mathews, *Religion in the Old South*, 185–86; Levine, *Black Culture and Black Consciousness*, 5–30; Genovese, *Roll, Jordan, Roll*, 240.

35. Southern, *Music of Black Americans*, 82–92; Raboteau, *Slave Religion*, 187–210; J. Campbell, *Songs of Zion*, 41; Martin, *For God and Race*, 120; Wright, *Bishops*, 20, 31–32; Angell, *Bishop Henry McNeal Turner*, 112; Taves, *Fits, Trances, and Visions*, 97; Spencer, *Black Hymnody*, 9, 11, 26–30, 48; Frey and Wood, *Come Shouting to Zion*, 181–83; Levine, *Black Culture and Black Consciousness*, 138–40; Nat L. Hent, "To Exist Is Not to Live," *African Expositor* 3 (Oct. 1880): 1; Holsey, *Colored Methodist Episcopal Hymnbook*, iii.

36. Spencer, *Black Hymnody*, 27.

37. J. Campbell, *Songs of Zion*, 32–43; Harvey, *Redeeming the South*, 30, 107, 110, 133; Harris, *Rise of Gospel Blues*, 7.

38. W. Barton, *Old Plantation Hymns*, 10, 45; Harris, *Rise of Gospel Blues*, 3–22, 109–14; Foote, *American Hymnody*, 272; Spencer, *Sing a New Song*, 199.

39. J. Warren, *O for a Thousand Tongues*, 119–20; Sizer, *Gospel Hymns*, 5; Breed, *History and Use of Hymns*, 331; Bradley, *Abide with Me*, 186; Brawley, *English Hymn*, 203.

40. Sankey, McGranahan, and Stebbins, *Church Hymns and Gospel Songs*, iii; Sankey, McGranahan, and Stebbins, *Gospel Hymns Nos. 1 to 6*, 98; Eva and Barr, *Hymns of Human Composition*, 4, 7. "I Need Thee Every Hour" ranked number 126 in Marini's "Hymnody Database" for the 1880s.

Chapter Eight

1. Julian, *Dictionary of Hymnology*, 971; G. Stevenson, *Methodist Hymn Book*, 415; Routley, *Hymns and Human Life*, 109; Dieter et al., *Five Views on Sanctification*, 51, 57, 72, 158.

2. Julian, *Dictionary of Hymnology*, 971; G. Stevenson, *Methodist Hymn Book*, 415; *Hymnal of the MEC*, 153.

3. *Hymnal of the MEC*, 153.

4. Parker, *Psalmody of the Church*, v; MacGill, *Songs of the Christian Creed*, iii; Benedict, *Hymns of Hildebert*, iii; Snepp, *Songs of Grace and Glory*, vii; Buell, *New England Literary Culture*, 54–60; Coultrap-McQuin, *Doing Literary Business*, 13–14, 28, 194; Brodhead, *Cultures of Letters*, 76–77.

5. Julian, *Dictionary of Hymnology*, 332; Brawley, *English Hymn*, 97; Routley, *Hymns and Human Life*, 74.

6. Julian, *Dictionary of Hymnology*, 337; Bradley, *Abide with Me*, 21; Snepp, *Songs of Grace and Glory*, viii–xii; F. Turner, *John Henry Newman*, 7, 74–79.

7. Ziff, "Upon What Pre-text?," 297–302; D. Hall, "Literacies," 3; Johnson, *Reading "Piers Plowman,"* 5, 18; Scudder, *Wesleyan Psalmist*, iii. 1 Cor. 14:15: "I will pray with the spirit, and I will pray with the understanding also: I will sing with the spirit, and I will sing with the understanding also."

8. Hull, *Pilgrim's Harp*, iii; G. Stevenson, *Methodist Hymn Book*, 6; B. Hill, *Hymns of Zion*, 5; Buck, *Baptist Hymn Book*, iv; Phillips, *Hallowed Songs*, iii; H. Beecher, *Revival Hymns*, iii; Picket, Bryant, and Knapp, *Tears and Triumphs*, iii; Tenney and Hoffman, *Songs of Faith*, iii; Hunt, *Grace-Culture*, 318; Aldrich, *Sacred Lyre*, iv; J. O. Murray, *Christian Hymnology*, 17, 25.

9. McDannell, *Material Christianity*, 5; Ricoeur, *Figuring the Sacred*, 243; Frei, *Eclipse of Biblical Narrative*, 25.

10. Bean, intro. to *Missouri Harmony*, by Allen D. Carden, x; Steinberg, *Printing*, 138; Tebbel, *Book Publishing*, 207; advertisement, in *Revision*, by Committee to the Bishops, back.

11. Inscription, in *Lyra Germanica: Hymns for the Sundays*, by Winkworth, front-ispiece, Widener Library, Harvard University; advertisement, *New Revival Melodies*, by Dadmun, back; H. Beecher, *Revival Hymns*, iii.

12. Advertisement, in *Palm Leaves*, by Hull, back; Scudder, *Wesleyan Psalmist*, iii; "New Hymn Book!" *Southern Baptist Messenger* 10 (15 June 1860): 96; Dadmun, *Revival Melodies*, iii; George Wallee, rev. of *The Baptist Hymn Book*, *Baptist Banner and Western Pioneer* 12 (2 Oct. 1845): 5; Vanmeter, *Pocket Hymns*, iii.

13. Southern, *Music of Black Americans*, 81–82; Bradley, *Abide with Me*, 59.

14. Hitchcock and Sadie, *Dictionary of American Music*, 2:446–55; Bucke, *History of American Methodism*, 1:285–86; Bird, "American Hymnody," 58; Spencer, *Black Hymnody*, 8.

15. Bird, "American Hymnody," 57; Julian, *Dictionary of Hymnology*, 339.

16. Bird, "American Hymnody," 57; *Annual Report of the PBP* (1843): 16, (1875): 19; speech by Rev. Dr. Skinner, in *Remarks on the Publication Cause*, 7–9, 16, 18, 20.

17. Hitchcock and Sadie, *Dictionary of American Music*, 2:446–55, 4:562.

18. Buck, *Baptist Hymn Book*, iii; Burrage, *Baptist Hymn Writers*, 655–58; Bird, "American Hymnody," 58; D. Stevens, *First Hundred Years*, 26, 41.

19. Committee to the Bishops, *Revision*, 6–7, 14; Duryea, *Presbyterian Hymnal*.

20. Committee to the Bishops, *Revision*, 6–7, 14; "Our New Hymn and Tune Book," *Sunday School Magazine* 6 (May 1876): 161; "New Hymn Book!" *Southern Baptist Messenger* 9 (15 June 1857): 96; T. Hastings, *Presbyterian Psalmodist*, 3; *AME Church Hymn Book*, iii–iv.

21. Committee to the Bishops, *Revision*, 6–7, 14; *Hymn and Tune Book of the MECS*, 3.

22. Agnew, "Report of the Committee," Presbyterian Historical Society; *Annual Report of the PBP* (1875): 17.

23. Marini, "Hymnody Database." Marini, in "Hymnody as History," 282–86, works from a list of the hymns most frequently reprinted between 1737 and 1860, but the rankings are similar enough for the 1830–90 time period that Marini's content analysis is germane.

24. Ricoeur, *Figuring the Sacred*, 240.

25. R. Palmer, *Book of Praise*, v; Haygood and McIntosh, *Prayer and Praise*, iii; Date, Hoffman, and Tenney, *Pentecostal Hymns*, iii; John Greenleaf Adams, *Sabbath School Melodist*, iii; T. Hastings and T. S. Hastings, *Church Melodies*, iii.

26. Advertisement, in *New Revival Melodies*, by Dadmun; rev. of *Gospel Temperance Songs*, *Western Christian Advocate* 46 (19 Mar. 1879): 3.

27. "From *Home Monthly Review*," in *Palm Leaves*, by Hull, back; H. Hastings, *Social Hymns*, iii.

28. Hull, *Pilgrim's Harp*, iii; advertisement, in *Psalmody of the Church*, by Parker, frontispiece; C. Robinson, *Annotations upon Popular Hymns*, 564; Burt, *Pastor's Selection*, 3.

29. Winkworth, *Lyra Germanica: Second Series*, vii–viii.

30. H. Beecher, *Revival Hymns*; B. Hill, *Hymns of Zion*; Cox, Varden, and Ridgely, *Revival Hymns*; Aldrich, *Sacred Lyre*; Phillips, *Hallowed Songs*.

31. Scudder, *Wesleyan Psalmist*, iii; Lorenz, *Glory Hallelujah*, 72; Bruce, *And They All Sang Hallelujah*, 5, 92.

32. "Union Prayer Meeting," *Carolina Baptist* 1 (Apr. 1846): 176–77; rev. of *Hymns for Social Worship*, *American Tract Magazine* 15 (Apr. 1840): back; "Abstract of the *Fifteenth Annual Report*," *American Tract Magazine* 15 (June 1840): 67.

33. Hitchcock and Sadie, *Dictionary of American Music*, 2:446–55; Caldwell and Gordon, *Service of Song*; Burrage, *Baptist Hymn Writers*, 477, 664.

34. J. O. Murray, *Christian Hymnology*, 19, 25; Lowry and Doane, *Pure Gold for the Sunday School*, 2–3; Committee to the Bishops, *Revision*, 20.

35. MacGill, *Songs of the Christian Creed*, iii; Committee to the Bishops, *Revision*, 22.

36. Bushman, *Refinement of America*, 313–52; Julian, *Dictionary of Hymnology*, 338; White, *Roman Catholic Worship*, 69–70; *Short Commentary*, iv–v.

37. Massie, *Lyra Domestica*, xii–xv; *Short Commentary*, iv–v; J. O. Murray, *Christian Hymnology*, 23–24; Charles, *Voice of Christian Life*, 177; Schaff, *Christ in Song*, 604; Winkworth, *Lyra Germanica: Hymns for the Sundays*, 83–84.

38. Benedict, *Hymns of Hildebert*, iii; Nelson, "Church Congress," xiii; Borthwick, *Hymns from the Land of Luther*, iii.

39. E. Andrews, *Revival Songs*, 3–4. Bird, "American Hymnody," 58, calculated that in the *Methodist Episcopal Hymnbook*, only 50 out of 1,148 hymns had an American author; for the *Baptist Hymn Book*, the ratio was 162 out of 1,000; for the *Presbyterian Hymnal*, Americans wrote 108 hymns out of 972; in the *Episcopal Hymnal*, Americans wrote 40 out of 520 hymns; and in the Congregationalist *Plymouth Collection*, Americans wrote 256 out of 1,374 hymns.

40. Marini, "Hymnody Database"; Bird, "American Hymnody," 58.

41. Marini, "Hymnody Database."

42. I based the discussion of hymn metaphors on my analysis of the 300 most often reprinted hymns for 1830 to 1890. Marini, "Hymnody Database."

43. "New Hymn and Tune Book," *Annual Report of the . . . ABPS* (1866): back; Phillips, *Hallowed Songs*; rev. of *Gospel Temperance Songs, Western Christian Advocate* 46 (19 Mar. 1879): 4; G. Henry, *Golden Harp*, 5, 15–16.

44. Marini, "Hymnody Database"; Julian, *Dictionary of Hymnology*, 792–93; G. Stevenson, *Methodist Hymn Book*, 497–98; Horder, *Hymn Lover*, 160; J. O. Murray, *Christian Hymnology*, 17.

45. J. Neale, *Hymns, Chiefly Mediaeval*, ix.

46. Bishop, *Isaac Watts's Hymns*, xv–xxii, 307; Julian, *Dictionary of Hymnology*, 332.

47. Kynaston, *Occasional Hymns*, v; W. Thompson, *Baptist Hymn Book*, iv–v.

48. Francis, *Collection of Psalms and Hymns*, iv.

49. G. Stevenson, *Methodist Hymn Book*, 497–98; Julian, *Dictionary of Hymnology*, 792–93.

50. J. O. Murray, *Christian Hymnology*, 39; Christophers, *Hymn Writers and Their Hymns*, iii.

51. Cleveland, *Lyra Sacra Americana*, vi; J. O. Murray, *Christian Hymnology*, 5; E. Long, *Illustrated History of Hymns*.

52. Hugg, *On Wings of Song*, iii; Dortch, *National Tidings of Joy*, iii.

53. Buck, *Baptist Hymn Book*, 5.

54. Committee to the Bishops, *Revision*, 20–25, 34–35.

Epilogue

1. Maryles, "Few Surprises in the Winners' Circle," 53; Rabey, "No Longer Left Behind"; Worth, "Spreading the Word."

2. Rabey, "No Longer Left Behind," 30, 33. Gutjahr, "No Longer Left Behind," 210, argues that American evangelicals have recently become more accepting of fiction because of its usefulness in explaining the "nonfictional content of the Bible."

3. Bercovitch, *American Jeremiad*, 16, 271.

4. Cavallo and Chartier, *History of Reading*, 26–29.

5. Marsden, *Religion and American Culture*, 279.

6. Ibid., 1–2, 283–90.

BIBLIOGRAPHY

Primary Sources

Manuscripts

Cambridge, Mass.
   Houghton Library, Harvard University
      Searle, Margaret Curson. Diary, 1 Jan. 1809–26 Nov. 1809. (bMS Am
         1175.1)
   Schlesinger Library, Harvard University
      Stearns, Rachel Willard. Diary, 3 Oct. 1834–17 Dec. 1837.
Philadelphia, Pa.
   Library Company
      Albums
         Harding, Sarah A. 1 Jan. 1837.
         May, Edna. 6 Sept. 1862–21 Feb. 1864.
   Presbyterian Historical Society
      Agnew, Benjamin Laskells. "Report of the Committee Appointed by the
         Presbyterian Ministerial Association of Philadelphia to Examine the
         New Hymnal." 1874.
      "Presbyterian General Assembly Centennial Meeting, Academy of Music,
         Horticultural Hall 1788–1888, May 24, 1888."
      "Psalms and Hymns for the Use of the First General Assembly of the Re-
         united Presbyterian Church in the USA, Held in the First Presbyte-
         rian Church, Washington Square, Philadelphia, May 19, 1870."
Rochester, N.Y.
   American Baptist Historical Society
      Griffin, Susan Elizabeth Cilley. Papers, 1851–1927. (RG-1038)
      Hartwell, Jesse. Papers, 1771–1860. (RG-1469)
      Hilton, Amos William. Papers, 1833–82. (RG-1361)
      Thresher, Ebenezer. Papers, 1798–1886. (RG-1372)
      Willmarth, James Willard. Papers, 1835–1911. (RG-1085)
Wheaton, Ill.
   Gebbie Archives and Special Collections, Wheaton College
      Mt. Temple Collection
Worcester, Mass.
   American Antiquarian Society
      Albums
         Barnes, Himkens. 1857.
         Barnes, Sarah. 17 Feb. 1859–13 June 1864.

Bonnton, Miss Catharine E. Nov. 1836.
Brooks, Marjorie. 31 Dec. 1832–15 July 1833.
Colesworthy, S. H. 1841.
Cowen, J. 1827.
Donaldson, Mary Eliza. 1832?
Everest, Helen M. 9 Jan. 1837–June 1842.
Gould, Thomas. 1830–40.
Hammond, Benjamin (Bennie) T. 1861.
Hubbard, Louisa M. 1866.
Londey, H. W. 17 May 1845–Aug. 1855.
Matlack, William. 1861.
Murray, Gertrude C. 1836–30 June 1837.
P. M. B. 1827.
Packard, Elizabeth B. 7 Sept. 1877.
Pluumer, Elizabeth S. 1840.
Prentiss, Lucretia J. Apr. 1832–12 July 1833.
Segu, Maria H. n.d.
Taft, Margaret S. 30 Sept. 1835–18 May 1839.
Taft, Rebeckah G. 1839–40.
Tenney, Lucy Maria. 1820?
Tyler, Ann Eugenia. 15 Aug. 1838–42.
Unsigned. 1832–30 July 1834.
Unsigned. 1841.
W., Anna. 1853.
Warner, Miss Jane R. 1 Jan. 1833.
Watson, Hannah E. 17 Mar. 1840?
Webb, Sarah E. 22 Oct. 1823–25 Mar. 1873.
Williams, Ezra S. n.d.
Young, Sarah L. 1846.
ATS Broadsides
Book Trades Collection, 1726–1939
Broadsides
Diaries and Papers
Blake, James Barnard. Diary. Worcester, Mass., 1851.
Bliss, Mrs. David [Sally Hitchcock]. Diary. Wilbraham, 1821–72.
Bowers, Mary L. Diary. Granville, Mass., 1870.
"Catalogue of Books in the High St. B. S.S. Library." Library Records.
    1859–60.
Greenwood, Mandana Street Ferry [Mrs. Arnold W.]. Diary. 1857–60.
Lee and Shepard Papers. 28 Jan. 1861–12 Oct. 1872.
Mellish, Martha A. Diary. Woodstock, N.Y., 1874–77.
Richardson, Benjamin Parker. Papers. 1814–57.
Second Baptist Sabbath School. Memorandum Book.
Smith, Elizabeth. Diary. 1820–54.

Periodicals

African [Baptist] Expositor. Raleigh, N.C., Oct. 1880–Jan. 1888.

Almanac and Baptist Register. Philadelphia: ABPS, 1851.

AME Church Review, The. Edited by L. J. Coppin, D.D. Philadelphia, Oct. 1891– Jan. 1892.

American Baptist. Philadelphia: ABPS, 1842–66.

American Baptist. St. Louis, 3 Oct. 1889.

American Baptist [Black] Missionary Convention [Report of the Fifteenth through Eighteenth Anniversaries of the]. 1855–58.

American Baptist Year-Book, The. Philadelphia: ABPS, 1873–98.

American Bookseller, The: A Semi-Monthly Journal Devoted to the Interests of the Book, Stationery, News and Music Trades. . . . New York, July 1876–Dec. 1876.

American Booksellers Guide, The. New York, 1 Jan. 1872.

American Journal of Science and Arts, The. Edited by Benjamin Silliman. New Haven: S. Converse, 1829.

American Messenger [Baptist]. New York, Mar. 1873.

American National [Black] Baptist Convention, The [Minutes and Addresses of the First through Third]. 1886–88.

American Primitive Methodist Magazine. Mineral Point, Wisc., Jan. 1863–Dec. 1863.

American Protestant Magazine. New York, June 1845–June 1849.

American Tract Magazine, The. New York: ATS, Jan. 1836–Mar. 1841.

Anglo-African Magazine, The. Jan.–Apr. 1859.

Annual Conference of the African Methodist Episcopal Zion Church in America, Minutes of the Philadelphia District. Philadelphia, 1859.

Annual Meeting of the Consolidated American [Black] Baptist Missionary Convention [Reports of the Thirtieth through Thirty-Ninth]. 1869–80.

Annual Report[s] of the American Tract Society . . . , [The First through Sixty-Fifth]. New York, 1826–90.

Annual Report[s] of the Board of Managers of the American Baptist Publication Society, [The First through Sixty-Second]. Philadelphia, 1840–86.

Annual Report[s] of the Board of Publication of the Presbyterian Church in the United States of America . . . , [The Fifth through Thirty-Seventh]. Philadelphia, 1843– 75.

Annual Report of the Board of Trustees of the Protestant Episcopal Tract Society, Instituted in New York, 1810, The Forty-Ninth. New York, 1858.

Annual Report[s] of the Congregational Board of Publication . . . , [The Twenty-Sixth through Thirtieth]. Boston, 1855–59.

Annual Report of the Missionary Society of the Methodist Episcopal Church, The Fortieth. New York, 1859.

Annual Report[s] of the Presbyterian Publication Committee . . . , [The Ninth through Eighteenth]. Philadelphia, 1861–70.

Arkansas Baptist, The: Denominational Organ of the State. Edited by P. S. G. Watson. Little Rock, 4 Mar. 1859–11 Mar. 1859.

Baltimore Literary and Religious Magazine, The. Edited by Robert J. Breckinridge and Andrew B. Cross. Baltimore, 1841.

Baptist Advocate, The. Cincinnati, Nov.–Dec. 1836.

Baptist Banner, The: A Religious and Literary Newspaper. Atlanta; Augusta, Ga., 4–6: 13 Dec. 1862–21 Jan. 1865.

Baptist Banner and Western Pioneer, The. Edited by W. C. Buck. Louisville, 2 Jan. 1840–2 Oct. 1845.

Baptist [Black] Foreign Mission Convention of the USA [Minutes of the Second through Sixth Annual Sessions of the]. 1881–85.

Baptist Layman, The. Winona, Miss., 1 July 1894.

Baptist Monthly, The. Edited by W. Pope Yeamean. Covington, Ky., Nov. 1865–May 1867.

Baptist Preacher, The. Edited by Rev. Henry Keeling. Richmond, Jan. 1844–Jan. 1857.

Baptist Preacher, The [Black/Missionary]. Edited by A. R. Griggs. Dallas, May 1886.

Baptist Preacher, The: Consisting of Monthly Sermons from Living Ministers. Edited by William Collier. Boston, Oct. 1829–July 1830.

Baptist Preacher [Old School]. Edited by Leonard Cox. Warwick, N.Y., 1 Apr. 1866–15 Aug. 1866.

Baptist Record, The. Edited by J. B. Hardwick. Parkersburg, W. Va., 4 May 1870–17 Aug. 1870.

Baptist Record, The. Edited by Wilson Jewell. Philadelphia: ABPS, 14 Apr. 1841–24 Dec. 1845.

Baptist Recorder, The: Devoted to Religion, the Interest of the Baptist Church, and General Intelligence. Fairmont, Va., 13 July 1848.

Baptist Sentinel, The. Dallas, Oreg.: North Pacific Coast Baptist Convention, 2 May 1895.

Baptist Sentinel, The. Lexington, Ky., Nov. 1869–Dec. 1871.

Beauty of Holiness, The: Devoted to the Sanctity of The Heart, The Life and The Sabbath. Edited by Rev. M. French and Mrs. A. French. Xenia, Ohio, Jan. 1855–Dec. 1856.

Biblical Repertory and Princeton Review, The. New York, Jan. 1837–Oct. 1871.

Budget, The: Containing the Annual Reports of the General Officers of the African Methodist Episcopal Church. . . . Edited by Bishop Benjamin W. Arnett. Xenia and Dayton, Ohio; Philadelphia, 1881–84.

Calvinistic Family Library, The: Devoted to the Republication of Standard Calvinistic Works. Edited by David Christy. Cadiz, Ohio, 1835–37.

Calvinistic Magazine, The [New School Presbyterian]. Edited by Isaac Anderson, D.D., Rev. Fred A. Ross, Rev. James King, and Rev. James McChain. Rogersville, Tenn.; Abingdon, Va., 1–n.s. 1, Jan. 1827–Dec. 1850.

Carolina Baptist, The: A Family Newspaper — Devoted to Religion, Religious Literature, Agriculture, and General Intelligence. Edited by James Blythe. Hendersonville, N.C., 22 Apr. 1857.

Carolina Baptist, The: A Monthly Magazine. Edited by T. W. Haynes. Charleston, S.C., Sept. 1845–Aug. 1846.

Cheap Religious Newspaper, A: Adapted to General Circulation in the Presbyterian Church. 1851.

Children's Magazine, The. New York: GPE SSU, Jan. 1838–Sept. 1838.

Child's Companion and Youth's Friend, The. Philadelphia: ASSU, Jan. 1846–Dec. 1851.

Christian Advocate and Journal and Zion's Herald, The. Edited by J. P. Durbin and T. Merritt; Thomas E. Bond and G. Coles; Daniel Curry, D.D., and W. H. De Puy, D.D.; C. H. Fowler, D.D., L.L.D., and W. H. De Puy, D.D.; J. M. Buckley, D.D. New York: MEC, 31 Aug. 1832–2 Jan. 1890.

Christian Diadem, and Family Keepsake, The: A Repository of Religious and Literary Gems. Edited by Z. Paten Hatch. New York, 1852.

Christian Intelligencer and Evangelical Guardian, The [Presbyterian]. Edited by David MacDill. Rossville, Ohio, Mar.–Apr. 1845.

Christian Keepsake, The: A Christmas and New Year's Gift. Edited by Lydia Huntley Sigourney. New York: Leavitt & Allen, 1858.

Christian Keepsake and Missionary Annual, The. Philadelphia: Brower, Hayes, 1849.

Christian Magazine of the South, The: Devoted to [Presbyterian] Religion, Literature and General Intelligence. Edited by J. Boyce. Columbia, S.C., Mar. 1843–Sept. 1851.

Christian Mirror, The. Edited by Andrew P. Gready. Charleston, 26 Mar. 1814–2 Apr. 1814.

Christian Offering, The. Boston: James B. Dow, 1831.

Christian Ornaments, and Sentiments of the Heart. Lowell: N. L. Dayton; Boston: Gould, Kendall & Lincoln, 1843.

Christian Parlor Book, The: Devoted to Science, Literature and Religion. New York: James H. Pratt, 1854.

Christian Press, The. Cincinnati: Western Tract and Book Society, May 1867.

Christian Recorder of the African Methodist Episcopal Church, The. Edited by Rev. J. P. Campbell; Rev. Elisha Weaver; Rev. Benjamin Tucker Tanner; Rev. Benjamin F. Lee. Philadelphia, 13 July 1854–8 Mar. 1888.

Christian's Gift, The. Edited by Rufus W. Clark. Boston: John P. Jewett; Cleveland: H. P. B. Jewett; New York: Sheldon, Blakeman, 1857.

Christian's Keepsake; Or, Friendship's Memorial: A Gift for All Seasons. Edited by Rev. Enoch Hutchinson. Nashua, N.H.: 1850.

Christian Souvenir, The: An Illustrated Annual, For All Seasons. New York: H. Dayton; Indianapolis: Dayton & Asher, 1858.

Christian Souvenir and Missionary Memorial, The. Auburn, N.Y.: Derby & Miller, 1851.

Christian Union, and Religious Review, The. Edited by Edward E. Orvis. New London, Penn., Mar. 1853.

Doctrinal Preacher: A Monthly Periodical, Devoted to the Support and Defence of Theological Truth. Edited by Leonard Parker. Washington, Ohio, Apr. 1851–June 1851.

Evangelical Guardian [Presbyterian]. May 1845.

Evangelical Repository, The: Devoted to the Principles of the Reformation as Set Forth in the Formularies of the Westminster Divines and Witnessed for by the Associate Synod of North America. Edited by Joseph T. Cooper. Philadelphia, Jan. 1842–June 1861.

Family Treasure, The [Presbyterian]: A Religious and Literary Monthly. Edited by

David McKinney, D.D., and I. N. McKinney. Pittsburgh, Jan. 1864–Dec. 1864.

Gem, The: A Literary Annual. 1835.

Georgia Baptist, The. Augusta, 24 Feb. 1898–5 May 1898.

Home Missionary, The. New York: Congregational Home Missionary Society, May 1828–Mar. 1909.

Home Monthly [MECS]: Devoted to Literature and Religion. Edited by Prof. A. B. Stark and Rev. Felix R. Hill. Nashville, Jan. 1867–Nov. 1867.

Hope [Baptist]. Plaquemine, La., Dec. 1885–Apr. 1886.

Journal of Education, The: Devoted to Educational Interests, Science, Literature and Art. Brooklyn, N.Y., Apr. 1875–Dec. 1875.

Journal of Proceedings of the Colored Shiloh Baptist Association of Virginia. . . . Richmond: V. I. Fore, 1868.

Journal of the American Temperance Union. Philadelphia, Jan. 1837–Mar. 1838.

Kind Words for the Sunday School Children. Edited by S. Boykin. Greenville, S.C.; Memphis: Southern Baptist Convention, Sept. 1866–1 Mar. 1872.

Kind Words Teacher for Baptist Sunday Schools, The. Edited by Basil Manly, D.D. Atlanta: Southern Baptist Convention, Jan. 1887.

Macedonian, The. Boston: American Baptist Missionary Union, Feb. 1851–May 1875.

Methodist Almanac. New York, 1847–1851.

Methodist Magazine, The. Edited by Alex W. McLeod, D.D. Baltimore: MECS, Jan. 1855–June 1856.

Methodist Magazine, The; The Methodist Magazine and Quarterly Review; The Methodist Quarterly Review; The Methodist Review. Edited by George Peck, D.D; J. M'Clintock; D. D. Whedon, D.D., L.L.D; Daniel Curry, L.L.D.; J. W. Mendenhal, D.D. New York: MEC, 1818–90.

Michigan Christian Herald. Detroit: Baptist State Convention, Mar. 1866–28 Dec. 1882.

Minutes and Proceedings of the Colored Shiloh Baptist Association of Virginia. . . . Richmond: Republic Book and Job Office, 1865.

Missionary, The. Baltimore: Presbyterian Church in the United States, July 1876.

Missionary Advocate. New York: MEC, 1 May 1854–16 July 1872.

Mississippi Baptist: A Religious Family Newspaper. Edited by John T. Freeman; Aaron Jones Jr. Jackson, 17 Sept. 1857–11 Oct. 1860.

Missouri Presbyterian Recorder, The [New School]. St. Louis: Synod of Missouri, Jan. 1855–Sept. 1855.

Mothers' Magazine, The. Edited by Mrs. A. G. Whittelsey. New York, 1849.

Mothers' Monthly Journal, The; The Mothers' Journal and Family Visitant. Edited by Mrs. Eliza C. Allen; Mrs. Mary G. Clarke; Mrs. Caroline O. Hiscox. Utica; Philadelphia; New York; Chicago: 1841–68.

Our Little Ones. Philadelphia: ABPS, 8 Oct. 1876–21 Oct. 1876.

Our Monthly. Edited by Rev. W. P. Jacobs. Clinton, S.C., July 1876.

Our Young People: An Illustrated Monthly. Edited by A. J. Rowland, D.D. Philadelphia: ABPS, Jan. 1881–Dec. 1883.

Pioneer Baptist, The: A Monthly Magazine. Coal Valley, W.Va.: Baptist State Convention Bible and Publication Board, Oct. 1884.

Presbyterial Reporter, The. Edited by Rev. W. H. Spencer. Milwaukee, Wisc., July 1852.

Presbyterian Parlor Magazine, The: Monthly Journal of Science, Literature, and Religion. Edited by Alfred Nevin, D.D. July 1860.

Presbyterian Sabbath School Visitor. Philadelphia; New York: PBP, 1851–75.

Presbyterian Standard, The. Paducah, Ga., June 1854–Dec. 1854.

Princeton Review, The. New York, Jan. 1845–Apr. 1849.

Religious Narrator, and Philadelphia [Baptist] Journal of Christian Effort, The. Edited by W. T. Brantly. Philadelphia: Central Union Association, 26 July 1833.

Repository of Religion and Literature, and of Science and Art. Edited by Rev. John M. Brown. Baltimore, Jan. 1862–Jan. 1863.

Sabbath at Home, The: An Illustrated Religious Magazine for the Family. Boston: ATS, Jan. 1867–Oct. 1870.

Sabbath-School Annual, The. Edited by Mrs. M. H. Adams. Boston: James M. Usher, 1848.

Sabbath School Visiter, The [Congregationalist]. Edited by Rev. Asa Bullard. Boston: MSSS, Jan. 1840–Dec. 1843.

Sacred Annual, The: A Gift for All Seasons. Edited by Rev. H. Hastings Weld. Philadelphia: T. K. Collins Jr., 1851.

Soldier's Friend, The [Baptist]. Edited by A. S. Worrell. Atlanta, Jan. 1863–9 July 1863.

Southern Baptist, The. Meridian, Miss., 4 Sept. 1878–7 Mar. 1889.

Southern Baptist Messenger, The: Devoted to the Service of the Old School Baptists. Edited by William Beebe. Covington, Ga., 1 Feb. 1857–1 May 1861.

Southern Christian Sentinel, The. Charleston: Union Presbytery, May 1841–Dec. 1841.

Southern Ladies' Book. Macon, Ga., Sept. 1840.

Southern Lady's Companion, The. Nashville: MECS, Jan. 1848–Dec. 1848.

Southern Methodist Pulpit, The. Edited by Charles F. Deems. Richmond, 1849–50.

Southern Presbyterian Review, The. 1 July 1863.

South-Western Baptist Chronicle: Devoted to Religion, Science, Literature, Commercial and General Intelligence. Edited by W. C. Duncan. New Orleans, 15 May 1847–11 Aug. 1849.

Southwestern Christian Advocate. New Orleans: MEC, Jan. 1877–7 Mar. 1878.

Sunday Scholar's Mirror, The: A Monthly Magazine for Children. Edited by Daniel P. Kidder. New York: MEC SSU, Jan. 1851–Dec. 1854.

Sunday-School Annual. New York: Dodd & Mead, 1874.

Sunday-School Journal. Philadelphia: ASSU, 3 Jan. 1849–19 Dec. 1855.

Sunday School Magazine, The. Edited by W. G. E. Cunnyngham, D.D. Nashville: MECS, May 1876.

Sunday School Magazine, The. New York: MEC SSU, Jan. 1839–Dec. 1839.

Sunday School Visitor. Edited by A. H. Redford. Nashville: MEC, June 1874.

Texas Baptist, The: Devoted Especially to the Religious and Educational Interests of the Baptist Denomination in Texas. Edited by George Baines. Anderson, Tex., 17 Oct. 1855–13 Feb. 1856.

True Union, The [Baptist]: A Religious and Family Newspaper. Edited by Rev. Franklin

Wilson; Rev. John Berg. Baltimore and Washington, 10 Jan. 1850–30 Dec. 1860.

United States Baptist Annual Register and Almanac, The. Edited by I. M. Allen. Philadelphia: ABPS, 1833–66.

Wesleyan Expositor, The. Edited by Rev. E. Smith. Mansfield, Ohio, June 1852.

Western Baptist Review, The. Edited by John L. Waller. Frankfort, Ky., July 1846– June 1850.

Western Christian, The. Edited by Rev. Spencer Carr. Elgin, Ill.: North-Western Baptist Anti-Slavery Convention, 28 June 1845–24 Sept. 1846.

Western Christian Advocate, The. Cincinnati: MEC, 19 Mar. 1879.

Western Presbyterian, The: A Religious Monthly. Edited by Rev. T. H. Cleveland and Rev. J. L. M'Kee. Louisville, Ky., 15 Jan.–Mar. 1864.

Western Watchman, The: A Religious Family Newspaper, for the Entertainment, Instruction and Salvation of All Classes of Readers Weekly. St. Louis, 29 Dec. 1853.

Youth's Companion, The: A Family Paper Devoted to Piety, Morality, Brotherly Love, — No Sectarianism, No Controversy. Boston, 4 Jan. 1834–1 Dec. 1870.

Youth's Magazine: A Monthly Miscellany. New York: MEC, Dec. 1838–Mar. 1839.

Zion's Advocate: Devoted to the Cause of God and Truth. Edited by J. Clark. Front Royal, Va., 1 Apr. 1876.

Books

A. E. C. *Hymns and Their Stories.* London: SPCK; New York: E. & J. B. Young, 1894.

A. L. O. E. [Charlotte M. Tucker]. *The Giant Killer; Or, the Battle Which All Must Fight.* Carter's Fireside Library. New York: Robert Carter & Bros., 1857.

Abbott, Jacob. *Congo; Or, Jasper's Experience in Command.* Harper's Story Books. New York: Harper & Bros., 1854.

———. *Fire-Side Piety; Or, The Duties and Enjoyments of Family Religion. . . .* Cooperstown, N.Y.: H. & E. Phinney, 1834.

———. *Malleville: A Franconia Story.* Harper's Story Books. New York: Harper & Bros., 1850.

———. *Mary Erskine: A Franconia Story.* Harper's Story Books. New York: Harper & Bros., 1850.

———. *Viola and Her Little Brother Arno.* Harper's Story Books. New York: Harper & Bros., 1854.

Abbott, Rev. Lyman, and Rev. T. J. Conant. *A Dictionary of Religious Knowledge: For Popular and Professional Use, Comprising Full Information on Biblical, Theological, and Ecclesiastical Subjects, with Several Hundred Maps and Illustrations.* New York: Harper & Bros., 1875.

Adams, John Greenleaf. *The Sabbath School Melodist: A Collection of Hymns and Tunes Designed for the Sabbath School and the Home.* Boston: R. A. Ballou, 1866.

Adams, John Quincy. *Sanctification: A Sermon, Preached in the North Baptist Church. . . .* New York: Sheldon, 1859.

Adams, Oscar Fay. *A Dictionary of American Authors.* Boston: Houghton, Mifflin; Cambridge: Riverside, 1897.

African Methodist Episcopal Church Hymn Book, The: Being a Collection of Hymns

Designed to Supersede All Others Hitherto Made Use of in That Church, Selected from Various Authors. Philadelphia: J. P. Campbell, 1856.

Aldrich, Rev. J. *The Sacred Lyre: A New Collection of Hymns and Tunes, for Social and Family Worship*. Boston: Andrew F. Graves; New York: Sheldon, Blakeman; Cincinnati: George S. Blanchard, 1858.

Alexander, Archibald, D.D. *A Selection of Hymns: Adapted to the Devotions of the Closet, the Family and the Social Circle. . . .* 3d ed. New York: Jonathan Leavitt, 1832.

Alexander, James W., D.D. *The Breaking Crucible and other Translations of German Hymns*. New York: A. D. F. Randolph, 1861.

———. *Frank Harper; Or, The Country-Boy in Town*. Library for Sunday-Schools. Philadelphia: ASSU, 1847.

Alfred Raymond; Or, A Mother's Influence. Philadelphia: ASSU, n.d.

Alleine, Joseph. *An Alarm to Unconverted Sinners: In a Serious Treatise on Conversion*. 1672. Evangelical Family Library, vol. 9. Reprint, New York: American Tract Society, 1834?.

Allen, Richard. *The Life Experience and Gospel Labor of the Rt. Rev. Richard Allen, Written by Himself*. Philadelphia: Martin & Boden, 1833.

American Clergyman, An, ed. *The Life and Writings of Bishop Heber: The Great Missionary to Calcutta. . . .* Boston: Albert Colby, 1856.

Andrew, James O., D.D. *Family Government: A Treatise on Conjugal, Parental, Filial and Other Duties; By One of the Bishops of the Methodist Episcopal Church, South. 3d enlarged ed.* Nashville: E. Stevenson & J. E. Evans, for the MECS, 1856.

Andrews, C. W., D.D. *An Apology: The Protestant Episcopal Society for the Promotion of Evangelical Knowledge; Its Origin, Constitution, Tendencies, and Work. . . .* New York: PESPEK, 1854.

Andrews, Charles Wesley. *Religious Novels: An Argument Against Their Use*. New York: A. D. F. Randolph, 1856.

Andrews, Rev. Emerson. *Revival Songs: A New Collection of Hymns and Spiritual Songs for Closet and Family Worship, Prayer, Conference, Revival and Protracted Meetings*. Boston: James H. Earle, 1870.

Anna Ross: A Story for Children. Philadelphia: ASSU, 1860.

Appleton's Library Manual: Containing a Catalogue Raisonne of Upwards of Twelve Thousand of the Most Important Works in Every Department of Knowledge, in All Modern Languages. New York: D. Appleton; Philadelphia: Geo. S. Appleton, 1847.

Arnett, Bishop Benjamin W., ed. *Proceedings of the Quarto-Centennial Conference of the African Methodist Episcopal Church, of South Carolina, at Charleston, S.C., May 15, 16, and 17, 1889*. Charleston, S.C.: AME Church, 1890.

Asbury, Rev. Francis. *The Journal of the Rev. Francis Asbury, Bishop of the Methodist Episcopal Church, from August 7, 1771, to December 7, 1815*. New York: N. Bangs & T. Mason, 1821.

Asher, Rev. Jeremiah. *An Autobiography, with Details of a Visit to England, and Some Account of the History of the Meeting Street Baptist Church, Providence, R.I., and of the Shiloh Baptist Church, Philadelphia, Penn*. Philadelphia: Jeremiah Asher, [1862].

Ayer, Sarah Newman [Connell]. *Diary of Sarah Connell Ayer [1791–1835]*. Portland, Maine: Lefavor-Tower Co., 1910.

Back Court, The; Or, Every-Day Work. Philadelphia: PBP, 1869.

Bacon, Henry. *The Christian Comforter: A Gift for the Afflicted and Bereaved*. Boston: Abel Tompkins, 1846.

Baillie, Rev. John. *A Memoir of Captain W. Thornton Bate, R.N.* New York: Robert Carter & Bros., 1859.

Baird, Rev. Robert. *Religion in America; Or, An Account of the Origin, Progress, Relation to the State, and Present Condition of the Evangelical Churches in the United States, with Notices of the Unevangelical Denominations*. New York: Harper & Bros., 1844.

Baldwin, Rev. P. C. *The Redemption of Sinners by the Free Grace of God; Or, the Doctrines of Unconditional Election, Perseverance of the Saints, Assurance of Hope, Sanctification and Glorification Freely Discussed*. Philadelphia: Henry Perkins, 1849.

Bangs, Nathan, D.D. *A History of the Methodist Episcopal Church*. 4 vols. New York: J. Collord, 1839.

———. "History of the Methodist Episcopal Church." In *Religious Denominations in the United States*, compiled by Israel Daniel Rupp, 357–79. Philadelphia: Charles Desilver; Savannah: John M. Cooper, 1861.

Banks, Louis Albert, D.D. *Immortal Hymns and Their Story: The Narrative of the Conception and Striking Experiences of Blessing Attending the Use of Some of the World's Greatest Hymns*. 2d ed. Cleveland: Burrows Brothers, 1897.

Bartlet, William S., A.M. *The Frontier Missionary: A Memoir of the Life of the Rev. Jacob Bailey, A [Protestant Episcopal] Missionary at Pownalborough, Maine, Cornwallis and Annapolis, N.S., with Illustrations, Notes, and an Appendix*. Boston: Ide & Dutton, 1853.

Bartley, Joseph D., A.M. *Songs for the School, Sacred and Secular*. New York, Chicago, and New Orleans: A. S. Barnes & Co., 1877.

Barton, Mrs. Parthena Rood. *Experiences of a Practical Christian Life: In Form of a Journal*. Utica, N.Y.: Curtiss & Childs, 1877.

Barton, William Eleazar, D.D. *Old Plantation Hymns: A Collection of Hitherto Unpublished Melodies of the Slave and the Freedman, with Historical and Descriptive Notes*. Boston: Lamson, Wolffe, 1899.

Bascom, John. "Professor Albert Hopkins." In *Book of Berkshire: Papers by its Historical and Scientific Society*, 39–59. Pittsfield, Mass.: Sun Printing, 1889.

Basset, Jonathan. *The Poor Man's Catechism: The Doctrine of the Church of Christ Explained*. Fall River, Mass.: Jonathan Bassett, 1857.

Bates, L. B. *Pocket Hymn Book for Social Worship Everywhere*. New Bedford, Mass.: n.p., 1869.

Beautifully Illustrated Juvenile Books. New York: Samuel Raynor, 1854.

Beecher, Rev. Henry Ward. *Revival Hymns*. Boston: Phillips & Sampson, 1858.

Beecher, Lyman. *The Autobiography of Lyman Beecher*. Edited by Barbara M. Cross. 2 vols. Cambridge: Harvard University Press, 1961.

Belcher, Joseph, D.D. "History of the Baptists." In *Religious Denominations in the United States*, compiled by Israel Daniel Rupp, 42–73. Philadelphia: Charles Desilver; Savannah: John M. Cooper, 1861.

Bell, Catherine D. *Horace and May; Or, Unconscious Influence.* New York: A. D. F. Randolph, 1859.

——. *Jane Thorn; Or, The Head or the Heart.* Boston: Henry Hoyt, 1869.

——. *Philip and Bessie; Or, Wisdom's Ways.* Boston: Henry Hoyt, 1861.

Bell, George A. *Book of Praise for the Sunday School with Hymns and Tunes Appropriate for the Prayer Meeting and the Home Circle.* New York and Chicago: Biglow & Main, 1875.

Benedict, Erastus C. *The Hymns of Hildebert and other Mediaeval Hymns with Translations.* New York: A. D. F. Randolph, 1867.

Benson, Louis F., D.D. *The Best Church Hymns.* Philadelphia: Westminster, 1899.

Berean Question Book (International Series) for 1875, The. . . . New York: Nelson & Philips; Cincinnati: Hitchcock & Walden, 1875.

Bibliotheca Munselliana: A Catalogue of the Books and Pamphlets Issued from the Press of Joel Munsell, from the Year 1828 to 1870. New York: Burt Franklin, 1872.

Biggs, Rev. Louis Coutier. *English Hymnology, Reprinted (with Additions and Corrections) from the "Monthly Packet."* London: Mozleys, 1873.

Blackburn, Alexander. *Financial Statement for the Year 1886 of the Baptist Foreign Missionary Convention of the USA.* . . . N.p., 1886.

Bliss, P. P. *"Hold the Fort" by P. P. Bliss, with Illustrations by Miss L. B. Humphrey and Robert Lewis.* Boston: William F. Gill; Cincinnati: John Church, 1876.

Boardman, Henry A. *The "Higher Life" Doctrine of Sanctification, Tried by the Word of God.* Philadelphia: PBP, 1877.

Boardman, William E. *The Higher Christian Life.* Boston: Henry Hoyt, 1858.

Boggs, W. B. *The Baptists: Who are They? and What Do They Believe?* 4th ed. Philadelphia: ABPS, 1898.

Bolton, Rev. James. *The Great Unpublished Book: A New Year's Address to Children.* New York: PESPEK, 1857.

Book Buyer's Manual, The: A Catalogue of Foreign and American Books in Every Department of Literature with a Classified Index. New York: G. P. Putnam, 1852.

Bookmakers, The: Reminiscences and Contemporary Sketches of American Publishers. New York: *New York Evening Post*, 1875.

Books for Children and Youth. Vol. 1. New York: ATS, 1848.

Books for Sunday Schools. New York: Carlton & Phillips, 1856.

Books Published. New York: Robert Carter & Bros., 1852, 1857, and 1859.

Books Published by Sheldon & Company. New York: Sheldon, 1873.

Books Published for the Sunday-School Union of the Methodist Episcopal Church. New York: Carlton & Phillips, 1854.

Booth, Samuel, comp. *Hanson-Place M.E. Sunday School Hymn Book.* New York: E. Goodenough, 1860.

Borthwick, Jane Laurie. *Hymns from the Land of Luther: Translated from the German.* New and enl. ed. New York: A. D. F. Randolph, 1862.

Bowdoin Street Church. *The Articles of Faith and Covenant of the Bowdoin Street Church, Boston, with a List of the Members.* Boston: T. R. Arvin, 1856.

Bowen, Rev. George. *Daily Meditations: By the Rev. George Bowen, the American Missionary, Bombay, India.* Philadelphia: PPC; New York: A. D. F. Randolph, 1865.

Boyd, Robert. *Food for the Lambs: Or, The Little Ones Invited to Jesus.* Chicago: Church & Goodman, 1865.

Brewer, S. S. *The Jubilee Harp: Revised and Enlarged, and for Tent, Conference, Prayer, and Congregational Meetings.* Concord, N.H.: Oliver Hart, 1855.

Brooks, Rev. Anson P. *Story of Sammy, the Sailor Boy: Designed to Promote the Welfare of Rail Road and Water Men, and Show the Influence of Piety in the Family Circle.* Rochester: M. T. Gardner, 1848.

Bryant, Rev. J. C. *A Journal of Rev. J. C. Bryant, Missionary of the American Board of Commissioners for Foreign Missions, Written on Board the Wm. H. Shaler, While on His Voyage to South Africa.* Manchester: Saturday Messenger Office, 1846.

Buck, William C. *The Baptist Hymn Book: Original and Select in Two Parts . . . For Public Worship . . . For Social Worship.* Louisville, Ky.: J. Eliot, 1842.

Bulkley, Rebekah Wheeler Pomeroy. *Memoir of Mrs. Lucy Gaylord Pomeroy, Wife of Hon. S. C. Pomeroy, Kansas, By His Sister.* New York: John W. Amerman, 1865.

Bulmer, Agnes. *Memoirs of Mrs. Elizabeth Mortimer, with Selections from Her Correspondence.* New York: T. Mason & G. Lane. 1836.

Bunyan, John. *The Pilgrim's Progress from This World to That Which is to Come: Delivered under the Similitude of a Dream, wherein is Discovered the Manner of His Setting out, His Dangerous Journey, and Safe Arrival at the Desired Country.* London: Nathan Ponder, 1678.

Burns, Rev. Jabez. *Death Bed Triumphs of Eminent Christians: Exemplifying the Power of Religion in a Dying Hour.* London: Joseph Smith; Philadelphia: PBP, 1842.

Burrage, Henry Sweetser, D.D. *Baptist Hymn Writers and Their Hymns.* Portland, Maine: Brown, Thurston, 1888.

Burt, Nathaniel Clark. *A Pastor's Selection of Hymns and Tunes for Worship in the Church and Family: The Hymns in the Body of the Work Being Taken From the Book of Psalms and Hymns of the Presbyterian Church; Those in the Supplement, From Various Sources.* Philadelphia: J. B. Lippincott, 1859.

Bush, Rev. Charles P. *Five Years in China; Or, The Factory Boy Made a Missionary: The Life and Observations of Rev. William Aitchison, Late Missionary to China.* Philadelphia: PPC; New York: A. D. F. Randolph, 1865.

Bushnell, Horace. *Christian Nurture.* Boston: MSSS, 1847; New York: Charles Scribner, 1860.

Butterworth, Hezekiah. *The Story of the Hymns; Or, Hymns That Have a History: An Account of the Origin of Hymns of Personal Religious Experience.* New York: ATS, 1875.

————. *The Story of the Tunes: For Home Reading, Praise Meetings, and Lectures on Sacred Music.* New York: ATS, 1890.

Caldwell, S. L., D.D., and A. J. Gordon, D.D. *The Service of Song, for Baptist Churches.* 1871. Boston: Gould & Lincoln, 1876.

Calvin, John. *Institutes of the Christian Religion.* 2 vols. Edited by John T. McNeill. Translated by Ford Lewis Battles. Library of Christian Classics, vols. 20–21. 1536. Reprint, Philadelphia: Westminster, 1960.

Campbell, Rev. T. G. *Sufferings of the Rev. T. G. Campbell and His Family, in Georgia.* Washington: Enterprise, 1877.

Carden, Allen D. *The Missouri Harmony; Or, a Collection of Psalm and Hymn Tunes, and Anthems.* . . . 1820. 9th ed. Cincinnati: Phillips & Reynolds, 1846.

Carroll, R. *Christ on the Cross: A Sermon Preached before the Baptist Educational, Missionary and Sunday School Convention of South Carolina, in Columbia, S.C., May 11, 1887.* Greenville, S.C.: Hoyt & Keys, 1887.

Cartwright, Peter. *Autobiography of Peter Cartwright, The Backwoods Preacher.* Edited by W. P. Strickland. Cincinnati: MEC Western Book Concern, 1856.

Catalogue. New York: D. Appleton, [1847?].

Catalogue. New York: Lane & Tippet, 1851.

Catalogue. New York: Carlton & Phillips, 1856.

Catalogue. Boston: D. Lothrop, 1871.

Catalogue of Books. Boston: Henry Hoyt, 1862.

Catalogue of Books and Other Publications of the American Sunday-School Union, Designed for Sunday-Schools, Juvenile, Family, and Parish Libraries, and for General Reading. Philadelphia: ASSU, 1851.

Catalogue of Books Belonging to the Burlington Library. Burlington, N.J.: Gazette Book and Job Printing Office, 1876.

Catalogue of Books, By the American Sunday School Union. Philadelphia: ASSU, 1856.

Catalogue of Books in the Library of the Second Reformed Church Sabbath School, Bethlehem, New York. Albany: Weed, Parsons, 1870.

Catalogue of Books Published. New York: Robert Carter & Bros., 1851.

Catalogue of Books Published and for Sale by Hurd & Houghton, A. . . . *Comprising Their Own Publications, and Those of P. Putnam and Warren F. Draper.* New York: Hurd & Houghton, 1866.

Catalogue of Standard and Miscellaneous Books Published by Dodd & Mead. . . . New York: Dodd & Mead, 1873.

Catalogue of the Apprentices' Library in New-York: Established and Supported by the General Society of Mechanics and Tradesmen, September 1865. New York: A. W. King, 1865.

Catalogue of the Juvenile, Sunday-School, and Family Library. Philadelphia: ASSU, 1845.

Catalogue of Valuable Standard Works, Comprising Theological, Religious, Classical, Musical, Etc. Boston: Crocker & Brewster, 1858.

Centennial of the Methodist Book Concern and Dedication of the New Publishing and Mission Building of the Methodist Episcopal Church. New York: Hunt & Eaton, 1890.

Chapel Hymnal, The. Philadelphia: PBPSSW, 1898.

Charles, Elizabeth Rundle. *Te Deum Laudamus: Christian Life in Song, the Song and the Singers.* 5th ed., rev. and enl. London: SPCK; New York: E & J. B. Young, 1897.

———. *The Voice of Christian Life in Song; Or, Hymns and Hymn-Writers of Many Lands and Ages.* New York: Robert Carter & Bros., 1866.

Charlie Scott; Or, There's Time Enough. London: RTS; Boston: Henry Hoyt, 1867.

Child's First Alphabet of Bible Names, The. Philadelphia: ASSU, 1827.

Child's Illustrated Scripture Question Book, The: Containing Forty-Five Lessons on the Gospels, Each Lesson Beautifully Illustrated. Boston: Henry Hoyt, 1860.

Choice Collection of Hymns, and Spiritual Songs, A: Designed for the Devotions of Israel, in Prayer, Conference, and Camp-Meetings; Also, A Suitable Pocket Companion for Christians of Every Denomination, Although Not Numbered among the Regular Tribes. Concord, N.H.: Hoag & Atwood, 1830.

Christmas Catalogue. Boston: Lockwood & Brooks, 1875.

Christophers, Rev. S. W. *The Epworth Singers and Other Poets of Methodism.* New York: A. D. F. Randolph, 1874.

———. *Hymn Writers and Their Hymns.* London: S. W. Partridge; New York: A. D. F. Randolph, 1867.

Clark, Alexander. *Workday Christianity; Or, The Gospel in the Trades.* Philadelphia: Claxton, Remsen & Haffelfinger; Springfield, Ohio: Methodist Publishing House; Pittsburgh: S. A. Clarke, 1871.

Clark, Rufus. *The New Serial Question Books on the Heroes of the Bible.* Boston: MSSS, and Henry Hoyt, and Graves & Young; New York: M. W. Dodd and A. D. F. Randolph; Philadelphia: W. S. & A. Martien; Albany: S. R. Gray and Fisk & Son, 1864.

Clergyman, A. *The Youth's Miscellany: For the Spiritual Advancement of the Young of all Classes.* Newburyport, Mass.: Huse & Bragdon, 1851.

Cleveland, Charles Dexter. *Lyra Sacra Americana: Or, Gems from American Sacred Poetry. Selected and Arranged, with Notes and Biographical Sketches.* New York: Charles Scribner; London: Sampson Low, Son, & Marston, 1868.

Coldstream, Rev. Peter Mearns. *Life of Mrs. Agnes Andrew, of Paisley: Illustrative of the Triumphs of Faith in Humble Life.* Philadelphia: PBP, n.d.

Coleman, Rev. William H., ed. *Casket of Pulpit Thought: Being a Collection of Sermons by Ministers of the Ohio, North Ohio and Other Conferences of the African Methodist Episcopal Church.* Newark, Ohio: Advocate, 1889.

Collection of Hymns and Sacred Songs, A: Suited to Both Private and Public Devotions, and Especially Adapted to the Wants and Uses of the Brethren of the Old German Baptist Church. Kinsey's Station, Ohio: Office of the Vindicator, 1882.

Colman, Miss. *Sunday Hymns: Selected from Heber, Sigourney, Howitt, and Others.* New York: Samuel Raynor, 1845.

Colonel, P. M. *Manual of Select Catholic Hymns and Devotions for the Use of Schools, Colleges, Academies, and Congregations: Compiled and Arranged from Approved Sources.* New York: C.S.S.R., 1885.

Committee of the Presbytery of Cleveland. *An Exposition of the Peculiarities, Difficulties and Tendencies of Oberlin Perfectionism.* Cleveland: T. H. Smead, 1841.

Committee on the Hymnal. *The Hymnal Revised and Enlarged as Adopted by the General Convention of the Protestant Episcopal Church in the United States of America.* . . . New York: James Pott, 1892.

Committee to the Bishops. *The Revision of the Hymn Book of the Methodist Episcopal Church.* . . . New York: Nelson & Philipps; Cincinnati: Hitchcock & Walden, 1878.

Cooke, Samuel, D.D. *The Gospel in Christ: A Sermon Preached before the Protestant Episcopal Society for the Promotion of Evangelical Knowledge, at its Twentieth Annual Meeting . . . Nov 5, 1867.* New York: PESPEK, 1867.

Cox, Rev. Luther J., Josiah Varden, and Charles W. Ridgely, comps. *Revival Hymns Designed for Protracted, Camp, Prayer, and Social Meetings, with a Supplement*

Containing Hymns for the Use of Sabbath Schools. Baltimore: Methodist Protestant Church, 1843.

Crane, William. *The Prayer Meeting Hymn Book: A Selection of Standard Evangelical Hymns, for Prayer and Conference Meetings, Revivals, and Family and Private Devotion.* Baltimore: Weishampel Jr.; Richmond: Wortham & Cotrell, 1858.

Crosby, Fanny [Mrs. Alexander Van Alstyne]. *Memories of Eighty Years.* Boston: James H. Earle, 1906.

Cross, Jonathan. *Five Years in the Alleghenies.* New York: ATS, 1863.

Cross, Marcus E., ed. *The Museum of Religious Knowledge: Designed to Illustrate Religious Truth.* Philadelphia: J. Whetham, 1839.

Crummell, Alexander. *A Defence of the Negro Race in America from the Assaults and Charges of Rev. J. L. Tucker, D.D., of Jackson, Miss., in His Paper before the "Church Congress" of 1882, "The Relations of the Church to the Colored Race," Prepared and Published at Request of the Colored Clergy of the Protestant Episcopal Church. . . .* Washington: Judd & Detweiler, 1883.

Cummings, Rev. Dr. *Songs for Catholic Schools and Aids to Memory for the Catechism, with Original Music by Domenico Speranza.* New York: O'Shea, 1860.

Cummings, Rev. Asa. *A Memoir of the Rev. Edward Payson, D.D., Late Pastor of the Second Church in Portland.* 1827. 3d ed. Boston: Crocker & Brewster, 1830.

——, comp. *Memoir, Select Thoughts and Sermons of the Late Rev. Edward Payson, D.D.* 3 vols. Portland, Maine: Hyde & Lord, 1846.

Cummins, Rev. George. *A Sketch of the Life of the Rev. William M. Jackson. . . .* New York: PESPEK, 1857.

Dabney, Jonathan Peele. *A Selection of Hymns and Psalms for Social and Private Worship.* 13th ed. Boston: Munroe & Francis, 1841.

Dadmun, J. W. *Musical String of Pearls: A Collection of Hymns and Tunes, Original and Selected, Adapted to All Occasions of Social Worship.* Boston: J. P. Magee and Russell & Patee; New York: Carlton & Porter; Buffalo: H. H. Otis; Pittsburg: J. L. Reed; Cincinnati: Poe & Hitchcock; Chicago: W. M. Doughty, 1862.

——. *The New Revival Melodies: A Collection of Some of the Most Popular Hymns and Tunes, Adapted to All Occasions of Social Worship.* Boston: J. P. Magee, 1860.

——. *Revival Melodies: A Collection of Some of the Most Popular Hymns and Tunes, Adapted to All Occasions of Social Worship.* Boston: J. P. Magee, 1858.

Daily Food for Christians: Being a Promise, and Another Scriptural Portion, for Every Day in the Year; Together with the Verse of a Hymn. New York: ATS, 1830.

Daily Steps Towards Heaven; Or, Practical Thoughts on the Gospel History, and Especially on The Life and Teaching of Our Lord Jesus Christ: For Every Day in the Year, According to the Christian Seasons. . . . 5th Am. ed., rev. and corr. by the 5th London ed. New York: GPE SSU and Church Book Society, 1869.

Date, Henry, selector, and E. A. Hoffman and J. H. Tenney, music eds. *Pentecostal Hymns No. 2: A Winnowed Collection for Evangelistic Services, Young People's Societies and Sunday Schools.* Chicago: Hope, 1898.

d'Aubigne, Jean Henri Merle. *History of the Reformation of the Sixteenth Century.* Translated by H. White. 5 vols. New York: ATS, 1847–53.

Davis, Caroline E. [Kelly]. *Little Apple Blossom.* The Hillside Library. Boston: Henry Hoyt, 1863.

Davis, James A., D.D. *The History of Episcopacy: Prelatic and Moderate.* Nashville: AME SSU, 1902.

Dayton, A. C. *Baptist Facts against Methodist Fictions.* Nashville: South-Western Publishing House; Graves & Marks, 1859.

DeBow, J. D. B. *The Seventh Census of the United States, 1850: Embracing a Statistical View of Each of the States and Territories.* Washington: Robert Armstrong, 1853.

Denison, M. A. *Kept from Idols.* Boston: Henry Hoyt, 1870.

De Pressense, Madame E. *Rosa.* Translated from the French. Philadelphia: PBP, 1868.

Derby, James C. *Fifty Years Among Authors, Books and Publishers.* New York: G. W. Carleton, 1884.

Derby & Miller's List of Popular Books. Auburn, N.Y.: Derby & Miller, 1853.

Descriptive Catalogue of the Books Published by the Congregational Board of Publication. Boston: MSSS, 1862.

Descriptive Catalogue of the Presbyterian Board of Publication. Boston: F. W. Walsh; Philadelphia: PBP, 1871.

Descriptive Catalogue of the Publications of Sheldon & Company, A. New York: Sheldon, 1871.

Descriptive Catalogue of the Publications of the Massachusetts Sabbath School Society, A. Boston: MSSS, 1854.

Descriptive Catalogue of Valuable Works with Illustrations . . . Many of Which are Admirably Adapted as "Gift Books," for the Approaching Season of Christmas and New Years. Boston: Gould & Lincoln, 1854.

Devotional Hymns Selected from Various Authors. New York: A. D. F. Randolph, 1859.

Deward, D., D.D., L.L.D. *The Holy Spirit: His Personality, Divinity, Office, and Agency, in the Regeneration and Sanctification of Man.* London: Ward, 1847.

Dexter, Henry Martyn. *Memoranda, Historical, Chronological, &c.: Prepared with the Hope to Aid Those Whose Interest in Pilgrim Memorials, and History, is Freshened by this Jubilee Year, And Who May Not Have a Large Historical Library at Hand.* Boston: Todd, 1870.

Dick, Thomas. *On the Improvement of Society by the Diffusion of Knowledge; Or, An Illustration of the Advantages Which Would Result from a More General Dissemination of Rational and Scientific Information among All Ranks.* New York: Harper & Bros., 1833.

Dickson, Rev. Andrew F. *Plantation Sermons; Or, Plain and Familiar Discourses for the Instruction of the Unlearned.* Philadelphia: PBP, 1856.

Doddridge, Philip. *Rise and Progress of Religion in the Soul: Illustrated in a Course of Serious and Practical Addresses, Suited to Persons of Every Character and Circumstance, with a Devout Meditation and Prayer Added to Each Chapter, to Which is Subjoined, a Sermon on the Care of the Soul.* 6th ed. Boston: D. Henchman, 1745.

Dortch, Rev. D. E. *National Tidings of Joy: A Choice Collection of Sacred Songs for Sunday Schools, Prayer and Praise Meetings, Revivals, Social Circles, Singing Classes, Choirs, etc., Original and Select.* Nashville: National Baptist Publishing Board, 1878.

Dowling, John, D.D. *The Conference Hymn Book: A New Edition Reissued and Improved, by the Addition of the Best of the New Revival and Conference Hymns.* New York: U. D. Ward, 1868.

Dunning, Mrs. A. K. *Grace Avery's Influence.* The Thousand Dollar Prize Series. Boston: D. Lothrop; Dover, N.H.: G. T. Day, 1873.

Duryea, Rev. Joseph T., comp. *The Presbyterian Hymnal.* Philadelphia: PBP, 1874.

Dwight, Sereno Edwards. *Memoirs of the Rev. David Brainerd: Missionary to the Indians.* . . . New Haven: S. Converse, 1822.

Dwight, William T., D.D. *Characteristics of New England Theology: A Discourse, Delivered at the First Public Anniversary of the Congregational Board of Publication.* . . . Boston: CBP, 1855.

E. O. P. *Gleams of Interest Across Hymns Ancient and Modern.* London: W. R. Russell, 1898.

Earler, A. B. *Revival Hymns.* Boston: n.p., 1865.

Easturn, Manton, D.D. *The Moderation of the Protestant Episcopal Church: The Second Annual Sermon before the Directors of the Protestant Episcopal Society for the Promotion of Evangelical Knowledge.* . . . Boston: James B. Dow, 1849.

Edgeworth, Maria. *Orlandino.* Chambers's Library for Young People. Boston: Gould, Kendall & Lincoln, 1848.

Edwards, Jonathan. *An Account of the Life of the Late Reverend Mr. David Brainerd, Minister of the Gospel, Missionary to the Indians.* . . . Boston: D. Henchman, 1749.

———. *The Treatise on Religious Affections.* . . . Evangelical Family Library, vol. 3. 1746. Reprint, New York: ATS, 1832?

Egliseau, S. S. *Lizzie Ferguson; Or, the Sabbath-School Scholar: A Narrative of Facts.* Philadelphia: PBP, 1856.

Elizabeth, Charlotte. *The Happy Mute; Or, The Dumb Child's Appeal.* New York: ATS, [1848–68?].

Ellen; Or, The Disinterested Girl. Philadelphia: ASSU, 1854.

Ellis, John Eimeo. *Life of William Ellis: Missionary to the South Seas and to Madagascar.* London: John Murray, 1873.

Emma Herbert; Or, Be Ye Perfect. Philadelphia: PBP, 1863.

Eva, W. T., and W. W. Barr. *Are Hymns of Human Composition Divinely Authorized?* . . . Philadelphia: Collins & McDill, 1884.

Evangelical Synod of North America. *Hymnal of the Evangelical Church.* St. Louis: Eden, 1899.

Evangelical Union Anti-Slavery Society of the City of New York. *Address to the Churches of Jesus Christ.* . . . New York: n.p., 1839.

Evans, Rev. Robert Wilson. *A Day in the Sanctuary, with an Introductory Treatise on Hymnology.* London: J. G. F. & J. Rivington, 1843.

Excell, E. O. *Triumphant Songs Nos. 3 and 4 Combined.* Chicago: E. O. Excell, n.d.

Father, A. *Pebbles from the Sea-Shore; Or, Lizzie's First Gleanings.* New York: Samuel Raynor, 1850.

Father William. *Recollections of Rambles at the South.* New York: Carlton & Phillips, for the MEC SSU, 1854.

Fénélon, François, and Jeanne Marie Guyon. *Spiritual Progress; Or, Instructions in the Divine Life of the Soul, from the French of Fénélon and Madame Guyon: Intended for Such as are Desirous to Count all Things But Loss That They May Win Christ.* Edited by James W. Metcalf. New York: M. W. Dodd, 1853.

Finney, Charles G. *Principles of Sanctification: Studies on Biblical Sanctification and Its Distinction from "Perfectionism."* Compiled and edited by Louis Gifford Parkhurst, Jr. 1840. Reprint, Mineapolis: Bethany, 1986.

Fitz, Asa. *The Congregational Singing Book: A Collection of the Most Approved Psalm and Hymn Tunes for Religious Worship.* Boston: Phillips & Sampson, 1848.

Francis, William Pitt Greenwood. *A Collection of Psalms and Hymns for Christian Worship.* 41st ed. Boston: Charles J. Hendee and Jenks & Palmer, 1835.

Free Reading Room Association of Spring Garden. *Constitution and By-laws.* . . . Philadelphia: n.p., 1856.

Friend to Youth, A. *Child's Own Hymn Book, with Engravings.* Truman's Entertaining Toy Books. Cincinnati: William T. Truman, 1844.

Fry, Caroline [Wilson]. *Christ Our Example, to Which is Prefixed an Autobiography of the Author.* New York: Robert Carter & Bros., 1852.

Fuller, Richard, et al. *The Baptist Praise Book.* New York: A. S. Barnes, 1872.

Ganse, Hervey Doddridge. *Poems and Hymns.* . . . Chicago: Young Men's Era, 1892.

Gibson, C. S. Preface to *Hymns and Their Stories,* by A. E. C. London: SPCK; New York: E. & J. B. Young, 1894.

Gillett, E. H., D.D. *History of the Presbyterian Church in the United States of America.* Philadelphia: PPC; New York: A. D. F. Randolph, 1864.

———. *Life Lessons in the School of Christian Duty.* Philadelphia: PBP; A. D. F. Randolph, 1864.

Gillmore, Calvin. *The Camp-Meeting Hymn Book: Selected from Various Authors, for the Use of Those Who Worship God in the Spirit.* Geneva, N.Y.: J. Bogert, 1830.

Godolphin, Mary. *Pilgrim's Progress in Words of One Syllable.* New York: George Routledge & Sons; Philadelphia: J. B. Lippincott, [1870?].

Goodrich, S. G. *Lives of Benefactors.* Boston: C. H. Peirce & G. C. Rand, 1844.

Goss, Rev. C. C. *Statistical History of the First Century of American Methodism, with a Survey of the Origin and Present Operations of Other Denominations.* New York: Carlton & Porter, 1866.

Gould, Nathaniel D. *Companion for the Psalmist: Containing Original Music, Arranged for Hymns in "The Psalmist," of Peculiar Character and Metre.* . . . Boston: Gould, Kendall & Lincoln, 1845.

Green, Rev. Augustus R. *The Life of the Rev. Dandridge F. Davis, of the African M.E. Church . . . Also, a Brief Sketch of the Life of the Rev. David Conyou, of the A.M.E. Church.* . . . Pittsburgh: Ohio Conference, 1850.

———, comp. *A Treatise on the Episcopacy of the African Methodist Episcopal Church: Duty of Parents and Churches to Baptized Children; An Examination of the Mother Church.* Pittsburg: N. Poindexter, 1845.

Griffiths, Rev. T. S. *Songs of the Sanctuary.* Baptist ed. New York: A. S. Barnes, 1869.

Guernsey, Lucy Ellen. *Winifred; Or, "After Many Days": A Story of Monmouth's Rebellion.* New York: Thomas Whittaker, 1869.

Hall, Charles Cuthbert, D.D., comp. *Twenty-Four Lessons to Illustrate Christian*

Belief and Christian Experience by Means of Christian Hymns. New York: YMCA, 1899.

Hall, E. B. *Hymns for Social Worship and Private Devotion.* Providence: B. Cranston, 1836.

Hall, John, D.D. *Sabbath-School Theology; Or, Conversations with a Class.* Philadelphia: PBP, 1856.

Hall, M. A. *Lizzie's Visit to New-York.* New York: PESPEK, [1886?].

Hamlin, H. *Questions on the Acts of the Apostles.* Boston: Henry Hoyt, 1861.

———. *The Youth's Scripture Question Book: On the New Testament.* Boston: Henry Hoyt, 1860.

Hammond, Edward Payson, ed. *The Revival Melodist: A Collection of Choice Hymns and Tunes, Especially Adapted to Seasons of Deep Religious Interest, and for Use in the Family and Sabbath School.* Boston: Henry Hoyt, 1864.

Hard Text, and Three Other Stories, The. New York: Carlton & Porter, for the MEC SSU, 1856.

Hare, Edward, ed. *An Epitome of the Art of Spiritual Navigation; Or, A Voyage to Heaven Recommended, by a Christian Mariner.* Philadelphia: James Harmstead, 1845.

Harper, Edward. *Strictures on "Hymns Ancient and Modern": Being an Exposure of the Errors, False Doctrines, and Heresies in That Compilation . . . Romist Services for Which They Had Been Appointed; Statistics of Popery in Great Britain.* 2d ed. London: W. Walborook, [1867?].

Hastings, Horace Lorenzo. *Social Hymns: Original and Selected.* Boston: H. L. Hastings, Scriptural Tract Repository, 1865.

Hastings, Thomas, Mus. Doc., ed. *The Presbyterian Psalmodist: A Collection of Tunes Adapted to the Psalms and Hymns of the Presbyterian Church in the United States of America, Approved by the General Assembly.* Philadelphia: PBP, 1865.

———. *Spiritual Songs, for Social Worship: Adapted to the Use of Familiar and Private Circles in Seasons of Revival, to Missionary Meetings, to the Monthly Concert, and Other Occasions of Special Interest.* 5th ed. Utica: Gardiner Tracy; New York: Robinson, Pratt, and F. J. Huntington, and Leavitt, Lord, and E. Collier, 1837.

Hastings, Thomas, Mus. Doc., and Rev. Thomas S. Hastings. *Church Melodies: A Collection of Psalms and Hymns, with Appropriate Music, For the Use of Congregations.* New York: A. D. F. Randolph; Chicago: William Tomlinson; Cincinnati: George Crosby; Boston: Henry Hoyt, 1859.

Hatfield, Edwin F., D.D. *The Poets of the Church. A Series of Biographical Sketches of Hymn-Writers with Notes on Their Hymns.* New York: A. D. F. Randolph, 1884.

Havergal, Rev. W. H. *A History of the Old Hundredth Psalm Tune, with Specimens.* New York: Mason Bros., 1854.

Haygood, Atticus G., D.D., and R. M. McIntosh, eds. *Prayer and Praise; Or, Hymns and Tunes for Prayer Meetings, Praise Meetings, Experience Meetings, Revivals, Missionary Meetings, and All Special Occasions of Christian Work and Worship.* Macon, Ga.: J. W. Burke; Nashville: MECS; St. Louis: Advocate, 1883.

Headley, Rev. P. C. *A New Series of Question Books on the Heroines of the Bible; Or, The*

Women of Sacred History: In Three Volumes, for the Infant School, Children under Fifteen Years, and Those of Maturer Age. Vol. 3. Boston: Henry Hoyt, 1867.

Henry, G. W., selector. *The Golden Harp: A Supplement to the First Edition of Camp-Meeting Hymns, to Which is Added the Opinion of 12 of the Early Fathers of Methodism on the Subject of Devotional Singing. . . .* Oneida: G. W. Henry, 1857.

———. *The Golden Harp; Or, Camp-Meeting Hymns, Old and New, Set to Music.* Oneida: G. W. Henry, 1857.

Henry, Thomas Charlton, D.D. *Etchings from "The Religious World."* Charleston: Observer Office, and D. W. Harrison; Philadelphia: E. Littell; New York: John P. Haven; Boston: Crocker & Brewster, 1828.

Henry A. Sumner's Catalogue of Publications. Chicago: Kenney & Sumner, 1871.

Hersey, John. *The Privilege of Those Who are Born of God; Or, A Plain Rational View of the Nature and Extent of Sanctification.* Baltimore: Armstrong & Berry, 1841.

Hill, Benjamin M. *Hymns of Zion: Being a Selection of Hymns for Social Worship, Compiled Chiefly for the Use of Baptist Churches.* New Haven: Durrie & Peck, 1830.

Hill, Levi L., comp. *The Baptist Scrap Book.* Lexington, N.Y.: Baptist Library Office, 1845.

Himes, Joshua V. *Millennial Harp: Designed for Meetings on the Second Coming of Christ.* Improved ed. Boston: Himes, 1843.

Hodge, Charles. *Systematic Theology.* London: T. Nelson & Sons, 1872–73.

Hoffman, Rev. Elisha A., and T. H. Tenney. *New Spiritual Songs.* Boston: Oliver Ditson; New York: C. H. Ditson; Chicago: Lyon & Healy; Philadelphia: J. E. Ditson, 1887.

Hoge, Moses D., D.D. *Mission Field of the South.* Richmond: Evangelical Alliance, 1873.

Holiday Gift Books. Boston: Roberts Bros., n.d.

Holsey, Lucius H. *Colored Methodist Episcopal Hymnbook.* Jackson, Tenn.: CME, 1891.

Holsinger, George B. *Shaped Notes: Gospel Songs, and Hymns No. 1.: For the Sunday School, Prayer Meeting, Social Meeting, General Song Service.* Mount Morris, Ill.: Brethren Publishing House, 1895.

Homes of the West, and How They Were Made Happy. Philadelphia: PBP, 1864.

Home Song Book: Prepared for the Use of the Children of the Home for the Friendless. New York: American Guardian Society, 1857.

Hooker, Edward, D.D. *Memoir of Mrs. Sarah L. Huntington Smith, Late of the American Mission in Syria.* 3d ed. New York: ATS, 1845.

Hopkins, Mrs. Louisa Payson. *Lessons on the Book of Proverbs, Topically Arranged: Forming a System of Practical Ethics, For the Use of Sabbath Schools and Bible Classes.* 1843. Boston: Tappan & Dennett, 1845.

———. *Scripture Questions.* Vol. 9, *On the Acts of the Apostles.* Boston: MSSS, 1845.

———. *Scripture Questions.* Vol. 12, *On The Book of Psalms, Topically Arranged: The Christian Life.* Boston: MSSS, 1846.

Horder, W. Garrett. *The Hymn Lover: An Account of the Rise and Growth of English Hymnody.* London: J. Curwen & Sons, 1889.

Hovey, Alvah. *The Doctrine of the Higher Christian Life Compared with the Teaching of the Holy Scriptures.* Boston: Henry A. Young, 1876.

Howitt, William. *History of Priestcraft in All Ages and Nations.* London and New York: E. Wilson, 1833.

Hubbard, Stephen. *The New Temperance Melodist: Consisting of Glees, Songs, and Pieces, Composed and Arranged for the Use of the Various Temperance Organizations in the United States and Canada.* Boston: Oliver Ditson, 1859.

Hugg, George C. *On Wings of Song: For Revival Meetings, Endeavor Societies, Epworth Leagues, Young People's Unions, Prayer Meetings, and the Sunday School.* Philadelphia: George C. Hugg, 1896.

Hull, Asa. *Palm Leaves of Sacred Melody: Suitable for Social Worship and Revival Occasions.* Boston: James P. Magee; New York: E. Goodnough and N. Tibbals; Cincinnati: George Crosby; Chicago: Poe & Hitchcock; St. Louis: B. St. J. Fry; Baltimore: T. Newton Kurtz; Philadelphia: Asa Hull, 1867.

——. *The Pilgrim's Harp: A Choice Collection of Sacred Music, Adapted to All Occasions of Social and Family Worship, and a Convenient Hand-Book for Church Choirs.* Philadelphia: Asa Hull; Boston: James P. Magee, 1869.

——. *The Sacred Harp: A Collection of Hymns and Tunes, Suitable for All Occasions of Social Worship, and Sabbath Schools.* Boston: Gilmore & Russell, 1859.

Hunt, Ezra M., M.D. *Grace-Culture; Or, Thoughts on Grace, Growth, and Glory.* Philadelphia: PBP, 1864.

Hurlbut, Jesse L., D.D., and Stephen V. R. Ford, eds. *Imperial Songs for Sunday Schools, Social Meetings, Epworth Leagues, Revival Services.* New York: Hunt & Eaton; Cincinnati: Cranston & Curts, 1894.

Hurst, John Fletcher, L.L.D. *Bibliotheca Theologica: A Select and Classified Bibliography of Theology and General Religious Literature.* New York: Charles Scribner's Sons, 1883.

Hutchins, Rev. Charles L. *Annotations of the Hymnal: Consisting of Notes, Biographical Sketches of Authors, Originals and References.* Hartford, Conn.: M. H. Mallory, 1872.

Hymnal of the Methodist Episcopal Church, with Tunes. Cincinnati: Jennings & Pye; New York: Eaton & Mains, 1878.

Hymnal of the Presbyterian Church: Ordered by the General Assembly. Philadelphia: PBP, 1867.

Hymn and Tune Book of the Methodist Episcopal Church, South. Character note ed. Nashville: MECS, 1889.

Hymns, Religious and Patriotic, for the Soldier and the Sailor. Boston: ATS, 1861.

Hymns for Anti-Slavery Prayer-Meetings. London: Jackson & Walford, 1838.

Hymns from the Land of Luther: Translated from the German, Taken from the Last Edinburgh Edition. New York: A. D. F. Randolph, 1857.

Illustrated Catalogue. London, Paris, and New York: Cassell, Petter, & Galpin, 1874.

Illustrated Works Published by Henry Hoyt. Boston: Henry Hoyt, 1870.

Influence; Or, The Little Silk-Winder. Philadelphia: ASSU, 1851.

J. B. Lippincott & Co.'s Catalogue of Publications and Importation, Embracing Valuable Standard Books in Historical, Law, Medical, School and General Literature, . . . A

Large Variety of Bibles, Testaments, and Episcopal Prayer Books, and Photograph Albums. Philadelphia: J. B. Lipincott, 1872.

Janvier, Emma. *Rulof and Ernestine: The Lost Children*. New York: PESPEK, 1870.

K. M. *Easter Day, And Other Stories, on the Book of Common Prayer*. New York: PESPEK, 1866.

Keble, Rev. John. *The Christian Year: Thoughts in Verse for the Sundays and Holydays throughout the Year*. . . . 1st American ed., from the 18th Oxford ed. Philadelphia: George & Wayne, 1844.

Kempis, Thomas à. *The Christian's Pattern; Or, A Treatise of the Imitation of Christ*. Translated by John Wesley. London: C. Rivington, 1735.

Kennedy, Grace. *Anna Ross: A Story for Children*. New York: Robert Carter & Bros., 1851; Philadelphia: ASSU, 1860.

Kenneth Forbes; Or, Fourteen Ways of Studying the Bible. Philadelphia: PBP, n.d.

Kinede, Bede. *Grebo Prayer Book*. Philadelphia: King & Baird, 1867.

Kurzenknabe, J. H., W. W. Bentley, and I. N. McHose. *Gospel Trio of Sacred Song for Gospel Meetings, Christian Associations and Young People's Societies for Christian Work*. Harrisburg, Pa.: J. H. Kurzenknabe & Sons, 1891.

Kynaston, Herbert, D.D. *Occasional Hymns (Original and Translated)*. England: R. Clay, Son, & Taylor, 1862.

Lady, A. *Catherine Brown, The Converted Cherokee: A Missionary Drama, Founded on Fact*. New Haven, Conn.: S. Converse, 1819.

Lamb, Mrs. Joseph. *Richard Owen's Choice*. New York: PESPEK, 1870.

Lee, Alfred, D.D., S.T.D. *The Life and Ministry of Benjamin Bosworth Smith, First Bishop of Kentucky*. . . . Louisville: John P. Norton, 1884.

———. *A Life Hid with Christ in God: Being a Memoir of Susan Allibone, Chiefly Compiled from Her Diary and Letters*. Philadelphia: Lippincott, 1856.

———. *The True Nature of the Kingdom of God: A Sermon Delivered at the Annual Meeting of the Protestant Episcopal Society for the Promotion of Evangelical Knowledge*. . . . New York: PESPEK, 1857.

Lee, Rev. Henry. *Prayers for Children*. 5th ed. New York: GPE SSU, 1853.

Lee, Jarena. *The Life and Religious Experience of Jarena Lee, A Coloured Lady: Giving an Account of Her Call to Preach the Gospel*. Rev. and corrected from the original manuscript. Philadelphia: Jarena Lee, 1836.

Leighton, Robert. *A Practical Commentary on the First Epistle of St. Peter*. 1694. Reprint of 1853 ed., Grand Rapids, Mich.: Kregel, 1972.

———. *The Whole Works of Robert Leighton: to Which is Prefixed a Memoir of the Author, by George Jerment*. 4 vols. New ed. London: Ogle & Duncan, 1820.

Leslie, Mrs. Madeline [Mrs. Harriette N. W. Baker]. *Howard and His Teachers, The Sister's Influence, and Other Stories*. Mrs. Leslie's Juvenile Series. Boston: Lee & Shepard; New York: Lee, Shepard & Dillingham, 1858.

———. *Virginia; Or, The Power of Grace*. Hillside Library. Boston: Henry Hoyt, 1862.

Lewis Colby's Book Establishment: For the Publication and Sale of Theological, Classical, Sunday-School, Miscellaneous, and School Books. New York: Lewis Colby, 1845.

Life and Light; Or, Every-Day Religion. Philadelphia: PBP, 1863.

Life of John Eliot, the Apostle of the Indians, The. New York: G. Lane & P. P. Sandford, for the MEC SSU, 1841.

Lintner, G. A., D.D. *A Memoir of the Rev. Walter Gunn, Late Missionary in India, from the Evangelical Lutheran Church of the United States.* Albany: E. H. Pease; Baltimore: T. Newton Kurtz, 1852.

List of Works Published by D. Appleton & Co. New York: D. Appleton, 1871.

Little Bill at the Pump. Philadelphia: ASSU, 1850.

Little Songs for Little People. New York: A. D. F. Randolph, 1866.

Liturgy and Hymns for Sunday Schools. New York: PESPEK, 1856.

Long, Rev. Edwin M. *Illustrated History of Hymns and Their Authors: Facts and Incidents of the Origin, Authors, Sentiments and Singing of Hymns, Which, with a Synopsis, Embrace Interesting Items Relating to Over Eight Hundred Hymn-Writers, with Many Portraits and Other Illustrations.* Philadelphia: P. W. Ziegler, 1876.

Lowry, Robert, D.D. and William Howard Doane. *Pure Gold for the Sunday School.* New York: Biglow & Main, 1871.

M. S. B. *The Temperance Lyre: A Collection of Temperance Songs Adapted to Popular Melodies.* N.p., [1852?].

MacGill, Hamilton M. *Songs of the Christian Creed and Life: Selected from Eighteen Centuries.* London: Basil, Montague, Pickering, 1876.

Magill, Mary Tucker. *A Story of Southern Life.* Philadelphia: PBPSSW, 1888.

Mahan, Asa. *Scripture Doctrine of Christian Perfection, with Other Kindred Subjects, Illustrated and Confirmed in a Series of Discourses Designed to Throw Light on the Way of Holiness.* 7th ed. Boston: Waite, Peirce, 1844.

Malcolm, Howard, D.D., L.L.D. *Theological Index: References to the Principal Works in Every Department of Religious Literature, Embracing Nearly Seventy Thousand Citations, Alphabetically Arranged under Two Thousand Heads.* Boston: Gould & Lincoln; London: Trubner, 1868.

Manning, Samuel. *Remarkable Escapes from Peril Illustrative of Divine Providence.* Philadelphia: PBP, 1858.

Marshall, Walter. *The Gospel-Mystery of Sanctification Opened, in Sundry Practical Directions: Suited Especially to the Case of Those Who Labour under the Guilt and Power of Indwelling-Sin, To Which is Added, a Sermon on Justification.* 1692. Reprint, New York: Southwick & Pelsur, 1811.

Mary and Frank; Or, A Mother's Influence. Philadelphia: Alfred Martien, 1870.

Mason, M. C. B. *In Dixie with the Spelling Book, the Bible, and the Plane.* Cincinnati: Freedmen's Aid and Southern Education Society of the MEC, n.d.

Massie, Richard. *Lyra Domestica: Translated from the "Psaltery and Harp" of C. J. P. Spittaby by Richard Massie, with Additional Selections by Rev. F. D. Huntington, D.D.* Boston: E. P. Dutton, 1863.

Matthews, John, D.D. *The Influence of the Bible in Improving the Understanding and Moral Character . . . with a Memoir of the Author, by James Wood, D.D.* Philadelphia: PBP, 1864.

M'Clellan, George Marion. *Poems.* Nashville: AME SSU, 1895.

M'Clellan, Kate. *Two Christmas Gifts.* New York: PESPEK, 1866.

Mears, John W., D.D. *From Exile to Overthrow: A History of the Jews from the Babylonian Captivity to the Destruction of the Second Temple.* Philadelphia: PBP, 1881.

Memoir of Jane Cornelia Judson. New York: ATS, 1854.

Mercein, Rev. T. F. Randolph. *Liberal and Evangelical Christianity.* . . . New York: Carlton & Philipps, 1854.

Messrs. Roberts Brothers' Publications. Boston: Roberts Bros., 1870.

Methodist Book Concern. *Descriptive Catalogue of the Sunday School Publications and Tracts of the Methodist Episcopal Church, by the Methodist Book Concern.* New York: Lane & Scott, 1849.

Milk-White Dove, The; Or, Little Jacob's Temptation. New York: n.p., 1868.

Miller, Josiah, M.A. *Singers and Songs of the Church: Being Biographical Sketches of the Hymn-Writers in All the Principal Collections, with Notes on Their Psalms and Hymns.* 2d ed. New York: A. D. F. Randolph; London: Spottiswoode, 1869.

Mills, Henry. *Horae Germanicae: A Version of German Hymns.* Auburn, N.Y.: H. and J. C. Ivision, 1845.

M'Ilvaine, Rev. J. H. *A Discourse upon the Power of Voluntary Attention, Delivered before the Rochester Atheneum & Mechanics' Association.* Rochester: D. M. Dewey, 1849.

Miner, Rev. Ovid. *A Strict Inquiry into the Doctrine of Sanctification as Revealed in the Bible, and Held by the Primitive Church, Together with Observations on the Present Position of Presbyterians and Congregationalists.* . . . New York: J. K. Wellman, 1846.

Missionary World: Being an Encyclopaedia of Information, Facts, Incidents, Sketches, and Anecdotes, Relating to Christian Missions, in All Ages and Countries, and of All Denominations. New York: A. D. F. Randolph, n.d.

Mitchell, Anne M. *The Freed Boy in Alabama.* Philadelphia: PBP, 1869.

Mitchell, Rev. Thomas. *The Old Paths: A Treatise on Sanctification, Scripture the Only Authority.* Albany, N.Y.: Charles van Bethuysen & Sons, 1869.

Moore, Charles H., M.D. *What to Read, and How to Read: Being Classified Lists of Choice Reading, with Appropriate Hints and Remarks, Adapted to the General Reader, to Subscribers to Libraries, and to Persons Intending to Form Collections of Books.* . . . New York: D. Appleton, 1871.

Moore, Rev. Henry. *The Life of Mrs. Mary Fletcher, Consort and Relict of the Rev. John Fletcher, Vicar of Madeley, Salop, Compiled from Her Journal and Other Authentic Documents.* New York: J. Soule & T. Mason, 1818.

More, Hannah. *Practical Piety; Or, the Influence of the Religion of the Heart on the Conduct of the Life.* 2 vols. New York: D. Appleton, 1851.

Muhlbach, Louisa. *Louisa of Prussia.* New York: D. Appleton, 1867.

Murray, James O., D.D. *Christian Hymnology: A Sermon Preached in the Brick Church, New York, December 12, 1869.* New York: Charles Scribner, 1870.

Murray, James Ramsey. *Murray's Songs for Sunday Schools and Gospel Meetings.* Boston: White, Smith, 1876.

Neale, John Mason, D.D., trans. and ed. *Hymns, Chiefly Mediaeval, on the Joys and Glories of Paradise.* London: J. T. Hayes, 1865.

Neale, Rev. R. H. *Revival Hymns: Principally Selected by the Rev. R. H. Neale; Set to Some of the Most Familiar and Useful Revival Tunes, Many of Which Have Never Before Been Published.* Boston: Hartley Wood, 1842.

Nelles, Annie. *Annie Nelles; Or, The Life of a Book Agent: An Autobiography.* 4th ed., rev. Cincinnati: Miami, 1869.

Nelson, Earl. "Church Congress at Nottingham, 1871." Frontispiece to *Annota-*

tions of the Hymnal, by Rev. Charles L. Hutchins, xii–xiv. Hartford, Conn.: M. H. Mallory, 1872.

New Books. New York: Robert Carter & Bros., 1873, 1874, 1876, and 1877.

New-England Sunday School Hymn Book, The: Prepared for the Board of Managers of the Hartford County Union. Ellington, Conn.: D. F. Robinson, 1830.

New England Tract Society. *Sanctified Afflictions.* 3d ed. Andover, Mass.: Flagg & Gould, 1822.

New Selection of Revival Hymns, A. Washington, D.C.: Columbian Office, 1827.

Nickle, William S., George J. Meyer, and O. F. Pugh. *Gospel Herald in Song: Compiled and Arranged for Use in Gospel Meetings, Sunday Schools, Prayer Meetings and other Religious Services.* Chicago: Meyer & Bro., 1899.

Norcross, C. T. *Sacred Songs: Being a Collection of Hymns for the Use of Christian Denominations.* Hallowell, Maine: Glazier, Masters, 1830.

Numerical Ordering Catalogue of the Books and Tracts of the Presbyterian Board of Publication. Philadelphia: PBP; New York: Dodd & Mead, n.d.

Ollier, Edmund. *The Doré Gallery: Containing Two Hundred and Fifty Beautiful Engravings . . . with Memoir of Doré, Critical Essay, and Descriptive Letterpress.* London and New York: Cassell, Petter & Galpin, [1870].

1000 Volumes Suitable for Sabbath School, Parish, Family, and District School Libraries. Boston: Tappan & Dennet, 1844.

Packard, J. B., and S. Hubbard. *The Songs of Canaan; Or, The Millennial Harmonist: A Collection of Hymns and Tunes Designed for Social Devotion.* Boston: D. S. King and Saxton & Pierce, 1842.

Palmer, Phoebe. *Faith and its Effects.* New York: Palmer & Hughes, 1867.

———. *Pioneer Experiences; Or, The Gift of Power Received by Faith, Illustrated and Confirmed by the Testimony of Eighty Living Ministers, of Various Denominations.* New York: W. C. Palmer, 1868.

———. *The Way of Holiness, with Notes by the Way: Being a Narrative of Religious Experience Resulting from a Determination to be a Bible Christian.* 52d ed. New York: Palmer & Hughes, 1867.

Palmer, Roundell. *The Book of Praise from the Best English Hymn-Writers.* Boston: Sever, Francis, 1870.

———. "Remarks on Hymnody at the Church Congress at York, 1866." Frontispiece to *Annotations of the Hymnal*, by Rev. Charles L. Hutchins, v–x. Hartford, Conn.: M. H. Mallory, 1872.

Park, Edwards A., Austin Phelps, and Lowell Mason. *The Sabbath Hymn Book: For the Service of Song in the House of the Lord.* New York: Mason Bros., 1858.

Parker, Rev. William H. *The Psalmody of the Church: Its Authors, Singers and Uses.* New York and Chicago: Fleming H. Revell, 1889.

Parlour and Kitchen; Or, the Story of Ann Connover. Philadelphia and New York: ASSU, 1835.

Parsons, Isaac. *Memoir of Amelia S. Chapman.* Books for Children and Youth, vol. 1. New York: ATS, 1848.

Parsons, Robert. *A Booke of Christian Exercise Appertaining to Resolution; That is, Shewing How That We Should Resolve Ourselves to Become Christians Indeede, Perused, and Accompanied Now with a Treatise Tending to Pacification by Edmund Bunny.* London: T. Dawson, 1585.

Payson, Edward Payson, D.D. *The Bible above All Price*. Tract No. 71. New York: ATS, [1827?].

———. *Sinners Willful and Perverse*. Doctrinal Tract No. 15. Boston: American Doctrinal Tract Society, [1830s].

Peck, George. *The Scripture Doctrine of Christian Perfection Stated and Defended, with a Critical and Historical Examination of the Controversy, Ancient and Modern; Also Practical Illustrations and Advices*. 3d ed., rev. New York: Lane & Scott, 1848.

Peloubet, Rev. Francis N. *The International Question Book: On the Uniform Series of Sabbath School Lessons, Adopted by the International Bible Lesson Committee for 1875. For Adult Scholars*. Vol. 1. Boston: Henry Hoyt, 1874.

Perfect Sanctification: An Article from the "Princeton Review" for July, 1842. Princeton, N.J.: John T. Robinson, 1842.

Phelps, Elizabeth Stuart [Ward]. *The Gates Ajar*. Boston: Fields, Osgood, 1868.

———. *Mercy Gliddon's Work*. The Sunday-School Series of Juvenile Religious Works. Boston: Henry Hoyt, 1865.

———. *Our Famous Women: An Authorized Record of the Lives and Deeds of Distinguished American Women of Our Times*. . . . Hartford, Conn.: A. D. Worthington, 1884.

Philes, George P. *How to Read a Book in the Best Way*. New York: George P. Philes, 1873.

Phillips, Philip. *Gospel Temperance Songs: A Choice Collection of Hymns and Songs with Tunes, for Use in Meetings and Conventions Conducted in the Interest of Temperance*. N.p., 1879.

———. *Hallowed Songs . . . Designed for Prayer Meetings, Young Men's Christian Associations, Sunday Schools, Religious Meetings, Family Worship, Praise Meetings, Etc.* Cincinnati: Hitchcock & Walden; New York: P. Phillips and Nelson & Phillips, 1874.

———. *The Singing Pilgrim; Or, Pilgrim's Progress Illustrated in Song, for the Sabbath School, Church and Family*. New York: Carlton & Porter; Cincinnati: Philip Phillips & Co., 1866.

Physician, A. *Confessions and Experience of a Novel Reader*. Chicago: William Stacy, 1855.

Picket, Rev. L. L., Jonathan R. Bryant, and Rev. Martin Wells Knapp. *Tears and Triumphs Combined: For Revivals, Sunday Schools and the Home, Unsectional, Loyal, Interdenominational*. Cincinnati: M. W. Knapp, Publisher of Gospel Literature, 1897.

Plans and Operations of the Board of Publication of the Presbyterian Church in the United States of America. Philadelphia: PBP, 1847.

Popular Miscellaneous Works Published by Messrs. Stringer & Townsend. New York: Stringer & Townsend, 1850.

Porter, Noah. *Books and Reading; Or, What Books Shall I Read and How Shall I Read Them?* New York: Charles Scribner's Sons, 1870.

Porter, William S. *Life of Rowland Hill*. Christian Library. New York: Lewis Colby, 1845.

Potter, A., D.D. "Preliminary Observations: On Reading." In *Discourses on the*

Objects and Uses of Science and Literature, edited by Henry Lord Brougham and G. C. Verplanck, ix–xxxi. New York: Harper & Bros., 1840.

Prentiss, Elizabeth. *Aunt Jane's Hero*. New York: A. D. F. Randolph, 1871.

———. *The Flower of the Family: A Book for Girls*. New York: A. D. F. Randolph, 1856.

———. *Henry and Bessie; Or, What They Did in the Country*. New York: A. D. F. Randolph, 1855.

———. *The Home at Greylock*. New York: A. D. F. Randolph, 1876.

———. *How Suffering Was Changed into Sympathy: Words of Cheer for Mothers Bereft of Little Children*. New York: A. D. F. Randolph, 1884.

———. *Little Susy's Little Servants, By Her Aunt Susan*. New York: A. D. F. Randolph, 1856.

———. *Little Susy's Six Birthdays, By Her Aunt Susan*. New York: A. D. F. Randolph, 1853.

———. *Little Susy's Six Teachers, By Her Aunt Susan*. New York: A. D. F. Randolph, 1856.

———. *Little Threads; Or, Tangle Thread, Silver Thread, and Golden Thread*. New York: A. D. F. Randolph, 1867.

———. *Mamma's Talks with Charlie, Reported by Aunt Susan*. Boston: Henry Hoyt, 1868.

———. *Nidworth and His Three Magic Wands*. Boston: Roberts Bros., 1869.

———. *Only a Dandelion and Other Stories*. New York: A. D. F. Randolph, 1854.

———. *The Percys*. New York: A. D. F. Randolph, 1870.

———. *Religious Poems*. New York: A. D. F. Randolph, 1873.

———. *Stepping Heavenward*. New York: A. D. F. Randolph, 1869.

———. *Urbane and His Friends*. New York: A. D. F. Randolph, 1874.

Prentiss, George Lewis. *A Discourse Delivered in the Mercer-Street Church, October 19, 1851*. . . . New York: John F. Trow, 1852.

———. *The Life and Letters of Elizabeth Prentiss*. New York: A. D. F. Randolph, 1882.

Presbyterian Church in the United States. *Psalms and Hymns for the Worship of God, Approved by the General Assembly*. . . . Richmond: Presbyterian Committee of Publication, 1867.

Presbyterian Church in the United States of America. *The Hymnal Published by Authority of the General Assembly*. . . . Philadelphia: PBPSSW, 1898.

Prescott, J. E., D.D. *Christian Hymns and Hymn Writers: A Course of Lectures*. Cambridge: Deighton, Bell; London: George Bell & Sons, 1883.

Price List. New York: Scribner, n.d.

Price List. New York: Scribner, Armstrong, n.d.

Professional Man, A. *Father's Pictures of Family Influence: For His Own Children to Read*. Holliston, Mass.: David Heart Jr., 1847.

Publications of Nelson & Phillips. New York: Nelson & Phillips, 1875.

Publications of the American Tract Society, The. Vols. 2–9. New York: ATS, 1838–54.

Ramsey, Mrs. Vienna G. Morrell. *Evenings with the Children; Or, Travels in South America*. Boston: D. Lothrop; Dover, N.H.: G. T. Day, 1871.

Rayne, Mrs. M. L. *Jennie and Her Mother and Other Stories*. Chicago: Kenney & Sumner, 1866.

Recent Publications of D. Appleton & Co. New York: D. Appleton, 1867.

Reid, Isaiah. *God's Way and Man's Methods of Becoming Holy, Contrasted.* Nevada, Iowa: n.p., 1880.

Remarkable Conversion, A. Tract No. 84. Philadelphia: Baptist General Tract Society, [1830?].

Remarks on the Publication Cause Made at the Sessions of the General Assembly. . . . Philadelphia: PPC; New York: A. D. F. Randolph, 1863.

Remembering Christ. New York: PESPEK, [1855?].

Retail Price List of the Publications of A. S. Barnes & Co., Publishers, Booksellers, and Stationers. Chicago: A. S. Barnes, 1874.

Reverend Dr. Sprague's Library: June 22–24, 1870. New York: Leavitt, Strebeigh, 1875.

Revival Melodies; Or, Songs of Zion, Dedicated to Elder Jacob Knapp. Boston: John Putnam, and New England SSU, and D. S. King, 1842.

Rice, Rev. Willard M., D.D. *History of the Presbyterian Board of Publication and Sabbath-School Work. . . .* Philadelphia: PBPSSW, 1888.

Richardson, Jacob D., Timothy Eatto, and J. C. Beaman. *A Collection of Hymns for the Use of the African Methodist Episcopal Church in America, Compiled from Various Authors.* New York: Marks, 1843.

Richardson, Wilson. *Catalogue of the Library of the University of Alabama, with an Index of Subjects.* Tuscaloosa: M. D. J. Slade, 1848.

Richmond, Legh. *Memoir of Wilberforce Richmond, Second Son of the Rev. Legh Richmond, Rector of Turvey, Bedfordshire, England, Drawn Chiefly from "Domestic Portraiture"; Or, The Successful Application of Religious Principle in the Education of a Family.* New York: ATS, 1848.

———. *The Rev. Legh Richmond's Letters and Counsels to His Children: Selected from His Memoir and "Domestic Portraiture," with an Account of the Closing Scene of His Life, Written by His Daughter.* New York: ATS, 1848.

Ritchie, Elizabeth. *Lessons of Life and Death: A Memorial of Sarah Ball, Who Died in Her Eighteenth Year.* Philadelphia: PBP, 1856.

Robert Carter: His Life and Work, 1870–1889. New York: A. D. F. Randolph, 1891.

Robert Carter & Brothers' Publications. New York: Robert Carter & Bros., 1865, 1866.

Roberts, Philetus. *Memoir of Mrs. Abigail Roberts: An Account of Her Birth, Early Education, Call to the Ministry, Varied and Extensive Labors, and the Success Which Attended Her in Several States, with Many Interesting Incidents of Her Life.* Irvington, N.H.: Moses Cummings, 1858.

Robinson, Charles Seymour, D.D., ed. *Annotations upon Popular Hymns . . . For Use in Praise Meetings.* New York: Hunt & Eaton; Cincinnati: Cranston & Curtis, 1893.

———. *A Selection of Spiritual Songs with Music for the Church and the Choir.* New York: Scribner, 1878.

———. *A Selection of Spiritual Songs with Music for Use in Social Meetings.* New York: Century, 1881.

Robinson, G. O., assisted by I. B. Woodbury. *"The Casket": Sacred Melodies for Public and Social Worship; Containing Many Choice Melodies from Eminent Ameri-*

can and European Composers. . . . Charleston, S.C.: Southern Baptist Publication Society, 1855.

Robinson, Rev. John J. *Memoir of Rev. Isaac Anderson, D.D. . . .* Knoxville, Tenn.: J. Addison Rayl, 1860.

Robinson, M. Lewis. *Sketch of the Life of Truman Pratt, the Centenarian, Including the History of Orchard-Steet Methodist Episcopal Church, Baltimore, Maryland; Also an Appendix, Containing an Account of the First Colored Methodist Episcopal Conference, with Brief Sketches of its Members, Father Pratt's Centennial Tea Party, etc.* Baltimore: James Young, 1876.

Rogers, E. P., D.D. *The Classmates; Or, The College Revival.* Philadelphia: PBP, 1856.

Rogers, Hester Ann. *A Short Account of the Experience . . . with a Brief Extract from Her Diary.* New York: MEC, 1804.

Roorbach, Orville A. *Addenda to The Bibliotheca Americana: A Catalogue of American Publications, (Reprints and Original Works,) from May, 1855 to March, 1858.* New York: Wiley & Halsted; London: Trubner, 1858.

———. *Bibliotheca Americana: A Catalogue of American Publications, Including Reprints and Original Works, from 1820 to 1852, Inclusive; Together with a List of Periodicals Published in the United States.* New York: Orville A. Roorbach, 1852.

———. *Supplement to The Bibliotheca Americana: A Catalogue of American Publications, (Reprints and Original Works), from October, 1852, to May, 1855, Including Also a Repetition of Such Books as Have Either Changed Prices or Publishers During That Period.* New York: O. A. Roorbach Jr., 1855.

Rupp, Israel Daniel, comp. *Religious Denominations in the United States: Their Past History, Present Condition, and Doctrines. . . .* Philadelphia: Charles Desilver; Savannah: John M. Cooper, 1861.

Ryle, Rev. J. C. *The Cross: A Call to the Fundamentals of Religion.* New York: PESPEK, 1852.

Sankey, Ira D., comp. *Sacred Songs and Solos: Nos. I and II Combined, Containing 441 Pieces.* London: Morgan & Scott, 1882.

Sankey, Ira D., and James McGranahan. *The Christian Choir.* London: Morgan & Scott, 1884.

Sankey, Ira D., James McGranahan, and George C. Stebbins. *Church Hymns and Gospel Songs for Use in Church Services, Prayer Meetings and Other Religious Gatherings.* New York and Chicago: Biglow & Main, 1898.

———. *Gospel Hymns Nos. 1 to 6 Complete (without Duplicates): For Use in Gospel Meetings and Other Religious Services.* New York: Biglow & Main; Chicago: John Church, 1894.

Sargent, John, ed. *Memoir of the Rev. Henry Martyn.* New York: PESPEK, 1858.

Schaff, Philip, D.D. *Christ in Song: Hymns of Immanuel, Selected from All Ages, with Notes.* New York: A. D. F. Randolph, 1870.

Schmidt, H. I. *Education: Part I. History of Education, Ancient and Modern; Part II. A Plan of Culture and Instruction, Based on Christian Principles. . . .* New York: Harper & Bros., 1842.

Schneider, W. F. *Catalogue of Books, Stationery and Miscellaneous Goods for Sale at the Publishing House of the Evangelical Association.* Cleveland, Ohio: Evangelical Association, [1870s?].

Scott, Clara H. *Truth in Song for the Lovers of Truth Everywhere*. Chicago: Stockham, 1896.

Scribner, Welford. *A Selection of Illustrated and Standard Works in Elegant and Substantial Bindings: Forming a Portion of the Importations of Scribner, Welford & Co., for the Holiday Season, 1871–72*. New York: Scribner, Welford, 1871.

Scudder, M. L. *The Wesleyan Psalmist; Or, Songs of Canaan: A Collection of Hymns and Tunes Designed to be Used at Camp-Meetings, and at Class and Prayer Meetings, and Other Occasions of Social Devotion*. Boston: D. S. King; Philadelphia: J. Harmstead; Albany: E. H. Pease, 1842.

Seasonable Supply, The. 3d ser., no. 302. Philadelphia: ASSU, n.d.

Selection from Hymns Authorized by the General Convention of 1871, A. New York: Lange, Little & Hillman, 1872.

Sewell, Mrs. *"Mother's Last Words": A Ballad for Boys*. New York: PESPEK, n.d.

Sheldon, Mrs. Electra Maria [Bronson]. *The Clevelands: Showing the Influence of a Christian Family in a New Settlement*. Boston: ATS, 1860.

Sherwood, Mary Martha. *The Infant's Progress from the Valley of Destruction to Everlasting Glory*. 1821. New York: Robert Carter & Bros., 1851.

Shields, Charles W., D.D. *The Book of Remembrance: A New Year's Gift*. Philadelphia: PBP, 1867.

Shoberl, Frederic. *Persecutions of Popery: Historical Narratives of the Most Remarkable Persecutions Occasioned by the Intolerance of the Church of Rome*. New York: Harper & Bros., 1844.

Short Commentary on the Hymnal Noted, from Ancient Sources, A: Intended Chiefly for the Use of the Poor. London: Joseph Masters, 1852.

Sigourney, Lydia Huntley. *Examples of Life and Death*. New York: Charles Scribner & Sons, 1851.

——. *The Farmer and Soldier; And, Louisa's Tenderness to the Little Birds in Winter*. New York: ATS, 1848.

——. *How to Be Happy: Written for the Children of Some Dear Friends*. Hartford, Conn.: D. F. Robinson, 1833.

——. *Poems*. New York: World Publishing House, 1841.

Simonds, William [Walter Aimwell, pseud.]. *Marcus; Or, The Boy-Tamer*. The Aimwell Stories. Boston: Gould & Lincoln; New York: Sheldon, Blakeman; Cincinnati: George S. Blanchard, 1857.

——. *The Unfinished Volume: Jerry; Or, The Sailor Boy Ashore. Being the Seventh — a Fragment — in the Series . . . to Which is Added a Memoir of the Author, with a Likeness*. The Aimwell Stories. Boston: Gould & Lincoln; New York: Sheldon; Cincinnati: George S. Blanchard, 1863.

Small, Bishop John B., D.D. *The Human Heart Illustrated by Nine Figures of the Heart, Representing the Different Stages of Life, and Two Death-Bed Scenes: The Wicked and the Righteous*. Salisbury, N.C.: York Dispatch, 1898.

Smith, Boston W. *Spicy Breezes from Minnesota Prairies*. Philadelphia: ABPS, 1885.

Smith, G. Barnett. *Eminent Christian Workers of the Nineteenth Century*. London: SPCK; New York: E. & J. B. Young, 1893.

Smith, Hannah Whitall. *The Christian's Secret of a Happy Life*. Boston: Christian Witness, 1885.

Smith, Lucius E., ed. *Heroes and Martyrs of the Modern Missionary Enterprise: A Record of *Their Lives and Labors, Including an Historical Review of Earlier Missions.* Hartford: P. Brockett, 1852.

Smith, Robert Pearsall. *Holiness Through Faith.* New York: A. D. F. Randolph, 1870.

Smithers, Nathaniel Barratt. *Translations of Latin Hymns of the Middle Ages.* Dover, Del.: James Kirk & Sons, 1881.

Snepp, Charles B., L.L.M., ed. *Songs of Grace and Glory for Private, Family and Public Worship: Hymnal Treasures of the Church of Christ from the Sixth to the Nineteenth Century.* London: W. Hunt, 1872.

Sommers, Charles George, and William R. Williams. *The Baptist Library: A Republication of Standard Baptist Works.* Prattsville, N.Y.: R. H. Hill, 1843; New York: Lewis Colby, 1846.

Southwark Temperance Society. *Anniversary Hymns. . . .* [Philadelphia]: n.p., 1837.

Sprague, William B., D.D. *Annals of the American Pulpit; Or, Commemorative Notices of Distinguished American Clergymen of Various Denominations. . . .* 9 vols. New York: Robert Carter & Bros., 1857–69.

Steele, Daniel. *Love Enthroned: Essays on Evangelical Perfection.* New York: Phillips & Hunt, 1880.

Steen, Rev. A., M.D. *Scriptural Sanctification!; Or, Personal Holiness.* Alamosa, Colo.: Earnest Presbyterian, 1885.

Stevens, Abel. *History of the Methodist Episcopal Church in the United States of America.* 4 vols. New York: Carlton & Porter, 1864–67.

——. *Tales from the Parsonage.* Boston: Waite & Peirce, 1846.

Stevens, William Bacon. *The Baptism of the Holy Ghost: The Great Need of the Church.* New York: PESPEK, 1857.

Stevenson, George John. *The Methodist Hymn Book: Illustrated with Biography, History, Incident, and Anecdote.* London: S. W. Partridge, [1883?].

Stories of Other Lands. New York: A. D. F. Randolph, 1859.

Stowe, Harriet Beecher. *The Minister's Wooing.* New York: Derby & Jackson, 1859.

——. *Oldtown Folks.* Boston: Fields, Osgood, 1869.

——. *Uncle Tom's Cabin; Or, Life Among the Lowly.* Boston: Jewett, 1852; New York: Harper & Row, 1965.

Strachan, Alexander. *The Doctrine of Entire Sanctification, Explained and Enforced.* 2d ed. London: J. Mason, 1843.

Stratton, Joseph Buck, D.D. *Hymns to the Holy Spirit.* Richmond, Va.: PCP, 1893.

Straub, S. W. *Temperance Battle Songs!: For the Use of Choirs and Glee Clubs in All Kinds of Temperance Meetings.* Chicago: S. W. Straub, 1883.

String of Pearls, A: Embracing a Scripture Verse and a Pious Reflection for Every Day in the Year. New York: Carlton & Phillips, for the MEC SSU, 1856.

Strong, Rev. J. D. *Child Life in Many Lands.* Boston: D. Lothrop, 1871.

Stryker, Melancthon Woosey. *Church Song: For the Uses of the House of God.* New York and Chicago: Biglow & Main, 1889.

Stuart, Arabella W. [Wilson]. *The Lives of Mrs. Ann H. Judson and Mrs. Sarah B. Judson, with a Biographical Sketch of Mrs. Emily C. Judson, Missionaries to Burmah.* Auburn, N.Y.: Derby & Miller; Buffalo: Derby, Orton & Mulligan; Cincinnati: Henry W. Derby, 1851.

Styles, John. *The Life of David Brainerd, Missionary to the Indians, with an Abridgment of His Diary and Journal, from President Edwards*. 2d Am. ed. Boston: Samuel T. Armstrong and Crocker & Brewster, 1821.

Summers, Rev. Thomas O. "History of the Methodist Episcopal Church, South." In *Religious Denominations in the United States*, compiled by Israel Daniel Rupp, 380–83. Philadelphia: Charles Desilver; Savannah: John M. Cooper, 1861.

Superbly Illustrated Works Suitable for HOLIDAY GIFT BOOKS. . . . New York: Charles Scribner, 1871.

Supplement to the Church Psalmist: Prepared by the Presbyterian Publication Committee, in Accordance with the Instructions of the General Assemblies of 1857 and 1858. New York: A. D. F. Randolph; Chicago: S. C. Griggs; Detroit: Rayong & Selleck; Cincinnati: Moore, Wilstach, Keys; St. Louis: Keith & Woods, 1859.

Supplement to the Collection of Hymns for the Use of the People Called Methodists, A. London: John Mason, 1830.

Sweney, John R., and William J. Kirkpatrick. *Melodious Sonnets for Sacred Service*. Philadelphia: John J. Hood, 1885.

———. *On Joyful Wing: A Book of Praise and Song*. Philadelphia: John J. Hood, 1886.

Sweney, John R., William J. Kirkpatrick, and H. L. Gilmour, eds. *Praise in Song: A Collection of Hymns and Sacred Melodies, Adapted for Use by Sunday Schools, Endeavor Societies, Epworth Leagues, Evangelists, Pastors, Choristers, etc.* Philadelphia: John J. Hood, 1893.

———. *Sunlit Songs: For Use In Meetings for Christian Worship or Work*. Philadelphia: John J. Hood, 1890.

Tanner, Bishop Benjamin Tucker. *Dispensations in the History of the Church and the Interregnums*. Vol. 1. Kansas City, Mo.: n.p., 1852.

———. *Paul and John vs. Pius IX: A Sermon Preached in Bethel Church, Baltimore*. . . . Baltimore: Innes, 1866.

Ten Books Beautifully Illustrated, for Children. New York: PESPEK, 1861.

Tenney, J. H., and Rev. E. A. Hoffman. *Songs of Faith: A Collection of Sacred Songs, Especially Adapted for Devotional, Revival and Camp Meetings*. Cleveland: S. Brainard's Sons, 1876.

Thayer, William. *Working and Winning; Or, The Deaf Boy's Triumph*. Boston: Henry Hoyt, 1862.

Their Father. Letters to Little Children, By Their Father. New York: ATS, 1847.

Theolinda. *Vail Family; Or, Doing Good*. Philadelphia: PBP, 1862.

Thompson, George. *Thompson in Africa: Or, An Account of the Missionary Labors, Sufferings, Travels, and Observations, of George Thompson in Western Africa, at the Mendi Mission*. 2d ed. Dayton, Ohio: George Thompson, 1857.

Thompson, Wilson, Elder. *A Baptist Hymn-Book: Designed Especially for the Regular Baptist Church, and all Lovers of Truth, Partly Selected from Approved Authors, and Partly Composed by the Compiler, Arranged to Suit All Occasions of Public or Private Worship*. Cincinnati: E. Shepard, 1844.

Three Darlings, The; Or, The Children of Adoption. New York: American Female Guardian Society, 1854.

Tillman, Charlie D. *The Revival No. 2, Suitable for All Kinds of Religious Meetings: A Wonderful Collection of Songs for Sunday Schools, Prayer and Praise Meetings,*

Revival and Camp Meetings, Christian Workers and Class Meetings. Atlanta and Cincinnati: Charlie D. Tillman, 1896.

———. *The Revival No. 3, Suitable for All Kinds of Religious Meetings: Songs for Sunday Schools and Special Services.* . . . Atlanta, Cincinnati, and Kansas City: n.p., n.d.

Todd, John, D.D. *The Raft; Or, The Widow's Two Sons.* Second Sabbath School Series, vol. 1. Pittsfield, Mass.: E. P. Little, 1844.

———. *Shaking Out the Reef, and Other "Gems."* Boston: Henry Hoyt, 1863.

Tom Bently; Or, The Story of a Prodigal. Boston: Henry Hoyt, 1870.

Towner, D. B. *Hymns New and Old: For Use in Gospel Meetings and Other Religious Services.* . . . Chicago and New York: Fleming H. Revell, Publisher of Evangelical Literature, 1887.

Tracey, Charles Chapin, of Marsovan, Turkey. *Myra: A Child's Story of Missionary Life.* Boston: CBP, 1876.

Ufford, Rev. E. S. *Converts' Praises: A Collection of Hymns by Rev. E. S. Ufford, As Sung by the Atlanta Colored Male Quartet.* Dedham, Mass.: Transcript Steam Job Printing, 1887.

Upham, Thomas C. *Life and Religious Opinions and Experience of Madame de la Mothe Guyon, Together with Some Account of the Personal History and Religious Opinions of Fénélon, Archbishop of Cambray.* 2 vols. New York: Harper & Bros., 1847.

Valuable Books for Sunday School and Family Reading. Philadelphia: ASSU, 1850.

Valuable Standard and Juvenile Books, Published by E. H. Pease & Co., Albany, New York. Albany, N.Y.: E. H. Pease, 1852.

Valuable Standard Works. New York: Harper & Bros., 1852.

Valuable Standard Works in the Several Departments of Literature. New York: Harper & Bros., 1842.

Valuable Works, in the Departments of Biography and History. New York: Harper & Bros., 1850.

Vanmeter, Isaac N., Elder. *Pocket Hymns, Original and Selected: Designed for the Use of the Regular [Primitive] Baptist Church, and All Who Love Our Lord Jesus Christ.* Galesburg, Ill.: Register, 1867.

Walker, William. *The Southern Harmony, and Musical Companion, Containing a Choice of Tunes, Hymns, Psalms, Odes, and Anthems . . . Well Adapted to Christian Churches of Every Denomination, Singing Schools, and Private Societies.* . . . Philadelphia: E. W. Miller, and Thomas, Cowperthwaite, and Lippincott, Grambo, and Troutman & Hayes; New York: A. S. Barnes; Pratt, Woodford; R. B. Collins; George F. Cooledge & Bros.; Charleston: A. Carter, McCarter & Allen, 1854.

Wallace, Rev. John H. *Entire Holiness: An Essay.* Auburn, N.Y.: William J. Moses, 1853.

Wallace, Lew. *Ben-Hur: A Tale of the Christ.* New York: Harper & Bros., 1880.

Warner, Susan. *Pine Needles.* New York: Robert Carter & Bros., 1877.

———. *Trading.* New York: Robert Carter & Bros., 1872.

———. *The Wide, Wide World.* New York: G. P. Putnam's Sons, 1850.

———. *Willow Brook.* New York: Robert Carter & Bros., 1874.

———. *The Word: Walks from Eden.* New York: Robert Carter & Bros., 1866.

Warren, George William. *Hymns and Tunes as Sung at St. Thomas's Church, New York, Music Composed and Adapted by George William Warren.* New York: Harper & Bros.; London: Novello, Ewer, 1888.

Warren, Rev. Israel P. *The Sisters: A Memoir of Elizabeth H., Abbie A., and Sarah F. Dickerman.* Boston: ATS, 1859.

Wayland, Francis. *A Memoir of the Life and Labors of the Rev. Adoniram Judson.* Boston: Phillips & Sampson, 1853.

Wayman, A. W. *Discourse on the Death of Rev. Walter Proctor, of Philadelphia.* [Washington, D.C.?]: n.p., 1862.

Webb, Rev. J. N. *Memoir of Miss Charity Richards; Or, Grace Reigning and Triumphing Under Complicated and Protracted Sufferings.* Adams, N.Y.: J. C. Hatch, 1845.

Wells, John D., D.D. *Saved by Grace; Or, The Last Week in the Life of Davis Johnson, Jr.* New York: Robert Carter & Bros., 1860.

Welsh, Rev. R. E., and F. G. Edwards. *Romance of Psalter and Hymnal: Authors and Composers.* New York: James Pott & Co., 1889.

Wesley, Charles. *A Short Account of the Death of Mrs. Hannah Richardson, Bristol, April 19, 1741.* 5th ed. Newcastle upon Tyne: Gooding, 1743.

Wesley, John. "The Character of a Methodist." In *The Works of the Reverend John Wesley, A.M., Sometime Fellow of Lincoln College, Oxford.* 1st American complete and standard ed., from the latest London ed. [1771–74]. 7 vols. 5:240–45. New York: J. Emery & B. Waugh, for the MEC, 1831.

———. *An Extract of the Life of the Late Rev. David Brainerd, Missionary to the Indians.* 4th ed. London: G. Whitfield, 1800.

———. *A Plain Account of Christian Perfection: As Believed and Taught by the Reverend Mr. John Wesley, from the Year 1725, to the Year 1777.* New York: G. Lane, 1844.

Western Harp, The: A Collection of Social and Revival Hymns. 3d ed., rev. and enl. St. Louis: P. M. Pinckard, 1867.

Williston, Seth. *Lectures on the Moral Imperfection of Christians: Designed to Show That While Sinless Perfection is Obligatory on All It is Attained by None.* New York: M. W. Dodd, 1846.

Winkworth, Catherine, trans. *Lyra Germanica: Hymns for the Sundays and Chief Festivals of the Christian Year.* 1855. New York: Stanford & Delisser, 1858.

———. *Lyra Germanica: Second Series: The Christian Life.* New York: A. D. F. Randolph, 1858.

Woods, Leonard, D.D. *An Examination of the Doctrine of Perfection, as Held by Rev. Asa Mahan. . . .* New York: W. R. Peters; London: Wiley & Putnam, 1841.

———. *Memoir of Mrs. Harriet Newell, Wife of the Rev. Samuel Newell, Missionary to India.* New York: ATS, 1813.

Woodworth, Francis. *The Girls' Story Book, with Illustrations.* Theodore Thinker's Tales. New York: Clark, Austin & Smith, 1851.

Young, Loyal. *The Hidden Treasure: An Allegory.* Philadelphia: PBP, 1860.

Secondary Sources

Ahlstrom, Sydney E. *A Religious History of the American People.* New Haven: Yale University Press, 1972.

Albaugh, Gaylord P. *History and Annotated Bibliography of American Religious Periodicals and Newspapers Established from 1740 through 1830.* Worcester, Mass.: AAS, 1994.

Amory, Hugh, and David D. Hall, eds. *A History of the Book in America.* Vol. 1, *The Colonial Book in the Atlantic World.* Cambridge: Cambridge University Press; Worcester, Mass.: AAS, 2000.

Anderson, Benedict. *Imagined Communities: Reflections on the Origin and Spread of Nationalism.* New York: Verso, 1983. Rev. ed., New York: Verso, 1991.

Angell, Stephen Ward. *Bishop Henry McNeal Turner and African-American Religion in the South.* Knoxville: University of Tennessee Press, 1992.

Augst, Thomas. "The Business of Reading in Nineteenth-Century America: The New York Mercantile Library." *American Quarterly* 50, no. 2 (1998): 267–305.

Bakhtin, Mikhail M. "Epic and Novel." In *The Dialogic Imagination: Four Essays,* edited by Michael Holquist and edited and translated by Caryl Emerson and Michael Holquist, 3–40. Austin: University of Texas Press, 1981.

Baldasty, Gerald. *The Commercialization of News in the Nineteenth Century.* Madison: University of Wisconsin Press, 1992.

Bauman, Richard. *Let Your Words Be Few: Symbolism of Speaking and Silence among Seventeenth-Century Quakers.* New York: Cambridge University Press, 1983.

Baym, Nina. *Woman's Fiction: A Guide to Novels by and about Women in America, 1820–1870.* Ithaca, N.Y.: Cornell University Press, 1978.

Bealle, John. *Public Worship, Private Faith: Sacred Harp and American Folksong.* Athens: University of Georgia Press, 1997.

Bean, Shirley. Intro. to *The Missouri Harmony; Or, a Collection of Psalm and Hymn Tunes, and Anthems . . . ,* by Allen D. Carden. 1835. Reprint, Lincoln: University of Nebraska Press, 1994.

Bell, Catherine. *Ritual Theory, Ritual Practice.* New York: Oxford University Press, 1992.

Bendroth, Margaret Lamberts. *Fundamentalism and Gender, 1875 to the Present.* New Haven: Yale University Press, 1993.

Bennett, Paula Bernat. "Not Just Filler and Not Just Sentimental: Women's Poetry in American Victorian Periodicals, 1860–1900." In *Periodical Literature in Nineteenth-Century America,* edited by Kenneth M. Price and Susan Belasco Smith, 202–19. Charlottesville: University Press of Virginia, 1995.

Bercovitch, Sacvan. *The American Jeremiad.* Madison: University of Wisconsin Press, 1978.

———. *Puritan Origins of the American Self.* New Haven: Yale University Press, 1975.

Bird, F. M., M.A. "American Hymnody." In *Dictionary of Hymnology,* edited by John Julian, 57–61. 1892. Rev. ed., with new supplement, London: John Murray, 1907.

Bishop, Selma L. *Isaac Watts's Hymns and Spiritual Songs (1707): A Publishing History and a Bibliography.* Ann Arbor, Mich.: Pierian, 1974.

Boylan, Ann. *Sunday School: The Formation of an American Institution, 1790–1880.* New Haven: Yale University Press, 1988.

Bradley, Ian. *Abide with Me: The World of Victorian Hymns.* London: SCM, 1997.

Brantley, Richard. "The Common Ground of Wesley and Edwards." *Harvard Theological Review* 83, no. 3 (1990): 271–303.

Braude, Ann. *Radical Spirits: Spiritualism and Women's Rights in Nineteenth-Century America.* Boston: Beacon, 1989.

Brawley, Benjamin. *History of the English Hymn.* New York: Abingdon, 1932.

Breed, David. *The History and Use of Hymns and Hymn-Tunes.* New York: Fleming H. Revell, 1903.

Brodhead, Richard H. *Cultures of Letters: Scenes of Reading and Writing in Nineteenth-Century America.* Chicago: University of Chicago Press, 1993.

[Brown], Candy Ann Gunther. "The Spiritual Pilgrimage of Rachel Stearns, 1834–1837: Reinterpreting Women's Religious and Social Experiences in the Methodist Revivals of Nineteenth-Century America." *Church History* 65 (Dec. 1996): 577–95.

Brown, Candy Gunther. "Domestic Nurture Versus Clerical Crisis: The Gender Dimension in Horace Bushnell's and Elizabeth Prentiss's Critiques of Revivalism." In *Embodying the Spirit: New Perspectives on North American Revivalism,* edited by Michael J. McClymond. Baltimore: Johns Hopkins University Press, 2004.

———. "Prophetic Daughter: Mrs. Mary Fletcher's Narrative and Women's Religious and Social Experiences in Eighteenth-Century British Methodism." In *Eighteenth-Century Women: Studies in Their Lives, Work, and Culture* 3 (2003): 77–98.

Brown, Richard D. *Knowledge Is Power: The Diffusion of Information in Early America, 1700–1865.* New York: Oxford University Press, 1989.

Bruce, Dickson D., Jr. *And They All Sang Hallelujah: Plain-Folk Camp-Meeting Religion, 1800–1845.* Knoxville: University of Tennessee Press, 1973.

Brumberg, Joan Jacobs. *Mission for Life: The Story of the Family of Adoniram Judson, the Dramatic Events of the First American Foreign Mission, and the Course of Evangelical Religion in the Nineteenth Century.* New York: Macmillan, 1980.

Bucke, Emory Stevens, et al., ed. *History of American Methodism.* 3 vols. New York: Abingdon, 1964.

Buell, Lawrence. "Calvinism Romanticized: Harriet Beecher Stowe, Samuel Hopkins, and 'The Minister's Wooing.'" In *Critical Essays on Harriet Beecher Stowe,* edited by Elizabeth Ammons, 259–75. Boston: G. K. Hall, 1980.

———. *New England Literary Culture: From Revolution Through Renaissance.* Cambridge Studies in American Literature and Culture. New York: Cambridge University Press, 1986.

Bushman, Richard L. *The Refinement of America: Persons, Houses, Cities.* New York: Knopf, 1992.

Bussy, R. Kenneth, ed. *Philadelphia's Publishers and Printers: An Informal History.* Philadelphia: Book Clinic, 1976.

Butler, Jon. *Awash in a Sea of Faith: Christianizing the American People.* Cambridge: Harvard University Press, 1990.

Calhoon, Robert M. *Evangelicals and Conservatives in the Early South, 1740–1861.* Columbia: University of South Carolina Press, 1988.

Calhoun, Daniel. *The Intelligence of a People*. Princeton: Princeton University Press, 1973.

Calhoun, David B. "David Brainerd: 'A Constant Stream.' " *Presbyterion* 13 (Spring 1987): 44–50.

Campbell, Colin. *The Romantic Ethic and the Spirit of Modern Consumerism*. New York: Basil Blackwell, 1987.

Campbell, James T. *Songs of Zion: The African Methodist Episcopal Church in the United States and South Africa*. New York: Oxford University Press, 1995.

Carey, James. *Communication as Culture: Essays on Media and Society*. Boston: Unwin Hyman, 1989.

Carnes, Tony. "Bush's Moment: The President's Faith in a Time of Crisis." *Christianity Today*, 12 Nov. 2001, 38–42.

Carwardine, Richard. " 'Antinomians' and 'Arminians': Methodists and the Market Revolution." In *The Market Revolution in America: Social, Political, and Religious Expression, 1800–1880*, edited by Melvyn Stokes and Stephen Conway, 282–307. Charlottesville: University Press of Virginia, 1996.

———. "Trauma in Methodism: Property, Church Schism, and Sectional Polarization in Antebellum America." In *God and Mammon*, edited by Mark A. Noll, 195–216. New York: Oxford University Press, 2002.

Casper, Scott E. *Constructing American Lives: Biography and Culture in Nineteenth-Century America*. Chapel Hill: University of North Carolina Press, 1999.

Cather, Willa, and Georgine Milmine. *The Life of Mary Baker G. Eddy and the History of Christian Science*. 1909. Reprint, Lincoln: University of Nebraska Press, 1993.

Cavalier, C. Acree. "Wesley's Reading as a Means of Grace." Paper presented in seminar on Lived Religion, Harvard University, Cambridge, 14 Apr. 1996.

Cavallo, Guglielmo, and Roger Chartier, eds. *A History of Reading in the West*. Translated by Lydia G. Cochrane. Cambridge: Polity, 1999.

Cavanaugh, Sister Mary Stephana. *Catholic Book Publishing History in the United States, 1785–1850*. Rochester: University of Rochester, 1954. Microfiche.

Cecil, Anthony C., Jr. *The Theological Development of Edwards Amasa Park: Last of the "Consistent Calvinists."* Missoula, Mont.: American Academy of Religion and Scholars' Press, 1974.

Chew, Samuel C. *Fruit among the Leaves: An Anniversary Anthology*. New York: Appleton-Century-Crofts, 1950.

Cmiel, Kenneth. *Democratic Eloquence: The Fight over Popular Speech in Nineteenth-Century America*. New York: William Morrow, 1990.

Conforti, Joseph A. *Jonathan Edwards, Religious Tradition, and American Culture*. Chapel Hill: University of North Carolina Press, 1995.

Conkin, Paul K. *American Originals: Homemade Varieties of Christianity*. Chapel Hill: University of North Carolina Press, 1997.

———. *The Uneasy Center: Reformed Christianity in Antebellum America*. Chapel Hill: University of North Carolina Press, 1995.

Cott, Nancy. *The Bonds of Womanhood: "Woman's Sphere" in New England, 1780–1835*. New Haven: Yale University Press, 1977.

Coultrap-McQuin, Susan. *Doing Literary Business: American Women Writers in the Nineteenth Century*. Chapel Hill: University of North Carolina Press, 1990.

Cross, Whitney R. *The Burned-Over District: The Social and Intellectual History of Enthusiastic Religion in Western New York, 1800–1850*. Ithaca, N.Y.: Cornell University Press, 1950; New York: Octagon, 1981.

Damrosh, Leopold, Jr. *God's Plot and Man's Stories: Studies in the Fictional Imagination from Milton to Fielding*. Chicago: University of Chicago Press, 1985.

Danky, James P., ed. *African-American Newspapers and Periodicals: A National Bibliography*. Cambridge: Harvard University Press, 1998.

Davidson, Cathy N. *Revolution and the Word: The Rise of the Novel in America*. New York: Oxford University Press, 1986.

Dieter, Melvin E., Anthony A. Hoekema, Stanley M. Horton, J. Robertson McQuilkin, and John F. Walvoord. *Five Views on Sanctification: Wesleyan, Reformed, Pentecostal, Keswick, Augustinian-Dispensational*. Grand Rapids, Mich.: Zondervan, Academie, 1987.

Donald, David, and Frederick A. Palmer. "Toward a Western Literature." *Mississippi Valley Historical Review* 35 (1948): 413–28.

Douglas, Ann. *The Feminization of American Culture*. New York: Doubleday Anchor, 1977.

Durden, Susan. "A Study of the First Evangelical Magazines." *Journal of Ecclesiastical History* 27 (1976): 255–75.

Eisenstein, Elizabeth L. *The Printing Press as an Agent of Change: Communications and Cultural Transformation in Early-Modern Europe*. 2 vols. New York: Cambridge University Press, 1979.

Epstein, Barbara Leslie. *The Politics of Domesticity: Women, Evangelism, and Temperance in Nineteenth-Century America*. Middletown, Conn.: Wesleyan University Press, 1981.

Epstein, Dena J. *Sinful Tunes and Spirituals: Black Folk Music to the Civil War*. Urbana: University of Illinois Press, 1977.

Exman, Eugene. *The House of Harper: One Hundred and Fifty Years of Publishing*. New York: Harper & Row, 1967.

Finke, Roger, and Rodney Stark. *The Churching of America, 1776–1990*. New Brunswick, N.J.: Rutgers University Press, 1992.

———. "How the Upstart Sects Won America: 1775–1850." *Journal for the Scientific Study of Religion* 28 (1989): 31.

Fish, Stanley. *Is There a Text in This Class? The Authority of Interpretive Communities*. Cambridge: Harvard University Press, 1980.

Fisher, Philip. *Hard Facts: Setting and Form in the American Novel*. New York: Oxford University Press, 1985.

Foote, Henry Wilder. *Three Centuries of American Hymnody*. Cambridge: Harvard University Press, 1940.

Frei, Hans W. *The Eclipse of Biblical Narrative: A Study in Eighteenth and Nineteenth Century Hermeneutics*. New Haven: Yale University Press, 1974.

Frey, Sylvia R., and Betty Wood. *Come Shouting to Zion: African American Protestantism in the American South and British Caribbean to 1830*. Chapel Hill: University of North Carolina Press, 1998.

Gabler-Hover, Janet. "The North-South Reconciliation Theme and the 'Shadow of the Negro' in *Century Illustrated Magazine.*" In *Periodical Literature in Nineteenth-Century America*, edited by Kenneth M. Price and Susan Belasco Smith, 239–56. Charlottesville: University Press of Virginia, 1995.

Gamble, Harry Y. *Books and Readers in the Early Church: A History of Early Christian Texts*. New Haven: Yale University Press, 1995.

Gaustad, Edwin Scott, and Philip L. Barlow. *New Historical Atlas of Religion in America*. New York: Oxford University Press, 2001.

Geertz, Clifford. *The Interpretation of Cultures: Selected Essays*. New York: Basic, 1973.

Genovese, Eugene. *Roll, Jordan, Roll: The World the Slaves Made*. New York: Pantheon, 1974.

Gill, Gillian. *Mary Baker Eddy*. Radcliffe Biography Series. Reading, Mass.: Perseus, 1998.

Gilmont, Jean-François. "Protestant Reformations and Reading." In *A History of Reading in the West*, edited by Guglielmo Cavallo and Roger Chartier, 213–37. Translated by Lydia G. Cochrane. Cambridge: Polity, 1999.

Gilmore, William J. *Reading Becomes a Necessity of Life*. Knoxville: University of Tennessee Press, 1989.

Gilreath, James. "American Book Distribution." In *Needs and Opportunities in the History of the Book*, edited by David D. Hall and John B. Hench, 103–83. Worcester, Mass.: AAS, 1987.

Green, Jay P., Sr., ed. *The Interlinear Bible: Hebrew-Greek-English, with Strong's Concordance Numbers above Each Word*. Lafayette, Ind.: Sovereign Grace, 1976.

Greengrass, Mark. *The European Reformation, c. 1500–1618*. New York: Longman, 1998.

Grimsted, David. "Books and Culture: Canned, Canonized, and Neglected." In *Needs and Opportunities in the History of the Book*, edited by David D. Hall and John B. Hench, 187–232. Worcester, Mass.: AAS, 1987.

Gura, Philip F. *The Wisdom of Words: Language, Theology, and Literature in the New England Renaissance*. Middletown, Conn.: Wesleyan University Press, 1981.

Gutjahr, Paul C. *An American Bible: A History of the Good Book in the United States, 1777–1880*. Stanford: Stanford University Press, 1999.

———. "No Longer Left Behind: Amazon.com, Reader-Response, and the Changing Fortunes of the Christian Novel in America." *Book History* 5 (2002): 209–36.

Hall, David D. *Cultures of Print: Essays in the History of the Book*. Amherst: University of Massachusetts Press, 1996.

———. "Literacies." Paper presented at Miami University, Miami, Ohio, May 2000.

———. "Readers and Reading in America: Historical and Critical Perspectives," *Proceedings of the American Antiquarian Society* 103 (1993): 337–57.

———. "Readers and Writers in Early New England." In *A History of the Book in America*, edited by Hugh Amory and David D. Hall, 117–51. Cambridge: Cambridge University Press; Worcester, Mass.: AAS, 2000.

———. *Worlds of Wonder, Days of Judgment: Popular Religious Belief in Early New England*. Cambridge: Harvard University Press, 1989.

———, ed. *Lived Religion in America: Toward a History of Practice.* Princeton: Princeton University Press, 1997.

Hall, David D., and Elizabeth Carroll Reilly. "Practices of Reading: Introduction." In *A History of the Book in America,* edited by Hugh Amory and David D. Hall, 377–80. Cambridge: Cambridge University Press; Worcester, Mass.: AAS, 2000.

Hall, David D., and John B. Hench, eds. *Needs and Opportunities in the History of the Book: America, 1639–1876.* Worcester, Mass.: AAS, 1987.

Halttunen, Karen. *Confidence Men and Painted Women: A Study of Middle-Class Culture in America, 1830–1870.* New Haven: Yale University Press, 1982.

Hambrick-Stowe, Charles. *The Practice of Piety: Puritan Devotional Disciplines in Seventeenth-Century New England.* Chapel Hill: University of North Carolina Press for the Institute of Early American History and Culture, Williamsburg, Va., 1982.

Hammack, Mary L. *A Dictionary of Women in Church History.* Chicago: Moody, 1984.

Handy, Robert T. *A Christian America: Protestant Hopes and Historical Realities.* New York: Oxford University Press, 1984.

Hansen, Klaus J. *Mormonism and the American Experience.* History of American Religion. Chicago: University of Chicago Press, 1981.

Harris, Michael W. *The Rise of Gospel Blues: The Music of Thomas Andrew Dorsey in the Urban Church.* New York: Oxford University Press, 1992.

Hart, William F. *Hymns in Human Experience.* New York: Harper & Bros., 1931.

Harvey, Paul. *Redeeming the South: Religious Cultures and Racial Identities among Southern Baptists, 1865–1925.* The Fred W. Morrison Series in Southern Studies. Chapel Hill: University of North Carolina Press, 1997.

Hatch, Nathan O. *The Democratization of American Christianity.* New Haven: Yale University Press, 1989.

Hedrick, Joan D. *Harriet Beecher Stowe: A Life.* New York: Oxford University Press, 1994.

Hendler, Glenn. *Public Sentiments: Structures of Feeling in Nineteenth-Century American Literature.* Chapel Hill: University of North Carolina Press, 2001.

Hewitt, Glenn A. *Regeneration and Morality: A Study of Charles Finney, Charles Hodge, John W. Nevin, and Horace Bushnell.* Brooklyn, N.Y.: Carlson, 1991.

Heyrman, Christine Leigh. *Southern Cross: The Beginnings of the Bible Belt.* New York: Knopf, 1997.

Hitchcock, H. Wiley, and Stanley Sadie. *The New Grove Dictionary of American Music.* 4 vols. New York: Grove, 1986.

Hobbs, June Hadden. *'I Sing for I Cannot Be Silent': The Feminization of American Hymnody, 1870–1920.* Pittsburgh: University of Pittsburgh Press, 1997.

Holland, Harold Edward. "Religious Periodicals in the Development of Nashville, Tennessee as a Regional Publishing Center, 1830–80." Ph.D. diss., Columbia University, 1976.

Howsam, Leslie. "The Nineteenth-Century Bible Society and 'The Evil of Gratuitous Distribution.'" In *Free Print and Non-Commercial Publishing since 1700,* edited by James Raven, 119–34. Burlington, Vt.: Ashgate, 2000.

Humphrey, Carol Sue. "Religious Newspapers and Antebellum Reform." In *Media and Religion in American History*, edited by William David Sloan, 104–18. Northport, Ala.: Vision, 2000.

Hutton, Frankie. *The Early Black Press in America, 1827 to 1860*. Westport, Conn.: Greenwood, 1993.

Jackson, George Pullen. *White and Negro Spirituals: Their Life Span and Kinship*. Locust Valley, N.Y.: Augustin, 1943.

Johns, Adrian. *The Nature of the Book: Print and Knowledge in the Making*. Chicago: University of Chicago Press, 1998.

Johnson, Barbara A. *Reading "Piers Plowman" and "The Pilgrim's Progress": Reception and the Protestant Reader*. Carbondale: Southern Illinois University Press, 1992.

Julian, John, ed. *A Dictionary of Hymnology: Setting Forth the Origin and History of Christian Hymns of All Ages and Nations*. 1892. Rev. ed., with new supplement, London: John Murray, 1907.

Kaestle, Carl. *Pillars of the Republic: Common Schools and American Society, 1780–1860*. Consulting ed. Eric Foner. New York: Hill & Wang, 1983.

Knott, John R., Jr. *The Sword of the Spirit: Puritan Responses to the Bible*. Chicago: University of Chicago Press, 1980.

Lehuu, Isabelle. *Carnival on the Page: Popular Print Media in Antebellum America*. Chapel Hill: University of North Carolina Press, 2000.

Levine, Lawrence. *Black Culture and Black Consciousness: Afro-American Folk Thought from Slavery to Freedom*. New York: Oxford University Press, 1977.

———. *Highbrow/Lowbrow: The Emergence of Cultural Hierarchy in America*. Cambridge: Harvard University Press, 1988.

Lewis, Donald, ed. *The Blackwell Dictionary of Evangelical Biography, 1730–1860*. 2 vols. Cambridge, Mass.: Blackwell, 1995.

Lindbeck, George A. *The Nature of Doctrine: Religion and Theology in a Postliberal Age*. Philadelphia: Westminster, 1984.

Long, Jason, and Joseph Ferrie. "Labour Mobility." In *The Oxford Encyclopedia of Economic History*, edited by Joel Mokyr, 3:248–50. New York: Oxford University Press, 2003.

Long, Kathryn Teresa. *The Revival of 1857–58: Interpreting an American Religious Awakening*. Religion in America Series. New York: Oxford University Press, 1998.

Lorenz, Ellen Jane. *Glory Hallelujah: The Story of the Campmeeting Spiritual*. Nashville: Abingdon, 1980.

Loughlin, Gerard. *Telling God's Story: Bible, Church and Narrative Theology*. New York: Cambridge University Press, 1996.

MacDonald, Ruth K. *Christian's Children: The Influence of John Bunyan's "The Pilgrim's Progress" on American Children's Literature*. American University Studies, ser. 24: American Literature, vol. 10. New York: Lang, 1989.

Machor, James L., ed. *Readers in History: Nineteenth-Century American Literature and the Contexts of Response*. Baltimore: Johns Hopkins University Press, 1993.

MacLeod, Anne Scott. *Children's Fiction and American Culture, 1820–1860*. Hamden, Conn.: Archon, 1975.

Madden, Etta M. *Bodies of Life: Shaker Literature and Literacies*. Study of Religion, vol. 52. Westport, Conn.: Greenwood, 1998.

Madison, Charles A. *Jewish Publishing in America: The Impact of Jewish Writing on American Culture*. New York: Sanhedrin, 1976.

Malone, Dumas, ed. *Dictionary of American Biography*. Vols. 14–15. New York: Charles Scribner's Sons, 1934–35.

Marini, Stephen A. "Hymnody as History: Early Evangelical Hymns and the Recovery of American Popular Religion." *Church History* 7 (June 2002): 273–306.

———. "Hymnody in American Protestantism Project Database." Institute for the Study of American Evangelicals, Wheaton College, Wheaton, Ill., 1999.

———. *Radical Sects of Revolutionary New England*. Cambridge: Harvard University Press, 1982.

Marsden, George M. *Fundamentalism and American Culture: The Shaping of Twentieth-Century Evangelicalism: 1870–1925*. New York: Oxford University Press, 1980.

———. *Religion and American Culture*. 2d ed. Fort Worth, Tex.: Harcourt, 2001.

Martin, Sandy Dwayne. *For God and Race: The Religious and Political Leadership of AMEZ Bishop James Walker Hood*. Columbia: University of South Carolina Press, 1999.

Maryles, Daisy, with research by Laurele Riippa. "Few Surprises in the Winners' Circle." *Publishers Weekly*, 18 Mar. 2002, 53–58.

Mathews, Donald G. *Religion in the Old South*. Chicago: University of Chicago Press, 1977.

McCrossen, Alexis. *Holy Day, Holiday: The American Sunday*. Ithaca, N.Y.: Cornell University Press, 2000.

McCue, George. *Music in American Society, 1776–1976: From Puritan Hymn to Synthesizer*. New Brunswick, N.J.: Transaction, 1977.

McDannell, Colleen. "Catholic Women Fiction Writers, 1840–1920." *Women's Studies* 19, nos. 3–4 (1991): 385–405.

———. *The Christian Home in Victorian America, 1840–1900*. Religion in North America. Bloomington: Indiana University Press, 1986.

———. *Material Christianity*. New Haven: Yale University Press, 1995.

McLoughlin, William G., ed. *The American Evangelicals, 1800–1900: An Anthology*. New York: Harper & Row, 1968.

———. *The Meaning of Henry Ward Beecher: An Essay on the Shifting Values of Mid-Victorian America, 1840–1870*. New York: Knopf, 1970.

Moore, R. Laurence. *Selling God: American Religion in the Marketplace of Culture*. New York: Oxford University Press, 1994.

Morgan, David. *Protestants and Pictures: Religion, Visual Culture, and the Age of American Mass Production*. New York: Oxford University Press, 1999.

Morgan, Edmund. *The Puritan Dilemma: The Story of John Winthrop*. Edited by Oscar Handlin. New York: HarperCollins, 1958.

Mott, Frank Luther. *Golden Multitudes: The Story of Best Sellers in the United States*. New York: Macmillan, 1947.

———. *A History of American Magazines*. 5 vols. Cambridge, Mass.: Harvard University Press, Belknap, 1938–68.

Niebuhr, H. Richard. *Christ and Culture*. New York: Harper, 1951.

Nischan, Bodo. *Lutherans and Calvinists in the Age of Confessionalism*. Variorum Collected Studies Series. Brookfield, Vt.: Ashgate, 1999.

Noll, Mark A. *America's God: From Jonathan Edwards to Abraham Lincoln*. New York: Oxford University Press, 2002.

——. *A History of Christianity in the United States and Canada*. Grand Rapids, Mich.: Eerdmans, 1992.

——, ed. *Charles Hodge: The Way of Life*. New York: Paulist, 1987.

——. *God and Mammon: Protestants, Money, and the Market, 1790–1860*. New York: Oxford University Press, 2002.

Noll, Mark A., George M. Marsden, and Nathan O. Hatch. *The Search for Christian America*. Westchester, Ill.: Crossway Books, 1983. Expanded ed., Colorado Springs: Helmers & Howard, 1989.

Nord, David Paul. "Benevolent Capital: Financing Evangelical Book Publishing in Early Nineteenth-Century America." In *God and Mammon*, edited by Mark A. Noll, 147–70. New York: Oxford University Press, 2002.

——. *Communities of Journalism*. Urbana: University of Illinois Press, 2001.

——. "The Evangelical Origins of Mass Media in America, 1815–1835." In *Media and Religion in American History*, edited by William David Sloan, 68–93. Northport, Ala.: Vision, 2000.

——. "Free Grace, Free Books, Free Riders: The Economics of Religious Publishing in Early Nineteenth Century America." *Proceedings of the American Antiquarian Society* 106 (1996): 241–72.

——. "Systematic Benevolence: Religious Publishing and the Marketplace in Early Nineteenth-Century America." In *Communication and Change in American Religious History*, edited by Leonard I. Sweet, 239–52. Grand Rapids, Mich.: Eerdmans, 1993.

Norton, Wesley. *Religious Newspapers in the Old Northwest to 1861: A History, Bibliography, and Record of Opinion*. Athens: Ohio University Press, 1977.

O'Brien, Susan. "Eighteenth-Century Publishing Networks in the First Years of Transatlantic Evangelicalism." In *Evangelicalism: Comparative Studies of Popular Protestantism in North America, the British Isles, and Beyond, 1700–1990*, edited by Mark A. Noll, David W. Bebbington, and George A. Rawlyk, 38–57. New York: Oxford University Press, 1994.

——. "A Transatlantic Community of Saints: The Great Awakening and the First Evangelical Network, 1735–1755." *American Historical Review* 91 (Oct. 1986): 811–32.

O'Connor, Leo F. *Religion in the American Novel: The Search for Belief, 1860–1920*. New York: University Press of America, 1984.

Ong, Walter J. *Orality and Literacy: The Technologizing of the Word*. New York: Routledge, 1982.

——. *The Presence of the Word: Some Prolegomena for Cultural and Religious History*. New Haven: Yale University Press, 1967.

Ortner, Sherry B. "Theory in Anthropology since the Sixties." *Comparative Studies in Society and History: An International Quarterly*. 26 (Jan. 1984): 126–66.

Pelikan, Jaroslav. *The Christian Tradition: A History of the Development of Doctrine*.

Vol. 4, *Reformation of Church and Dogma (1300–1700)*. Chicago: University of Chicago Press, 1984.

Peters, Erskine, ed. *Lyrics of the Afro-American Spiritual: A Documentary Collection.* The Greenwood Encyclopedia of Black Music. Westport, Conn.: Greenwood, 1993.

Pettit, Norman. Intro. to *The Life of David Brainerd, by Jonathan Edwards.* The Works of Jonathan Edwards, vol. 7. New Haven: Yale University Press, 1985.

Pilkington, James Penn. *The Methodist Publishing House: A History.* Vol. 1, *Beginnings to 1870.* Nashville: Abingdon, 1968.

Price, Kenneth M., and Susan Belasco Smith, eds. *Periodical Literature in Nineteenth-Century America.* Charlottesville: University Press of Virginia, 1995.

Rabey, Steve. "No Longer Left Behind: An Insider's Look at How Christian Books Are Agented, Acquired, Packaged, Branded, and Sold in Today's Marketplace." *Christianity Today,* 22 Apr. 2002, 26–33.

Rabinowitz, Richard. *The Spiritual Self in Everyday Life: The Transformation of Personal Religious Experience in Nineteenth-Century New England.* Boston: Northeastern University Press, 1989.

Raboteau, Albert J. *Slave Religion: The "Invisible Institution" in the Antebellum South.* New York: Oxford University Press, 1978.

Reardon, Bernard M. G. *Religious Thought in the Reformation.* 2d ed. 1981. Reprint, New York: Longman, 1995.

Reeves, Jeremiah Bascom. *The Hymn as Literature.* New York: Century, 1922.

Reilly, Elizabeth Carroll, and David D. Hall. "Customers and the Market for Books." In *A History of the Book in America,* edited by Hugh Amory and David D. Hall, 387–99. Cambridge: Cambridge University Press; Worcester, Mass.: AAS, 2000.

———. "Modalities of Reading." In *A History of the Book in America,* edited by Hugh Amory and David D. Hall, 404–10. Cambridge: Cambridge University Press; Worcester, Mass.: AAS, 2000.

Reynolds, David S. *Beneath the American Renaissance: The Subversive Imagination in the Age of Emerson and Melville.* New York: Knopf, 1988.

———. *Faith in Fiction: The Emergence of Religious Literature in America.* Cambridge, Mass.: Harvard University Press, 1981.

Richey, Russell E. "Denominations and Denominationalism: An American Morphology." In *Reimagining Denominationalism: Interpretive Essays,* edited by Robert Bruce Mullin and Russell E. Richey, 74–98. New York: Oxford University Press, 1994.

Ricoeur, Paul. *Figuring the Sacred: Religion, Narrative, and Imagination.* Translated by David Pellauer. Edited by Mark I. Wallace. Minneapolis: Fortress, 1995.

Rogal, Samuel J. *Sisters of Sacred Song: A Select Listing of Women Hymnodists in Great Britain and America.* New York: Garland, 1981.

Routley, Erik. *Church Music and Theology.* London: SCM, 1959.

———. *Hymns and Human Life.* Grand Rapids, Mich.: Eerdmans, 1952.

Rubin, Joan Shelley. *The Making of Middle/Brow Culture.* Chapel Hill: University of North Carolina Press, 1992.

Ruffin, Bernard. *Fanny Crosby: The Hymn Writer*. Uhrichsville, Ohio: Barbour, 1945.

Ryan, James Emmett. "Inventing Catholicism: Nineteenth-Century Literary History and the Contest for American Religion." Ph.D. diss., University of North Carolina, 2000.

Sadie, Stanley, ed. *The New Grove Dictionary of Music and Musicians*. 29 vols. 2d ed. New York: Grove, 2001.

Sallee, James. *A History of Evangelistic Hymnody*. Grand Rapids, Mich.: Baker, 1978.

Schmidt, Leigh Eric. *Consumer Rites: The Buying and Selling of American Holidays*. Princeton, N.J.: Princeton University Press, 1995.

———. *Hearing Things: Religion, Illusion, and the American Enlightenment*. Cambridge: Harvard University Press, 2000.

———. *Holy Fairs: Scotland and the Making of American Revivalism*. 2d ed., with a new preface. Grand Rapids, Mich.: Eerdmans, 2001.

Schneider, A. Gregory. *The Way of the Cross Leads Home: The Domestication of American Methodism*. Religion in North America. Bloomington: Indiana University Press, 1993.

Secord, James A. *Victorian Sensation: The Extraordinary Publication, Reception, and Secret Authorship of "Vestiges of the Natural History of Creation."* Chicago: University of Chicago Press, 2000.

Sellers, Charles Grier. *The Market Revolution: Jacksonian America, 1815–1846*. New York: Oxford University Press, 1991.

Showalter, Elaine. *A Literature of Their Own: British Women Novelists from Brontë to Lessing*. London: Virago, 1978.

Sizer, Sandra S. *The Gospel Hymns and Social Religion: The Rhetoric of Nineteenth-Century Revivalism*. Philadelphia: Temple University Press, 1978.

Sloan, William David, ed. *Media and Religion in American History*. Northport, Ala.: Vision, 2000.

Smith, Christian. *Christian America? What Evangelicals Really Want*. Berkeley and Los Angeles: University of California Press, 2000.

Smith, Jonathan Z., ed. *Harper Collins Dictionary of Religion*. San Francisco: Harper, 1995.

Smith, Susan Belasco. "Serialization and the Nature of *Uncle Tom's Cabin*." In *Periodical Literature in Nineteenth-Century America*, edited by Kenneth M. Price and Susan Belasco Smith, 69–89. Charlottesville: University Press of Virginia, 1995.

Smith, Timothy L. *Revivalism and Social Reform: American Protestantism on the Eve of the Civil War*. New York: Abingdon, 1957. Reprint, with a new afterword by the author, Baltimore: Johns Hopkins University Press, 1980.

Southern, Eileen. *The Music of Black Americans: A History*. 2d ed. New York: Norton, 1983.

Spencer, Jon Michael. *Black Hymnody: A Hymnological History of the African-American Church*. Knoxville: University of Tennessee Press, 1992.

———. *Sing a New Song: Liberating Black Hymnody*. Minneapolis: Fortress, 1995.

Steinberg, S. H. *Five Hundred Years of Printing*. New ed., rev. by John Trevitt. New Castle, Del.: British Library and Oak Knoll, 1996.

Stevens, Daniel Gurden. *The First Hundred Years of The American Baptist Publication Society*. Philadelphia: ABPS, [1924].

Stevenson, Louise. *Scholarly Means to Evangelical Ends: The New Haven Scholars and the Transformation of Higher Learning in America, 1830–1890.* Baltimore: Johns Hopkins University Press, 1986.

Stout, Harry S., and Nathan O. Hatch. "The Religious Press in Early America." Paper presented at Conference on Needs and Opportunities in the History of the Book, AAS, 1–3 Nov. 1984.

Stowe, Charles Edward. *Life of Harriet Beecher Stowe: Compiled from Her Letters and Journals.* Boston: Houghton, Mifflin, 1891.

Stroupe, Henry Smith. *The Religious Press in the South Atlantic States, 1802–1865: An Annotated Bibliography with Historical Introduction and Notes.* Durham, N.C.: Duke University Press, 1956.

Sutton, Walter. *The Western Book Trade: Cincinnati as a Nineteenth-Century Publishing and Book-Trade Center. . . .* Columbus: Ohio State University Press for the Ohio Historical Society, 1961.

Sweet, William Warren. *Methodism in American History.* New York: MEC, 1938; rev. ed., New York: Abingdon, 1954.

———. *Religion in the Development of American Culture, 1765–1840.* New York: Charles Scribner's Sons, 1952.

Taves, Ann. *Fits, Trances, and Visions: Experiencing Religion and Explaining Experience from Wesley to James.* Princeton: Princeton University Press, 1999.

Tebbel, John. *A History of Book Publishing in the United States.* Vol. 1, *The Creation of an Industry, 1630–1865.* New York: R. R. Bowker, 1972.

Thomas, Amy. "Who Makes the Text? The Production and Use of Literature in Antebellum America." Ph.D. diss., Duke University, 1992.

Thompson, Lawrence. "The Printing and Publishing Activities of the American Tract Society from 1825 to 1850." *The Papers of the Bibliographical Society of America* 35 (second quarter 1941): 81–114.

Tompkins, Jane. *Sensational Designs: The Cultural Work of American Fiction, 1790–1860.* New York: Oxford University Press, 1985.

Tracy, David. *The Analogical Imagination: Christian Theology and the Culture of Pluralism.* New York: Crossroad, 1981.

Tripp, Bernell E. "The Origins of the Black Press." In *Media and Religion in American History,* edited by William David Sloan, 94–103. Northport, Ala.: Vision, 2000.

Turner, Frank M. *John Henry Newman: The Challenge to Evangelical Religion.* New Haven: Yale University Press, 2002.

Turner, Victor, and Edith Turner. *Image and Pilgrimage in Christian Culture: Anthropological Perspectives.* New York: Columbia University Press, 1978.

Unger, Merrill F. *The New Unger's Bible Dictionary.* Edited by R. K. Harrison. Chicago: Moody, 1957.

Wacker, Grant. *Heaven Below: Early Pentecostals and American Culture.* Cambridge: Harvard University Press, 2001.

Walsham, Alexandra. *Providence in Early Modern England.* New York: Oxford University Press, 1999.

Walters, Ronald. *American Reformers, 1815–1860.* Consulting ed. Eric Foner. New York: Hill & Wang, 1978. Rev. ed., New York: Hill & Wang, 1997.

Warren, James I., Jr. *O for a Thousand Tongues: The History, Nature, and Influence of Music in the Methodist Tradition*. Grand Rapids, Mich.: Francis Asbury, 1988.

Watt, Tessa. *Cheap Print and Popular Piety, 1550–1640*. New York: Cambridge University Press, 1991.

Westerhoff, John H., III. *McGuffey and His Readers: Piety, Morality, and Education in Nineteenth-Century America*. Nashville: Abingdon, 1978.

White, James F. *Roman Catholic Worship: Trent to Today*. New York: Paulist, 1995.

Winship, Michael. *American Literary Publishing in the Mid-Nineteenth Century: The Business of Ticknor and Fields*. New York: Cambridge University Press, 1995.

——— . *Ticknor and Fields: The Business of Literary Publishing in the United States of the Nineteenth Century*. The Ninth Hanes Lecture: Presented by the Hanes Foundation for the Study of the Origin and Development of the Book. Chapel Hill: Hanes Foundation, Rare Book Collection/University Library and University of North Carolina, 1992.

Winslow, Ola Elizabeth. "Elizabeth Prentiss." In *Notable American Women: A Biographical Dictionary*, edited by Edward T. James, 3:95–96. Cambridge: Harvard University Press, Belknap, 1971.

Wittmann, Reinhard. "Was There a Reading Revolution at the End of the Eighteenth Century?" In *A History of Reading in the West*, edited by Guglielmo Cavallo and Roger Chartier, 284–312. Translated by Lydia G. Cochrane. Cambridge: Polity, 1999.

Work, John W. *American Negro Songs: 230 Folk Songs and Spirituals, Religious and Secular*. New York: Howell, Soskin, 1940; Mineola, N.Y.: Dover, 1998.

Worth, Robert F. "Spreading the Word in Just-the-Basics Style." *New York Times*, 2 Nov. 2002.

Wosh, Peter J. *Spreading the Word: The Bible Business in Nineteenth-Century America*. Ithaca, N.Y.: Cornell University Press, 1994.

Wright, Bishop Richard R., Jr. *The Bishops of the African Methodist Episcopal Church*. Nashville: AME SSU, 1963.

Zboray, Ronald J. *A Fictive People: Antebellum Economic Development and the American Reading Public*. New York: Oxford University Press, 1993.

Ziff, Larzer. "Upon What Pre-Text? The Book and Literary History." *Proceedings of the American Antiquarian Society* 95 (1985): 297–302.

INDEX

(*what evdg to the bk — see p.247*)

17–18: CGB seeking to "rehabilitate" the analytical usefulness of the term 'evangelical' and also explore what people meant when they called themselves evangelical, emphasizing the variety in this term, the overlapping and cultural crossings, etc.

19 – Douglas's "feminization" argument invoked as a "secularization" thesis. (But see 87 when CGB restates a point made by Douglas.) P. 99 – again, though Douglas not cited.

— The book seems to leave out any seamy side of evangelical publishing (anti-Catholicism, e.g.) — Comp to frontlist. Attractions of Cath.: 131–132.

83 – Popularity of history for 19th-c. evangelicals

86–87 – 1832: beginning of the Evangelical Family Library (modified & abridged many texts)

88ff – memoirs, children's stories, missionary me[...] (women & A-A's rec. mention here, but no analysis of race or [...] ↳ see p. 95 too.